Shojo Beat

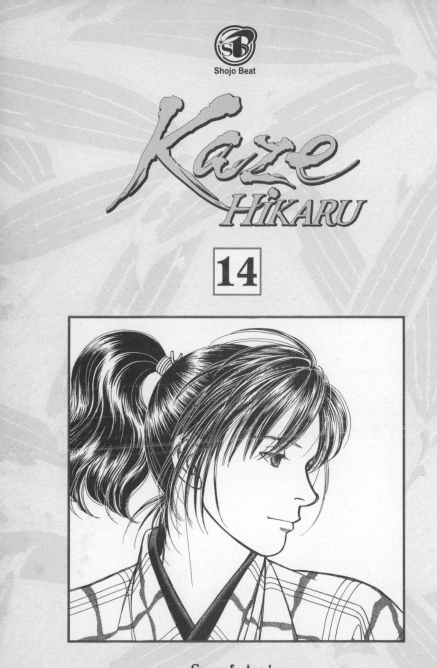

Kaze Hikaru

14

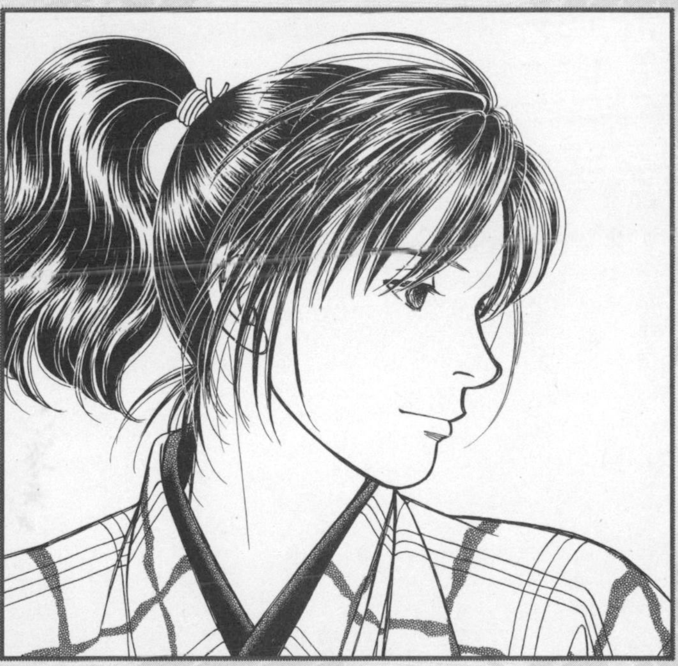

Story & Art by

Taeko Watanabe

Contents

Story Thus Far

It is the end of the Bakufu era, the 3rd year of Bunkyu (1863) in Kyoto. The Shinsengumi is a band of warriors formed to protect the Shogun.

Tominaga Sei, the daughter of a former Bakufu bushi, joined the Shinsengumi disguised as a boy by the name of Kamiya Seizaburo to avenge her father and brother. She has continued her training under the only person in the Shinsengumi who knows her true identity, Okita Soji, and she aspires to become a true *bushi*.

The Shinsengumi prove their worth through their success in the Ikedaya Affair and the *Kinmon no Hen*. Ito Kashitaro and his men join the Shinsengumi as part of the troop expansion. However, their disgust at the Bakufu drives them to plot to change the philosophy of the Shinsengumi.

Yamanami commits seppuku after sympathizing with Ito, who has anti-Bakufu inclinations. The aftermath leaves the troop shaken, but amidst looming doubts, the Shinsengumi move their headquarters to Nishi Honganji—a place considered enemy territory. Okita is ordered to go to Edo to recruit new troops. Worried about Sei's well-being in his absence, he suggests she leave the troop. He says the only way she can stay is if she defeats him in combat!

Characters

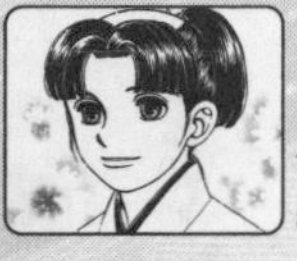

Tominaga Sei
She is secrectly in love with Soji and stays with the troop solely out of a desire to protect him. She struggles to prove herself as a true bushi.

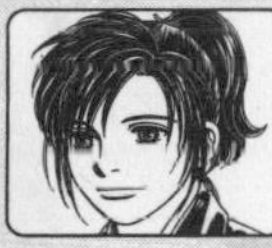

Okita Soji
Assistant vice captain of the Shinsengumi and licensed master of the Ten'nen Rishin-Ryu. He supports the troop alongside Kondo and Hijikata and guides Seizaburo with a kind yet firm hand.

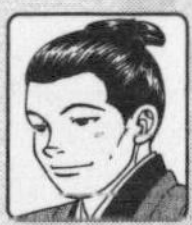

Kondo Isami
Captain of the Shinsengumi and fourth grandmaster of the Ten'nen Rishin-ryu. A passionate, warm and well-respected leader.

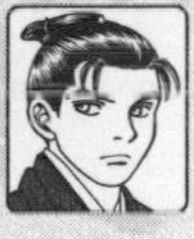

Hijikata Toshizo
Vice captain of the Shinsengumi. He commands both the group and himself with a rigid strictness. He is also known as the "Oni vice captain."

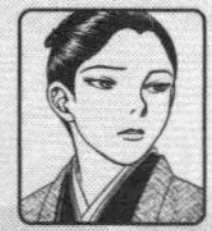

Ito Kashitaro
Councilor of the Shinsengumi. A skilled swordsman yet also an academic with anti-Bakufu sentiments, he plots to sway the direction of the troop.

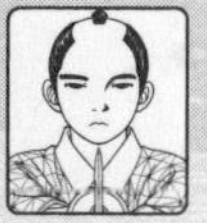

Saito Hajime
Assistant vice captain. He was a friend of Sei's older brother. Sei is attached to him in place of her lost brother.

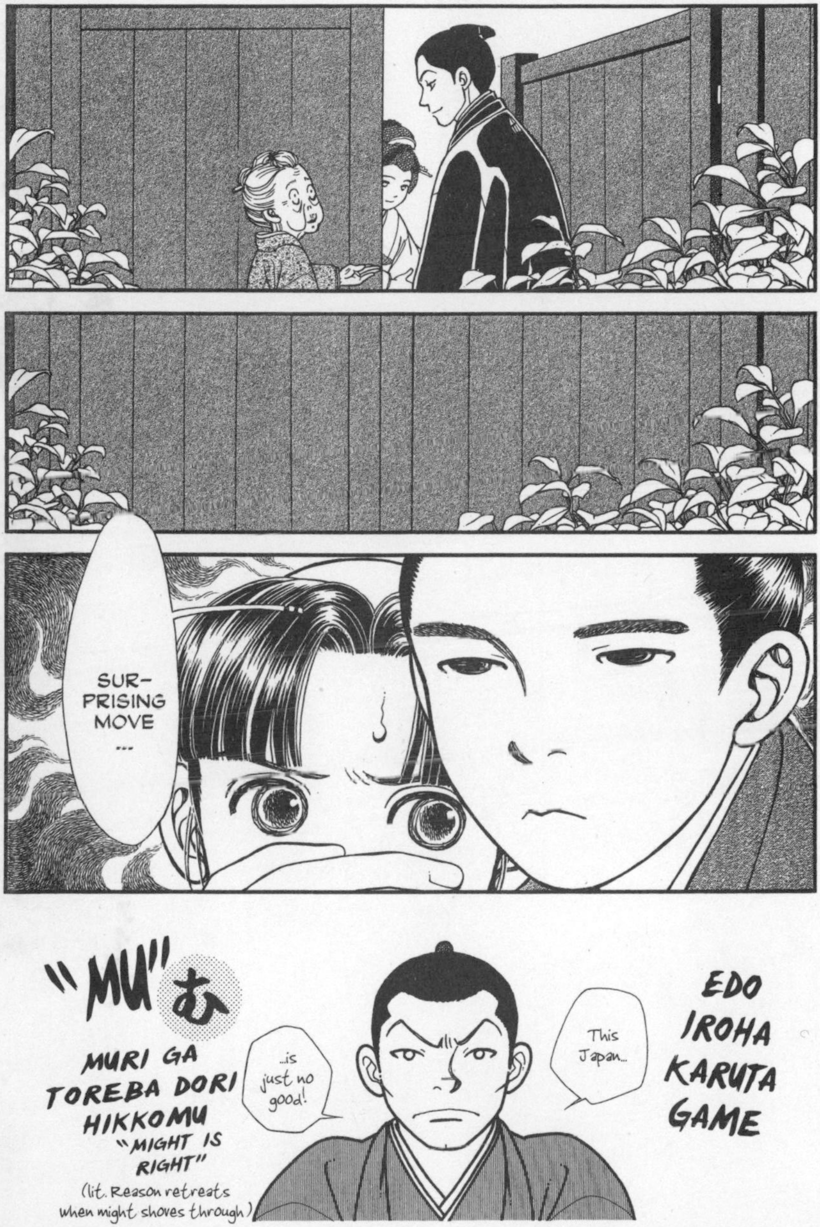
SUR-PRISING MOVE ...
EDO IROHA KARUTA GAME
This Japan...
...is just no good!
"MU" む
MURI GA TOREBA DORI HIKKOMU "MIGHT IS RIGHT"
(lit. Reason retreats when might shoves through)

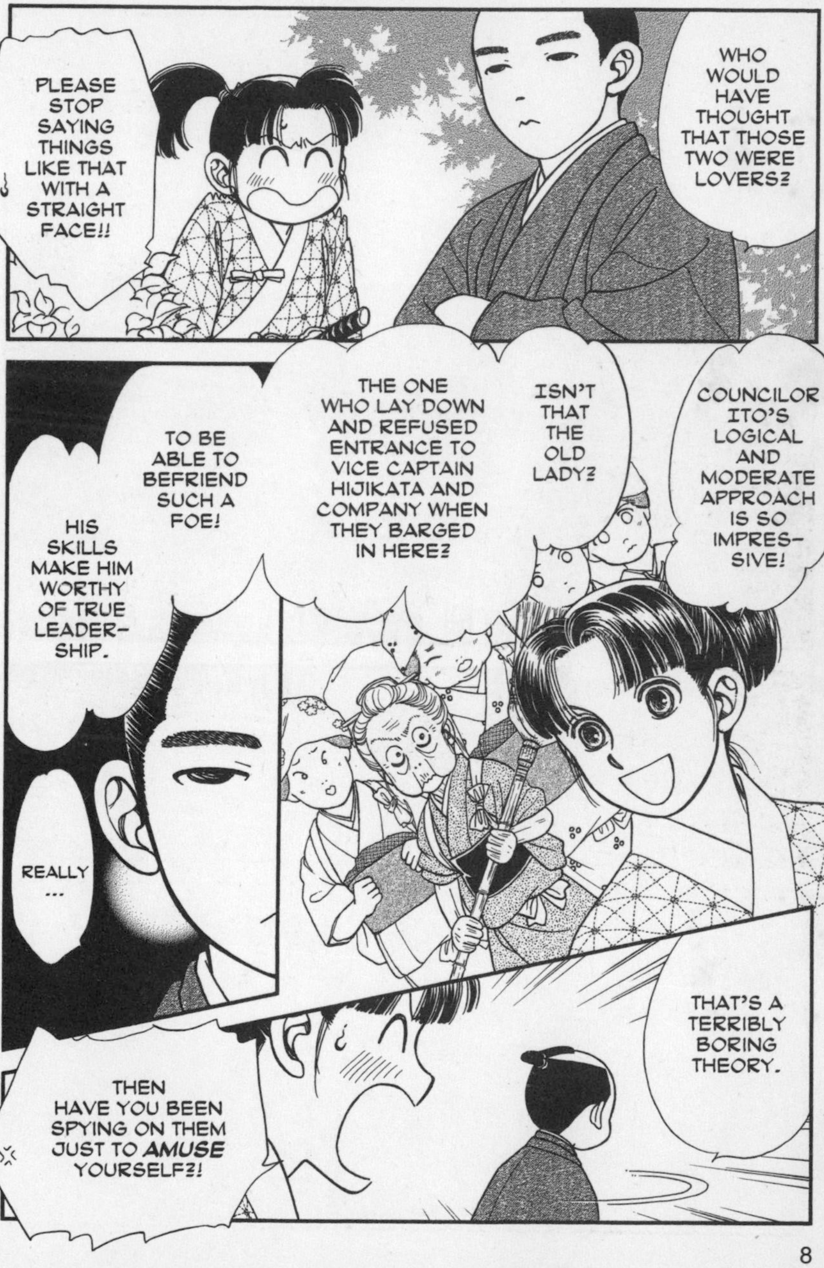
WHO WOULD HAVE THOUGHT THAT THOSE TWO WERE LOVERS?
PLEASE STOP SAYING THINGS LIKE THAT WITH A STRAIGHT FACE!!
COUNCILOR ITO'S LOGICAL AND MODERATE APPROACH IS SO IMPRES-SIVE!
ISN'T THAT THE OLD LADY?
THE ONE WHO LAY DOWN AND REFUSED ENTRANCE TO VICE CAPTAIN HIJIKATA AND COMPANY WHEN THEY BARGED IN HERE?
TO BE ABLE TO BEFRIEND SUCH A FOE!
HIS SKILLS MAKE HIM WORTHY OF TRUE LEADER-SHIP.
REALLY ...
THAT'S A TERRIBLY BORING THEORY.
THEN HAVE YOU BEEN SPYING ON THEM JUST TO *AMUSE* YOURSELF?!

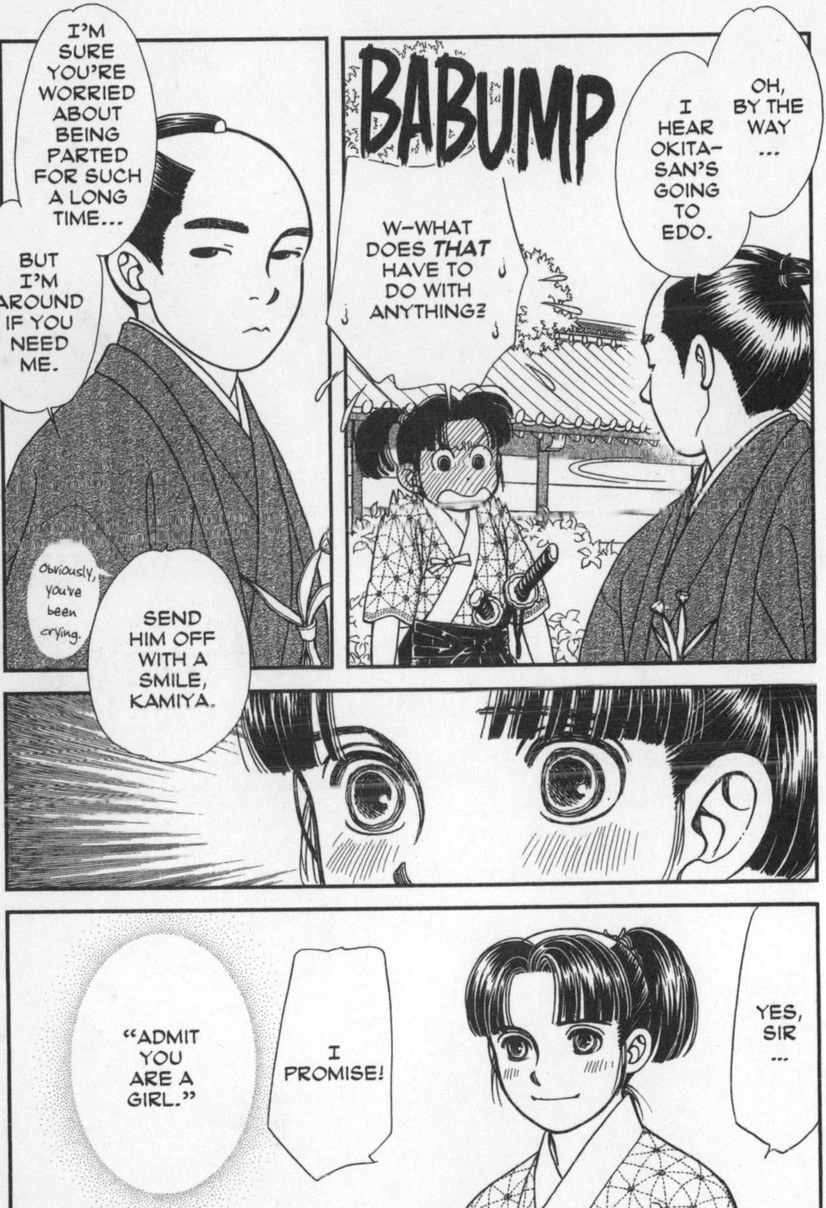
OH, BY THE WAY...
I HEAR OKITA-SAN'S GOING TO EDO.
BABUMP
W-WHAT DOES THAT HAVE TO DO WITH ANYTHING!?
I'M SURE YOU'RE WORRIED ABOUT BEING PARTED FOR SUCH A LONG TIME...
BUT I'M AROUND IF YOU NEED ME.
Obviously, you've been crying.
SEND HIM OFF WITH A SMILE, KAMIYA.
YES, SIR...
I PROMISE!
"ADMIT YOU ARE A GIRL."

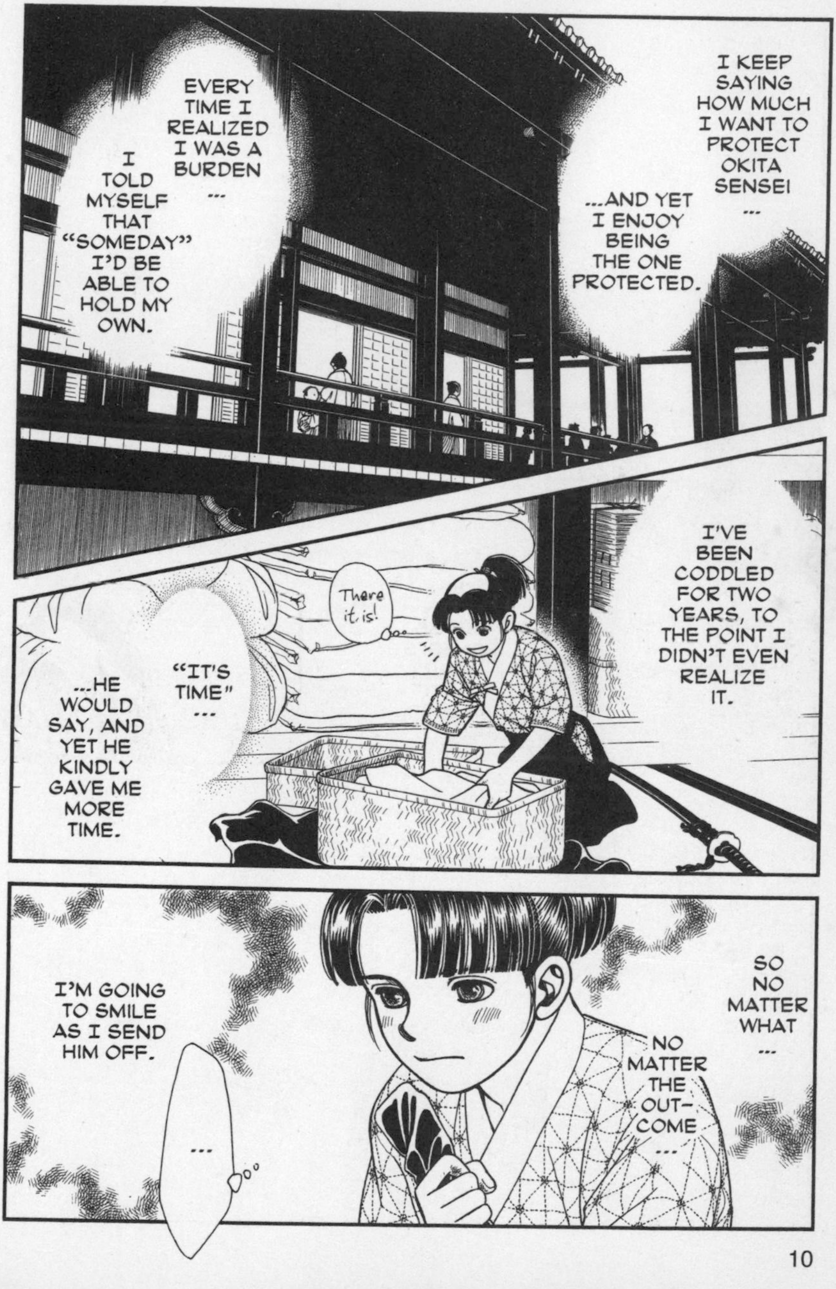
I KEEP SAYING HOW MUCH I WANT TO PROTECT OKITA SENSEI ...
...AND YET I ENJOY BEING THE ONE PROTECTED.
EVERY TIME I REALIZED I WAS A BURDEN ...
I TOLD MYSELF THAT "SOMEDAY" I'D BE ABLE TO HOLD MY OWN.
I'VE BEEN CODDLED FOR TWO YEARS, TO THE POINT I DIDN'T EVEN REALIZE IT.
There it is!
"IT'S TIME" ...
...HE WOULD SAY, AND YET HE KINDLY GAVE ME MORE TIME.
SO NO MATTER WHAT ...
NO MATTER THE OUT-COME ...
I'M GOING TO SMILE AS I SEND HIM OFF.
...

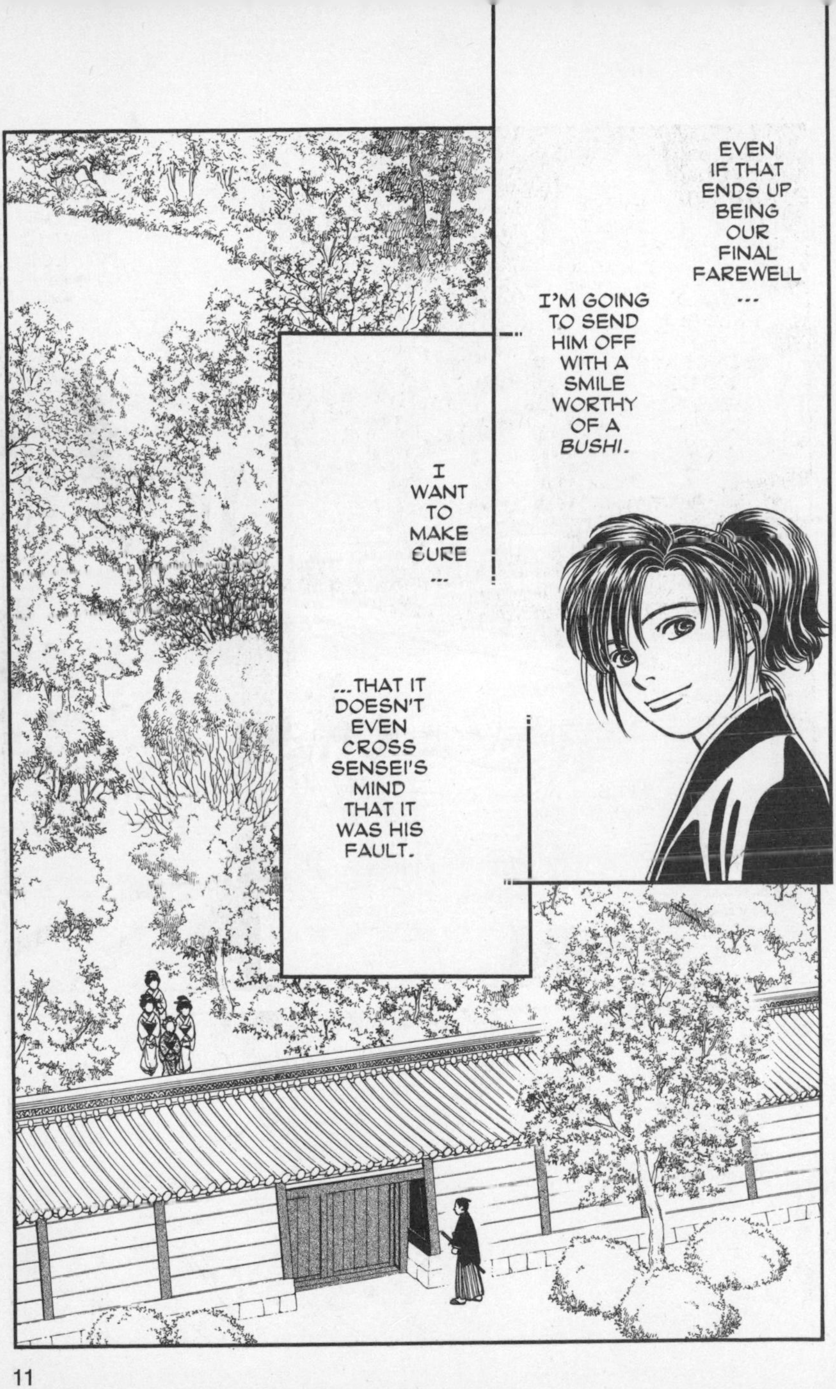
EVEN IF THAT ENDS UP BEING OUR FINAL FAREWELL...
I'M GOING TO SEND HIM OFF WITH A SMILE WORTHY OF A *BUSHI*.
I WANT TO MAKE SURE...
...THAT IT DOESN'T EVEN CROSS SENSEI'S MIND THAT IT WAS HIS FAULT.

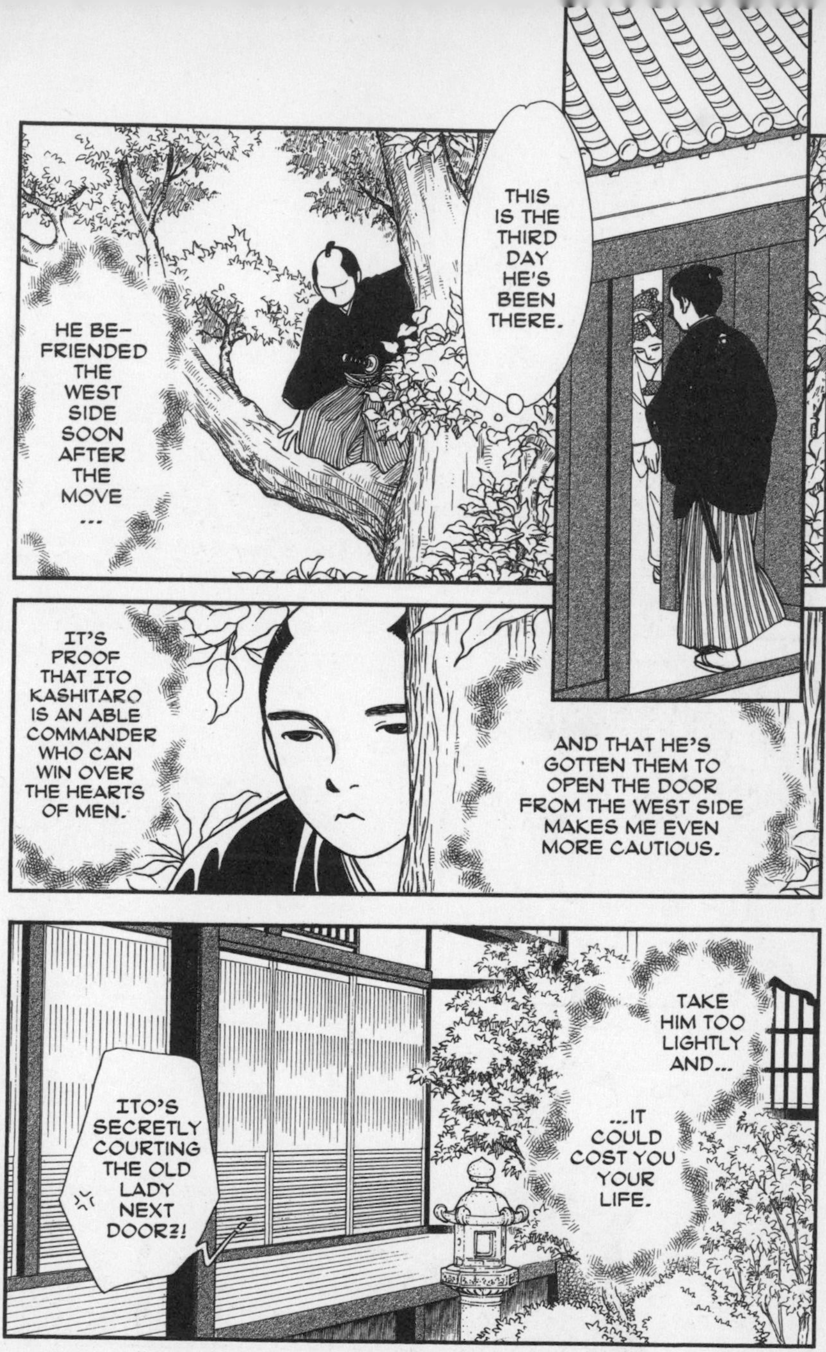
THIS IS THE THIRD DAY HE'S BEEN THERE.
HE BE-FRIENDED THE WEST SIDE SOON AFTER THE MOVE...
IT'S PROOF THAT ITO KASHITARO IS AN ABLE COMMANDER WHO CAN WIN OVER THE HEARTS OF MEN.
AND THAT HE'S GOTTEN THEM TO OPEN THE DOOR FROM THE WEST SIDE MAKES ME EVEN MORE CAUTIOUS.
TAKE HIM TOO LIGHTLY AND...
...IT COULD COST YOU YOUR LIFE.
ITO'S SECRETLY COURTING THE OLD LADY NEXT DOOR?!

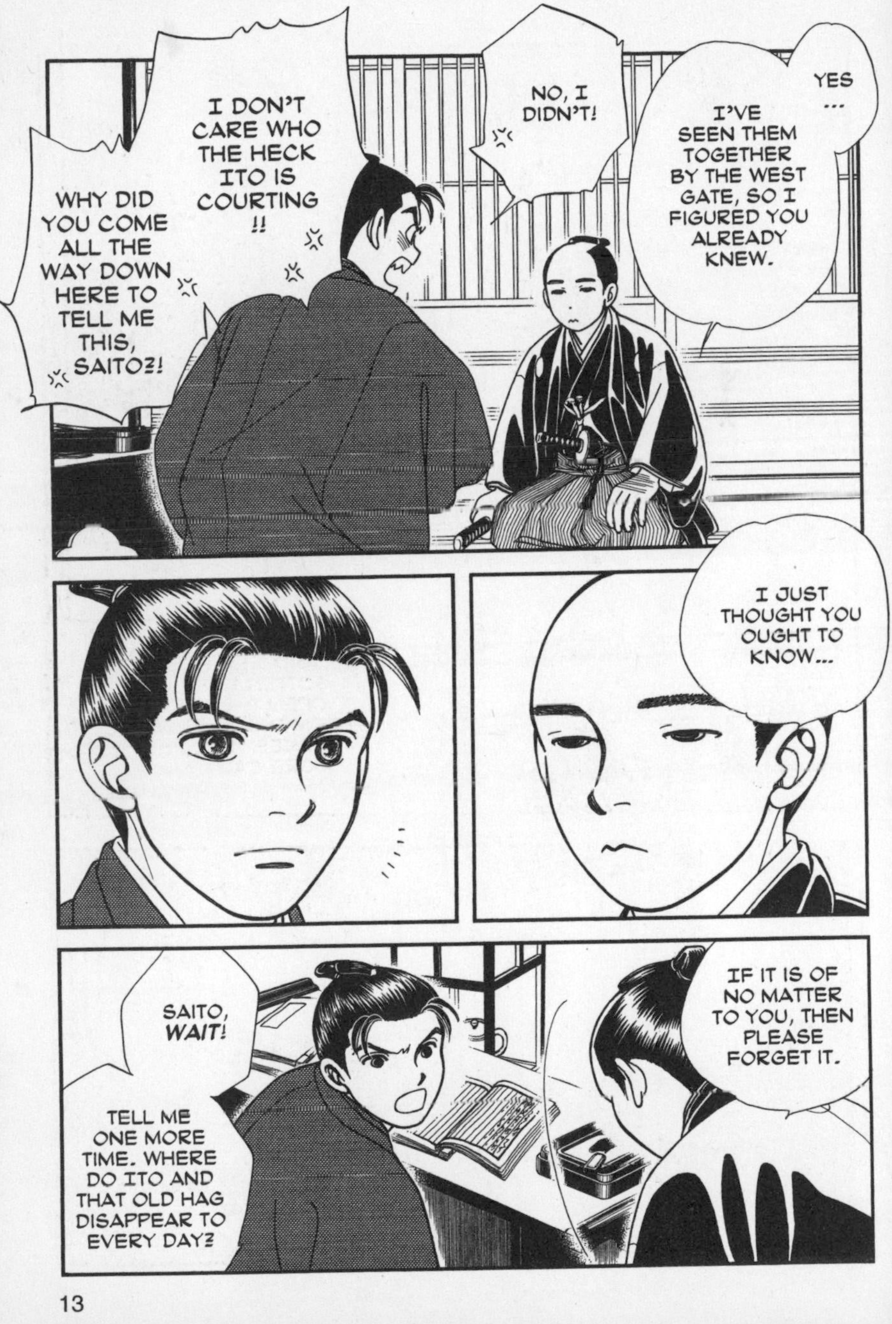
YES ...
I'VE SEEN THEM TOGETHER BY THE WEST GATE, SO I FIGURED YOU ALREADY KNEW.
NO, I DIDN'T!
I DON'T CARE WHO THE HECK ITO IS COURTING!!
WHY DID YOU COME ALL THE WAY DOWN HERE TO TELL ME THIS, SAITO?!
I JUST THOUGHT YOU OUGHT TO KNOW...
IF IT IS OF NO MATTER TO YOU, THEN PLEASE FORGET IT.
SAITO, *WAIT!*
TELL ME ONE MORE TIME. WHERE DO ITO AND THAT OLD HAG DISAPPEAR TO EVERY DAY?

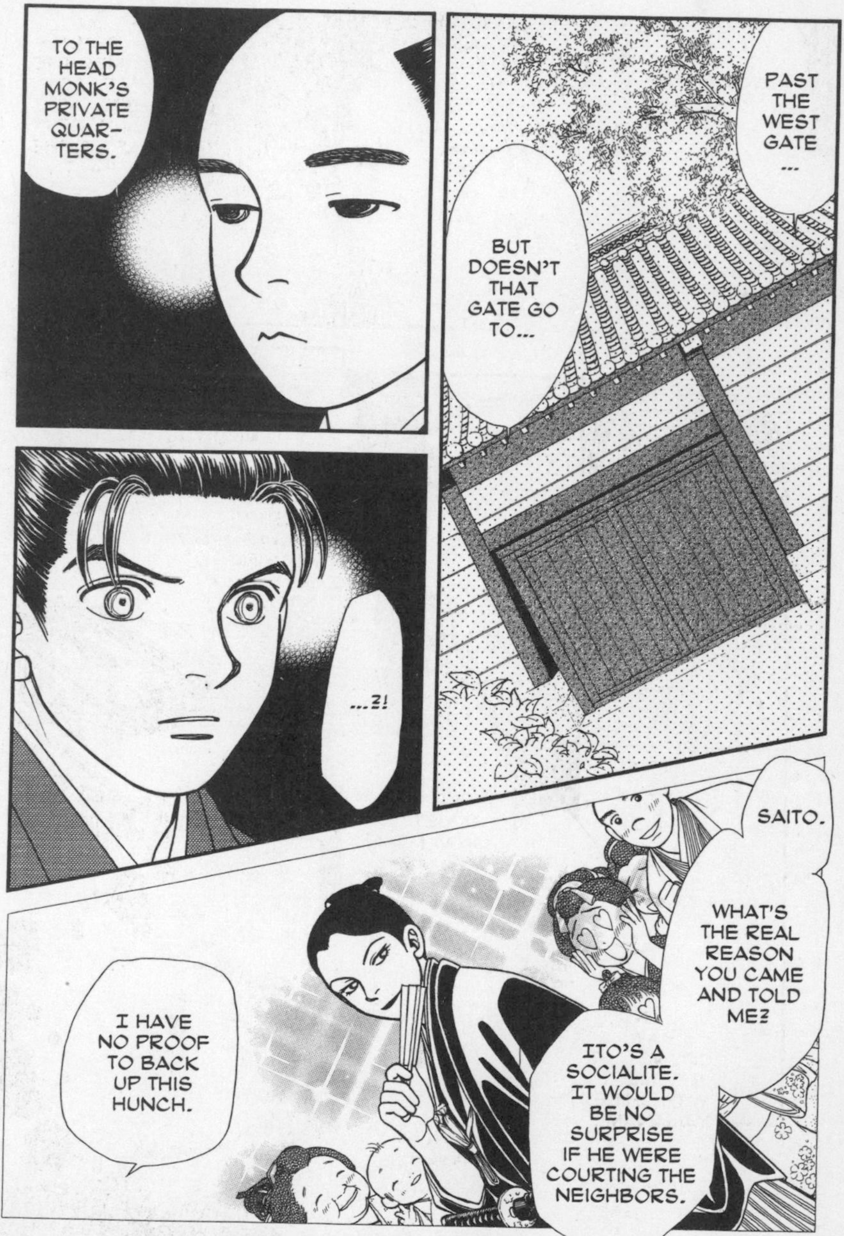
PAST THE WEST GATE ...
BUT DOESN'T THAT GATE GO TO...
TO THE HEAD MONK'S PRIVATE QUARTERS.
...?!
SAITO.
WHAT'S THE REAL REASON YOU CAME AND TOLD ME?
ITO'S A SOCIALITE. IT WOULD BE NO SURPRISE IF HE WERE COURTING THE NEIGHBORS.
I HAVE NO PROOF TO BACK UP THIS HUNCH.

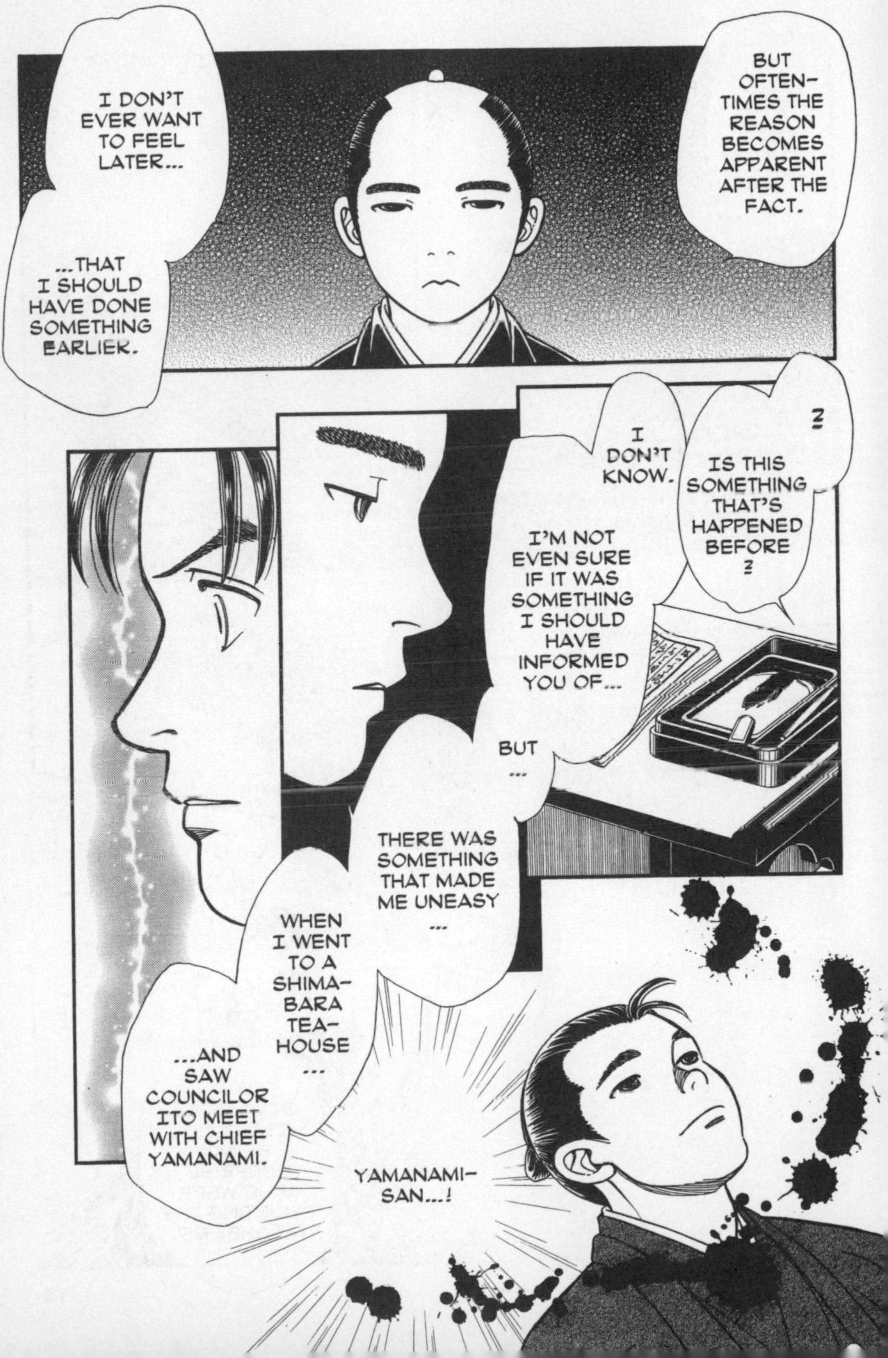
BUT OFTEN-TIMES THE REASON BECOMES APPARENT AFTER THE FACT.
I DON'T EVER WANT TO FEEL LATER...
...THAT I SHOULD HAVE DONE SOMETHING EARLIER.
IS THIS SOMETHING THAT'S HAPPENED BEFORE?
I DON'T KNOW.
I'M NOT EVEN SURE IF IT WAS SOMETHING I SHOULD HAVE INFORMED YOU OF...
BUT...
THERE WAS SOMETHING THAT MADE ME UNEASY...
WHEN I WENT TO A SHIMABARA TEAHOUSE...
...AND SAW COUNCILOR ITO MEET WITH CHIEF YAMANAMI.
YAMANAMI-SAN...!

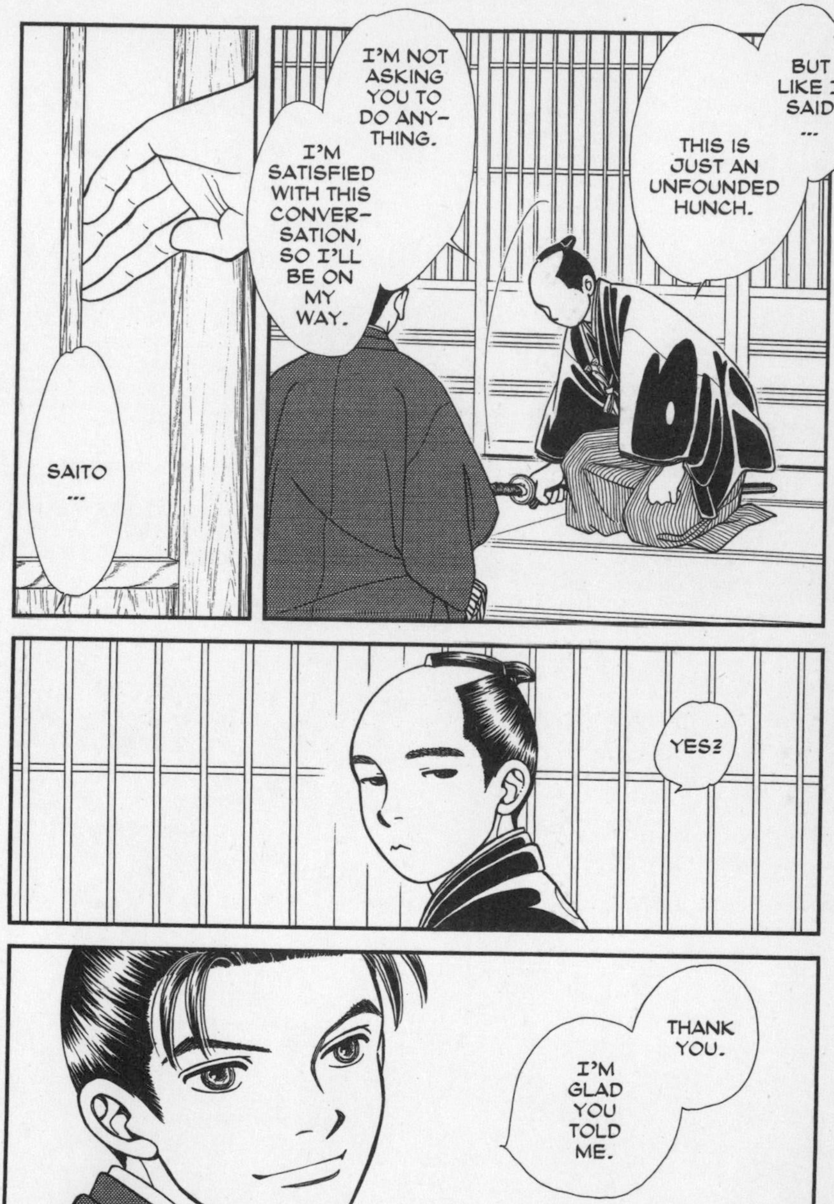

BUT LIKE I SAID ...
THIS IS JUST AN UNFOUNDED HUNCH.
I'M NOT ASKING YOU TO DO ANYTHING.
I'M SATISFIED WITH THIS CONVERSATION, SO I'LL BE ON MY WAY.
SAITO ...
YES?
THANK YOU.
I'M GLAD YOU TOLD ME.

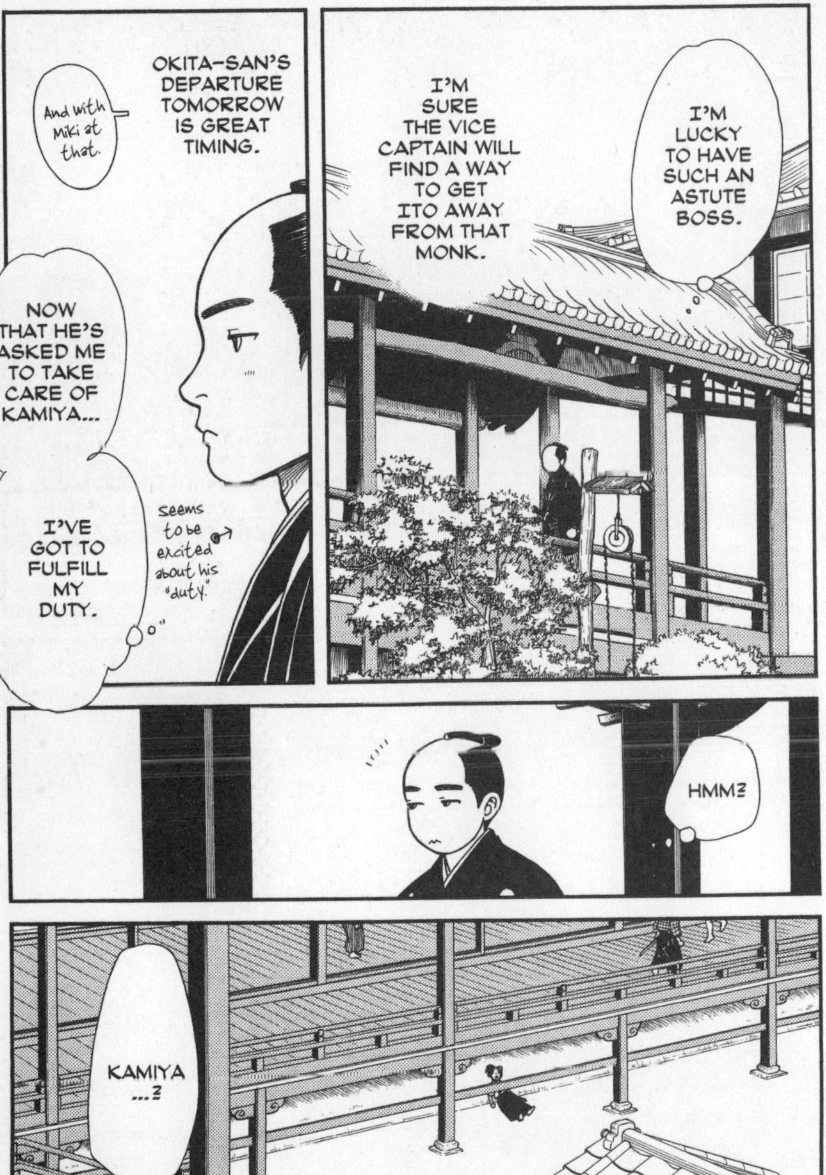
I'M LUCKY TO HAVE SUCH AN ASTUTE BOSS.
I'M SURE THE VICE CAPTAIN WILL FIND A WAY TO GET ITO AWAY FROM THAT MONK.
OKITA-SAN'S DEPARTURE TOMORROW IS GREAT TIMING.
And with Miki at that.
NOW THAT HE'S ASKED ME TO TAKE CARE OF KAMIYA...
I'VE GOT TO FULFILL MY DUTY.
Seems to be excited about his "duty."
HMM?
KAMIYA...?

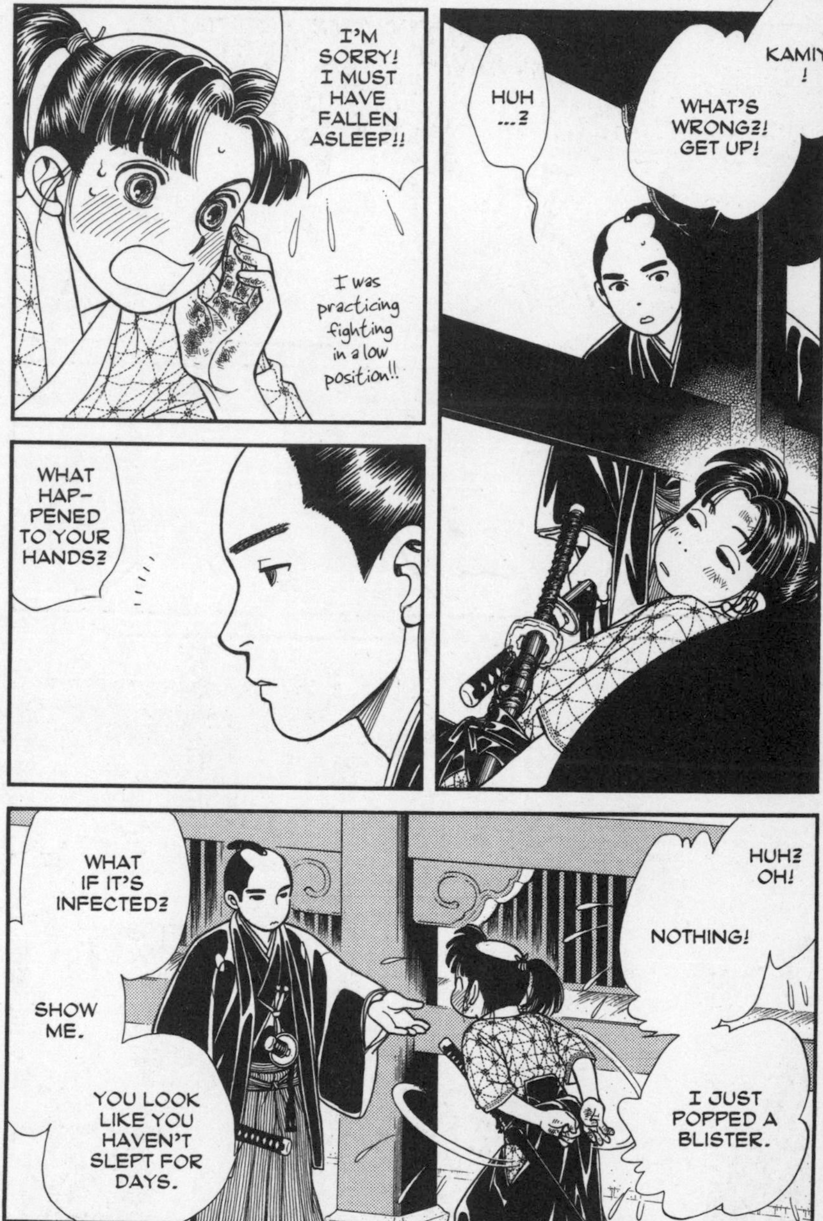
KAMIYA!
WHAT'S WRONG?! GET UP!
HUH...?
I'M SORRY! I MUST HAVE FALLEN ASLEEP!!
I was practicing fighting in a low position!!
WHAT HAPPENED TO YOUR HANDS?
HUH? OH!
NOTHING!
I JUST POPPED A BLISTER.
WHAT IF IT'S INFECTED?
SHOW ME.
YOU LOOK LIKE YOU HAVEN'T SLEPT FOR DAYS.

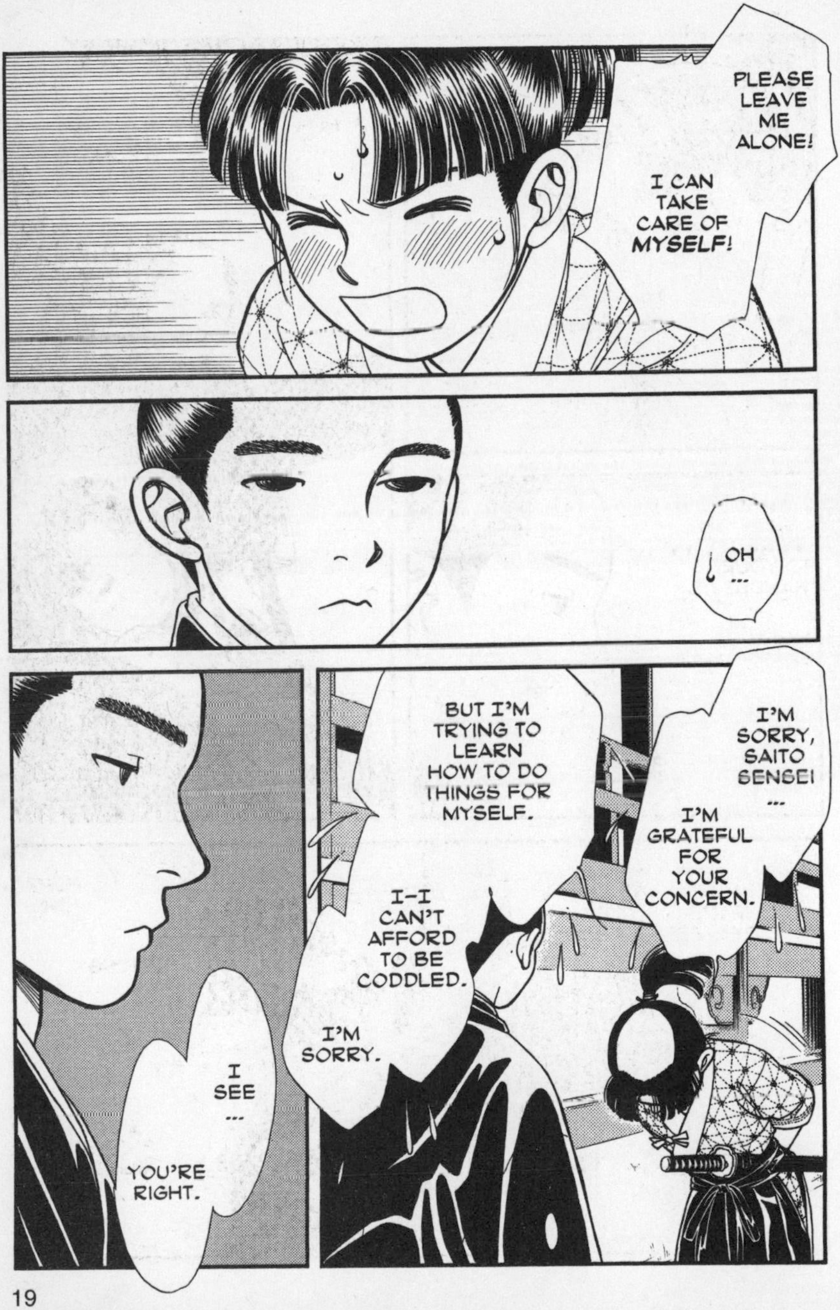
PLEASE LEAVE ME ALONE!
I CAN TAKE CARE OF *MYSELF*!
OH ...
I'M SORRY, SAITO SENSEI ...
I'M GRATEFUL FOR YOUR CONCERN.
BUT I'M TRYING TO LEARN HOW TO DO THINGS FOR MYSELF.
I-I CAN'T AFFORD TO BE CODDLED.
I'M SORRY.
I SEE ...
YOU'RE RIGHT.

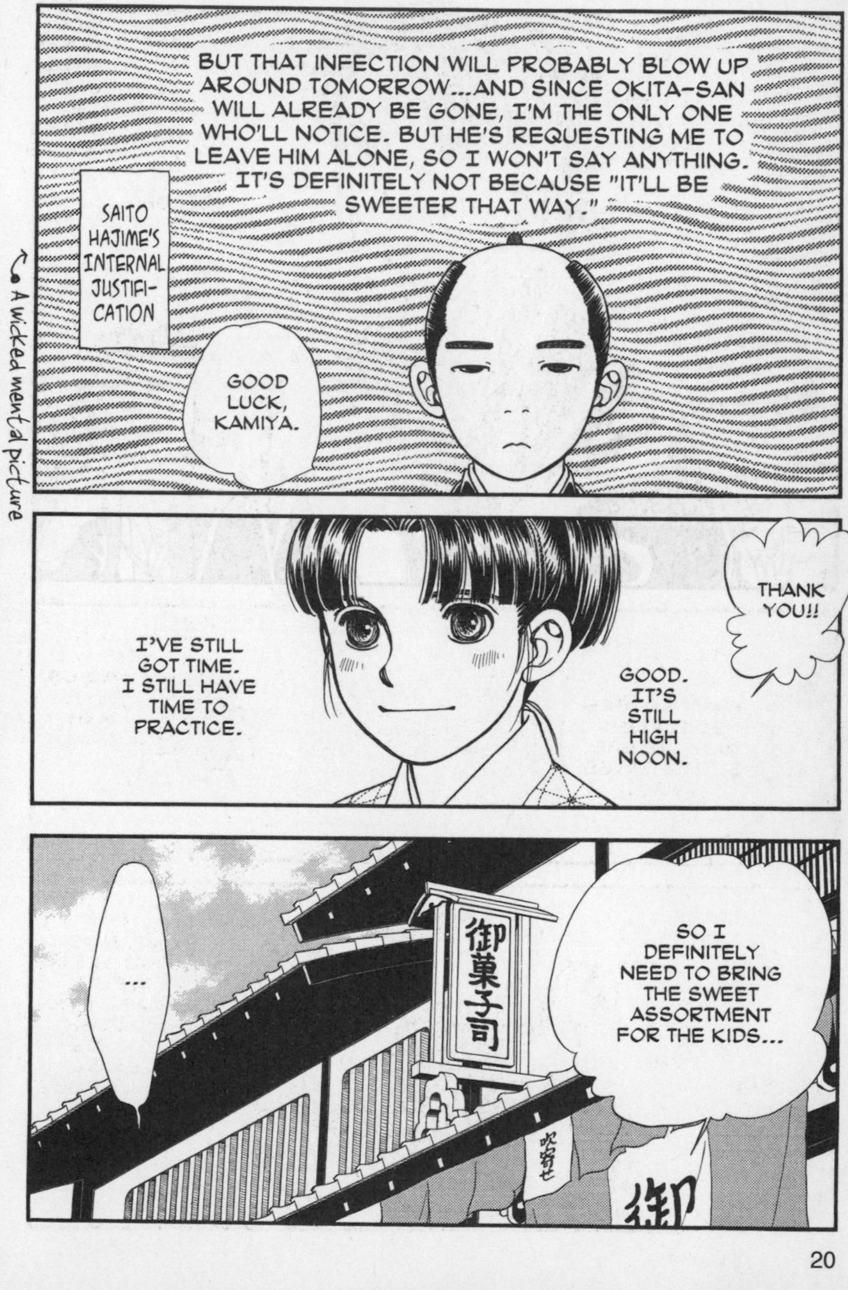
BUT THAT INFECTION WILL PROBABLY BLOW UP AROUND TOMORROW...AND SINCE OKITA-SAN WILL ALREADY BE GONE, I'M THE ONLY ONE WHO'LL NOTICE. BUT HE'S REQUESTING ME TO LEAVE HIM ALONE, SO I WON'T SAY ANYTHING. IT'S DEFINITELY NOT BECAUSE "IT'LL BE SWEETER THAT WAY."
GOOD LUCK, KAMIYA.
SAITO HAJIME'S INTERNAL JUSTIFICATION
A wicked mental picture
THANK YOU!!
GOOD. IT'S STILL HIGH NOON.
I'VE STILL GOT TIME. I STILL HAVE TIME TO PRACTICE.
SO I DEFINITELY NEED TO BRING THE SWEET ASSORTMENT FOR THE KIDS...
御菓子司
吹寄せ
御
...

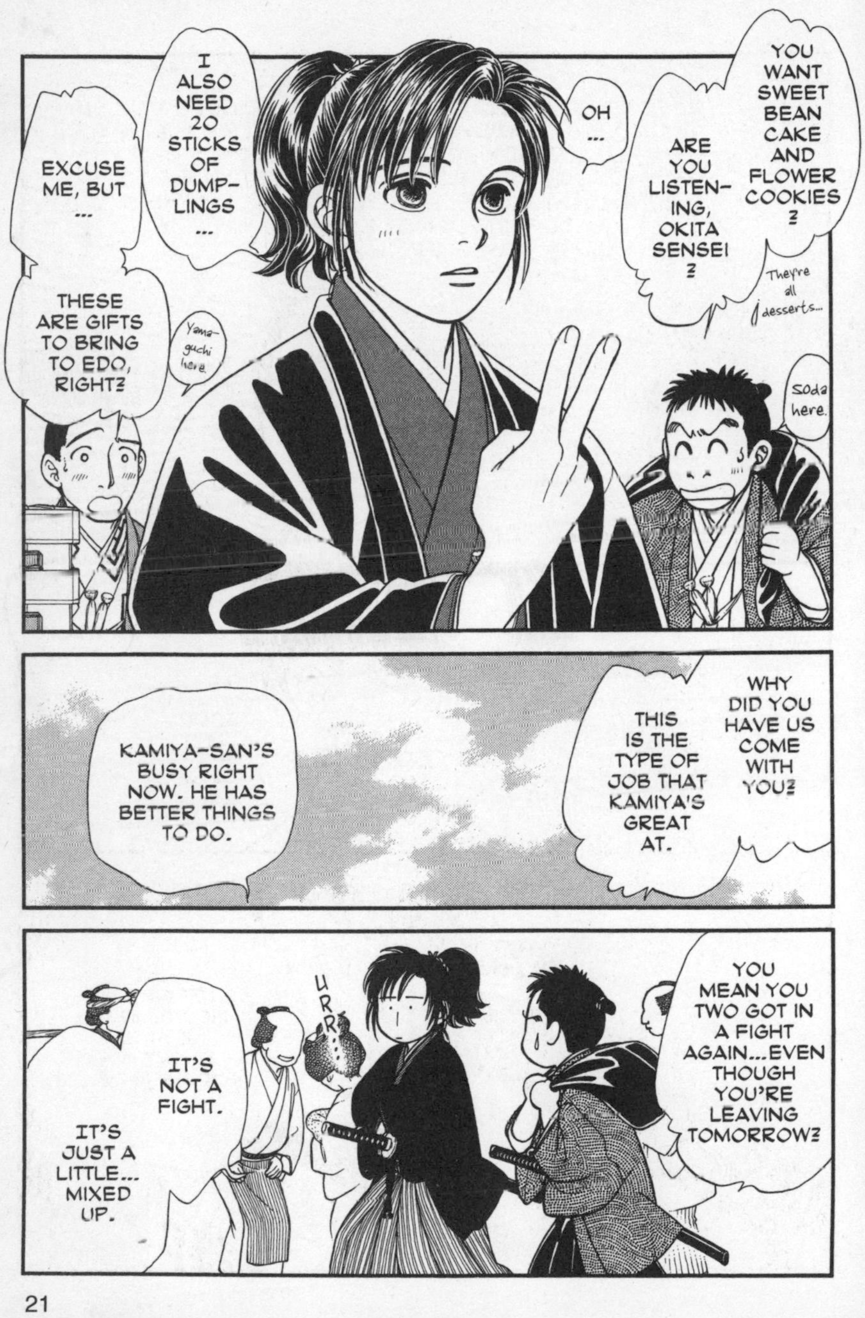
YOU WANT SWEET BEAN CAKE AND FLOWER COOKIES?
They're all desserts...
ARE YOU LISTENING, OKITA SENSEI?
OH ...
Soda here.
I ALSO NEED 20 STICKS OF DUMPLINGS ...
EXCUSE ME, BUT ...
THESE ARE GIFTS TO BRING TO EDO, RIGHT?
Yamaguchi here.
WHY DID YOU HAVE US COME WITH YOU?
THIS IS THE TYPE OF JOB THAT KAMIYA'S GREAT AT.
KAMIYA-SAN'S BUSY RIGHT NOW. HE HAS BETTER THINGS TO DO.
YOU MEAN YOU TWO GOT IN A FIGHT AGAIN...EVEN THOUGH YOU'RE LEAVING TOMORROW?
URR...
IT'S NOT A FIGHT.
IT'S JUST A LITTLE... MIXED UP.

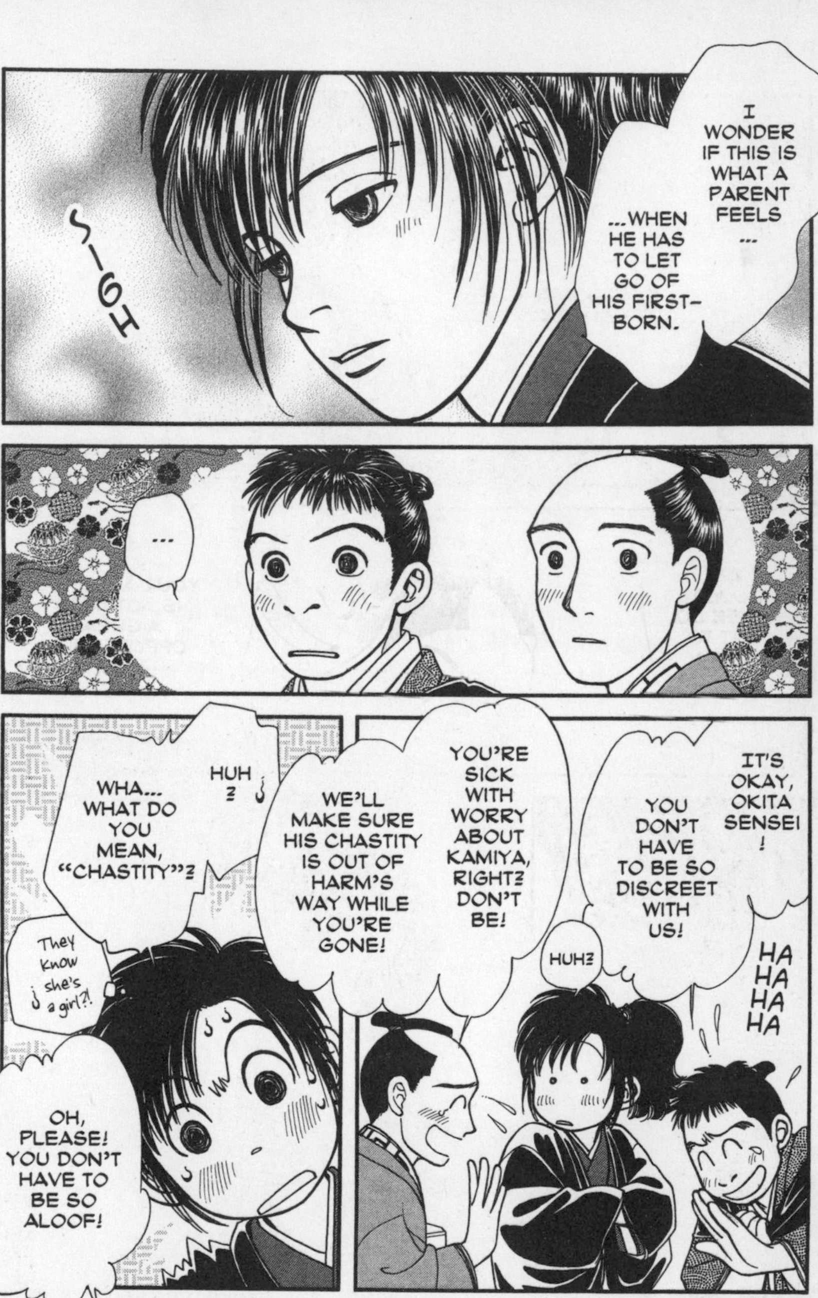

I WONDER IF THIS IS WHAT A PARENT FEELS...
...WHEN HE HAS TO LET GO OF HIS FIRSTBORN.
SIGH
...
IT'S OKAY, OKITA SENSEI!
YOU DON'T HAVE TO BE SO DISCREET WITH US!
YOU'RE SICK WITH WORRY ABOUT KAMIYA, RIGHT? DON'T BE!
WE'LL MAKE SURE HIS CHASTITY IS OUT OF HARM'S WAY WHILE YOU'RE GONE!
HUH?
HA HA HA HA
HUH?
WHA... WHAT DO YOU MEAN, "CHASTITY"?
They know she's a girl?!
OH, PLEASE! YOU DON'T HAVE TO BE SO ALOOF!

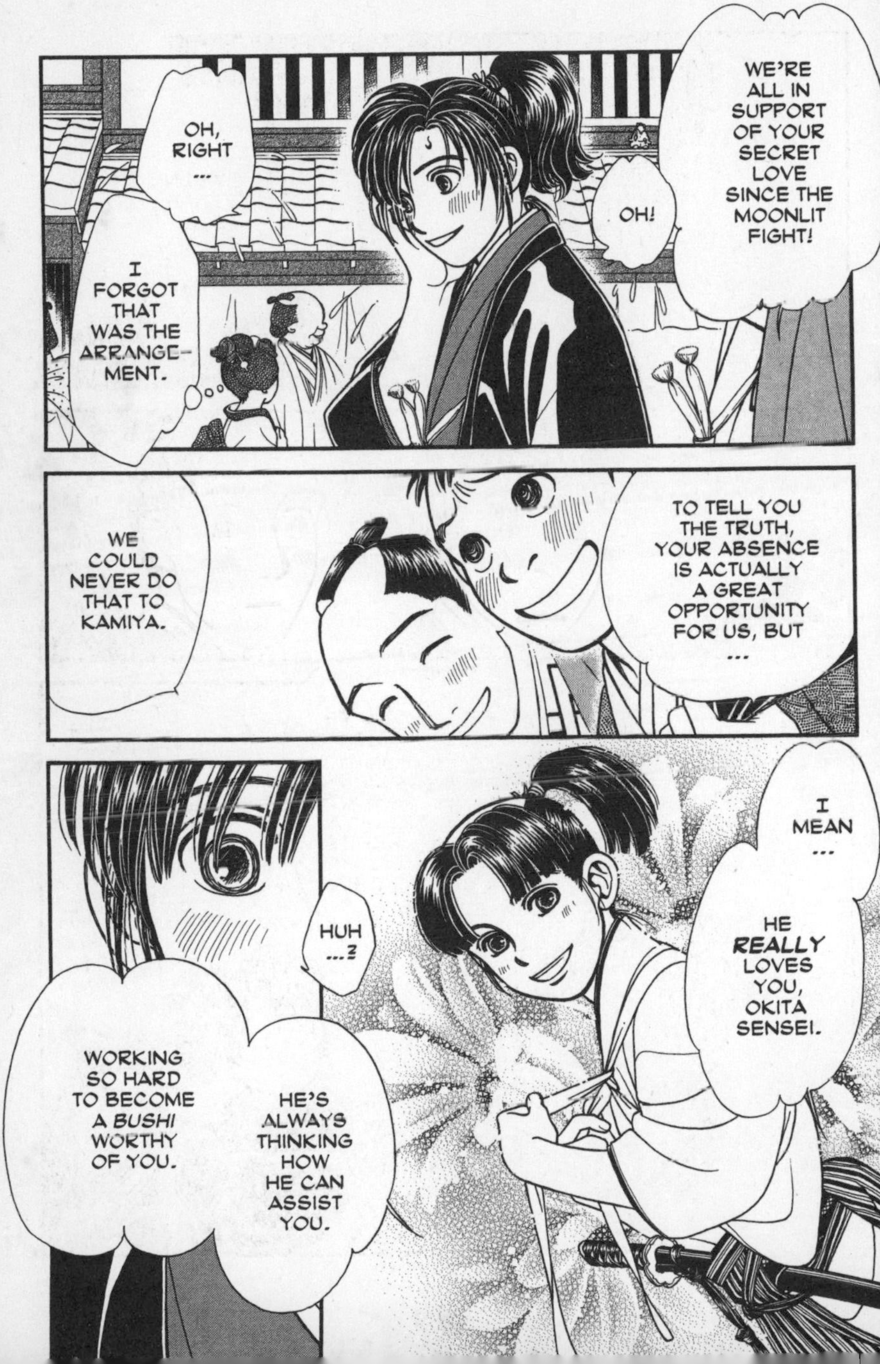
WE'RE ALL IN SUPPORT OF YOUR SECRET LOVE SINCE THE MOONLIT FIGHT!
OH!
OH, RIGHT ...
I FORGOT THAT WAS THE ARRANGEMENT.
TO TELL YOU THE TRUTH, YOUR ABSENCE IS ACTUALLY A GREAT OPPORTUNITY FOR US, BUT ...
WE COULD NEVER DO THAT TO KAMIYA.
I MEAN ...
HE *REALLY* LOVES YOU, OKITA SENSEI.
HUH ...?
HE'S ALWAYS THINKING HOW HE CAN ASSIST YOU.
WORKING SO HARD TO BECOME A *BUSHI* WORTHY OF YOU.

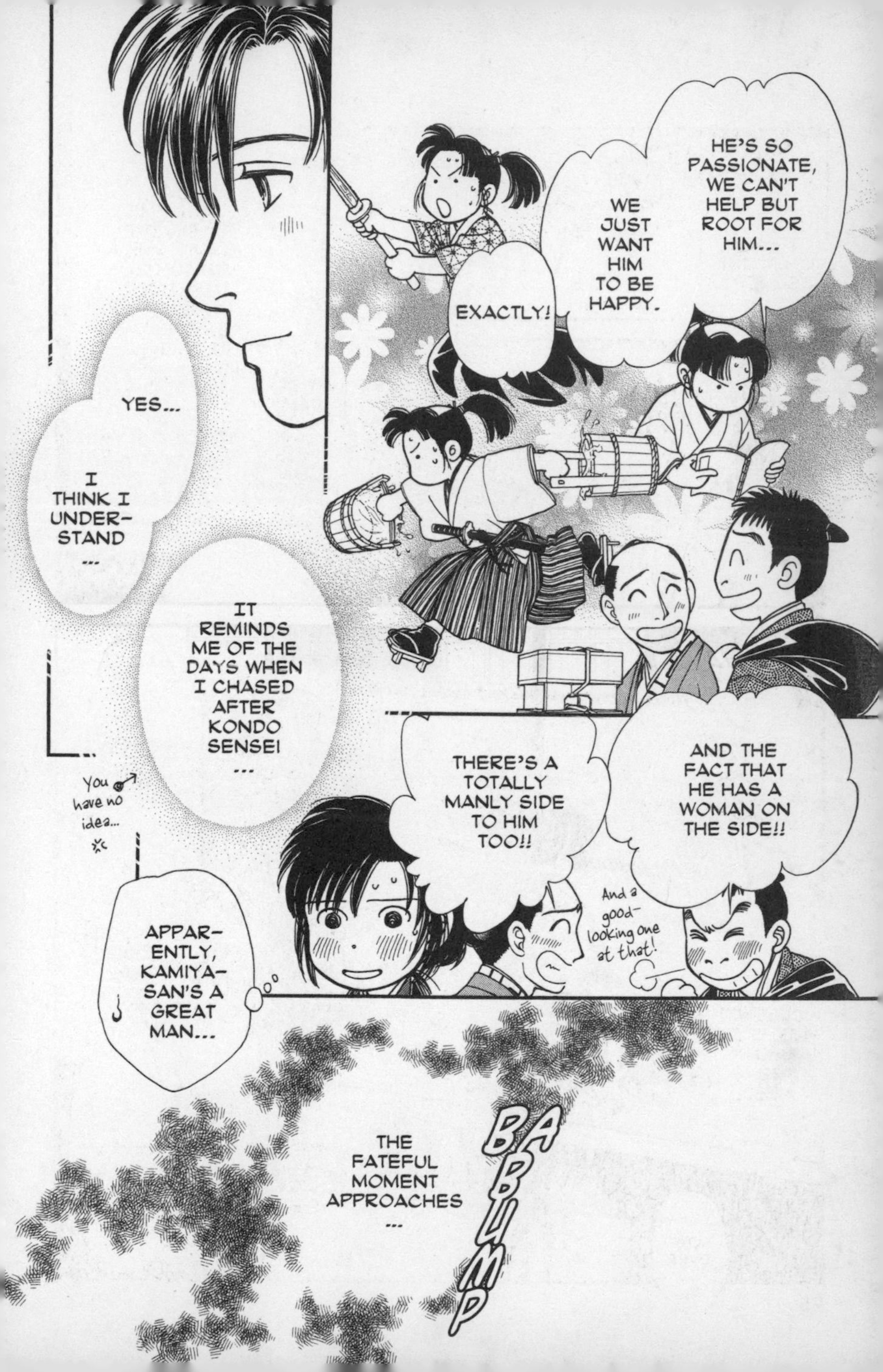

HE'S SO PASSIONATE, WE CAN'T HELP BUT ROOT FOR HIM...
WE JUST WANT HIM TO BE HAPPY.
EXACTLY!
YES...
I THINK I UNDERSTAND...
IT REMINDS ME OF THE DAYS WHEN I CHASED AFTER KONDO SENSEI...
AND THE FACT THAT HE HAS A WOMAN ON THE SIDE!!
And a good-looking one at that!
THERE'S A TOTALLY MANLY SIDE TO HIM TOO!!
You have no idea...
APPARENTLY, KAMIYA-SAN'S A GREAT MAN...
BABUMP
THE FATEFUL MOMENT APPROACHES...

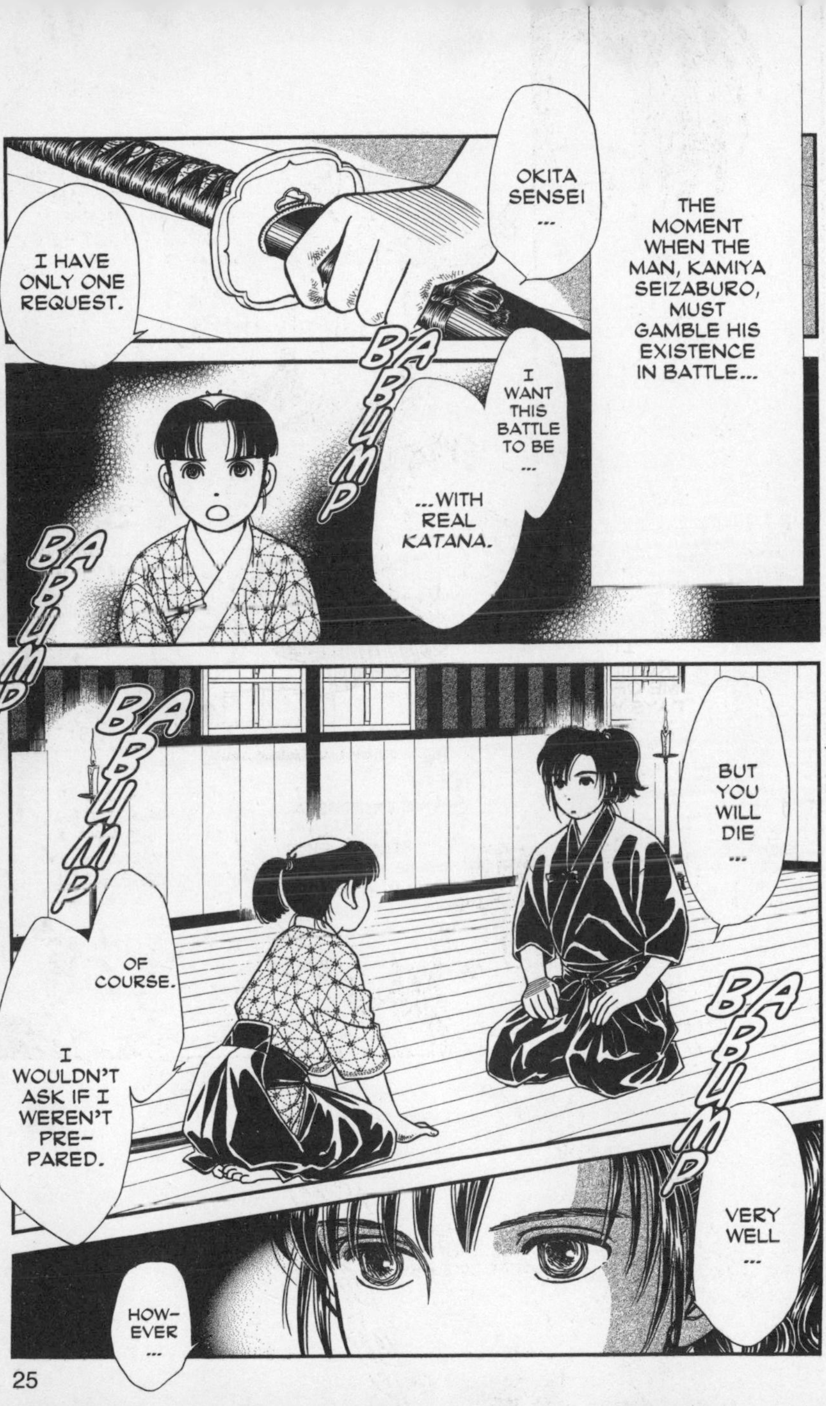
THE MOMENT WHEN THE MAN, KAMIYA SEIZABURO, MUST GAMBLE HIS EXISTENCE IN BATTLE...
OKITA SENSEI ...
I HAVE ONLY ONE REQUEST.
BABUMP
I WANT THIS BATTLE TO BE ...
...WITH REAL KATANA.
BABUMP
BABUMP
BUT YOU WILL DIE ...
OF COURSE.
I WOULDN'T ASK IF I WEREN'T PRE-PARED.
BABUMP
VERY WELL ...
HOW-EVER ...

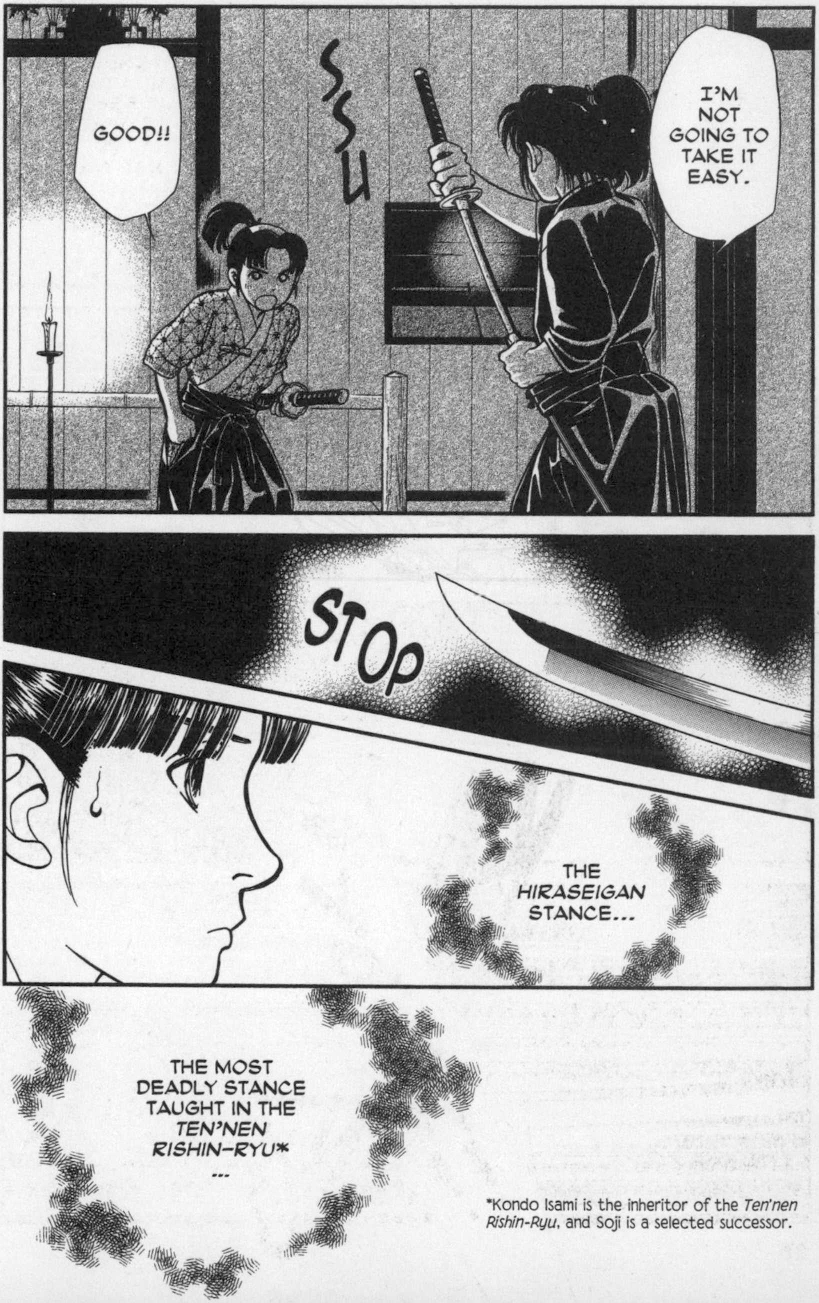
I'M NOT GOING TO TAKE IT EASY.
SSU
GOOD!!
STOP
THE HIRASEIGAN STANCE...
THE MOST DEADLY STANCE TAUGHT IN THE *TEN'NEN RISHIN-RYU** ...

*Kondo Isami is the inheritor of the *Ten'nen Rishin-Ryu*, and Soji is a selected successor.

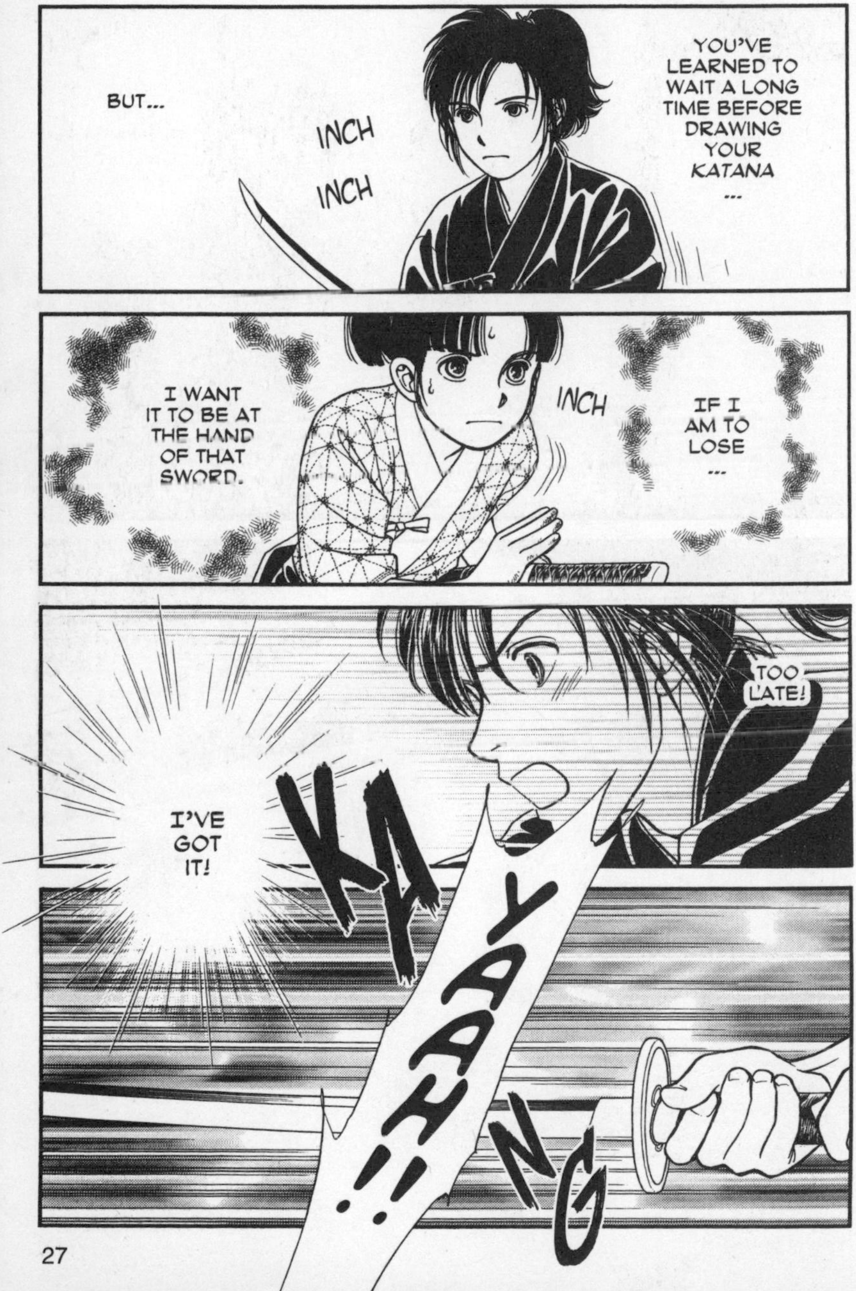
YOU'VE LEARNED TO WAIT A LONG TIME BEFORE DRAWING YOUR KATANA ...
INCH
INCH
BUT...
IF I AM TO LOSE ...
INCH
I WANT IT TO BE AT THE HAND OF THAT SWORD.
TOO LATE!
I'VE GOT IT!
KA
YAAHNG!!!

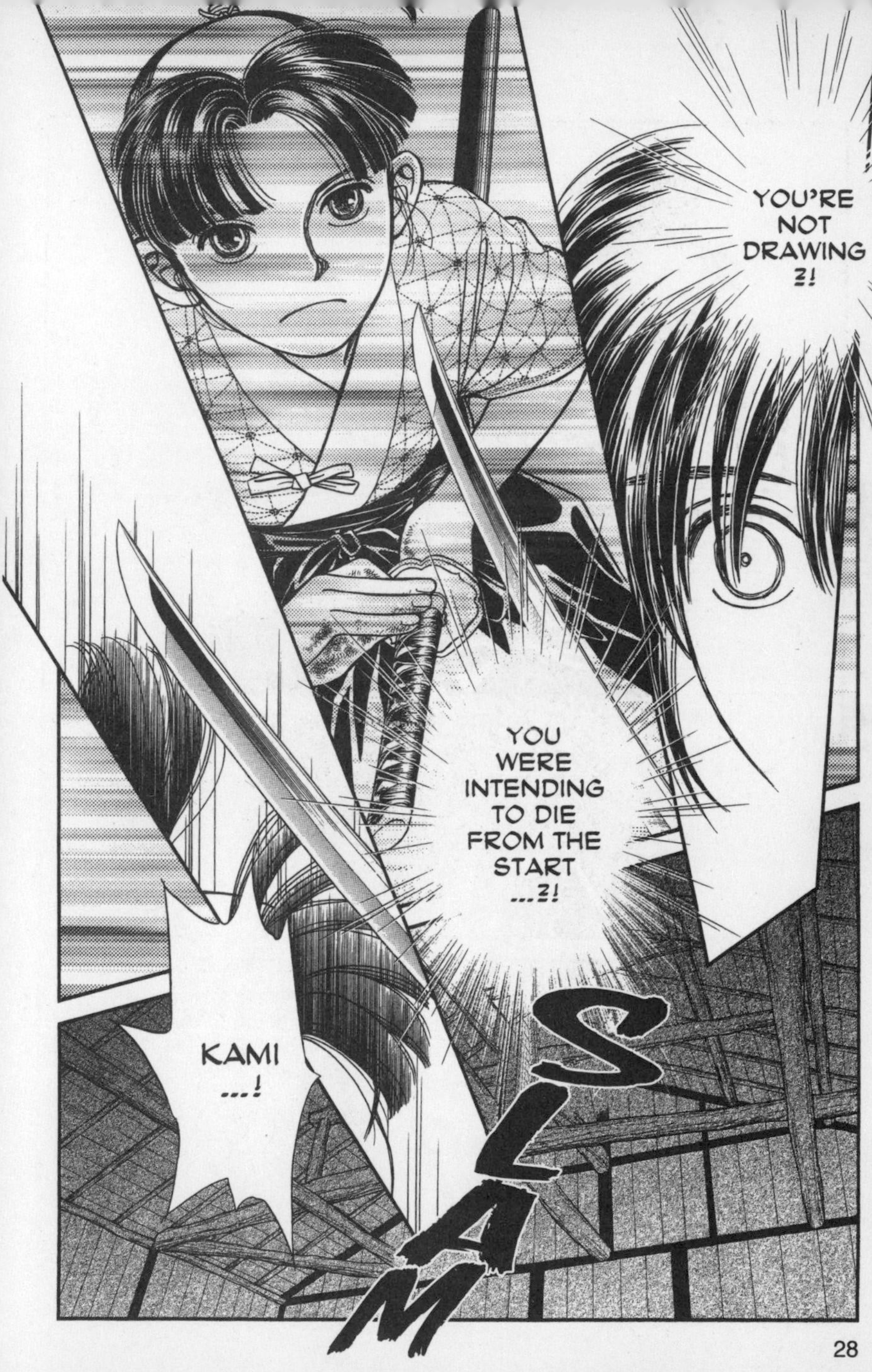
YOU'RE NOT DRAWING ?!
YOU WERE INTENDING TO DIE FROM THE START ...?!
SLAM
KAMI ...!

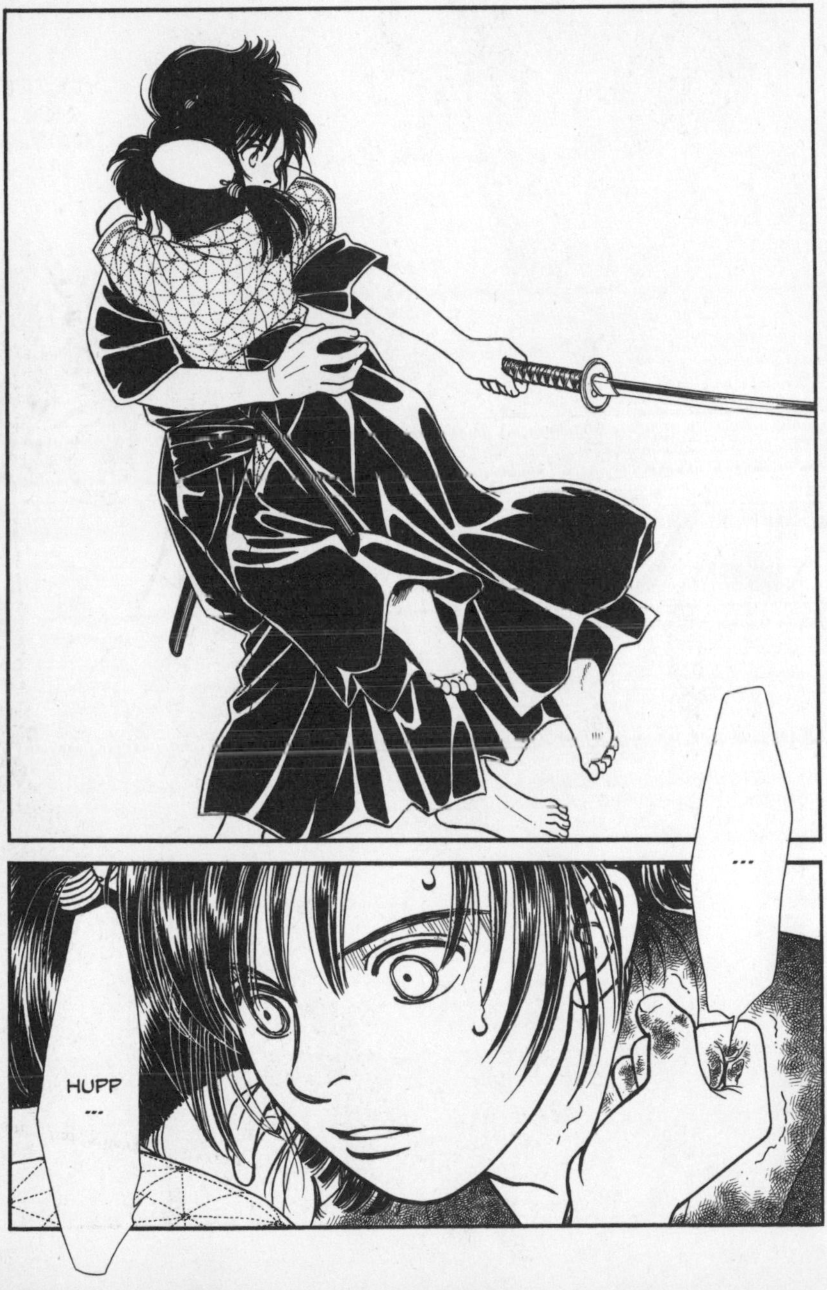
...
HUPP ...

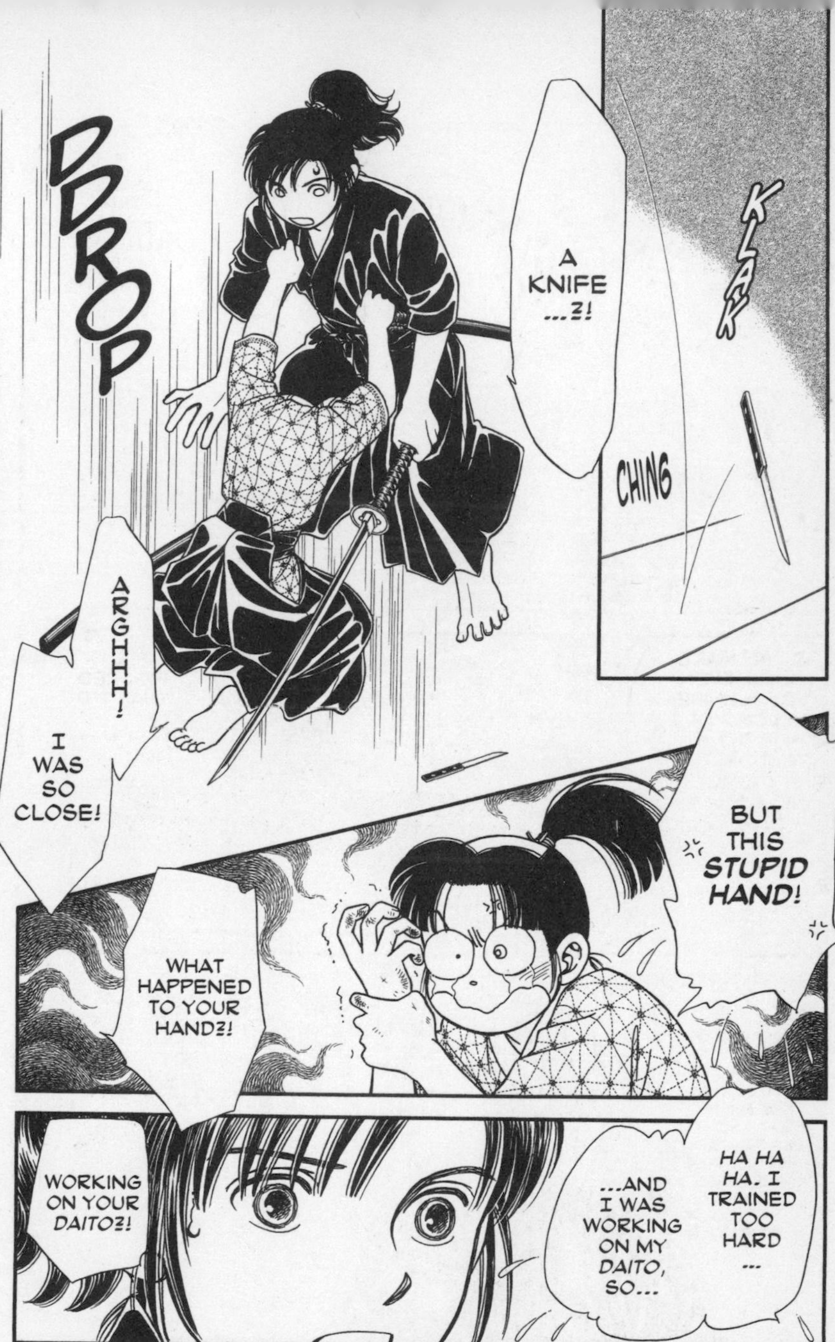
KLAK
A KNIFE ...?!
CHING
DROP
ARGHHH!
I WAS SO CLOSE!
BUT THIS STUPID HAND!
WHAT HAPPENED TO YOUR HAND?!
HA HA HA. I TRAINED TOO HARD ...
...AND I WAS WORKING ON MY DAITO, SO...
WORKING ON YOUR DAITO?!

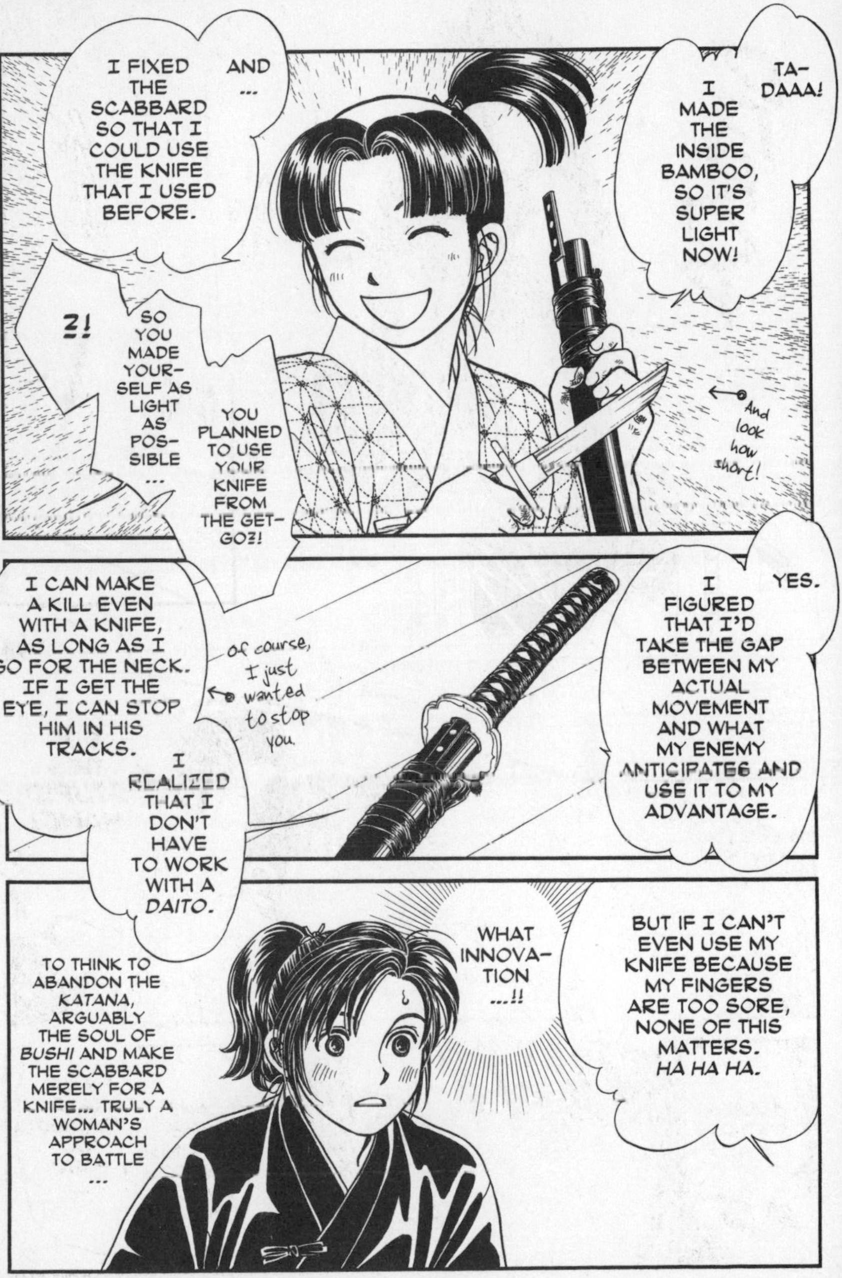
TA-DAAA! I MADE THE INSIDE BAMBOO, SO IT'S SUPER LIGHT NOW!
And look how short!
AND ... I FIXED THE SCABBARD SO THAT I COULD USE THE KNIFE THAT I USED BEFORE.
Z!
SO YOU MADE YOURSELF AS LIGHT AS POSSIBLE ...
YOU PLANNED TO USE YOUR KNIFE FROM THE GET-GO?!
YES. I FIGURED THAT I'D TAKE THE GAP BETWEEN MY ACTUAL MOVEMENT AND WHAT MY ENEMY ANTICIPATES AND USE IT TO MY ADVANTAGE.
I CAN MAKE A KILL EVEN WITH A KNIFE, AS LONG AS I GO FOR THE NECK. IF I GET THE EYE, I CAN STOP HIM IN HIS TRACKS.
Of course, I just wanted to stop you.
I REALIZED THAT I DON'T HAVE TO WORK WITH A *DAITO*.
BUT IF I CAN'T EVEN USE MY KNIFE BECAUSE MY FINGERS ARE TOO SORE, NONE OF THIS MATTERS. *HA HA HA.*
WHAT INNOVATION ...!!
TO THINK TO ABANDON THE *KATANA*, ARGUABLY THE SOUL OF *BUSHI* AND MAKE THE SCABBARD MERELY FOR A KNIFE... TRULY A WOMAN'S APPROACH TO BATTLE ...

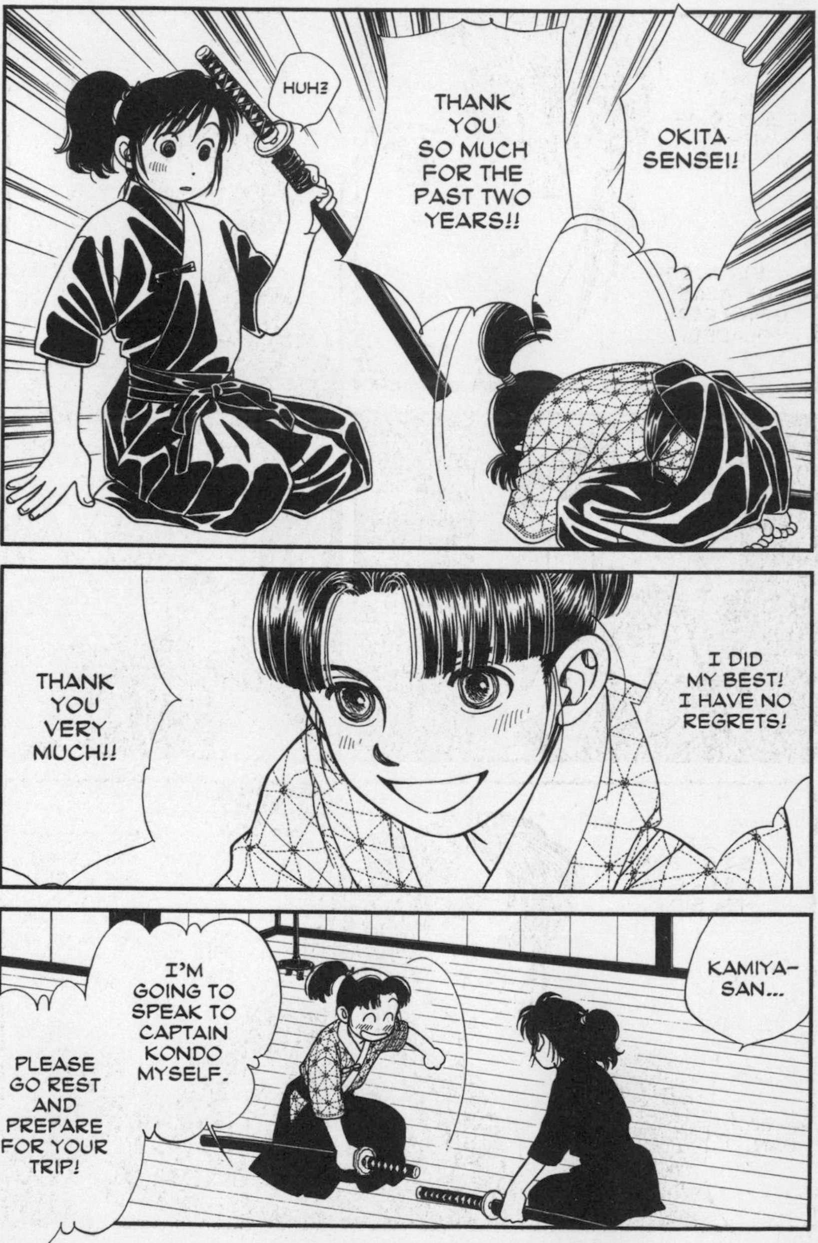
OKITA SENSEI!
THANK YOU SO MUCH FOR THE PAST TWO YEARS!!
HUH?
I DID MY BEST! I HAVE NO REGRETS!
THANK YOU VERY MUCH!!
KAMIYA-SAN...
I'M GOING TO SPEAK TO CAPTAIN KONDO MYSELF.
PLEASE GO REST AND PREPARE FOR YOUR TRIP!

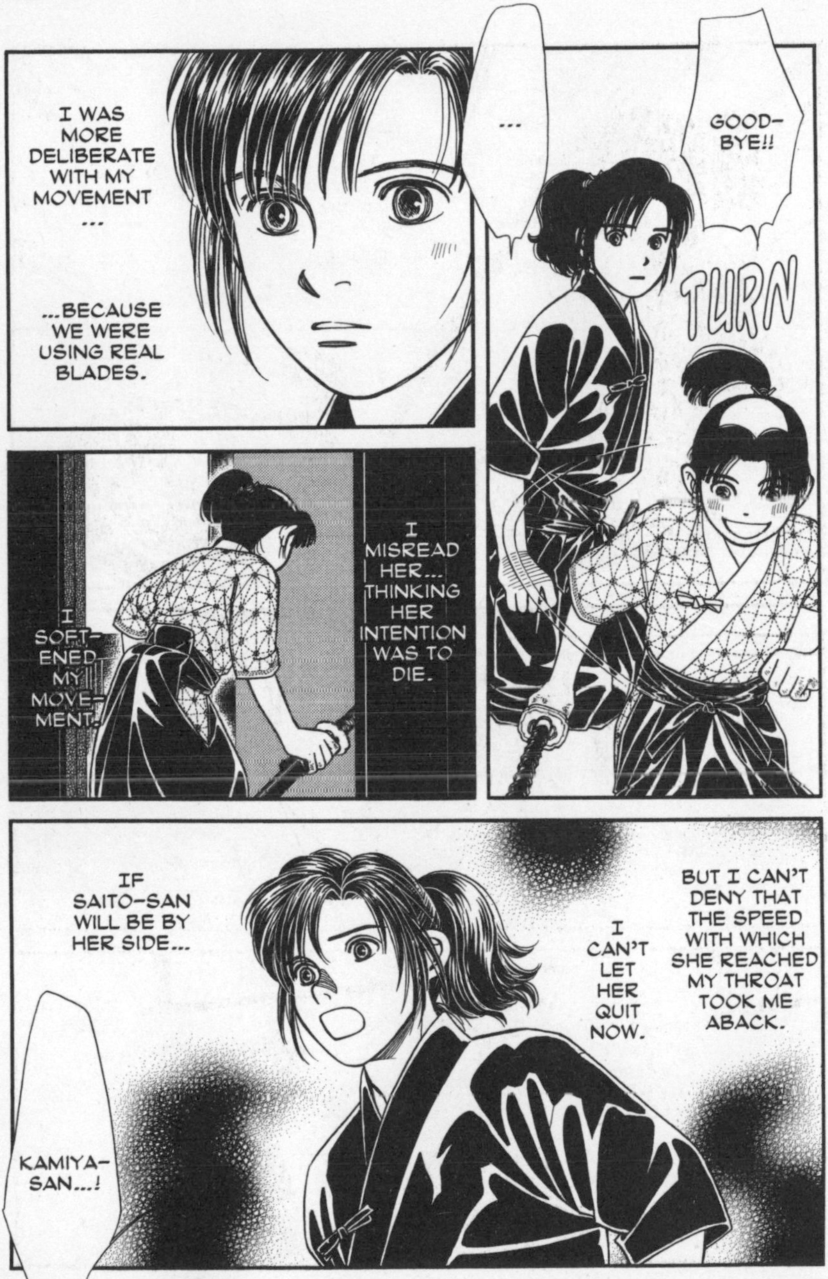
GOOD-BYE!!
TURN
...
I WAS MORE DELIBERATE WITH MY MOVEMENT...
...BECAUSE WE WERE USING REAL BLADES.
I MISREAD HER... THINKING HER INTENTION WAS TO DIE.
I SOFTENED MY MOVEMENT.
BUT I CAN'T DENY THAT THE SPEED WITH WHICH SHE REACHED MY THROAT TOOK ME ABACK.
I CAN'T LET HER QUIT NOW.
IF SAITO-SAN WILL BE BY HER SIDE...
KAMIYA-SAN...!

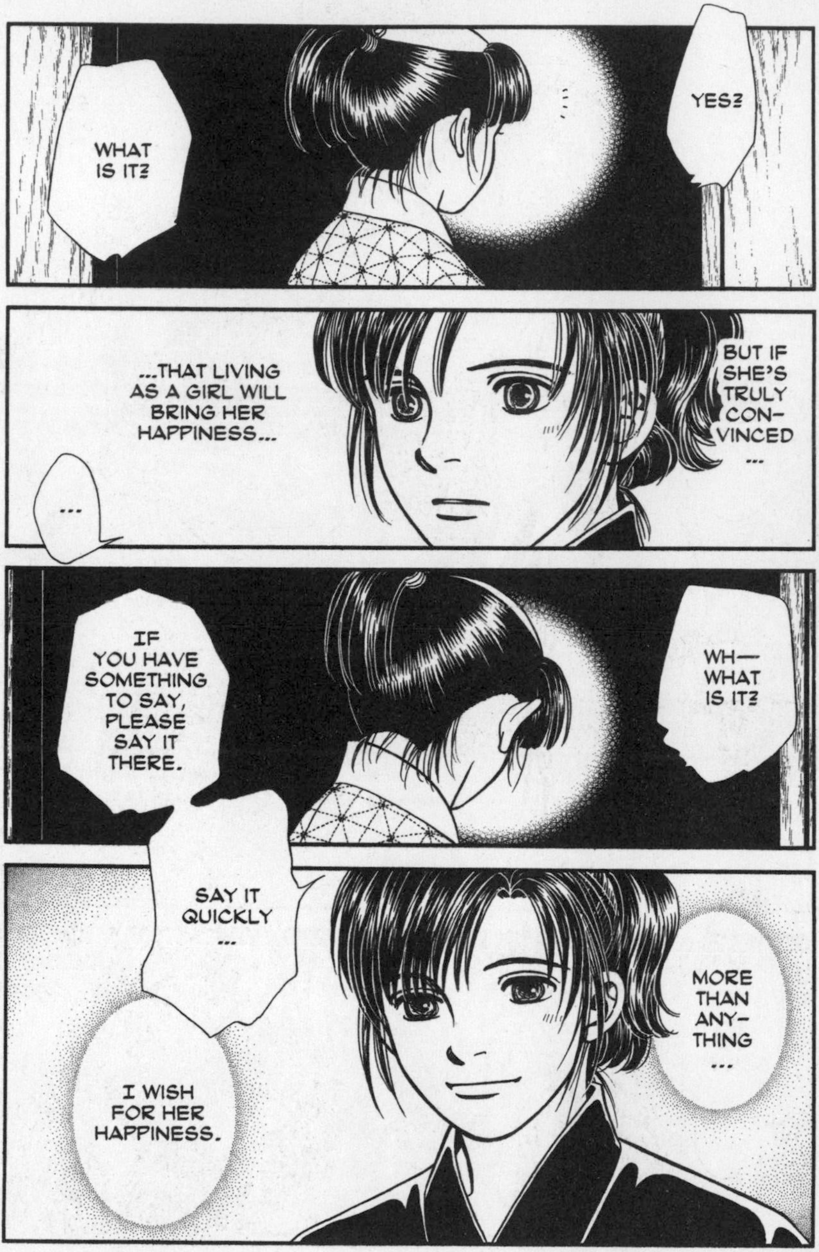

YES?
WHAT IS IT?
BUT IF SHE'S TRULY CON-VINCED ...
...THAT LIVING AS A GIRL WILL BRING HER HAPPINESS...
...
WH— WHAT IS IT?
IF YOU HAVE SOMETHING TO SAY, PLEASE SAY IT THERE.
SAY IT QUICKLY ...
MORE THAN ANY-THING ...
I WISH FOR HER HAPPINESS.

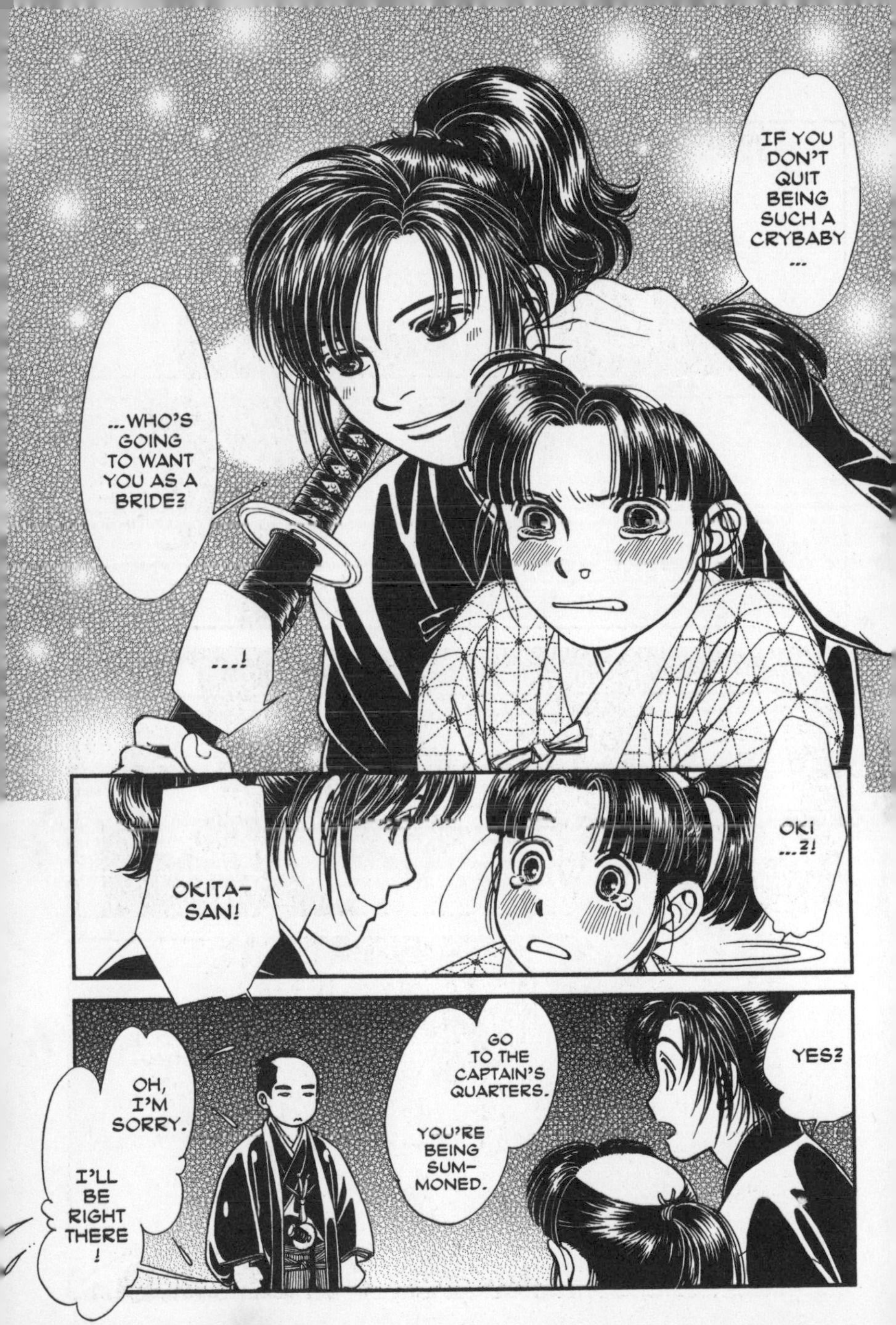
IF YOU DON'T QUIT BEING SUCH A CRYBABY ...
...WHO'S GOING TO WANT YOU AS A BRIDE?
...!
OKI ...?!
OKITA-SAN!
YES?
GO TO THE CAPTAIN'S QUARTERS.
YOU'RE BEING SUM-MONED.
OH, I'M SORRY.
I'LL BE RIGHT THERE!

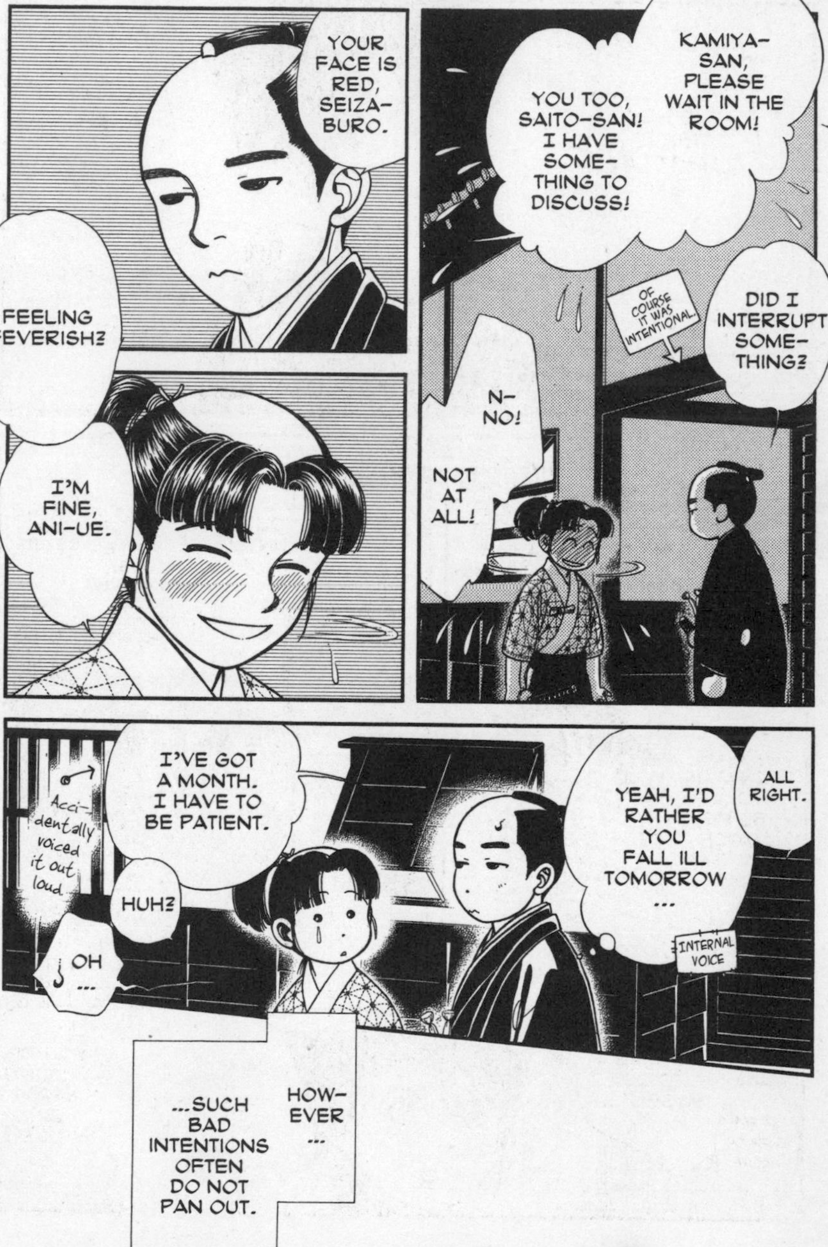
KAMIYA-SAN, PLEASE WAIT IN THE ROOM!
YOU TOO, SAITO-SAN! I HAVE SOMETHING TO DISCUSS!
DID I INTERRUPT SOMETHING?
OF COURSE IT WAS INTENTIONAL.
N-NO!
NOT AT ALL!
YOUR FACE IS RED, SEIZABURO.
FEELING FEVERISH?
I'M FINE, ANI-UE.
ALL RIGHT.
YEAH, I'D RATHER YOU FALL ILL TOMORROW ...
INTERNAL VOICE
I'VE GOT A MONTH. I HAVE TO BE PATIENT.
Accidentally voiced it out loud
HUH?
OH ...
HOWEVER ...
...SUCH BAD INTENTIONS OFTEN DO NOT PAN OUT.

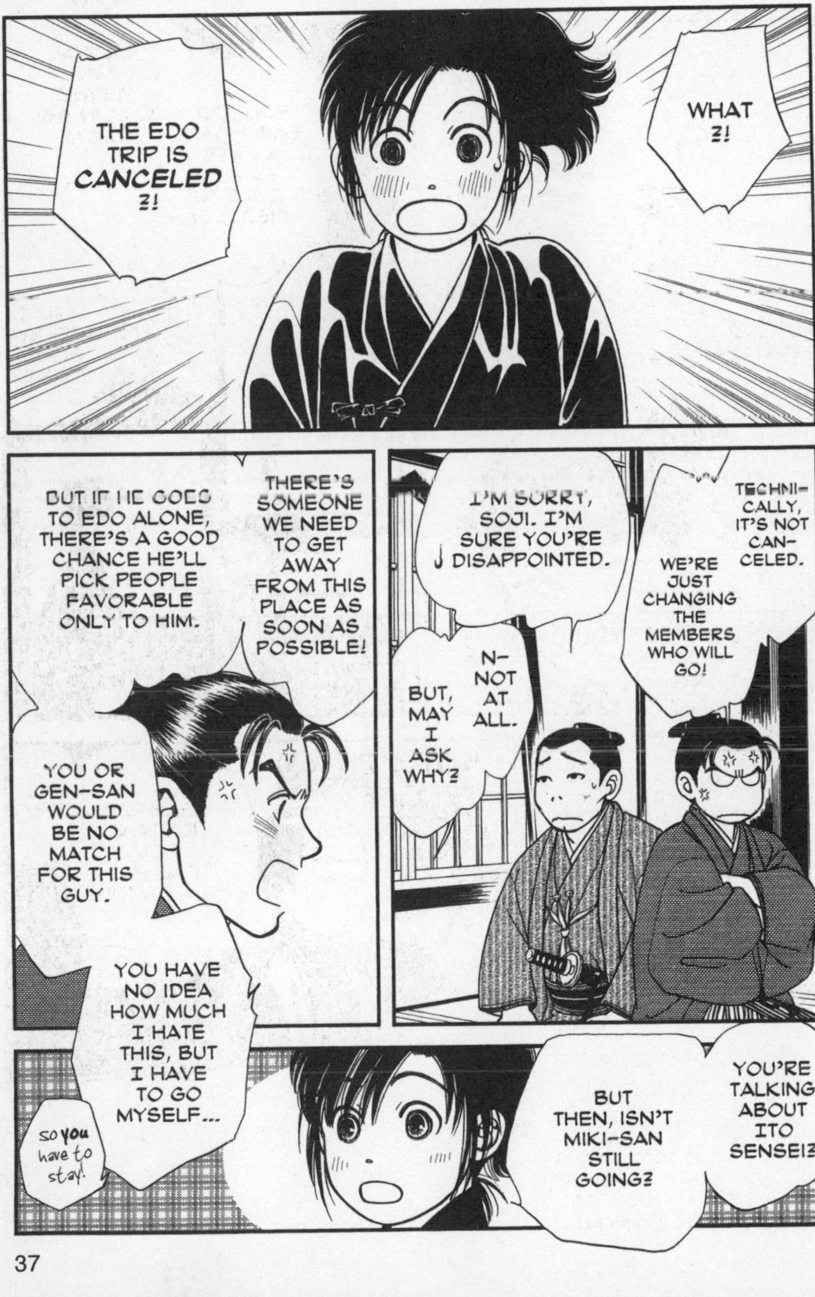
WHAT?!
THE EDO TRIP IS CANCELED?!
TECHNICALLY, IT'S NOT CANCELED.
WE'RE JUST CHANGING THE MEMBERS WHO WILL GO!
I'M SORRY, SOJI. I'M SURE YOU'RE DISAPPOINTED.
N-NOT AT ALL.
BUT, MAY I ASK WHY?
THERE'S SOMEONE WE NEED TO GET AWAY FROM THIS PLACE AS SOON AS POSSIBLE!
BUT IF HE GOES TO EDO ALONE, THERE'S A GOOD CHANCE HE'LL PICK PEOPLE FAVORABLE ONLY TO HIM.
YOU OR GEN-SAN WOULD BE NO MATCH FOR THIS GUY.
YOU HAVE NO IDEA HOW MUCH I HATE THIS, BUT I HAVE TO GO MYSELF...
so you have to stay!
YOU'RE TALKING ABOUT ITO SENSEI?
BUT THEN, ISN'T MIKI-SAN STILL GOING?

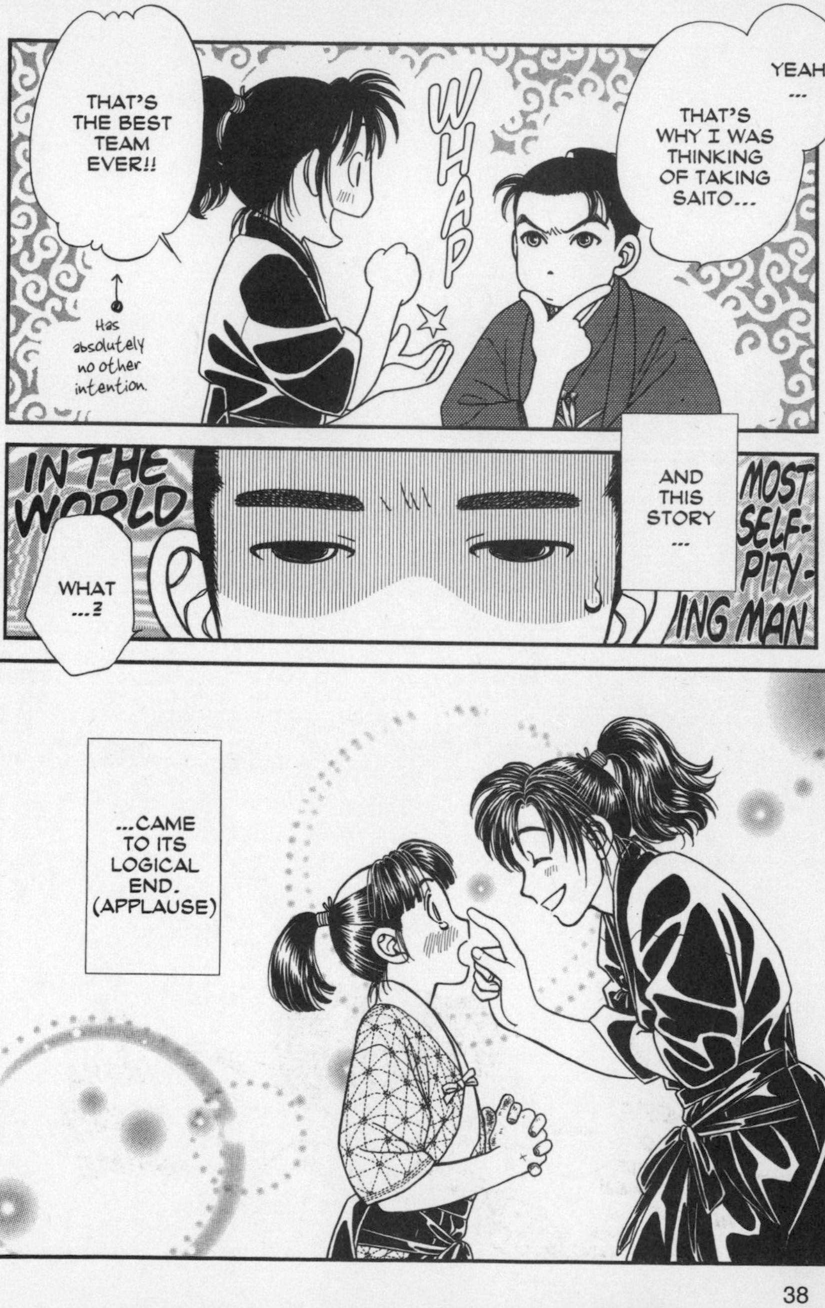

YEAH ... THAT'S WHY I WAS THINKING OF TAKING SAITO...
WHAP
THAT'S THE BEST TEAM EVER!!
Has absolutely no other intention.
AND THIS STORY ...
MOST SELF-PITYING MAN
IN THE WORLD
WHAT ...?
...CAME TO ITS LOGICAL END. (APPLAUSE)

EDO
IROHA
KARUTA
GAME

"U" う

USO
KARA DETA
MAKOTO
"MANY A TRUE
WORD IS SPOKEN
IN JEST"
(lit. Truth
born from a lie)

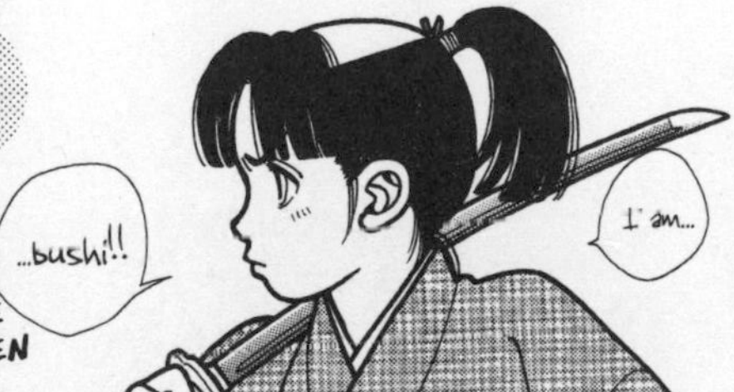
I am...
...bushi!!

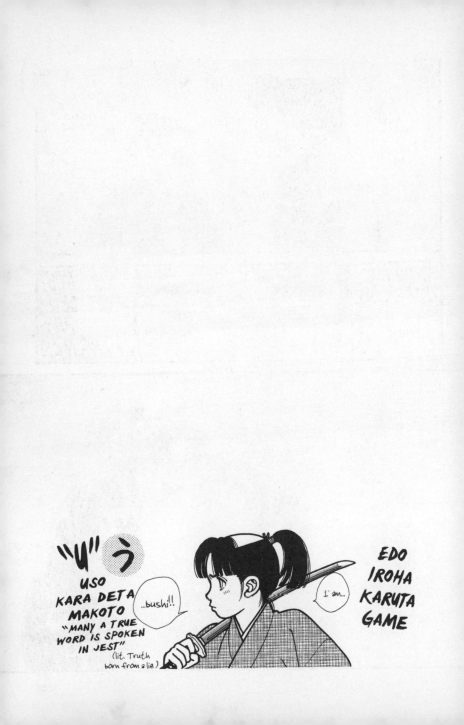

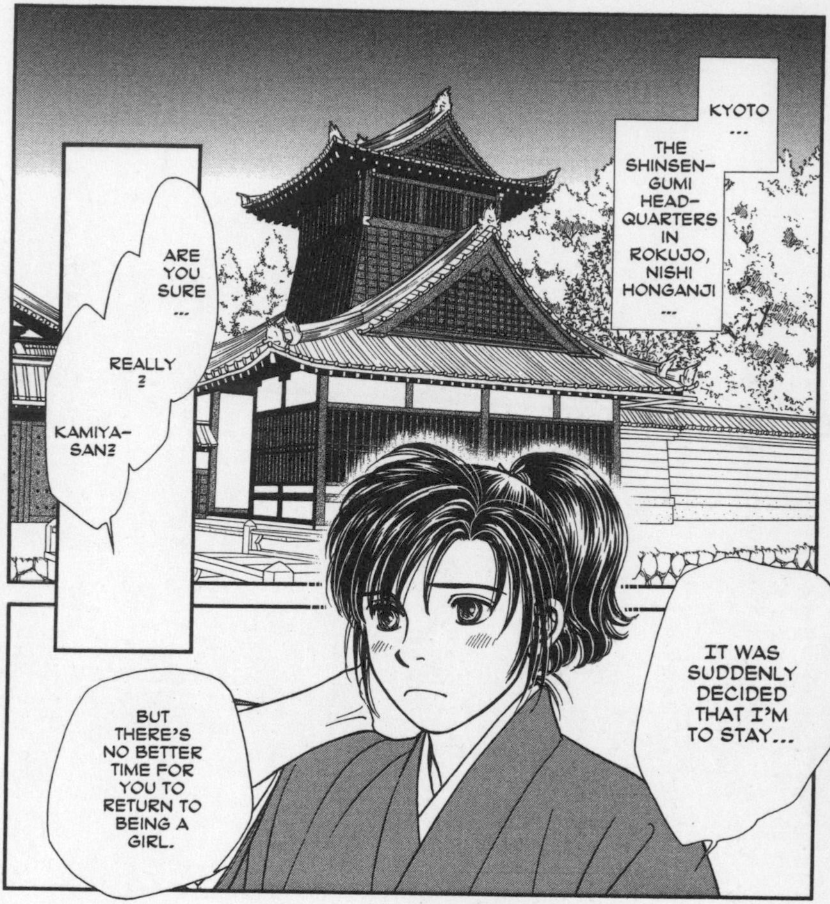
KYOTO ...
THE SHINSEN-GUMI HEAD-QUARTERS IN ROKUJO, NISHI HONGANJI ...
ARE YOU SURE ... REALLY? KAMIYA-SAN?
IT WAS SUDDENLY DECIDED THAT I'M TO STAY...
BUT THERE'S NO BETTER TIME FOR YOU TO RETURN TO BEING A GIRL.

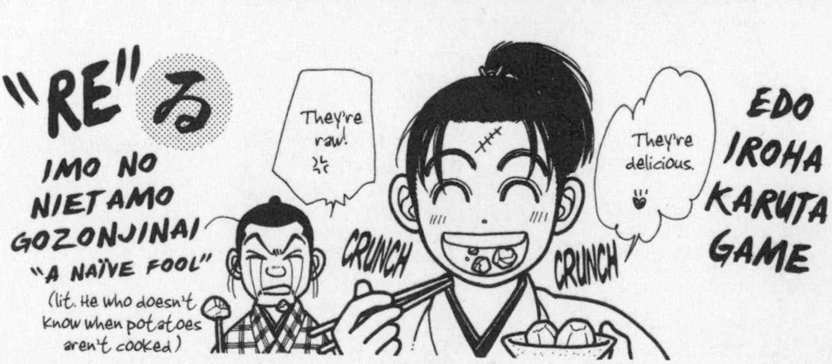
EDO IROHA KARUTA GAME
"RE" る
IMO NO NIETAMO GOZONJINAI
"A NAÏVE FOOL"
(lit. He who doesn't know when potatoes aren't cooked)
They're delicious.
CRUNCH
They're raw!
CRUNCH

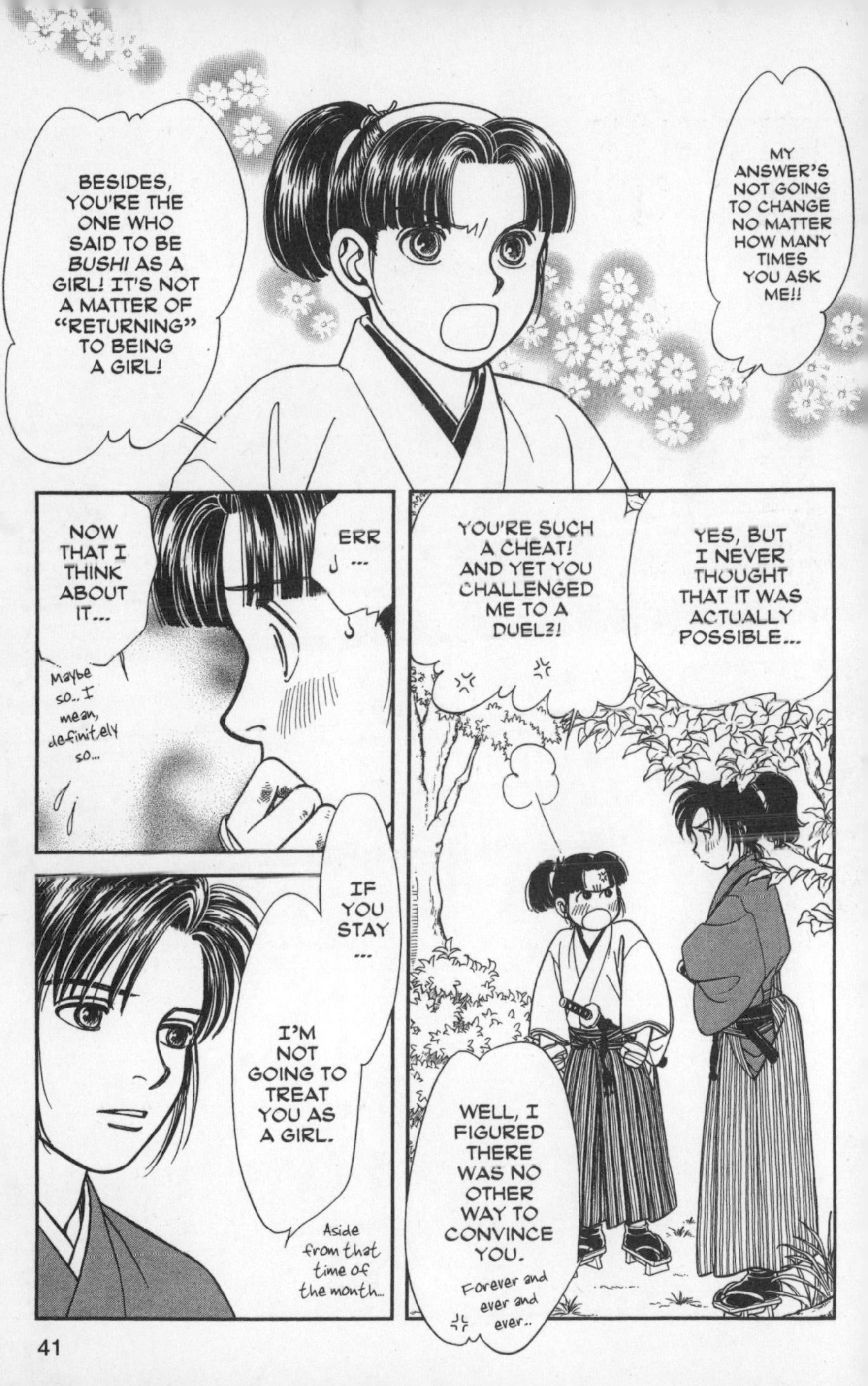
MY ANSWER'S NOT GOING TO CHANGE NO MATTER HOW MANY TIMES YOU ASK ME!!
BESIDES, YOU'RE THE ONE WHO SAID TO BE *BUSHI* AS A GIRL! IT'S NOT A MATTER OF "RETURNING" TO BEING A GIRL!
YES, BUT I NEVER THOUGHT THAT IT WAS ACTUALLY POSSIBLE...
YOU'RE SUCH A CHEAT! AND YET YOU CHALLENGED ME TO A DUEL?!
WELL, I FIGURED THERE WAS NO OTHER WAY TO CONVINCE YOU.
Forever and ever and ever..
ERR ...
NOW THAT I THINK ABOUT IT...
Maybe so.. I mean, definitely so...
IF YOU STAY ...
I'M NOT GOING TO TREAT YOU AS A GIRL.
Aside from that time of the month...

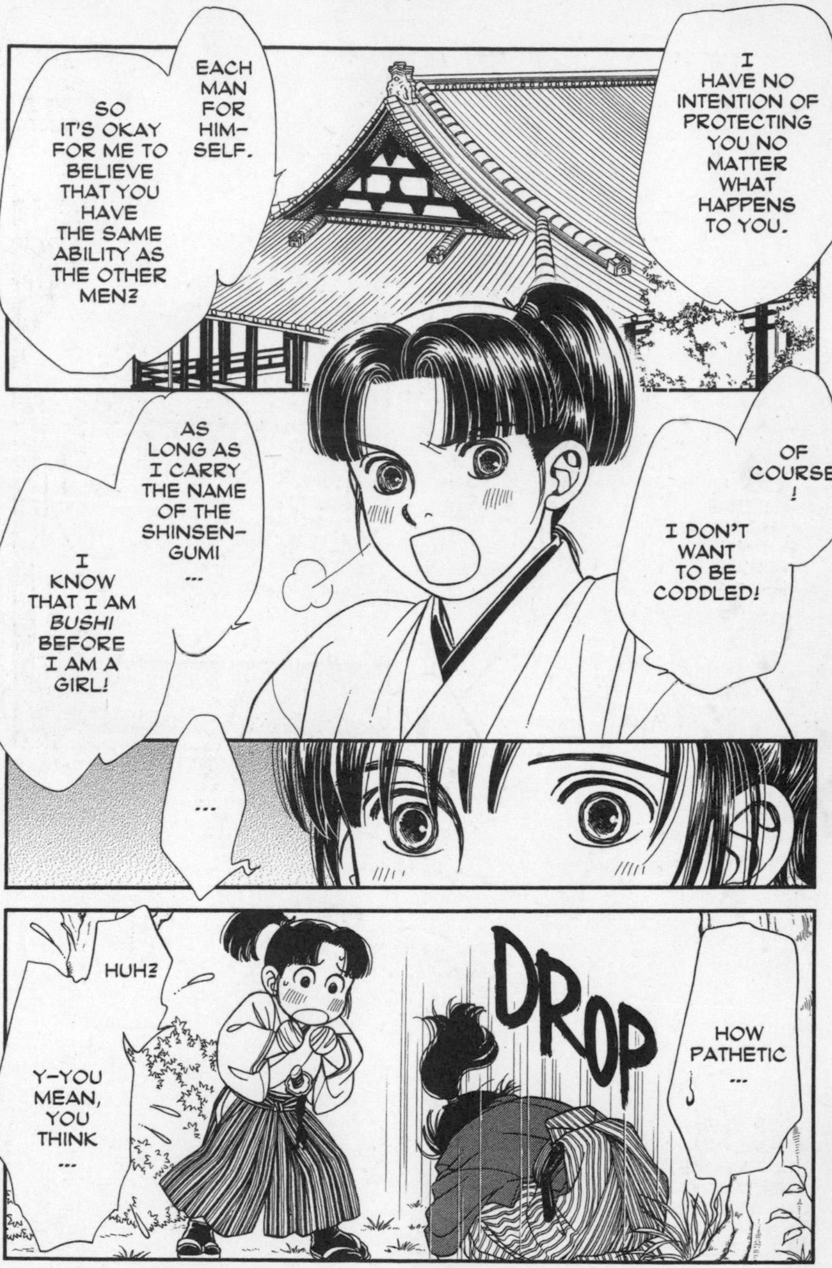
I HAVE NO INTENTION OF PROTECTING YOU NO MATTER WHAT HAPPENS TO YOU.
EACH MAN FOR HIM-SELF.
SO IT'S OKAY FOR ME TO BELIEVE THAT YOU HAVE THE SAME ABILITY AS THE OTHER MEN?
OF COURSE!
I DON'T WANT TO BE CODDLED!
AS LONG AS I CARRY THE NAME OF THE SHINSEN-GUMI...
I KNOW THAT I AM *BUSHI* BEFORE I AM A GIRL!
...
HOW PATHETIC...
DROP
HUH?
Y-YOU MEAN, YOU THINK...

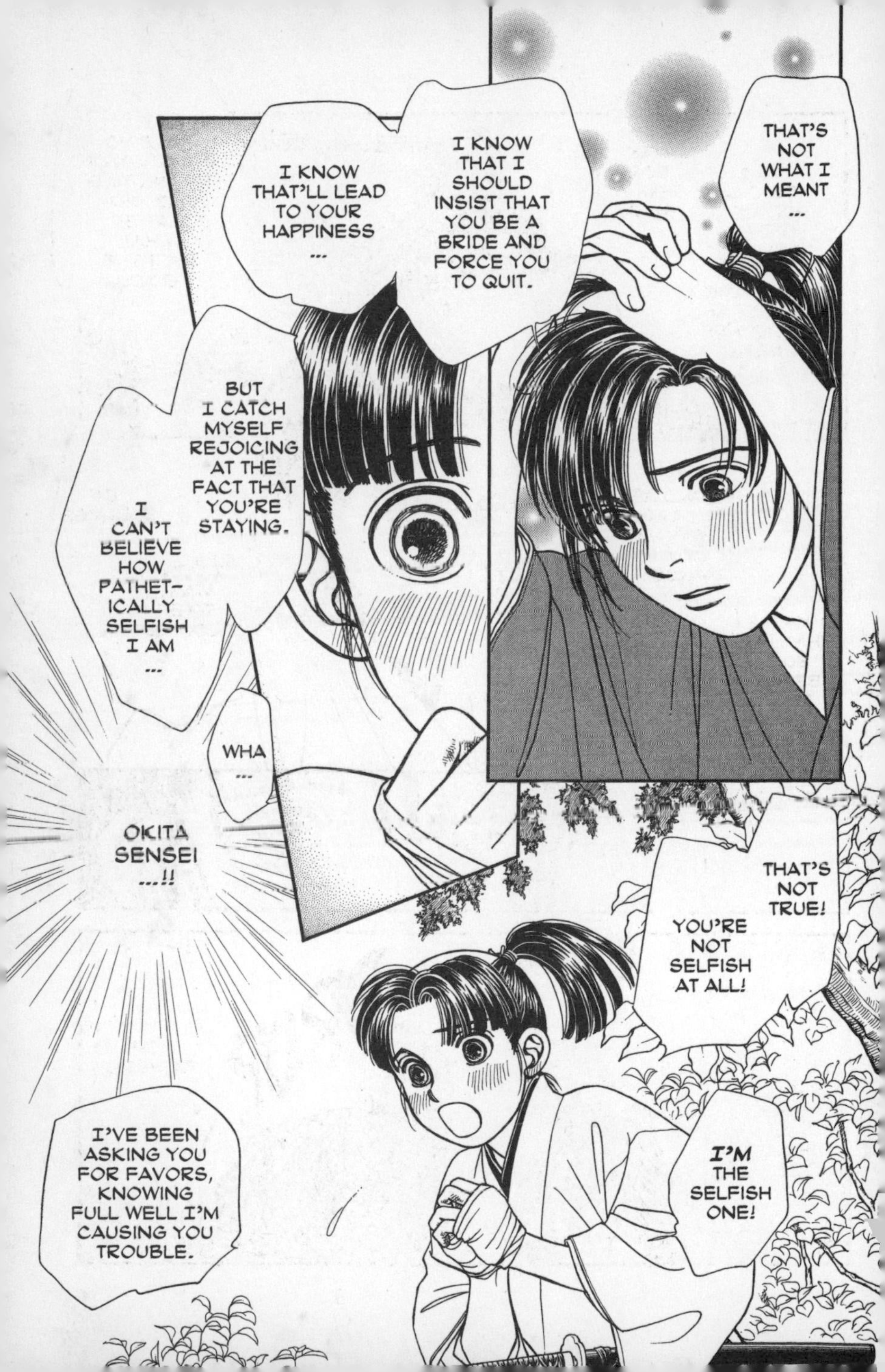
THAT'S NOT WHAT I MEANT ...
I KNOW THAT I SHOULD INSIST THAT YOU BE A BRIDE AND FORCE YOU TO QUIT.
I KNOW THAT'LL LEAD TO YOUR HAPPINESS ...
BUT I CATCH MYSELF REJOICING AT THE FACT THAT YOU'RE STAYING.
I CAN'T BELIEVE HOW PATHET-ICALLY SELFISH I AM ...
WHA ...
OKITA SENSEI ...!!
THAT'S NOT TRUE!
YOU'RE NOT SELFISH AT ALL!
I'M THE SELFISH ONE!
I'VE BEEN ASKING YOU FOR FAVORS, KNOWING FULL WELL I'M CAUSING YOU TROUBLE.

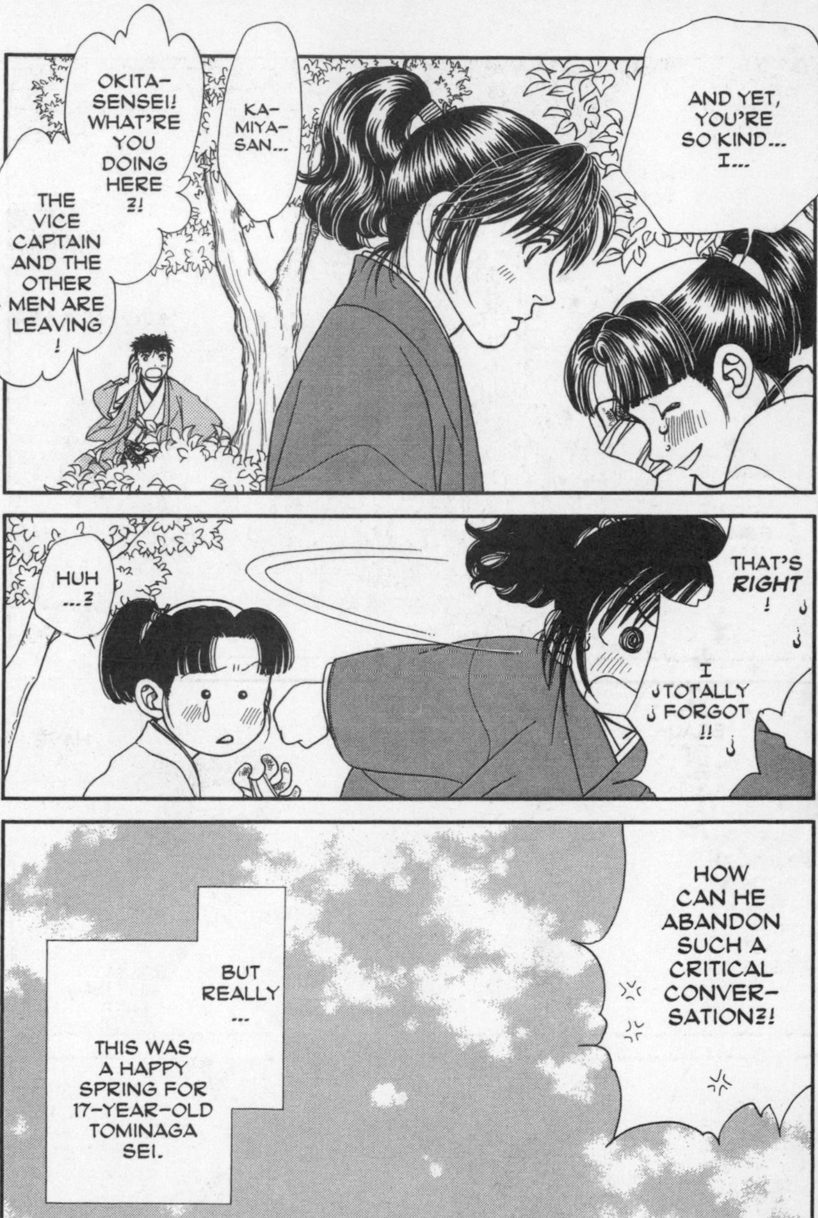
AND YET, YOU'RE SO KIND... I...
KA-MIYA-SAN...
OKITA-SENSEI! WHAT'RE YOU DOING HERE?!
THE VICE CAPTAIN AND THE OTHER MEN ARE LEAVING!
THAT'S RIGHT!
I TOTALLY FORGOT!!
HUH...?
HOW CAN HE ABANDON SUCH A CRITICAL CONVER-SATION?!
BUT REALLY...
THIS WAS A HAPPY SPRING FOR 17-YEAR-OLD TOMINAGA SEI.

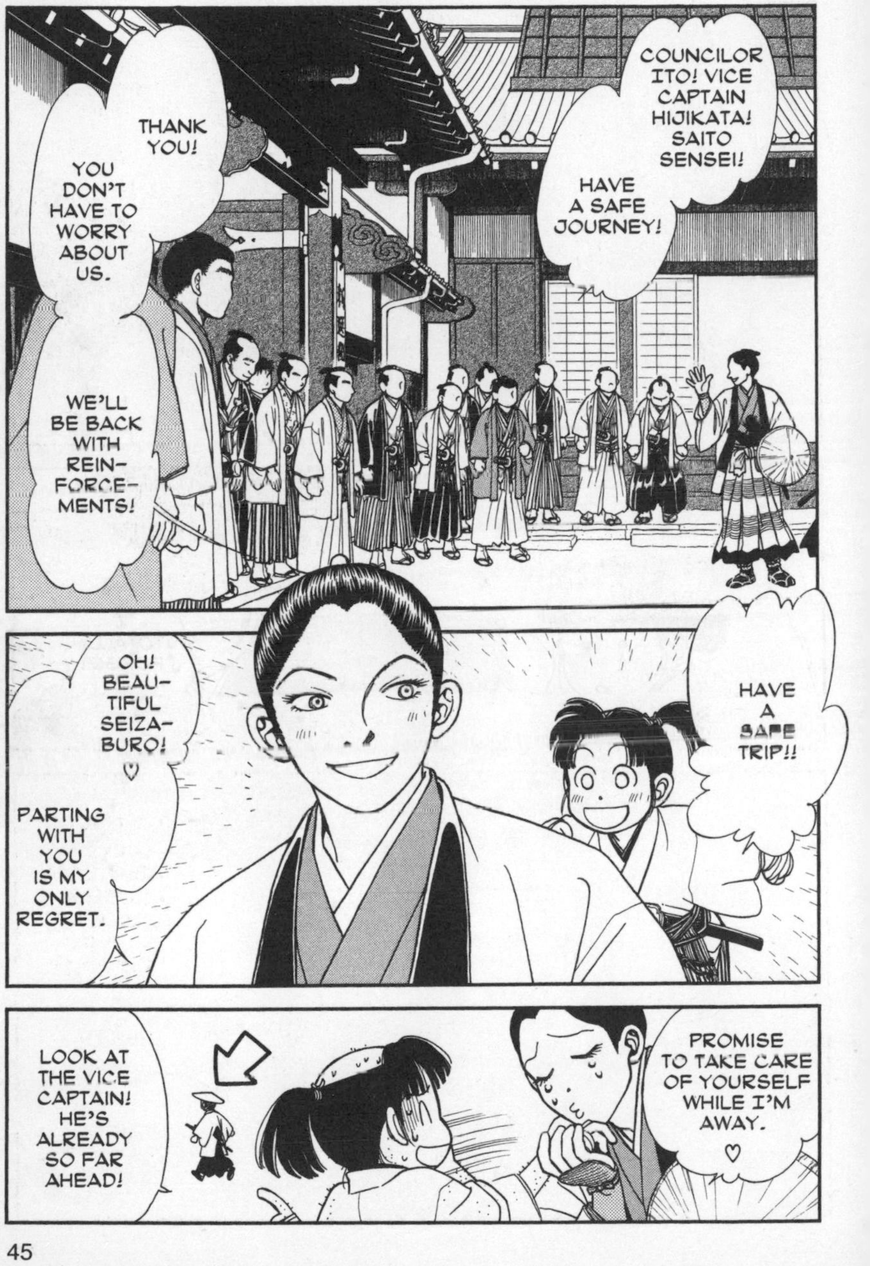
COUNCILOR ITO! VICE CAPTAIN HIJIKATA! SAITO SENSEI!
HAVE A SAFE JOURNEY!
THANK YOU!
YOU DON'T HAVE TO WORRY ABOUT US.
WE'LL BE BACK WITH REINFORCEMENTS!
HAVE A SAFE TRIP!!
OH! BEAUTIFUL SEIZABURO! ♡
PARTING WITH YOU IS MY ONLY REGRET.
PROMISE TO TAKE CARE OF YOURSELF WHILE I'M AWAY. ♡
LOOK AT THE VICE CAPTAIN! HE'S ALREADY SO FAR AHEAD!

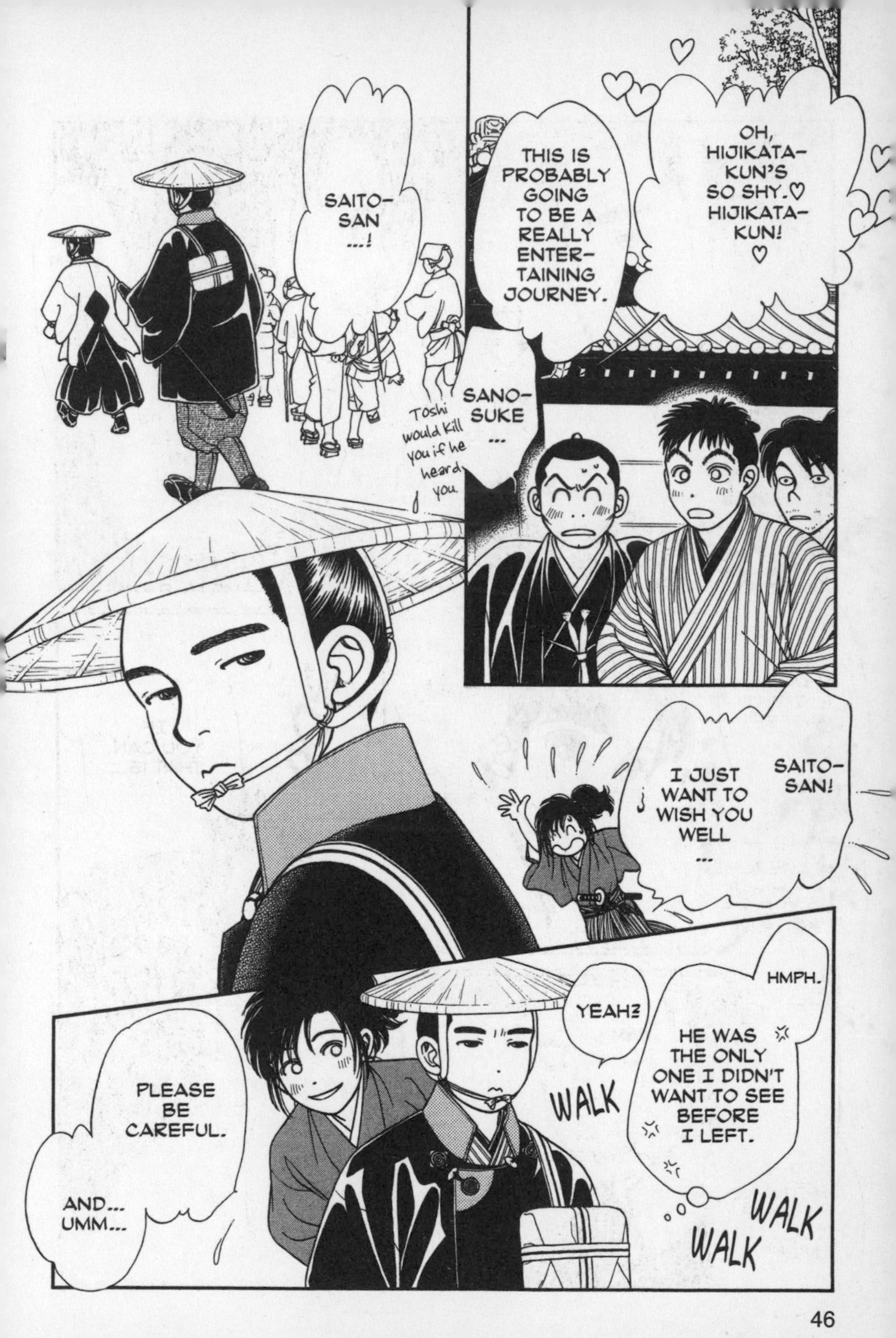
OH, HIJIKATA-KUN'S SO SHY.♡ HIJIKATA-KUN! ♡
THIS IS PROBABLY GOING TO BE A REALLY ENTERTAINING JOURNEY.
SANO-SUKE ...
Toshi would kill you if he heard you.
SAITO-SAN ...!
SAITO-SAN!
I JUST WANT TO WISH YOU WELL ...
HMPH.
HE WAS THE ONLY ONE I DIDN'T WANT TO SEE BEFORE I LEFT.
YEAH?
WALK
WALK
WALK
PLEASE BE CAREFUL.
AND... UMM...

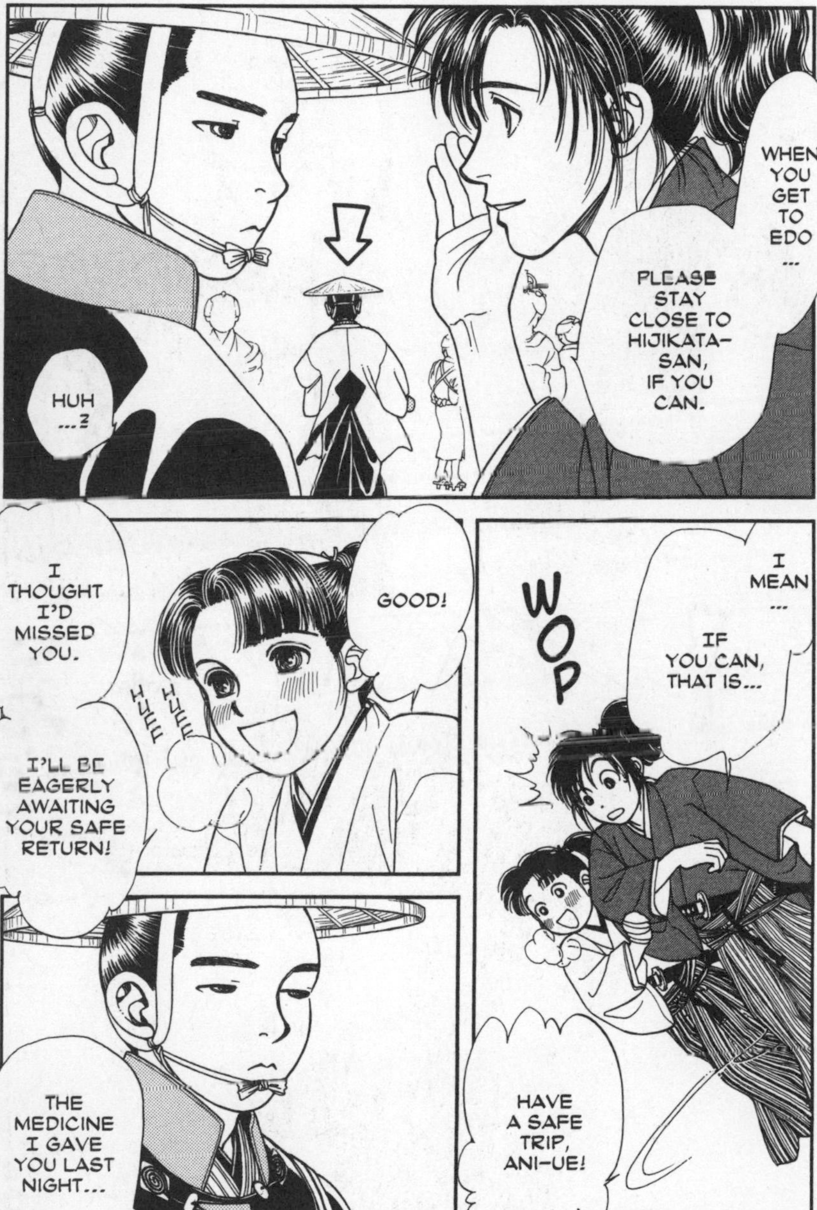
WHEN YOU GET TO EDO ...
PLEASE STAY CLOSE TO HIJIKATA-SAN, IF YOU CAN.
HUH ...?
I MEAN ...
IF YOU CAN, THAT IS...
WOP
HAVE A SAFE TRIP, ANI-UE!
GOOD!
I THOUGHT I'D MISSED YOU.
HUFF HUFF
I'LL BE EAGERLY AWAITING YOUR SAFE RETURN!
THE MEDICINE I GAVE YOU LAST NIGHT...

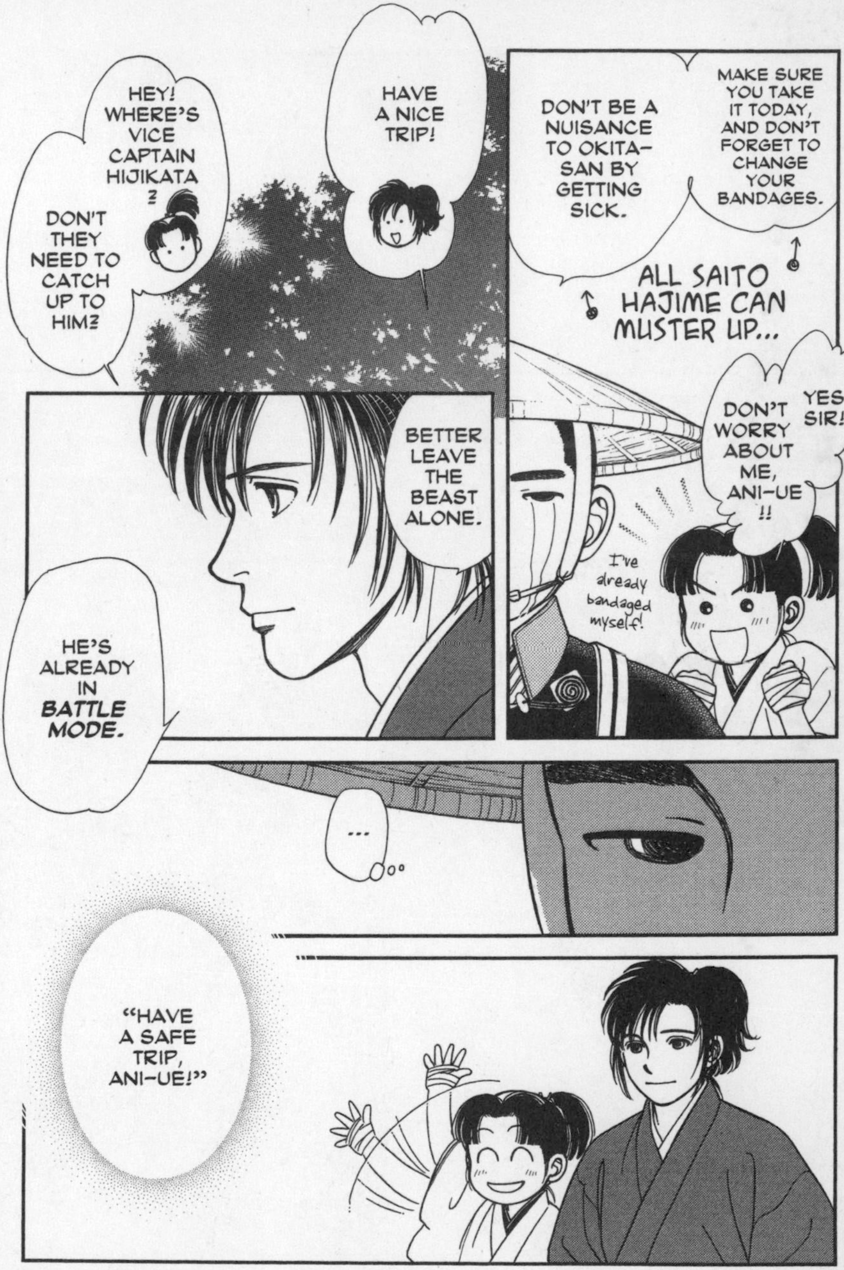
MAKE SURE YOU TAKE IT TODAY, AND DON'T FORGET TO CHANGE YOUR BANDAGES.
DON'T BE A NUISANCE TO OKITA-SAN BY GETTING SICK.
ALL SAITO HAJIME CAN MUSTER UP...
YES SIR!
DON'T WORRY ABOUT ME, ANI-UE!!
I've already bandaged myself!
HAVE A NICE TRIP!
HEY! WHERE'S VICE CAPTAIN HIJIKATA? DON'T THEY NEED TO CATCH UP TO HIM?
BETTER LEAVE THE BEAST ALONE.
HE'S ALREADY IN BATTLE MODE.
...
"HAVE A SAFE TRIP, ANI-UE!"

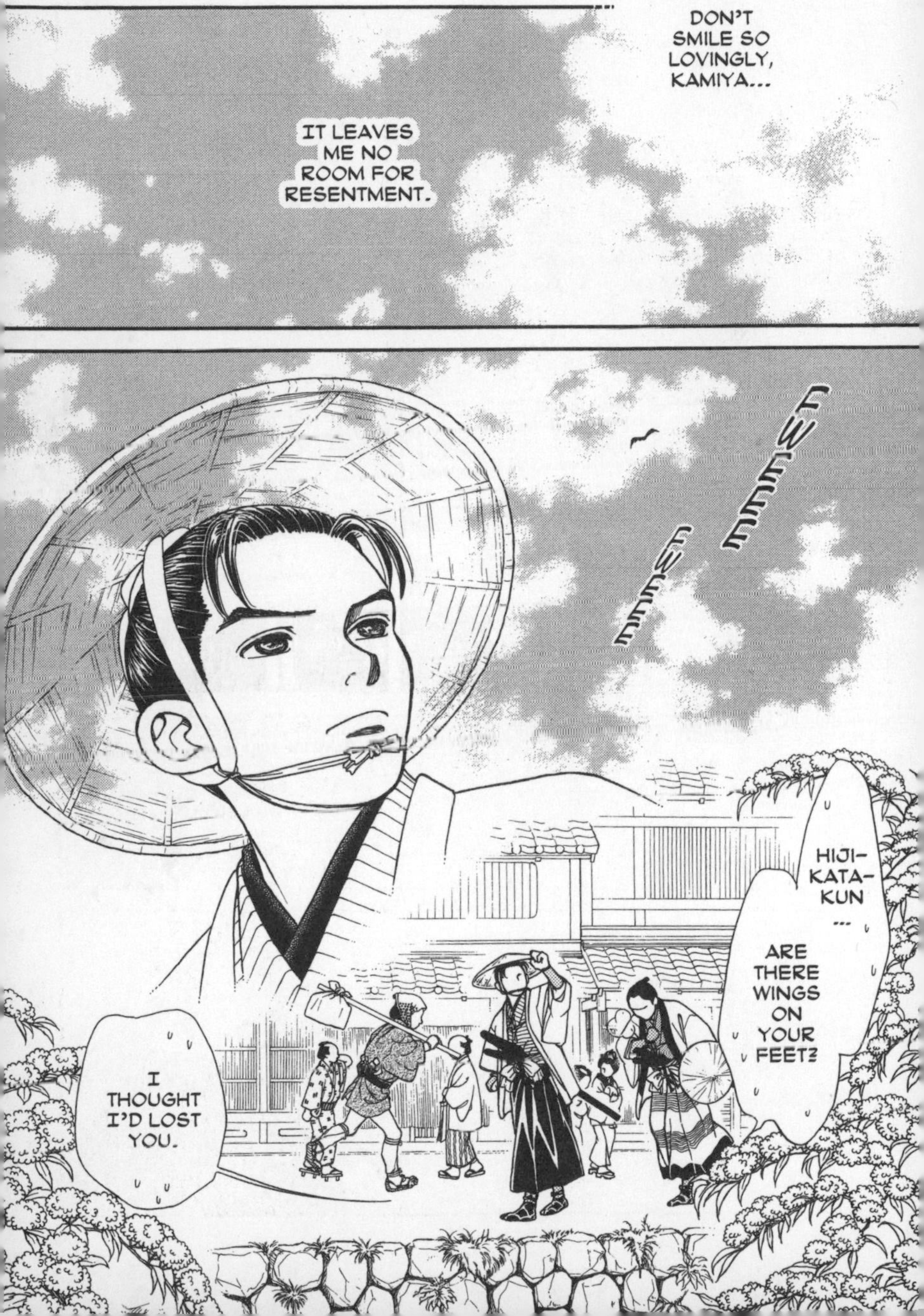
DON'T SMILE SO LOVINGLY, KAMIYA...
IT LEAVES ME NO ROOM FOR RESENTMENT.
FWEEEEEE
FWEEEE
HIJI-KATA-KUN ... ARE THERE WINGS ON YOUR FEET?
I THOUGHT I'D LOST YOU.

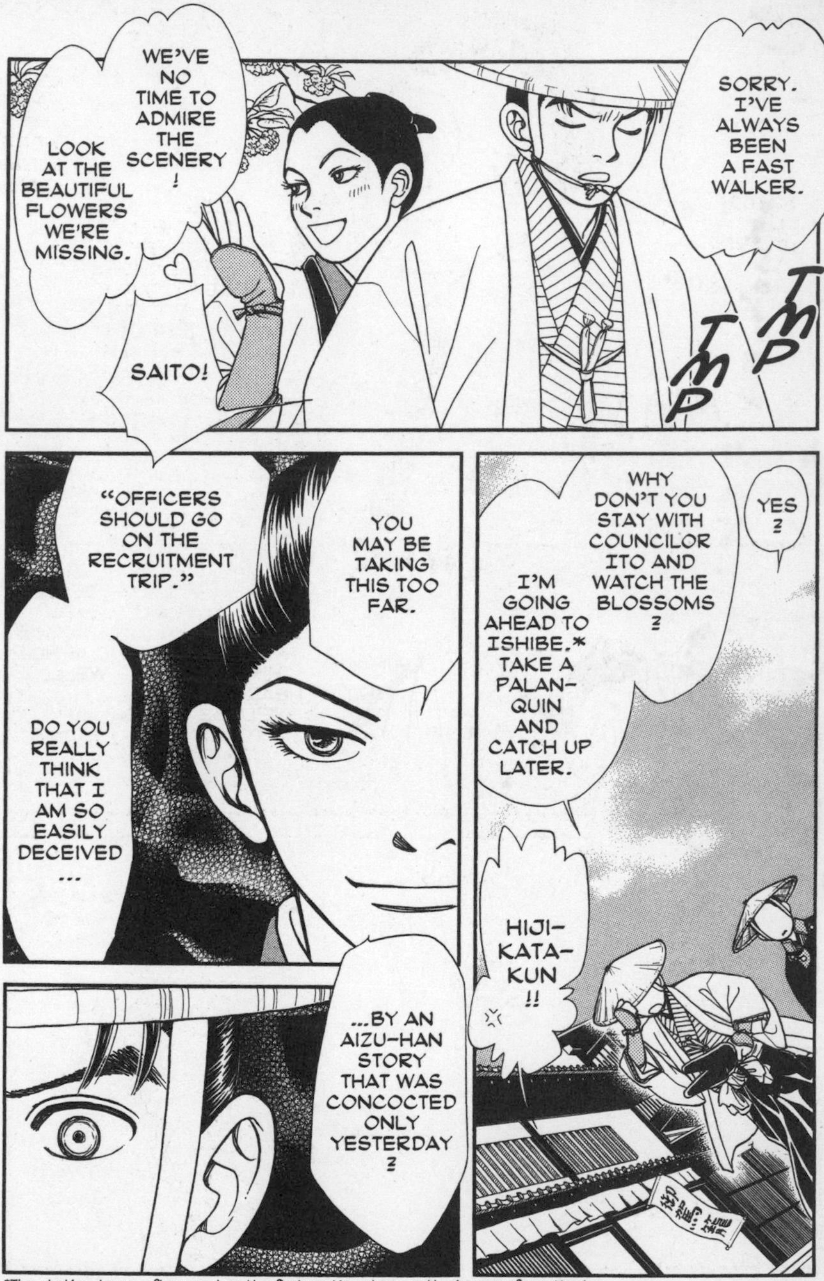
SORRY. I'VE ALWAYS BEEN A FAST WALKER.
TMP TMP
WE'VE NO TIME TO ADMIRE THE SCENERY!
LOOK AT THE BEAUTIFUL FLOWERS WE'RE MISSING.
SAITO!
YES?
WHY DON'T YOU STAY WITH COUNCILOR ITO AND WATCH THE BLOSSOMS?
I'M GOING AHEAD TO ISHIBE.* TAKE A PALANQUIN AND CATCH UP LATER.
HIJI-KATA-KUN!!
YOU MAY BE TAKING THIS TOO FAR.
"OFFICERS SHOULD GO ON THE RECRUITMENT TRIP."
DO YOU REALLY THINK THAT I AM SO EASILY DECEIVED...
...BY AN AIZU-HAN STORY THAT WAS CONCOCTED ONLY YESTERDAY?

*The station town often used as the first resting stop on the journey from Kyoto.

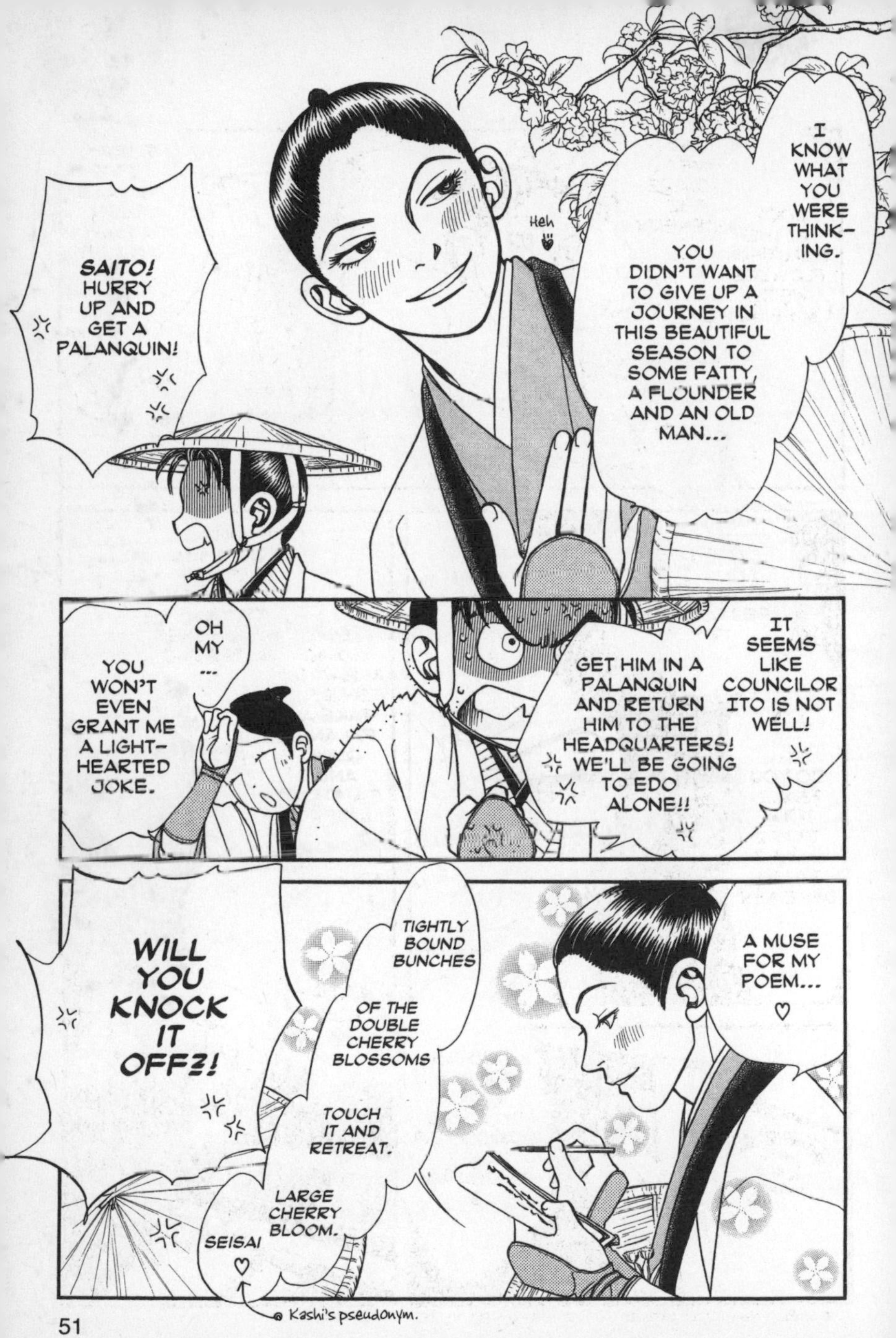
I KNOW WHAT YOU WERE THINKING.
YOU DIDN'T WANT TO GIVE UP A JOURNEY IN THIS BEAUTIFUL SEASON TO SOME FATTY, A FLOUNDER AND AN OLD MAN...
Heh
SAITO! HURRY UP AND GET A PALANQUIN!
IT SEEMS LIKE COUNCILOR ITO IS NOT WELL!
GET HIM IN A PALANQUIN AND RETURN HIM TO THE HEADQUARTERS! WE'LL BE GOING TO EDO ALONE!!
OH MY ...
YOU WON'T EVEN GRANT ME A LIGHT-HEARTED JOKE.
A MUSE FOR MY POEM... ♡
TIGHTLY BOUND BUNCHES
OF THE DOUBLE CHERRY BLOSSOMS
TOUCH IT AND RETREAT.
LARGE CHERRY BLOOM.
SEISAI ♡
WILL YOU KNOCK IT OFF?!
Kashi's pseudonym.

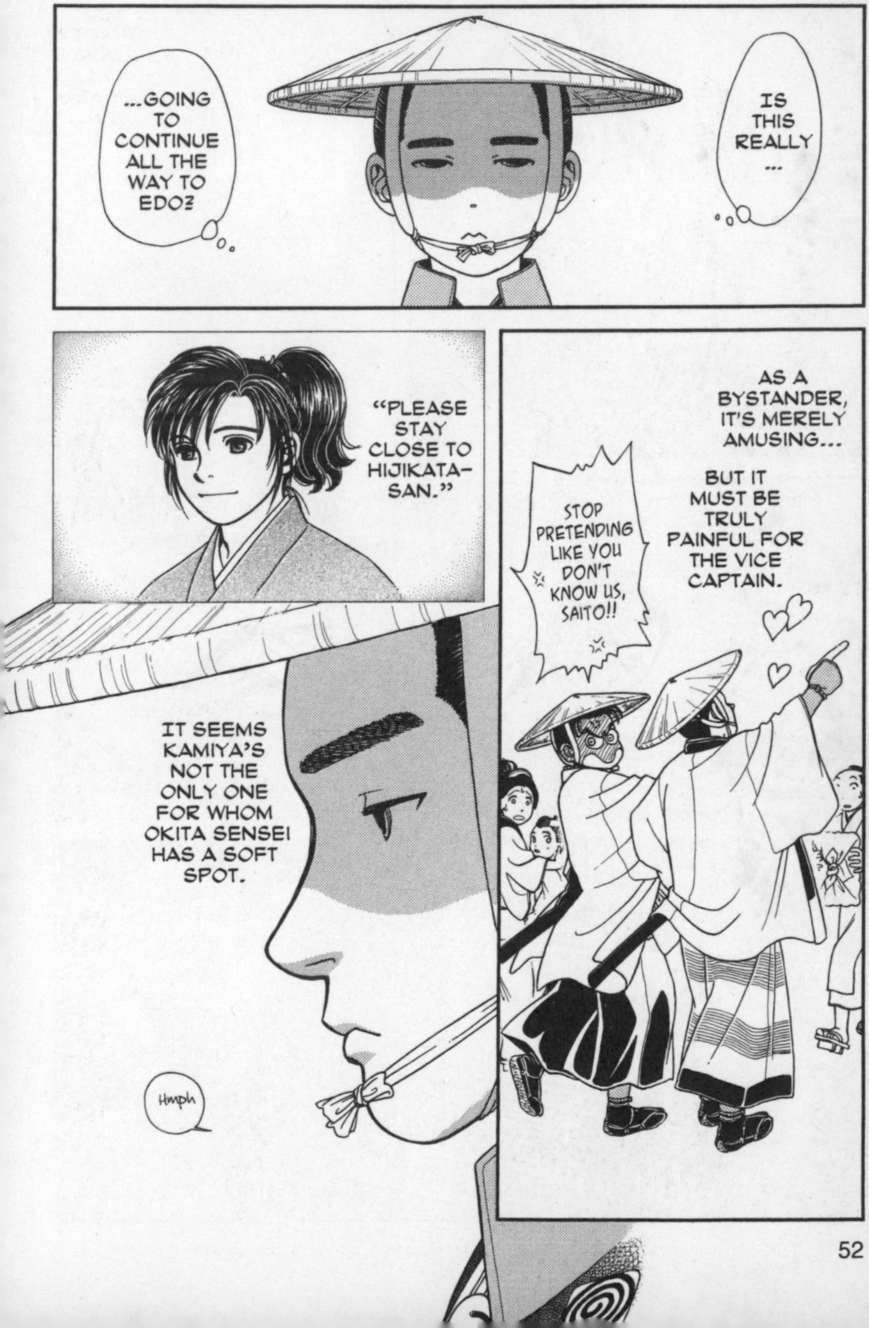
IS THIS REALLY ...
...GOING TO CONTINUE ALL THE WAY TO EDO?
AS A BYSTANDER, IT'S MERELY AMUSING...
BUT IT MUST BE TRULY PAINFUL FOR THE VICE CAPTAIN.
STOP PRETENDING LIKE YOU DON'T KNOW US, SAITO!!
"PLEASE STAY CLOSE TO HIJIKATA-SAN."
IT SEEMS KAMIYA'S NOT THE ONLY ONE FOR WHOM OKITA SENSEI HAS A SOFT SPOT.
Hmph

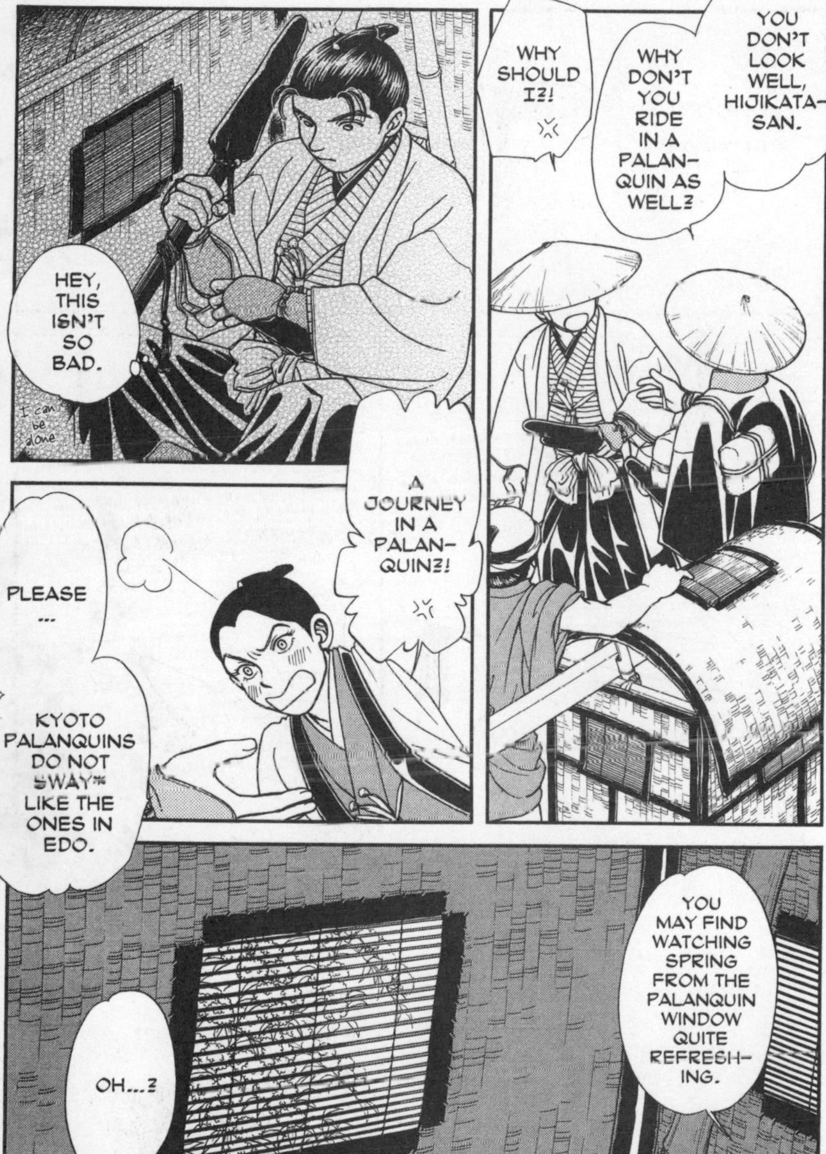
YOU DON'T LOOK WELL, HIJIKATA-SAN.
WHY DON'T YOU RIDE IN A PALANQUIN AS WELL?
WHY SHOULD I?!
HEY, THIS ISN'T SO BAD.
I can be alone
A JOURNEY IN A PALANQUIN?!
PLEASE ...
KYOTO PALANQUINS DO NOT SWAY* LIKE THE ONES IN EDO.
YOU MAY FIND WATCHING SPRING FROM THE PALANQUIN WINDOW QUITE REFRESHING.
OH...?

*Edo palanquins were prized for their speed, but Kyoto was much smaller and palanquins there were prized for the comfort of the ride.

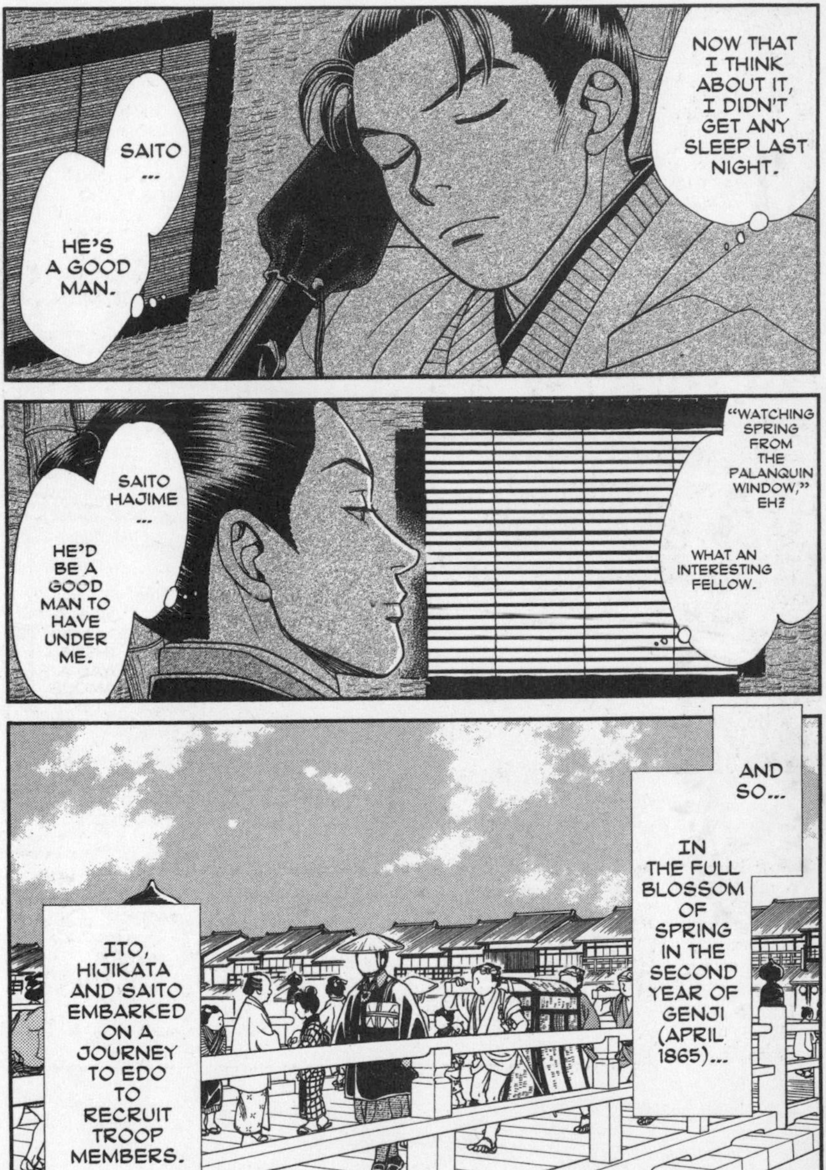
NOW THAT I THINK ABOUT IT, I DIDN'T GET ANY SLEEP LAST NIGHT.
SAITO ...
HE'S A GOOD MAN.
"WATCHING SPRING FROM THE PALANQUIN WINDOW," EH?
WHAT AN INTERESTING FELLOW.
SAITO HAJIME ...
HE'D BE A GOOD MAN TO HAVE UNDER ME.
AND SO...
IN THE FULL BLOSSOM OF SPRING IN THE SECOND YEAR OF GENJI (APRIL 1865)...
ITO, HIJIKATA AND SAITO EMBARKED ON A JOURNEY TO EDO TO RECRUIT TROOP MEMBERS.

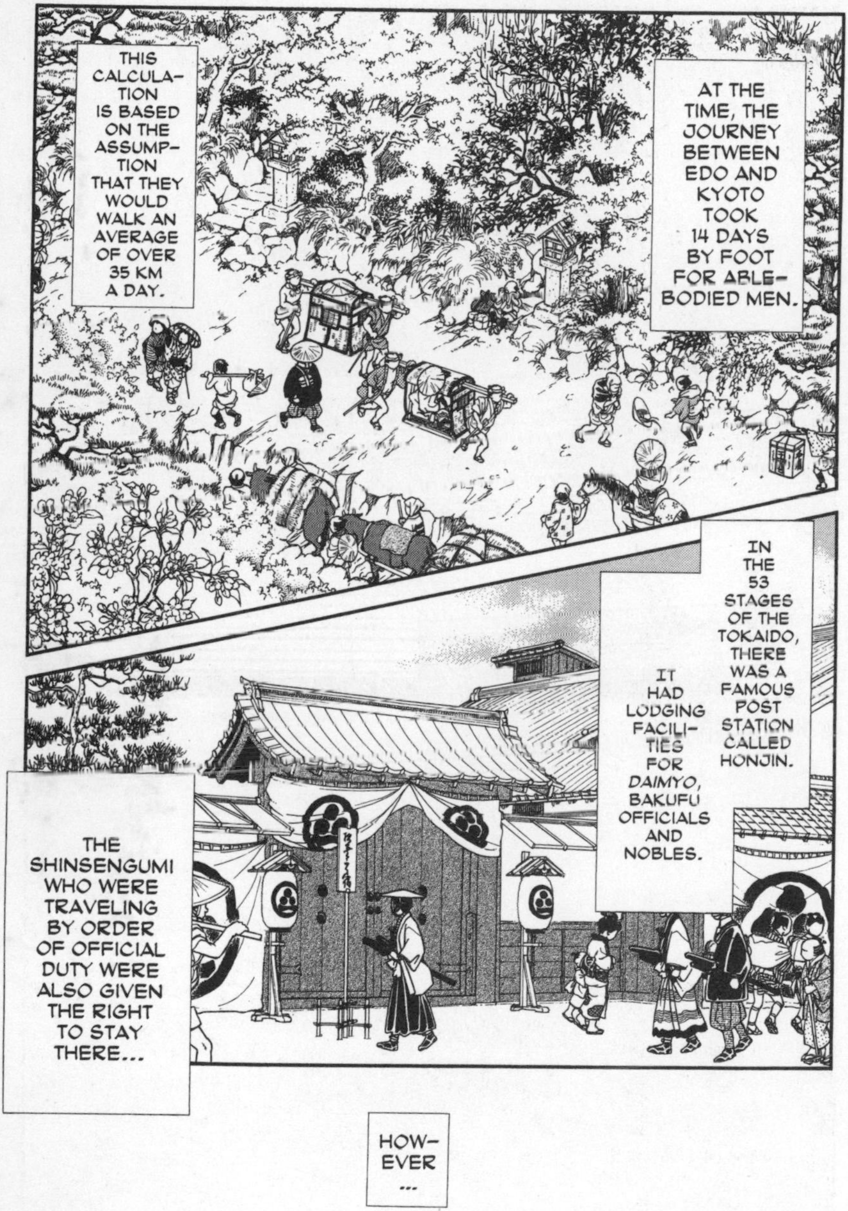
AT THE TIME, THE JOURNEY BETWEEN EDO AND KYOTO TOOK 14 DAYS BY FOOT FOR ABLE-BODIED MEN.
THIS CALCULATION IS BASED ON THE ASSUMPTION THAT THEY WOULD WALK AN AVERAGE OF OVER 35 KM A DAY.
IN THE 53 STAGES OF THE TOKAIDO, THERE WAS A FAMOUS POST STATION CALLED HONJIN.
IT HAD LODGING FACILITIES FOR *DAIMYO*, BAKUFU OFFICIALS AND NOBLES.
THE SHINSENGUMI WHO WERE TRAVELING BY ORDER OF OFFICIAL DUTY WERE ALSO GIVEN THE RIGHT TO STAY THERE...
HOWEVER...

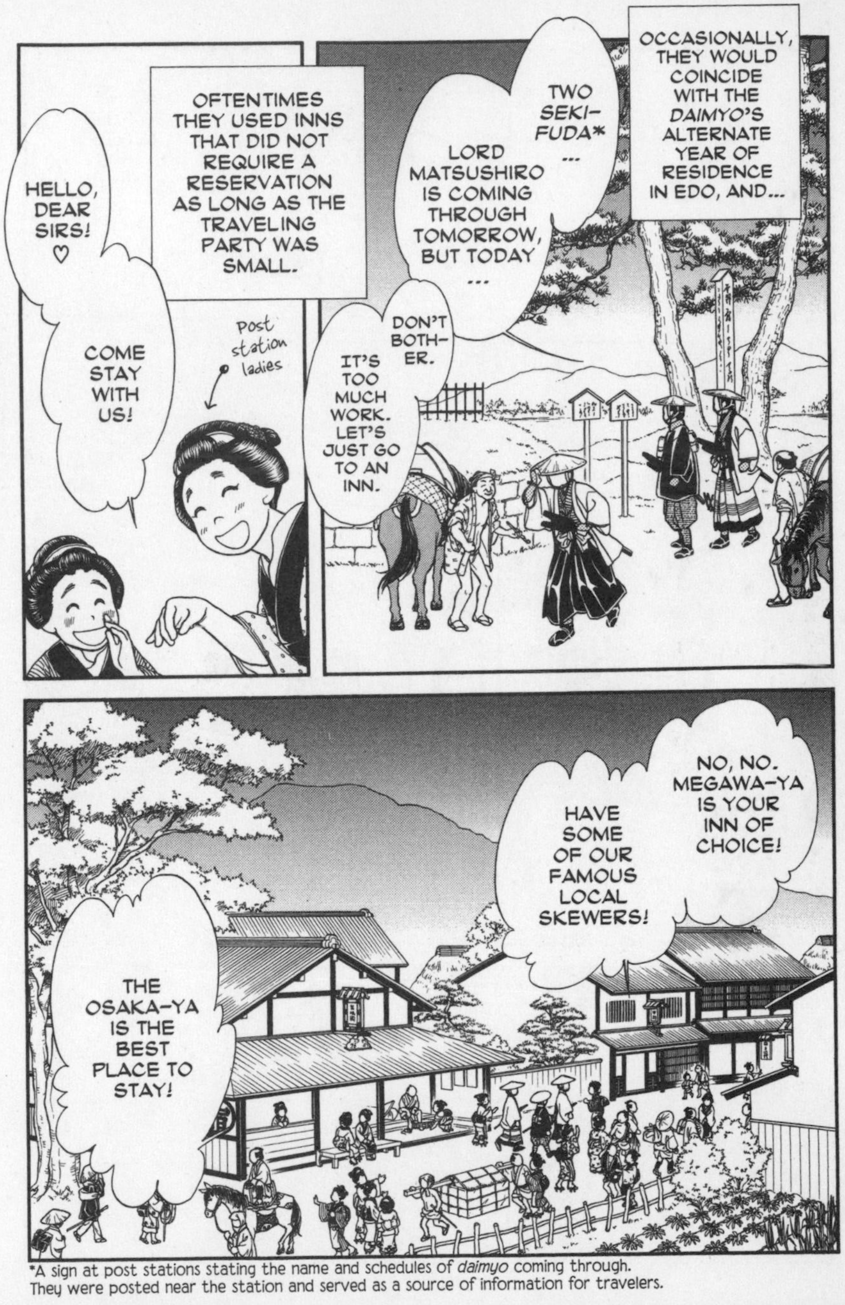
OCCASIONALLY, THEY WOULD COINCIDE WITH THE *DAIMYO*'S ALTERNATE YEAR OF RESIDENCE IN EDO, AND...
TWO *SEKI-FUDA** ...
LORD MATSUSHIRO IS COMING THROUGH TOMORROW, BUT TODAY ...
DON'T BOTHER.
IT'S TOO MUCH WORK. LET'S JUST GO TO AN INN.
OFTENTIMES THEY USED INNS THAT DID NOT REQUIRE A RESERVATION AS LONG AS THE TRAVELING PARTY WAS SMALL.
HELLO, DEAR SIRS! ♡
COME STAY WITH US!
Post station ladies
NO, NO. MEGAWA-YA IS YOUR INN OF CHOICE!
HAVE SOME OF OUR FAMOUS LOCAL SKEWERS!
THE OSAKA-YA IS THE BEST PLACE TO STAY!

*A sign at post stations stating the name and schedules of *daimyo* coming through. They were posted near the station and served as a source of information for travelers.

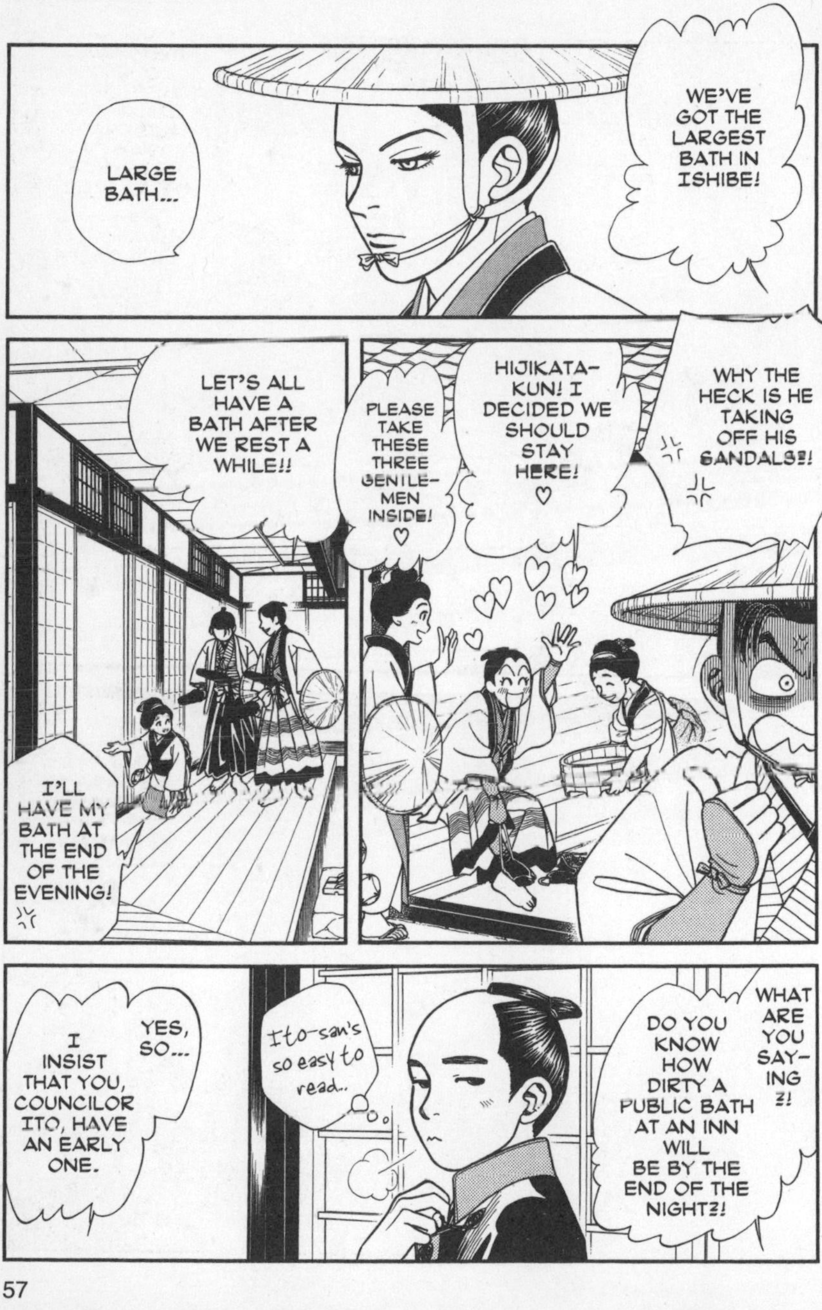
WE'VE GOT THE LARGEST BATH IN ISHIBE!
LARGE BATH...
WHY THE HECK IS HE TAKING OFF HIS SANDALS?!
HIJIKATA-KUN! I DECIDED WE SHOULD STAY HERE! ♡
PLEASE TAKE THESE THREE GENTLEMEN INSIDE! ♡
LET'S ALL HAVE A BATH AFTER WE REST A WHILE!!
I'LL HAVE MY BATH AT THE END OF THE EVENING!
WHAT ARE YOU SAYING?!
DO YOU KNOW HOW DIRTY A PUBLIC BATH AT AN INN WILL BE BY THE END OF THE NIGHT?!
Ito-san's so easy to read..
YES, SO...
I INSIST THAT YOU, COUNCILOR ITO, HAVE AN EARLY ONE.

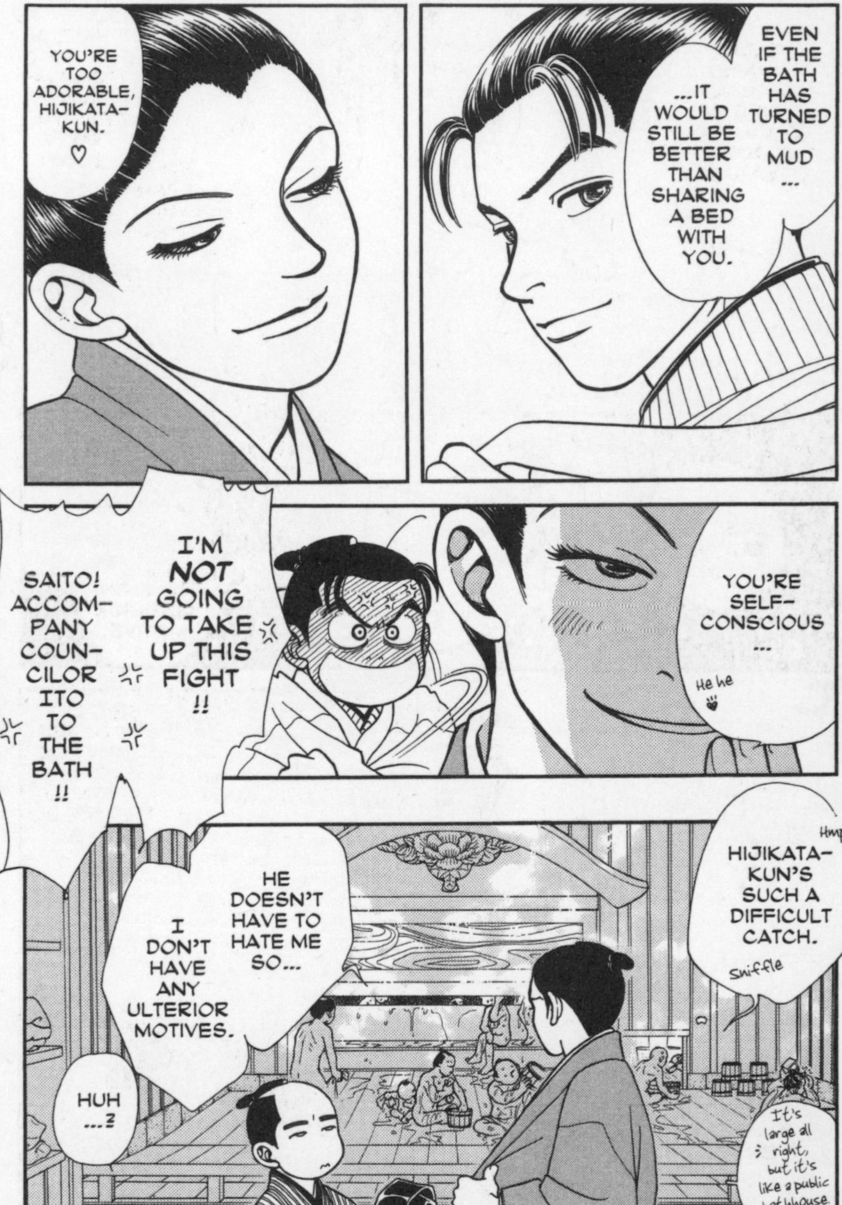
EVEN IF THE BATH HAS TURNED TO MUD...
...IT WOULD STILL BE BETTER THAN SHARING A BED WITH YOU.
YOU'RE TOO ADORABLE, HIJIKATA-KUN. ♡
YOU'RE SELF-CONSCIOUS...
He he
I'M **NOT** GOING TO TAKE UP THIS FIGHT!!
SAITO! ACCOMPANY COUNCILOR ITO TO THE BATH!!
Hmph.
HIJIKATA-KUN'S SUCH A DIFFICULT CATCH.
Sniffle
HE DOESN'T HAVE TO HATE ME SO...
I DON'T HAVE ANY ULTERIOR MOTIVES.
It's large all right, but it's like a public bathhouse.
HUH...?

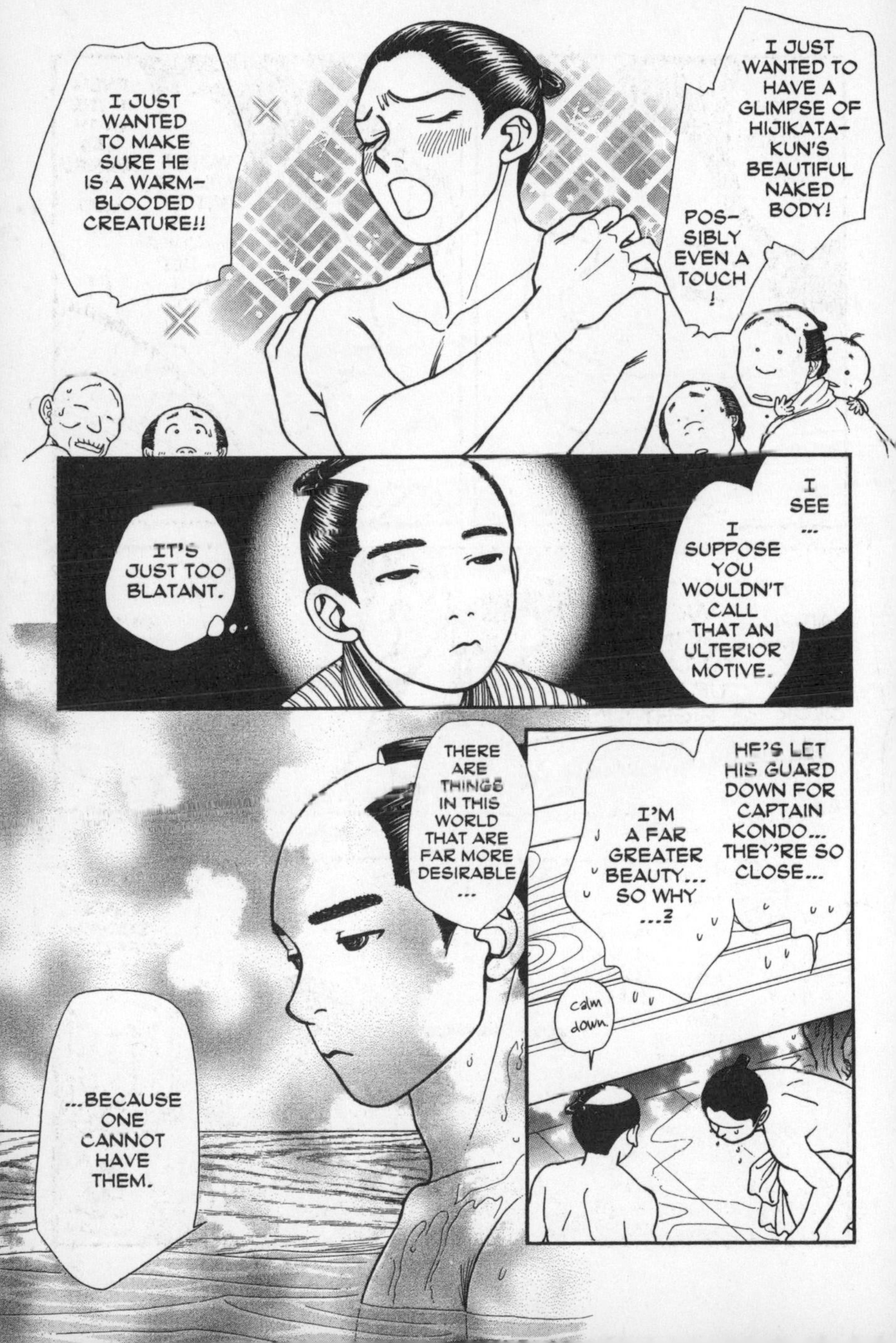
I JUST WANTED TO HAVE A GLIMPSE OF HIJIKATA-KUN'S BEAUTIFUL NAKED BODY!
POSSIBLY EVEN A TOUCH!
I JUST WANTED TO MAKE SURE HE IS A WARM-BLOODED CREATURE!!
I SEE...
I SUPPOSE YOU WOULDN'T CALL THAT AN ULTERIOR MOTIVE.
IT'S JUST TOO BLATANT.
HE'S LET HIS GUARD DOWN FOR CAPTAIN KONDO... THEY'RE SO CLOSE...
I'M A FAR GREATER BEAUTY... SO WHY...?
calm down.
THERE ARE THINGS IN THIS WORLD THAT ARE FAR MORE DESIRABLE...
...BECAUSE ONE CANNOT HAVE THEM.

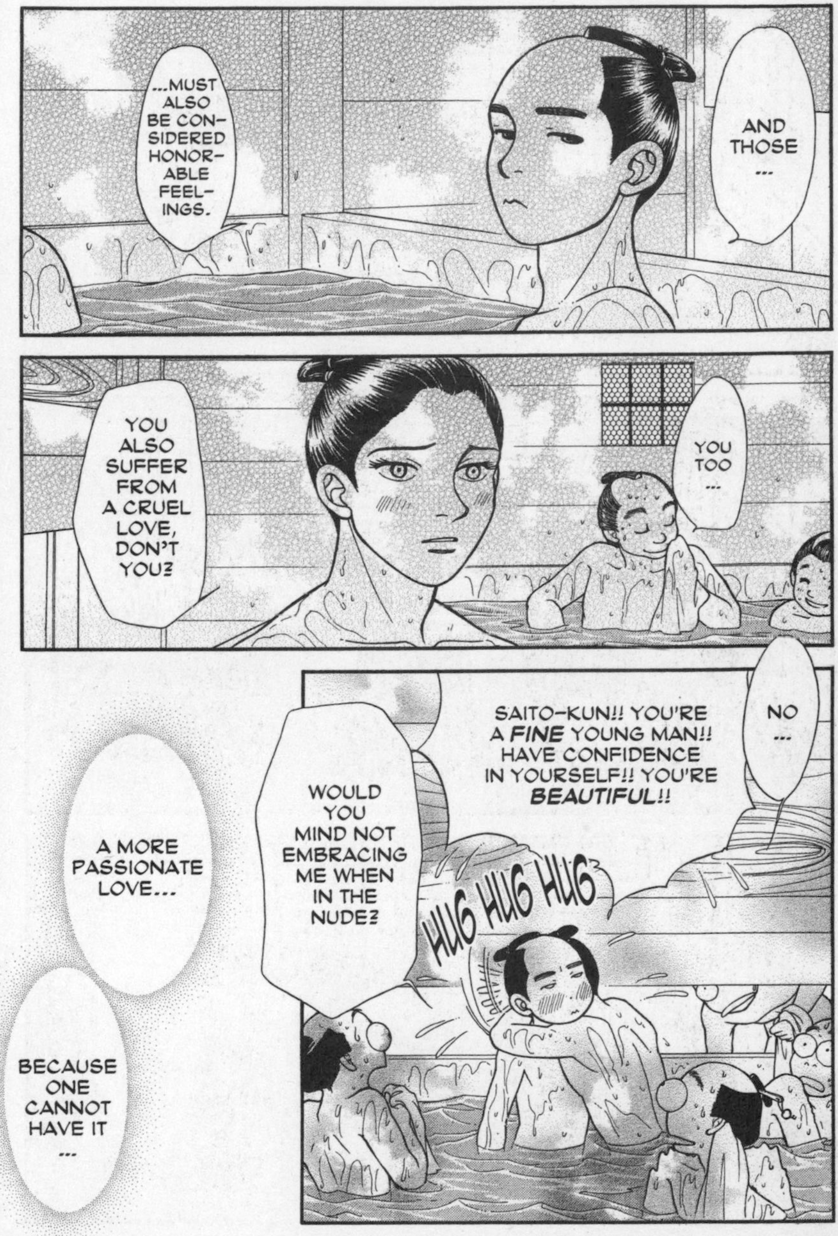
AND THOSE ...
...MUST ALSO BE CONSIDERED HONORABLE FEELINGS.
YOU TOO ...
YOU ALSO SUFFER FROM A CRUEL LOVE, DON'T YOU?
NO ...
SAITO-KUN!! YOU'RE A *FINE* YOUNG MAN!! HAVE CONFIDENCE IN YOURSELF!! YOU'RE *BEAUTIFUL*!!
HUG HUG HUG
WOULD YOU MIND NOT EMBRACING ME WHEN IN THE NUDE?
A MORE PASSIONATE LOVE...
BECAUSE ONE CANNOT HAVE IT ...

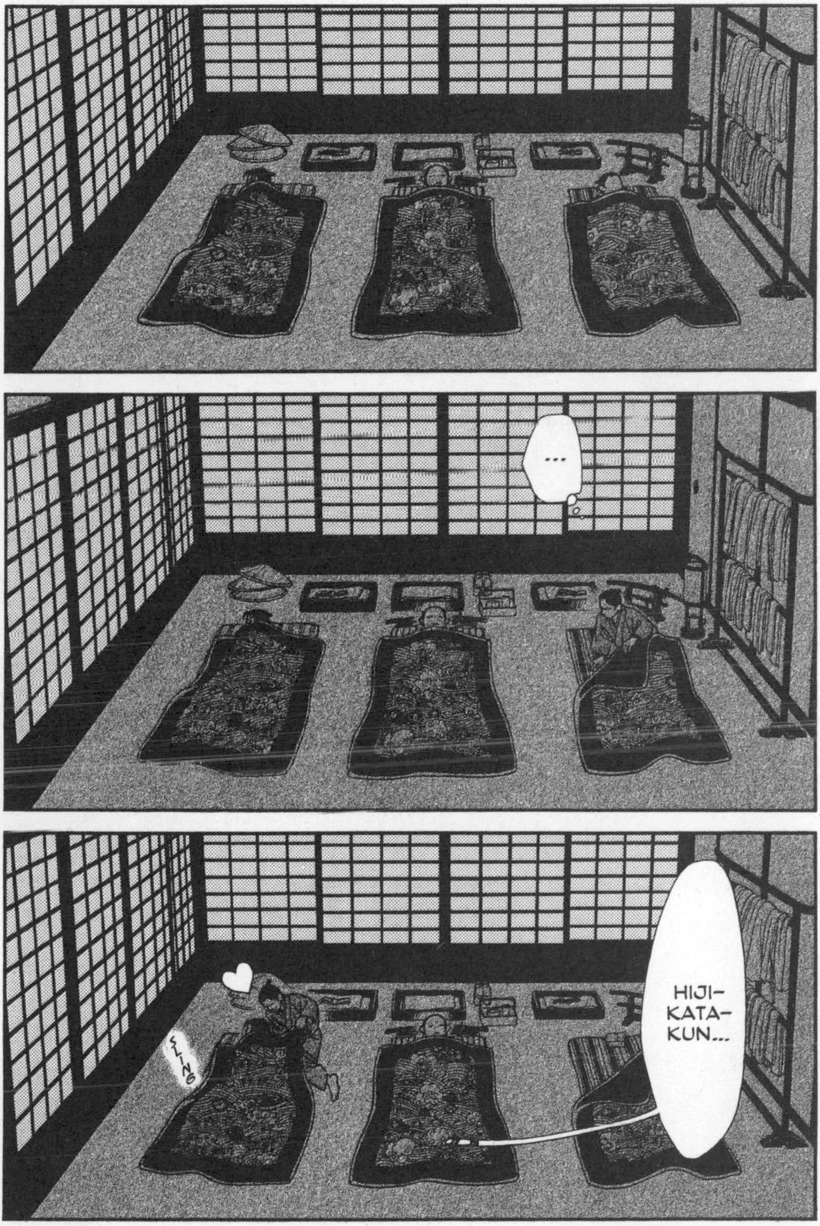
...
HIJI-KATA-KUN...
SLING

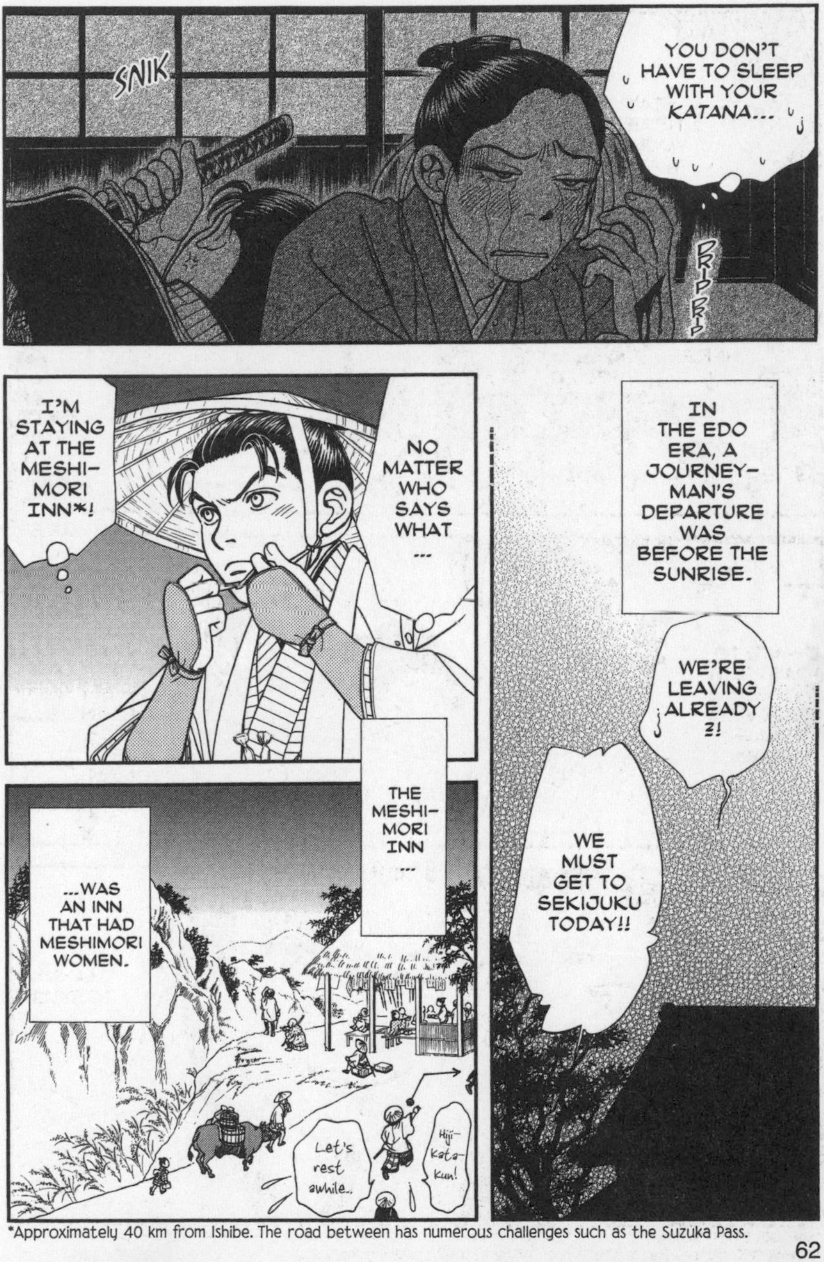
YOU DON'T HAVE TO SLEEP WITH YOUR *KATANA*...
SNIK
DRIP DRIP
IN THE EDO ERA, A JOURNEYMAN'S DEPARTURE WAS BEFORE THE SUNRISE.
WE'RE LEAVING ALREADY?!
WE MUST GET TO SEKIJUKU TODAY!!
NO MATTER WHO SAYS WHAT...
I'M STAYING AT THE MESHIMORI INN*!
THE MESHIMORI INN...
...WAS AN INN THAT HAD MESHIMORI WOMEN.
Hijikata-kun!
Let's rest awhile..

*Approximately 40 km from Ishibe. The road between has numerous challenges such as the Suzuka Pass.

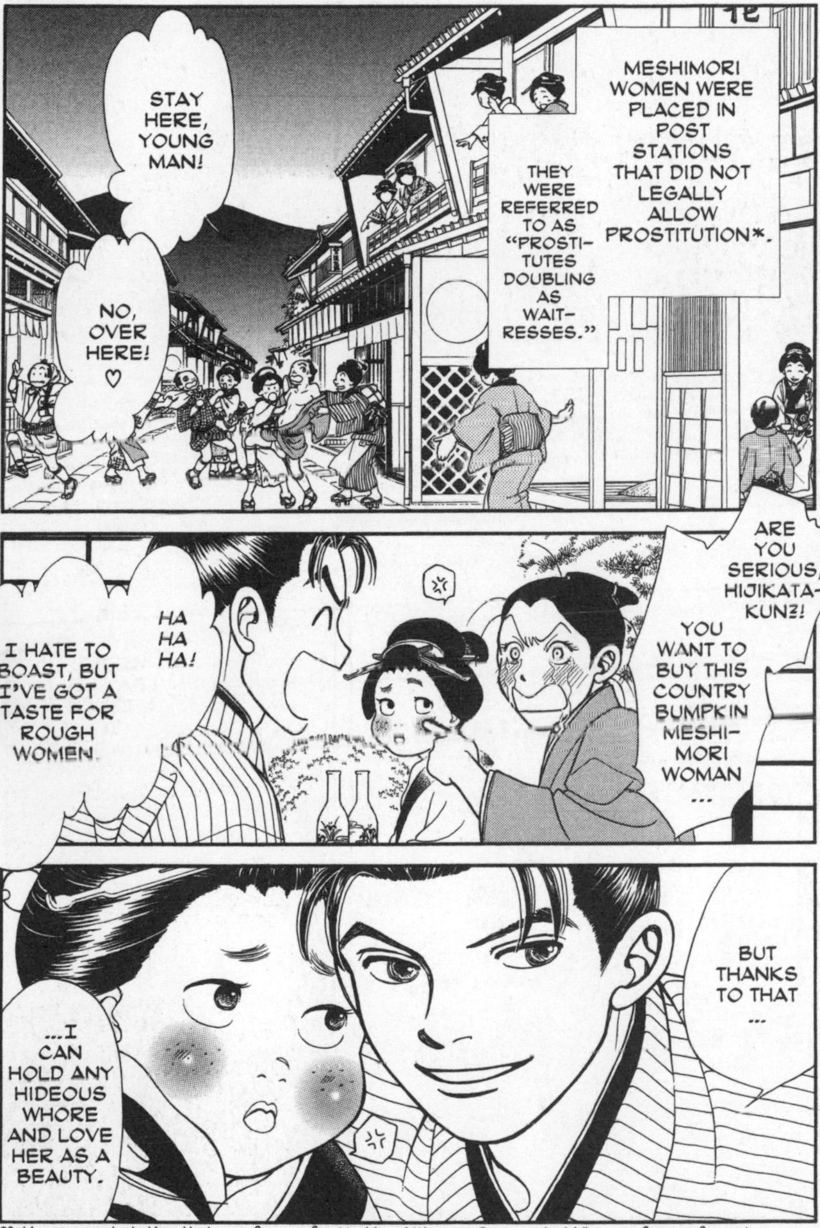
MESHIMORI WOMEN WERE PLACED IN POST STATIONS THAT DID NOT LEGALLY ALLOW PROSTITUTION*.
THEY WERE REFERRED TO AS "PROSTITUTES DOUBLING AS WAITRESSES."
STAY HERE, YOUNG MAN!
NO, OVER HERE! ♡
ARE YOU SERIOUS, HIJIKATA-KUN?!
YOU WANT TO BUY THIS COUNTRY BUMPKIN MESHIMORI WOMAN...
HA HA HA!
I HATE TO BOAST, BUT I'VE GOT A TASTE FOR ROUGH WOMEN.
BUT THANKS TO THAT...
...I CAN HOLD ANY HIDEOUS WHORE AND LOVE HER AS A BEAUTY.

*Seki was a post station that was famous for Meshimori Women. Conversely, Ishibe was famous for not allowing prostitutes. Hence the saying, "Ishibe Kinkichi," meaning a prude.

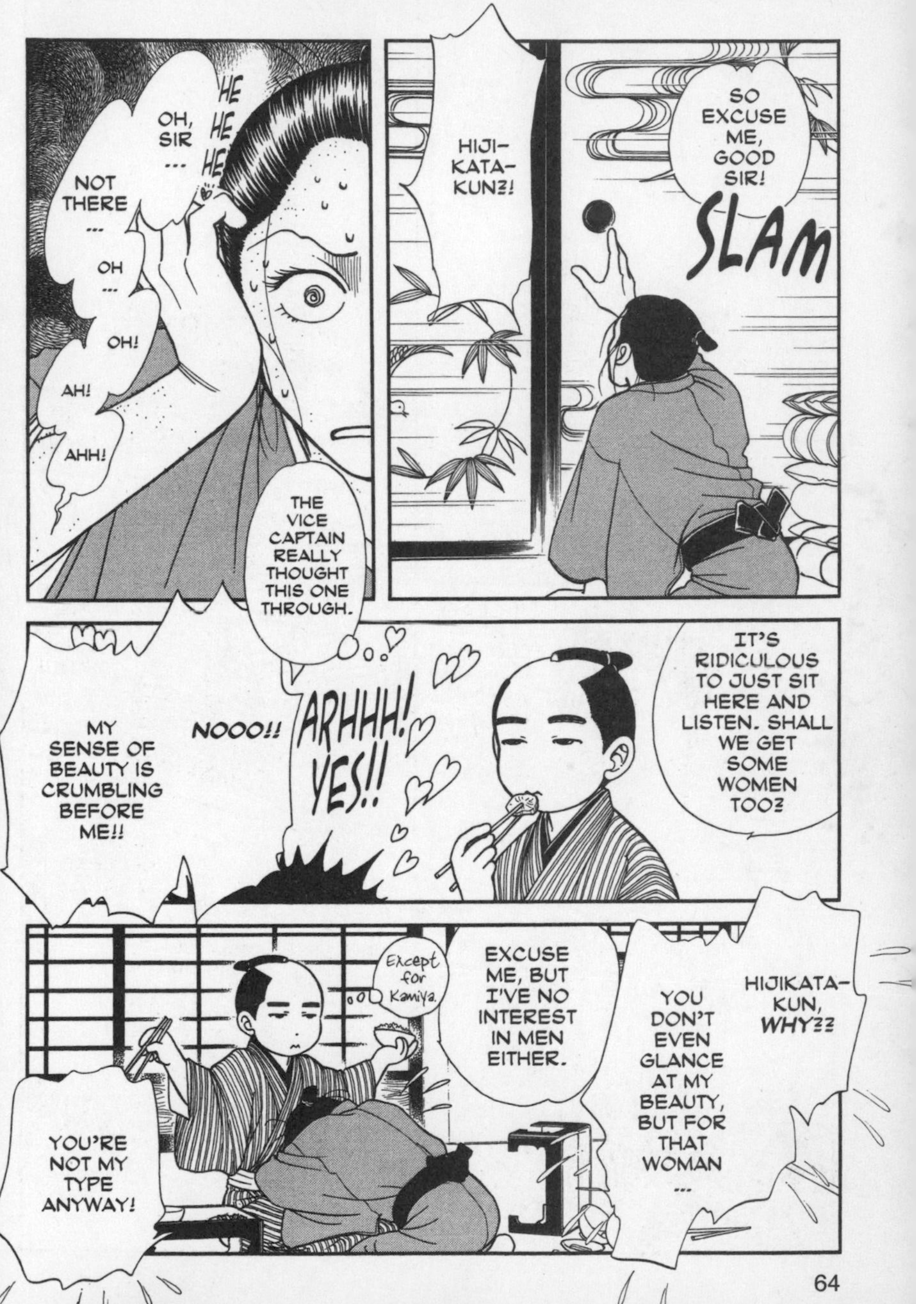
SO EXCUSE ME, GOOD SIR!
SLAM
HIJI-KATA-KUN?!
HE HE HE
OH, SIR ... NOT THERE ... OH ... OH! AH! AHH!
THE VICE CAPTAIN REALLY THOUGHT THIS ONE THROUGH.
IT'S RIDICULOUS TO JUST SIT HERE AND LISTEN. SHALL WE GET SOME WOMEN TOO?
ARHHH! YES!!
NOOO!!
MY SENSE OF BEAUTY IS CRUMBLING BEFORE ME!!
HIJIKATA-KUN, WHY??
YOU DON'T EVEN GLANCE AT MY BEAUTY, BUT FOR THAT WOMAN ...
EXCUSE ME, BUT I'VE NO INTEREST IN MEN EITHER.
Except for Kamiya.
YOU'RE NOT MY TYPE ANYWAY!

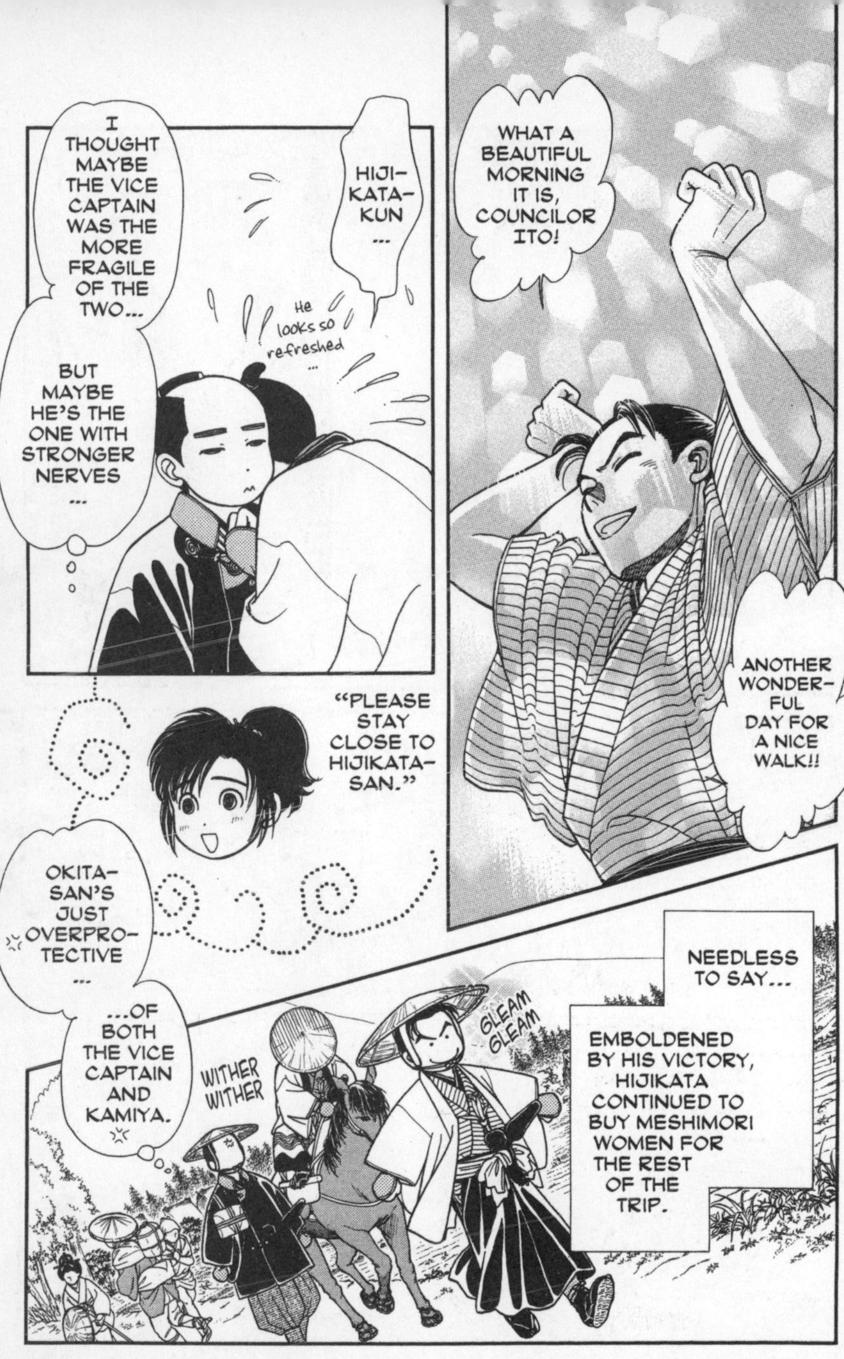
WHAT A BEAUTIFUL MORNING IT IS, COUNCILOR ITO!
ANOTHER WONDERFUL DAY FOR A NICE WALK!!
HIJIKATA-KUN...
He looks so refreshed...
I THOUGHT MAYBE THE VICE CAPTAIN WAS THE MORE FRAGILE OF THE TWO...
BUT MAYBE HE'S THE ONE WITH STRONGER NERVES...
"PLEASE STAY CLOSE TO HIJIKATA-SAN."
OKITA-SAN'S JUST OVERPROTECTIVE...
...OF BOTH THE VICE CAPTAIN AND KAMIYA.
NEEDLESS TO SAY...
EMBOLDENED BY HIS VICTORY, HIJIKATA CONTINUED TO BUY MESHIMORI WOMEN FOR THE REST OF THE TRIP.
GLEAM GLEAM
WITHER WITHER

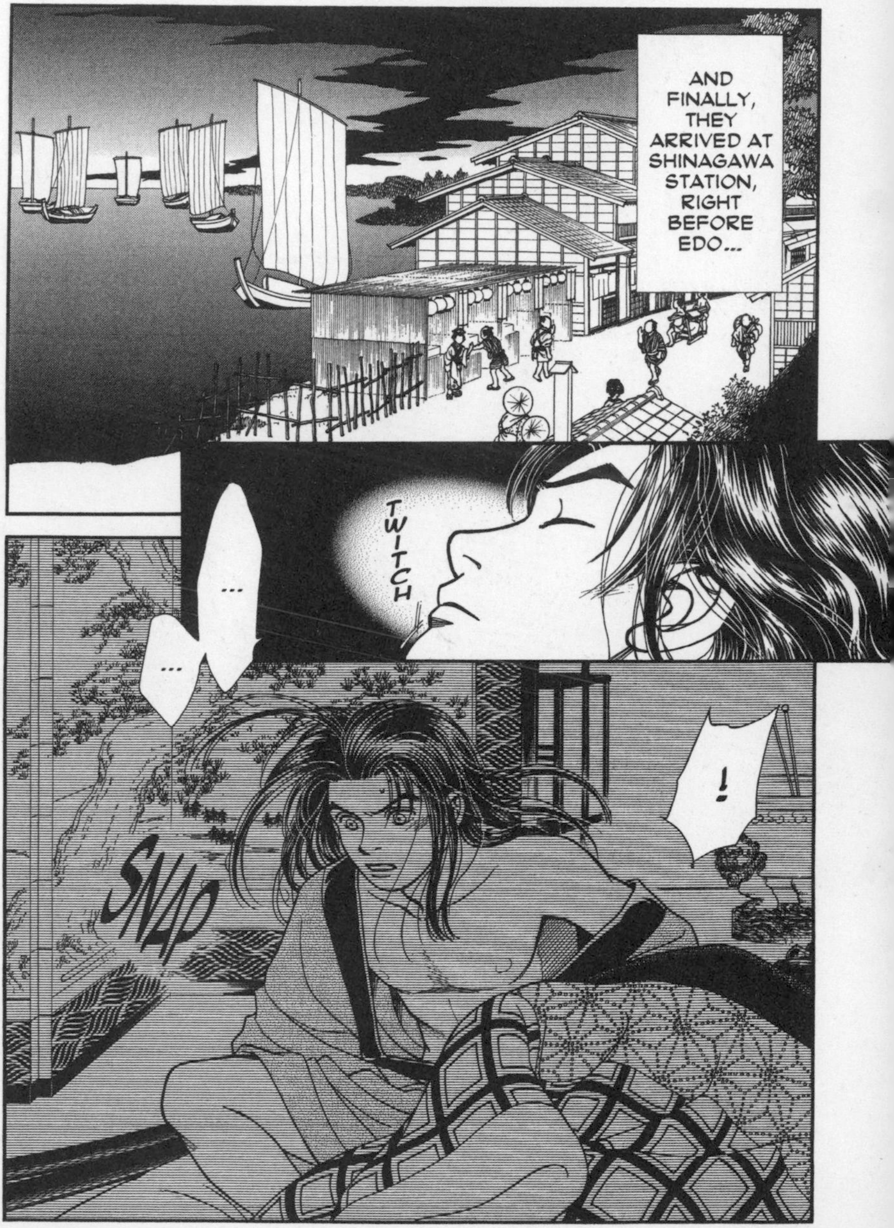
AND FINALLY, THEY ARRIVED AT SHINAGAWA STATION, RIGHT BEFORE EDO...
TWITCH
...
...
!
SNAP

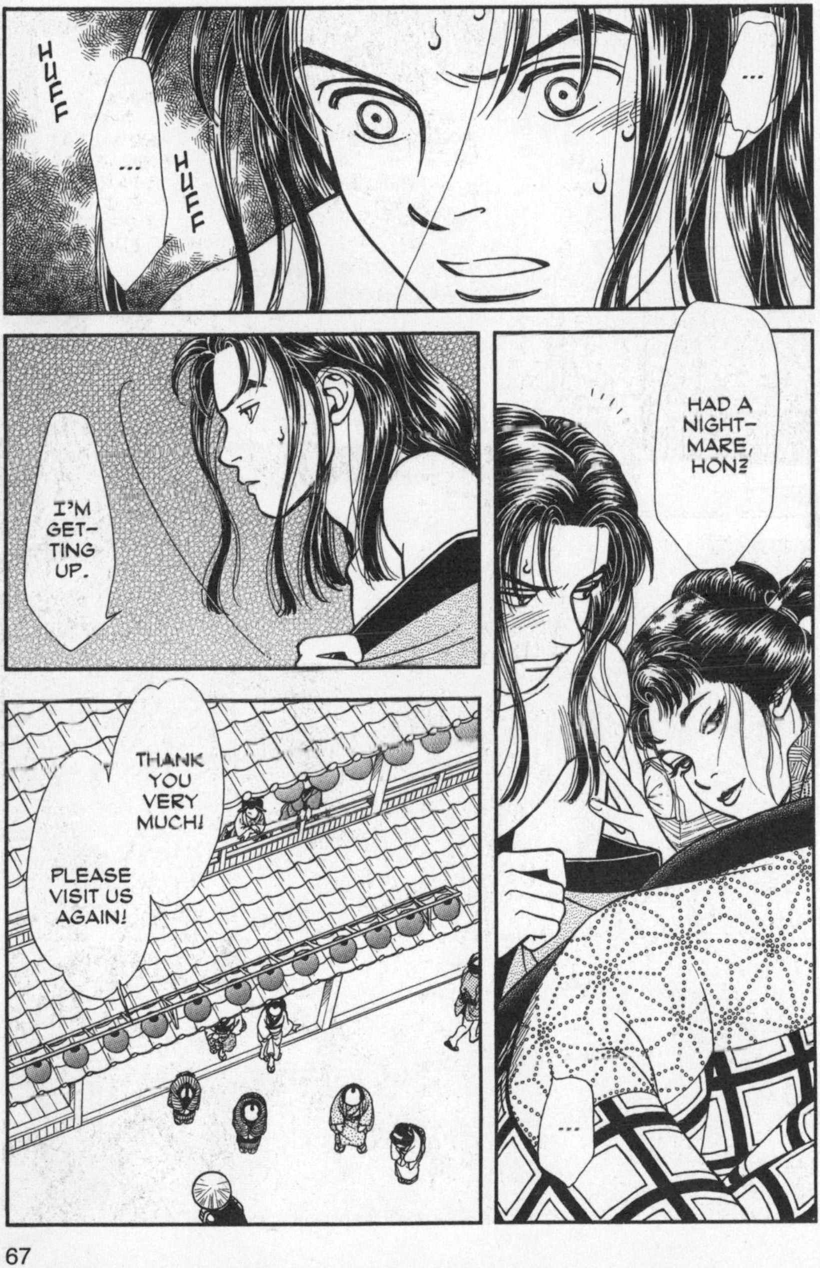
...
HUFF
...
HUFF
HAD A NIGHT-MARE, HON?
...
I'M GET-TING UP.
THANK YOU VERY MUCH!
PLEASE VISIT US AGAIN!

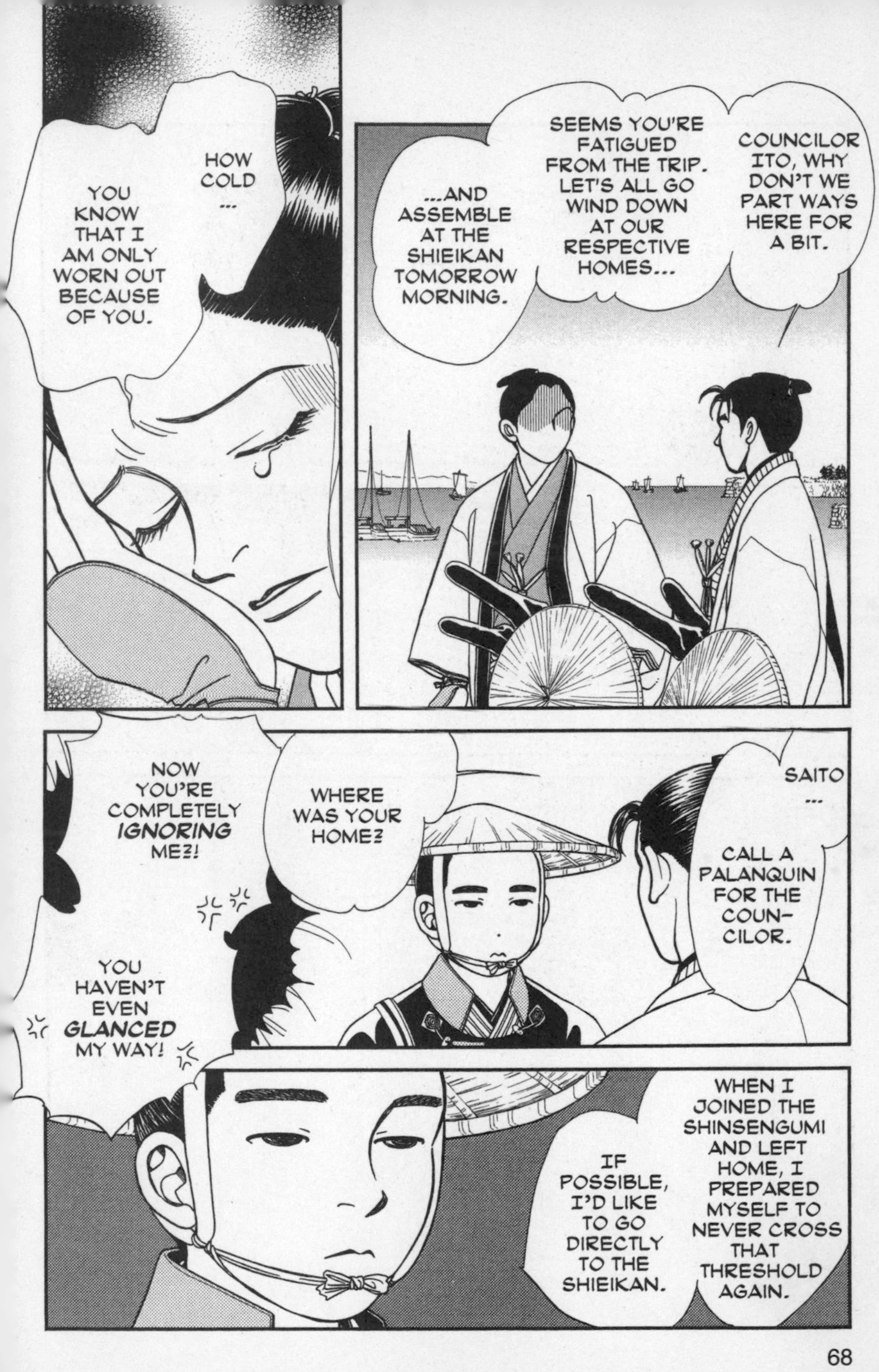
COUNCILOR ITO, WHY DON'T WE PART WAYS HERE FOR A BIT.
SEEMS YOU'RE FATIGUED FROM THE TRIP. LET'S ALL GO WIND DOWN AT OUR RESPECTIVE HOMES...
...AND ASSEMBLE AT THE SHIEIKAN TOMORROW MORNING.
HOW COLD...
YOU KNOW THAT I AM ONLY WORN OUT BECAUSE OF YOU.
SAITO... CALL A PALANQUIN FOR THE COUN-CILOR.
WHERE WAS YOUR HOME?
NOW YOU'RE COMPLETELY *IGNORING* ME?!
YOU HAVEN'T EVEN *GLANCED* MY WAY!
WHEN I JOINED THE SHINSENGUMI AND LEFT HOME, I PREPARED MYSELF TO NEVER CROSS THAT THRESHOLD AGAIN.
IF POSSIBLE, I'D LIKE TO GO DIRECTLY TO THE SHIEIKAN.

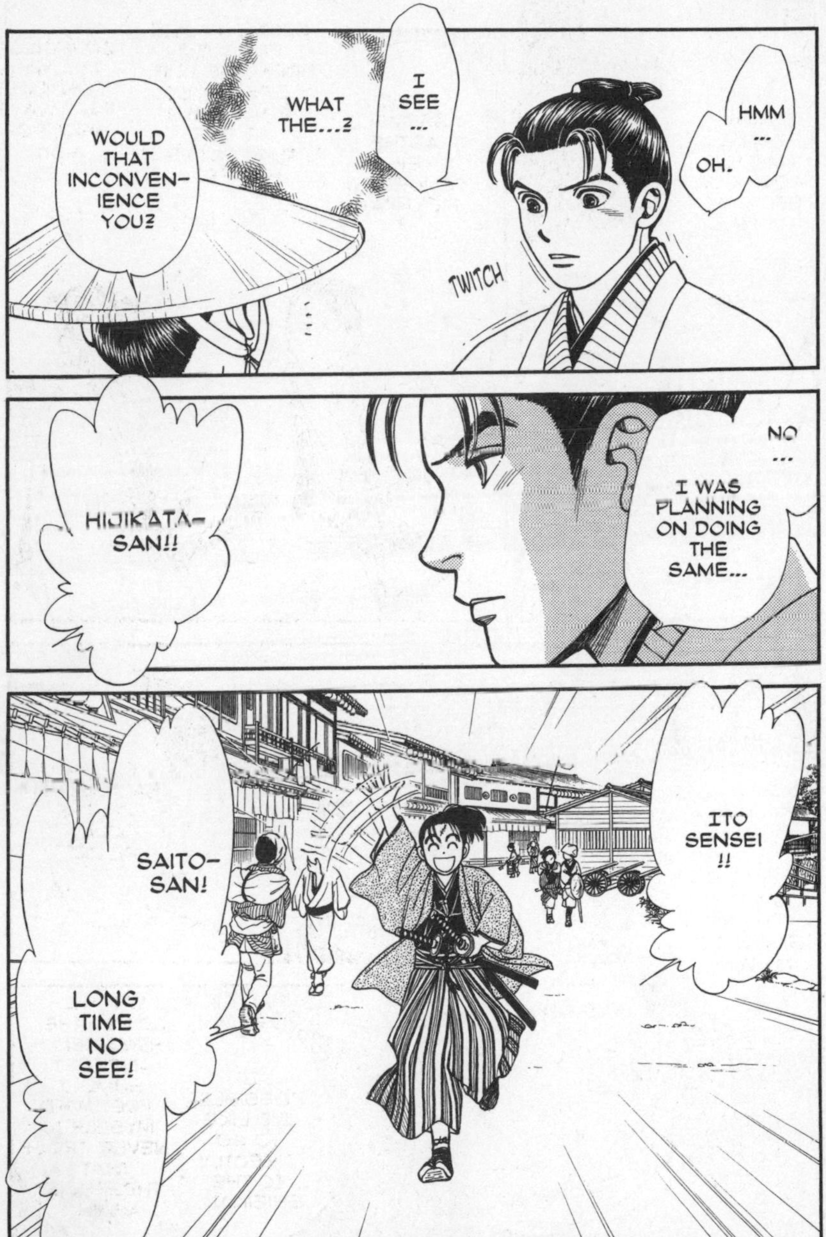
HMM ... OH.
I SEE ...
WHAT THE...?
WOULD THAT INCONVENIENCE YOU?
TWITCH
NO ... I WAS PLANNING ON DOING THE SAME...
HIJIKATA-SAN!!
ITO SENSEI !!
SAITO-SAN!
LONG TIME NO SEE!

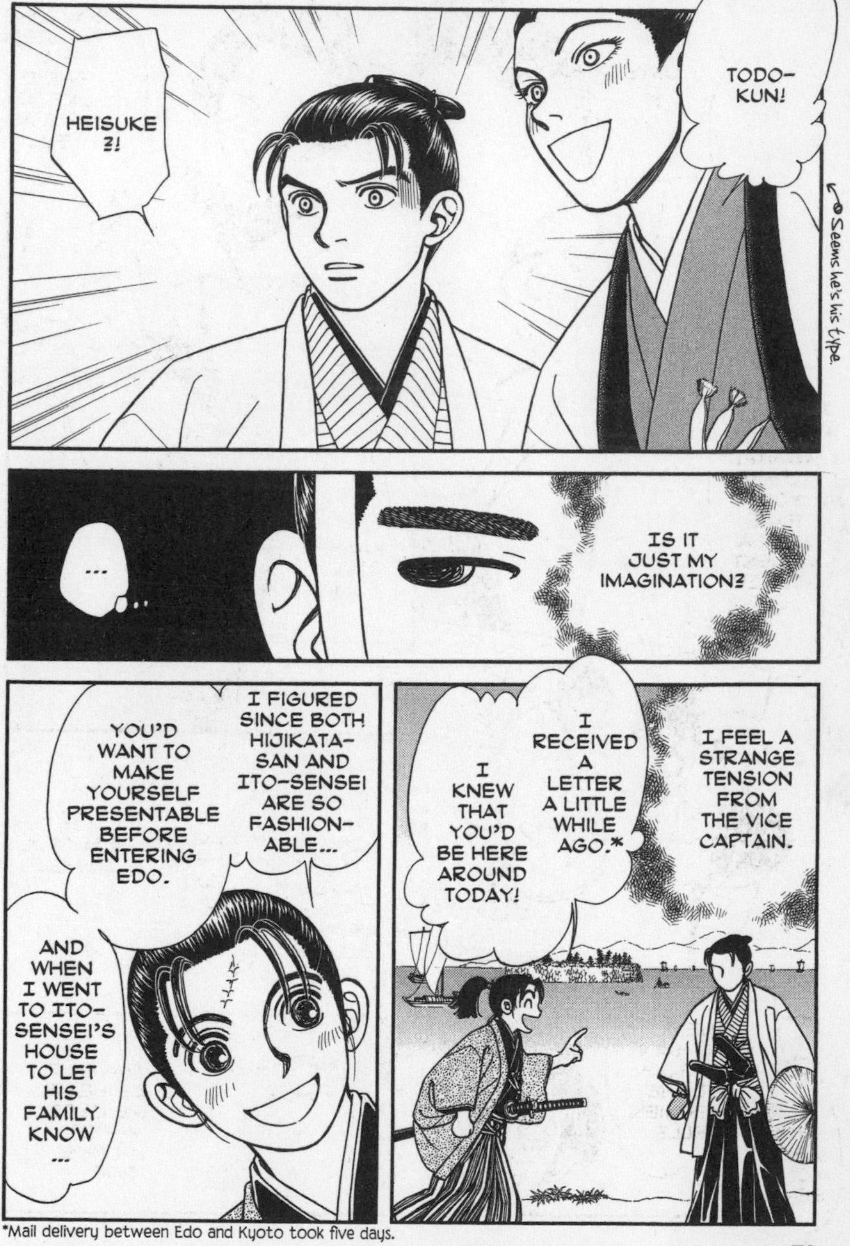
TODO-KUN!
HEISUKE?!
Seems he's his type.
IS IT JUST MY IMAGINATION?
...
...
I FEEL A STRANGE TENSION FROM THE VICE CAPTAIN.
I RECEIVED A LETTER A LITTLE WHILE AGO.*
I KNEW THAT YOU'D BE HERE AROUND TODAY!
I FIGURED SINCE BOTH HIJIKATA-SAN AND ITO-SENSEI ARE SO FASHIONABLE...
YOU'D WANT TO MAKE YOURSELF PRESENTABLE BEFORE ENTERING EDO.
AND WHEN I WENT TO ITO-SENSEI'S HOUSE TO LET HIS FAMILY KNOW ...

*Mail delivery between Edo and Kyoto took five days.

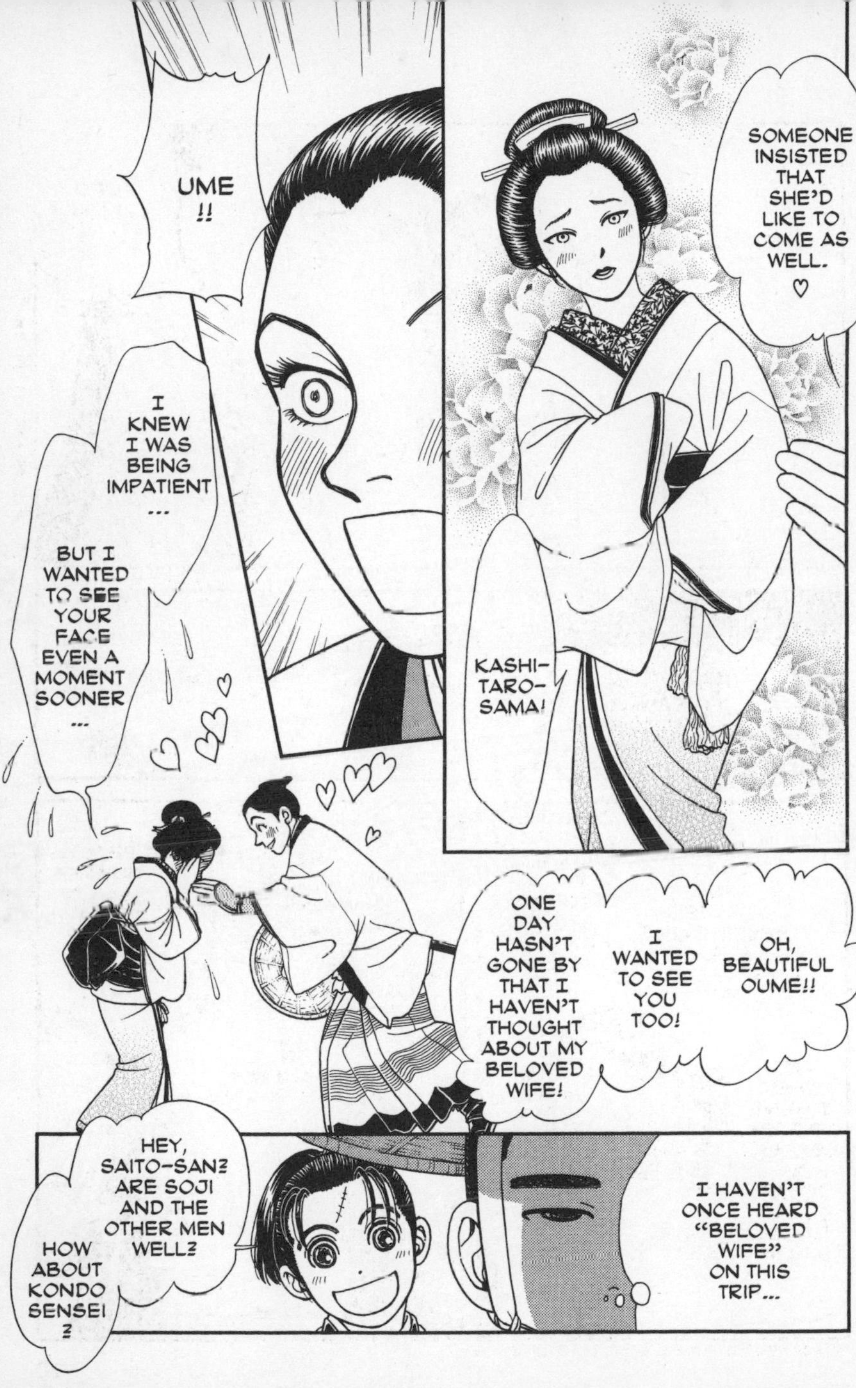
SOMEONE INSISTED THAT SHE'D LIKE TO COME AS WELL. ♡
KASHI-TARO-SAMA!
UME !!
I KNEW I WAS BEING IMPATIENT...
BUT I WANTED TO SEE YOUR FACE EVEN A MOMENT SOONER...
OH, BEAUTIFUL OUME!!
I WANTED TO SEE YOU TOO!
ONE DAY HASN'T GONE BY THAT I HAVEN'T THOUGHT ABOUT MY BELOVED WIFE!
I HAVEN'T ONCE HEARD "BELOVED WIFE" ON THIS TRIP...
HEY, SAITO-SAN? ARE SOJI AND THE OTHER MEN WELL?
HOW ABOUT KONDO SENSEI?

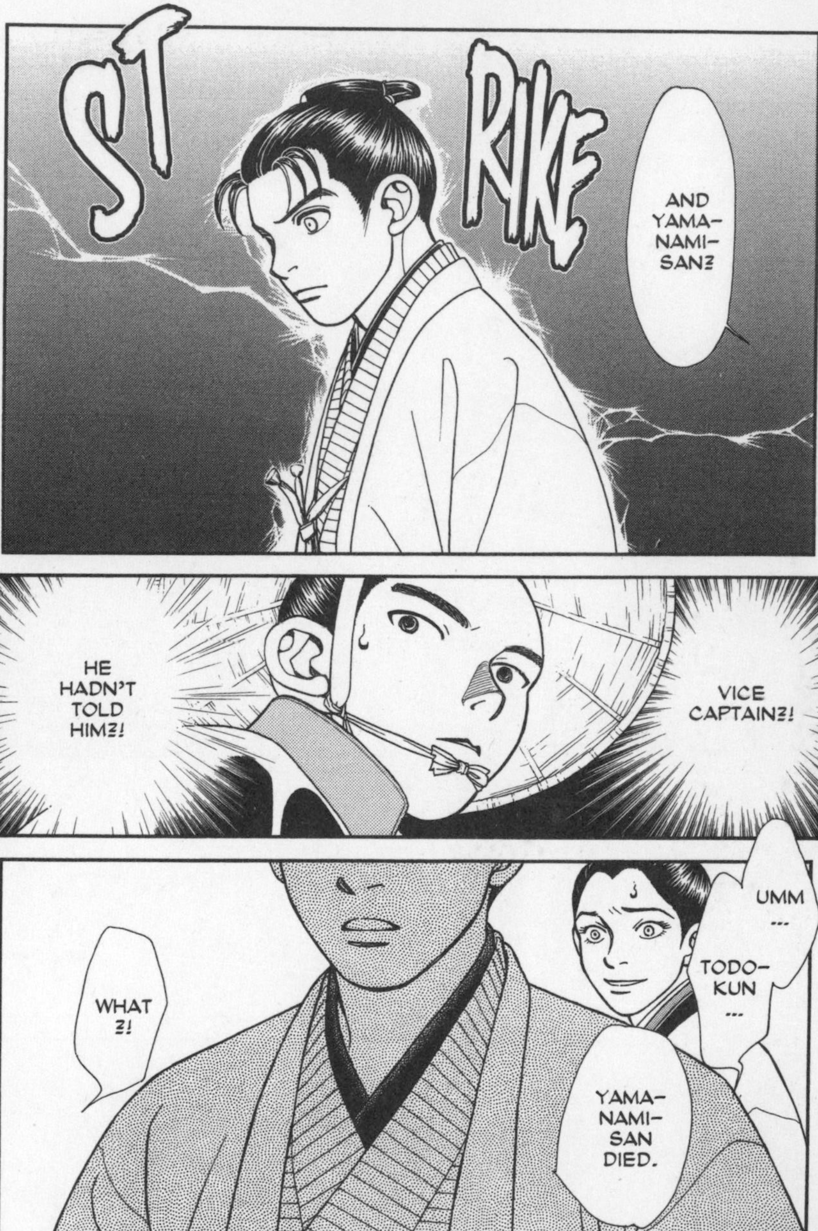
STRIKE
AND YAMA-NAMI-SAN?
VICE CAPTAIN?!
HE HADN'T TOLD HIM?!
UMM... TODO-KUN...
YAMA-NAMI-SAN DIED.
WHAT?!

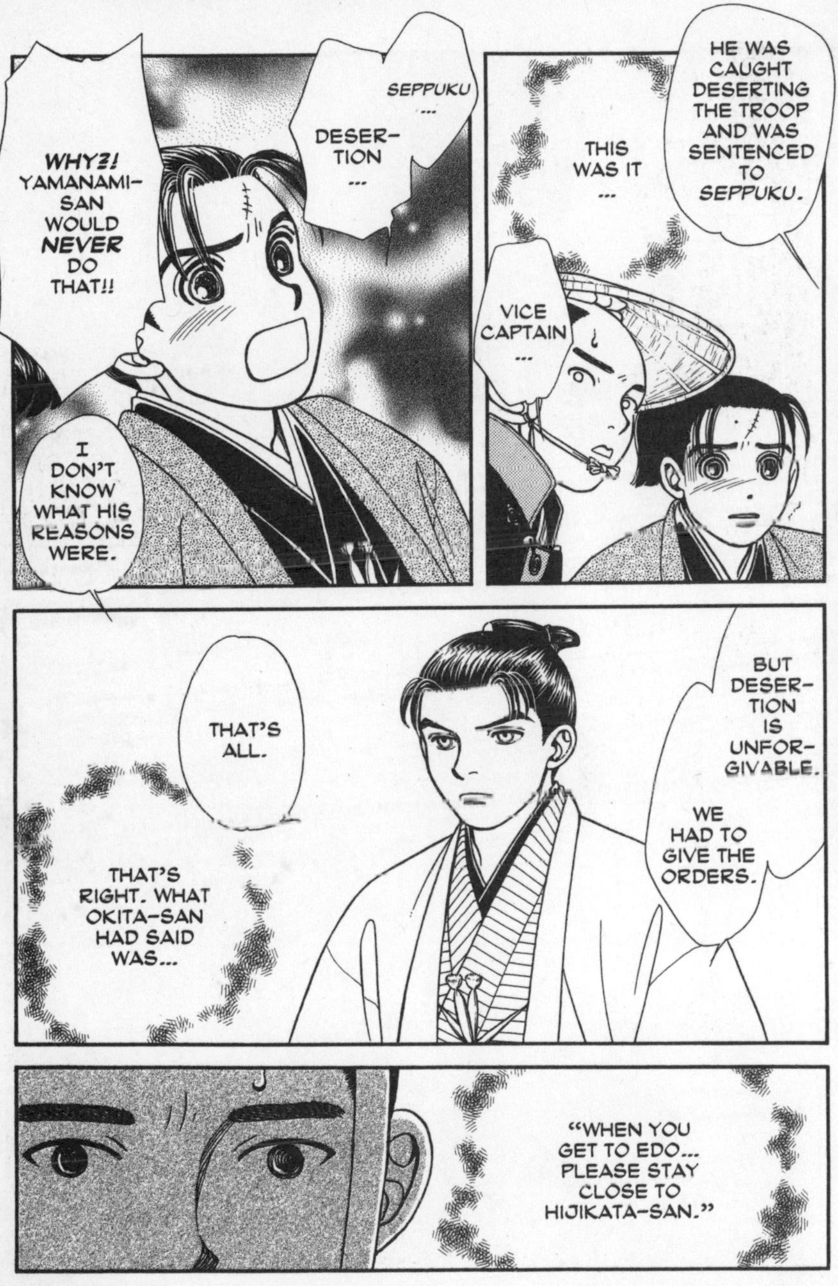
HE WAS CAUGHT DESERTING THE TROOP AND WAS SENTENCED TO SEPPUKU.
THIS WAS IT ...
VICE CAPTAIN ...
SEPPUKU ...
DESERTION ...
WHY?! YAMANAMI-SAN WOULD NEVER DO THAT!!
I DON'T KNOW WHAT HIS REASONS WERE.
BUT DESERTION IS UNFORGIVABLE.
WE HAD TO GIVE THE ORDERS.
THAT'S ALL.
THAT'S RIGHT. WHAT OKITA-SAN HAD SAID WAS...
"WHEN YOU GET TO EDO... PLEASE STAY CLOSE TO HIJIKATA-SAN."

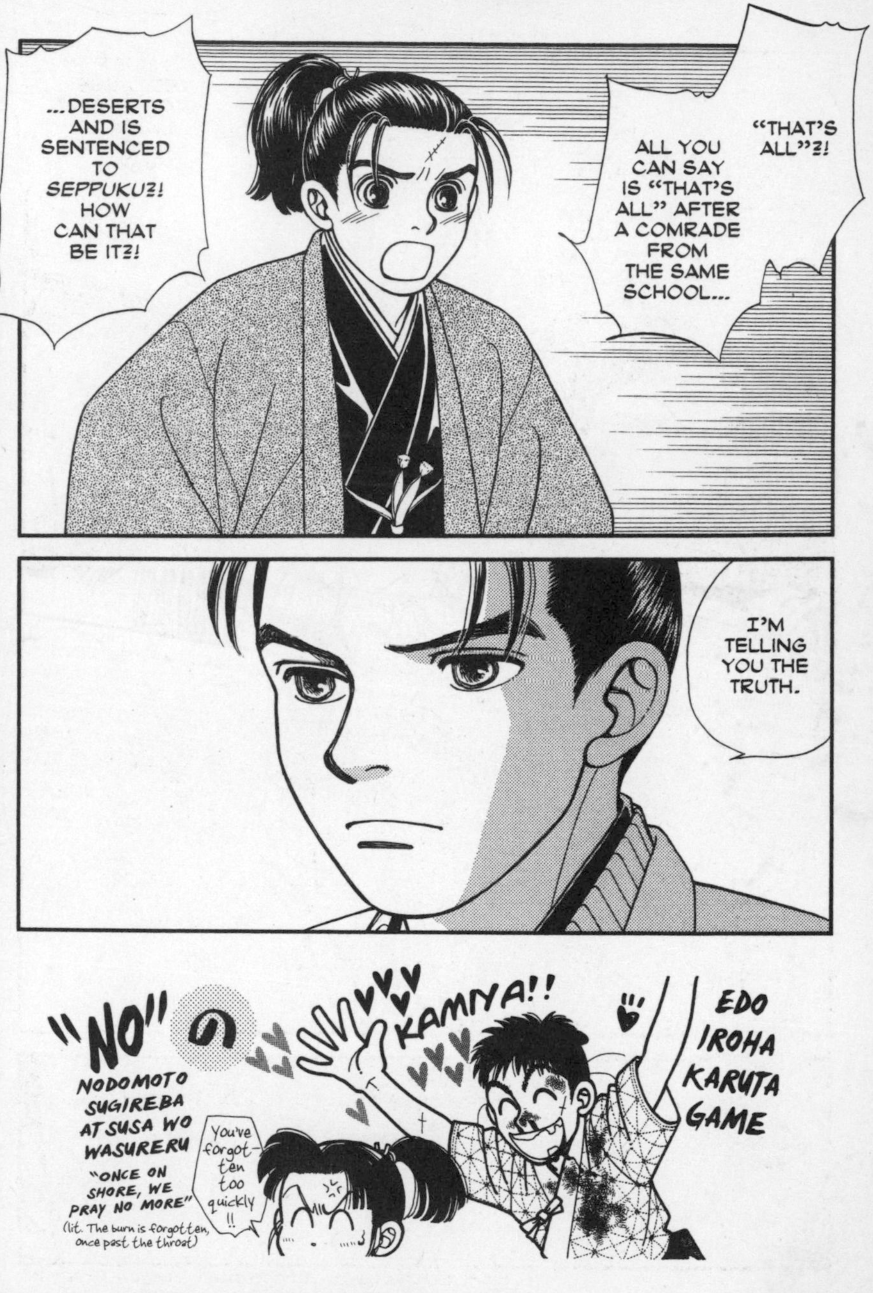
"THAT'S ALL"?!
ALL YOU CAN SAY IS "THAT'S ALL" AFTER A COMRADE FROM THE SAME SCHOOL...
...DESERTS AND IS SENTENCED TO SEPPUKU?! HOW CAN THAT BE IT?!
I'M TELLING YOU THE TRUTH.
EDO IROHA KARUTA GAME
KAMIYA!!
"NO" の
NODOMOTO SUGIREBA ATSUSA WO WASURERU
"ONCE ON SHORE, WE PRAY NO MORE"
(lit. The burn is forgotten, once past the throat)
You've forgotten too quickly!!

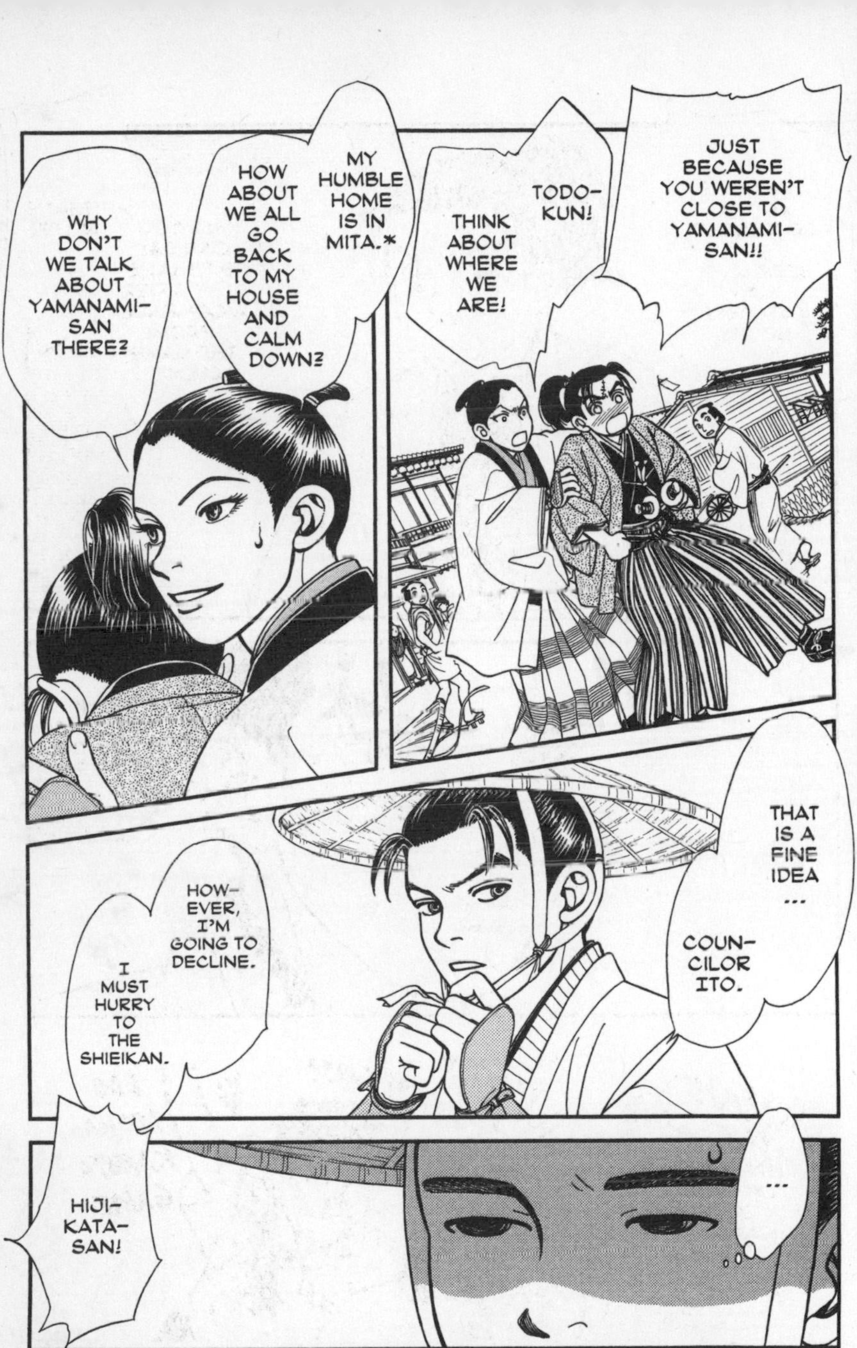
JUST BECAUSE YOU WEREN'T CLOSE TO YAMANAMI-SAN!!
TODO-KUN!
THINK ABOUT WHERE WE ARE!
MY HUMBLE HOME IS IN MITA.*
HOW ABOUT WE ALL GO BACK TO MY HOUSE AND CALM DOWN?
WHY DON'T WE TALK ABOUT YAMANAMI-SAN THERE?
THAT IS A FINE IDEA ...
COUNCILOR ITO.
HOWEVER, I'M GOING TO DECLINE.
I MUST HURRY TO THE SHIEIKAN.
...
HIJI-KATA-SAN!

*He closed the Furukawa *dojo* and moved when joining the Shinsengumi. Mita and Shinagawa were close, with Takanawa in between.

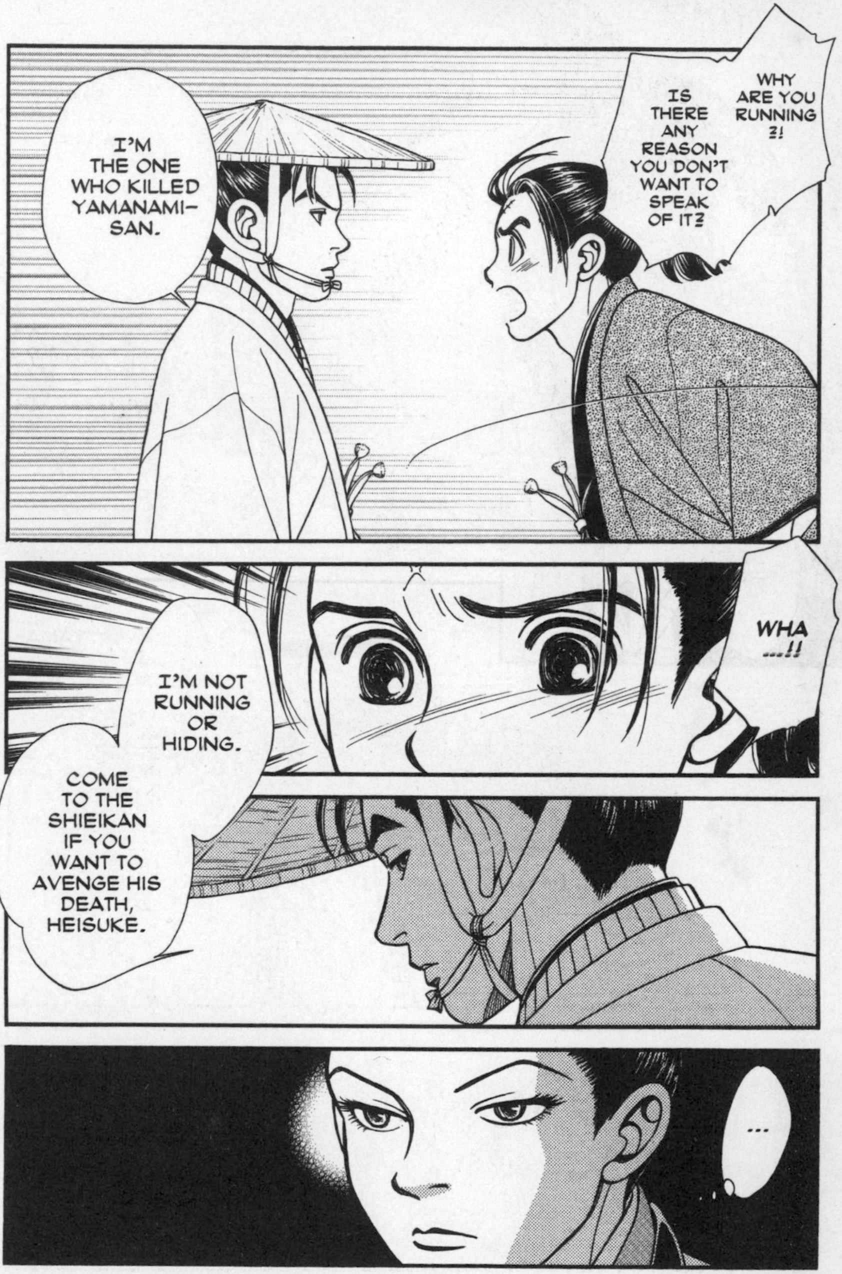
WHY ARE YOU RUNNING ?!
IS THERE ANY REASON YOU DON'T WANT TO SPEAK OF IT?
I'M THE ONE WHO KILLED YAMANAMI-SAN.
WHA...!!
I'M NOT RUNNING OR HIDING.
COME TO THE SHIEIKAN IF YOU WANT TO AVENGE HIS DEATH, HEISUKE.
...

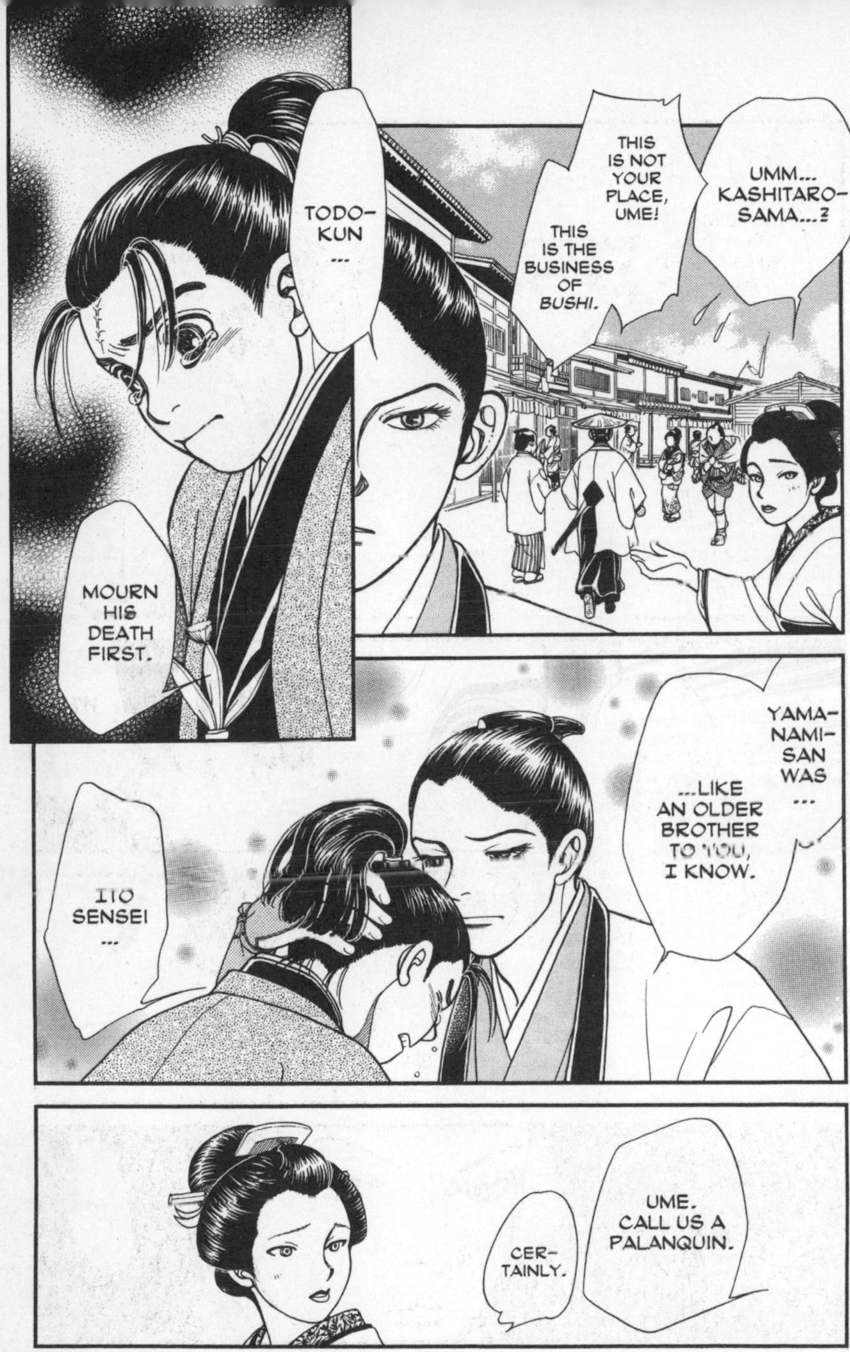
UMM... KASHITARO-SAMA...?
THIS IS NOT YOUR PLACE, UME!
THIS IS THE BUSINESS OF BUSHI.
TODO-KUN ...
MOURN HIS DEATH FIRST.
YAMANAMI-SAN WAS ...
...LIKE AN OLDER BROTHER TO YOU, I KNOW.
ITO SENSEI ...
UME. CALL US A PALANQUIN.
CER-TAINLY.

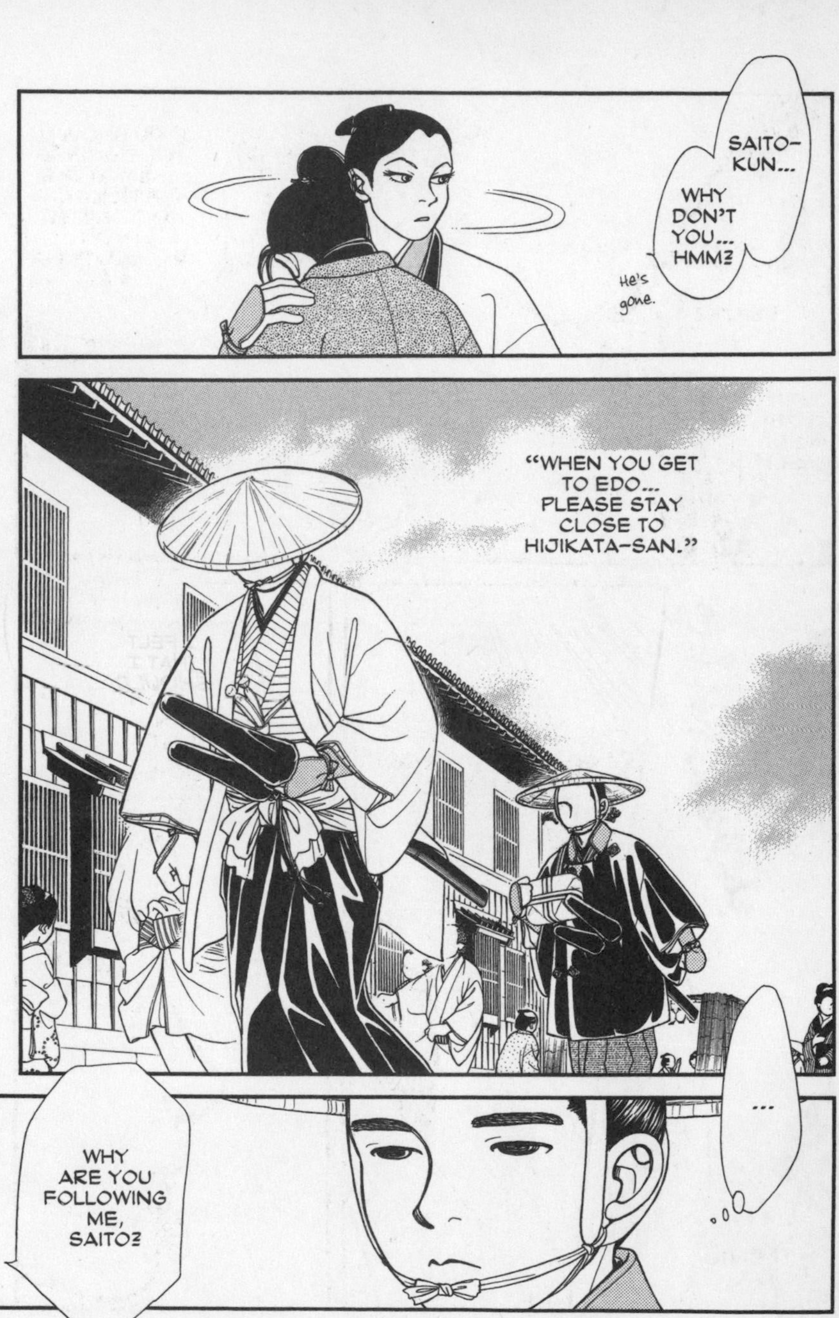
SAITO-KUN...
WHY DON'T YOU... HMM?
He's gone.
"WHEN YOU GET TO EDO... PLEASE STAY CLOSE TO HIJIKATA-SAN."
...
WHY ARE YOU FOLLOWING ME, SAITO?

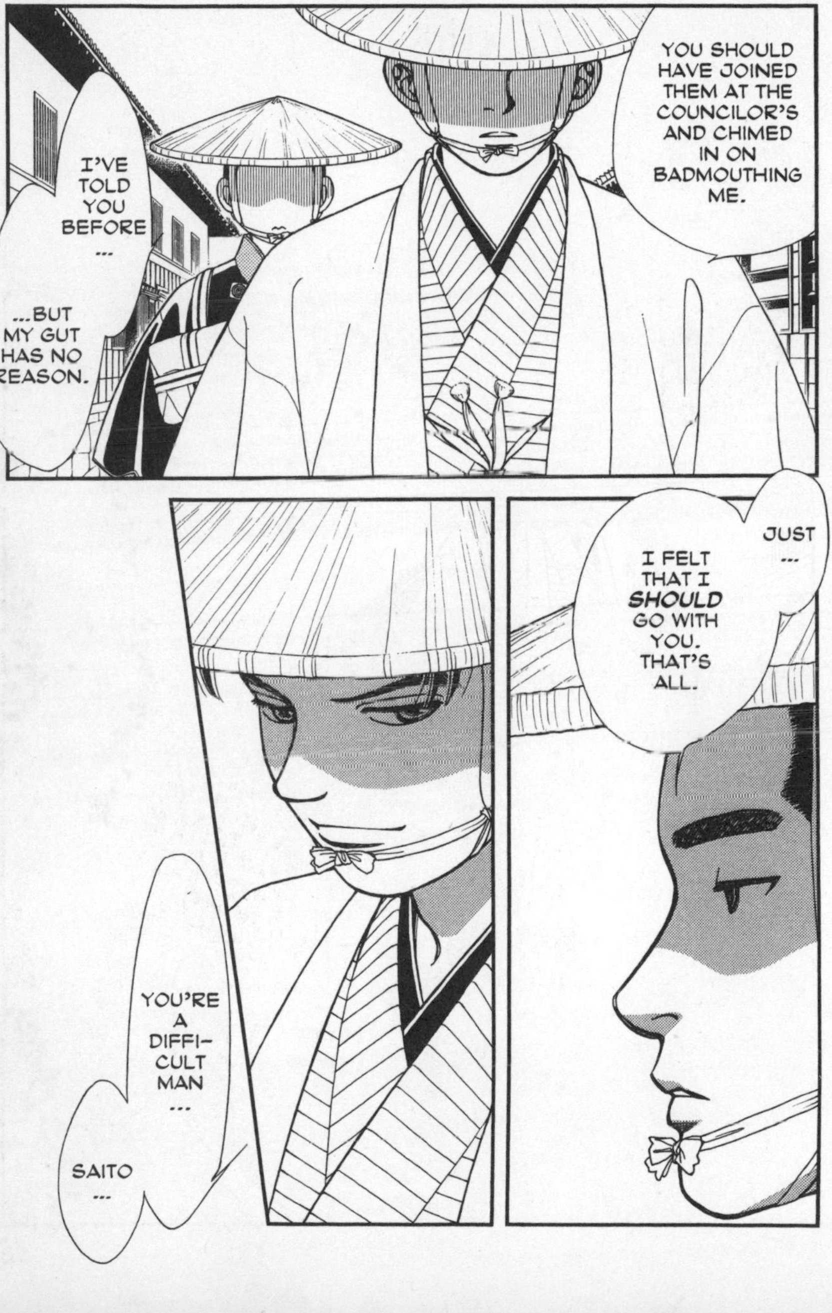
YOU SHOULD HAVE JOINED THEM AT THE COUNCILOR'S AND CHIMED IN ON BADMOUTHING ME.
I'VE TOLD YOU BEFORE ...
...BUT MY GUT HAS NO REASON.
JUST ...
I FELT THAT I ***SHOULD*** GO WITH YOU. THAT'S ALL.
YOU'RE A DIFFI- CULT MAN ...
SAITO ...

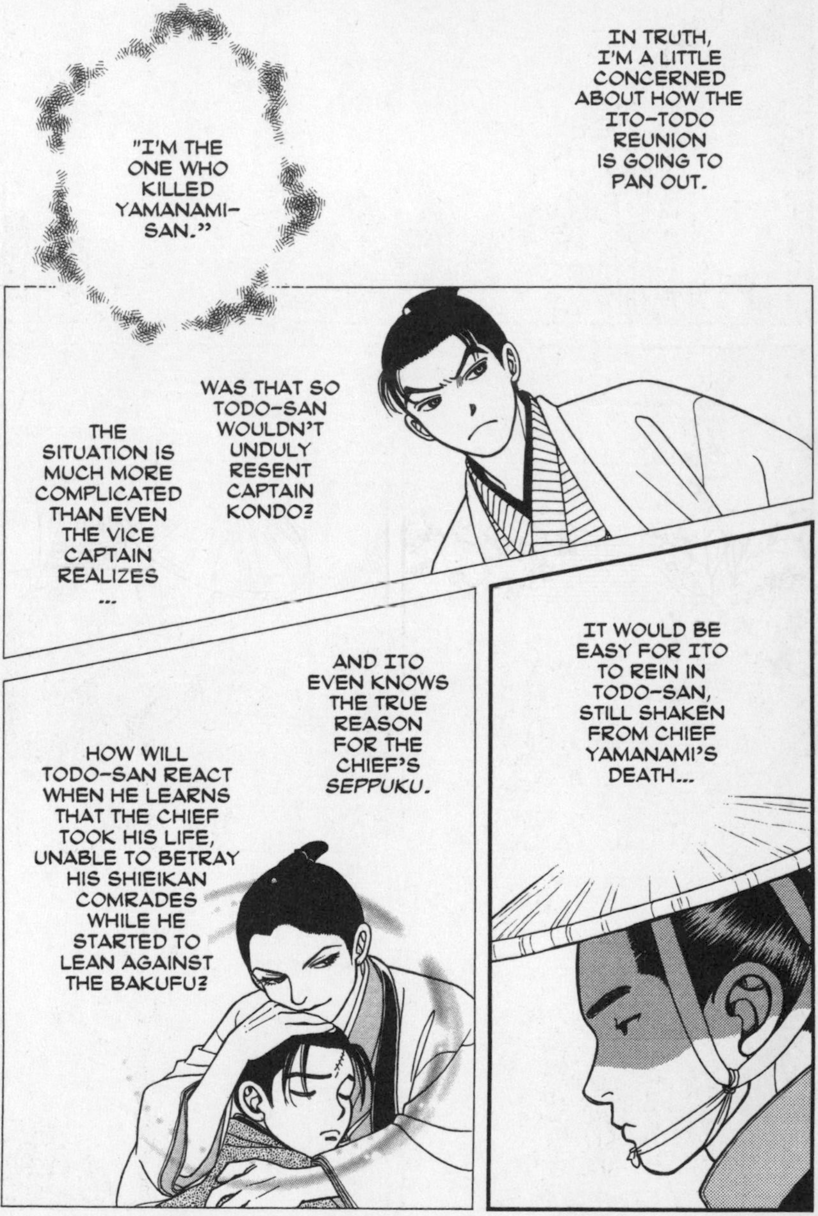
IN TRUTH, I'M A LITTLE CONCERNED ABOUT HOW THE ITO-TODO REUNION IS GOING TO PAN OUT.
"I'M THE ONE WHO KILLED YAMANAMI-SAN."
WAS THAT SO TODO-SAN WOULDN'T UNDULY RESENT CAPTAIN KONDO?
THE SITUATION IS MUCH MORE COMPLICATED THAN EVEN THE VICE CAPTAIN REALIZES...
IT WOULD BE EASY FOR ITO TO REIN IN TODO-SAN, STILL SHAKEN FROM CHIEF YAMANAMI'S DEATH...
AND ITO EVEN KNOWS THE TRUE REASON FOR THE CHIEF'S *SEPPUKU*.
HOW WILL TODO-SAN REACT WHEN HE LEARNS THAT THE CHIEF TOOK HIS LIFE, UNABLE TO BETRAY HIS SHIEIKAN COMRADES WHILE HE STARTED TO LEAN AGAINST THE BAKUFU?

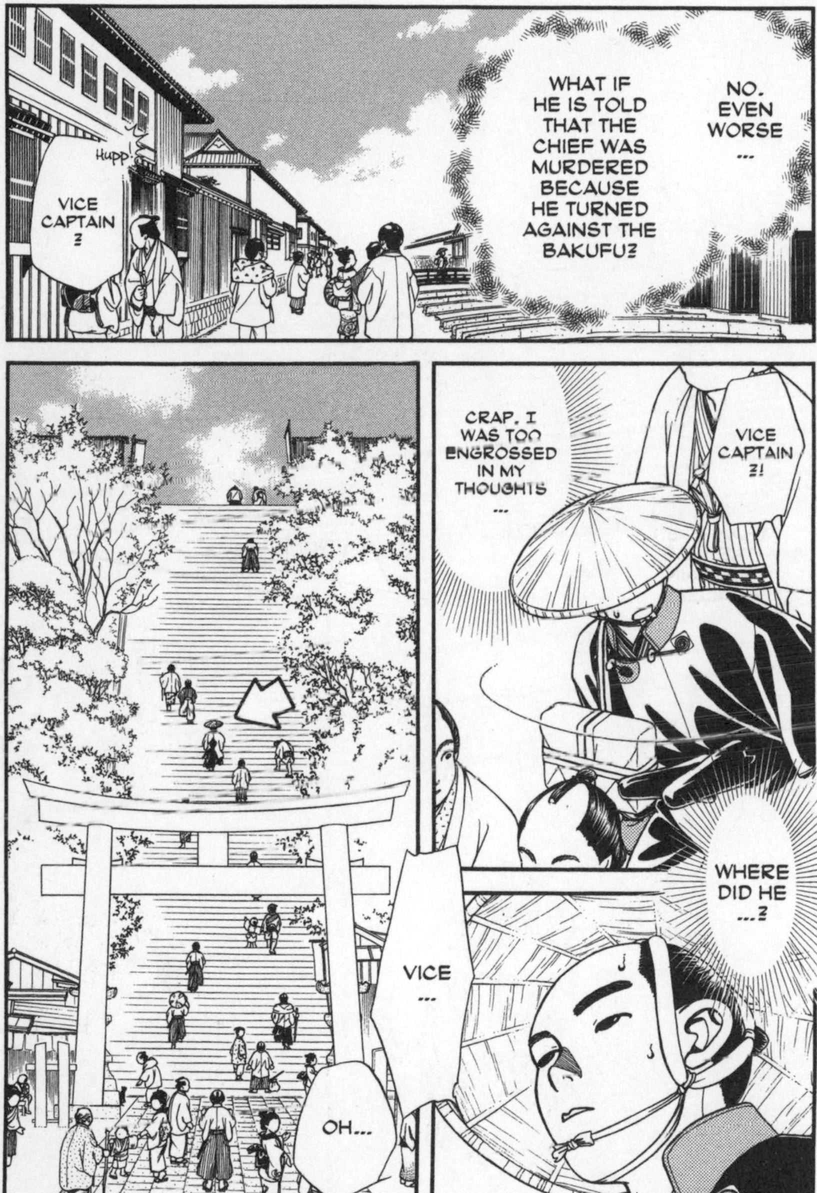
WHAT IF HE IS TOLD THAT THE CHIEF WAS MURDERED BECAUSE HE TURNED AGAINST THE BAKUFU?
NO. EVEN WORSE ...
HUPP!
VICE CAPTAIN?
VICE CAPTAIN?!
CRAP. I WAS TOO ENGROSSED IN MY THOUGHTS ...
WHERE DID HE ...?
VICE ...
OH...

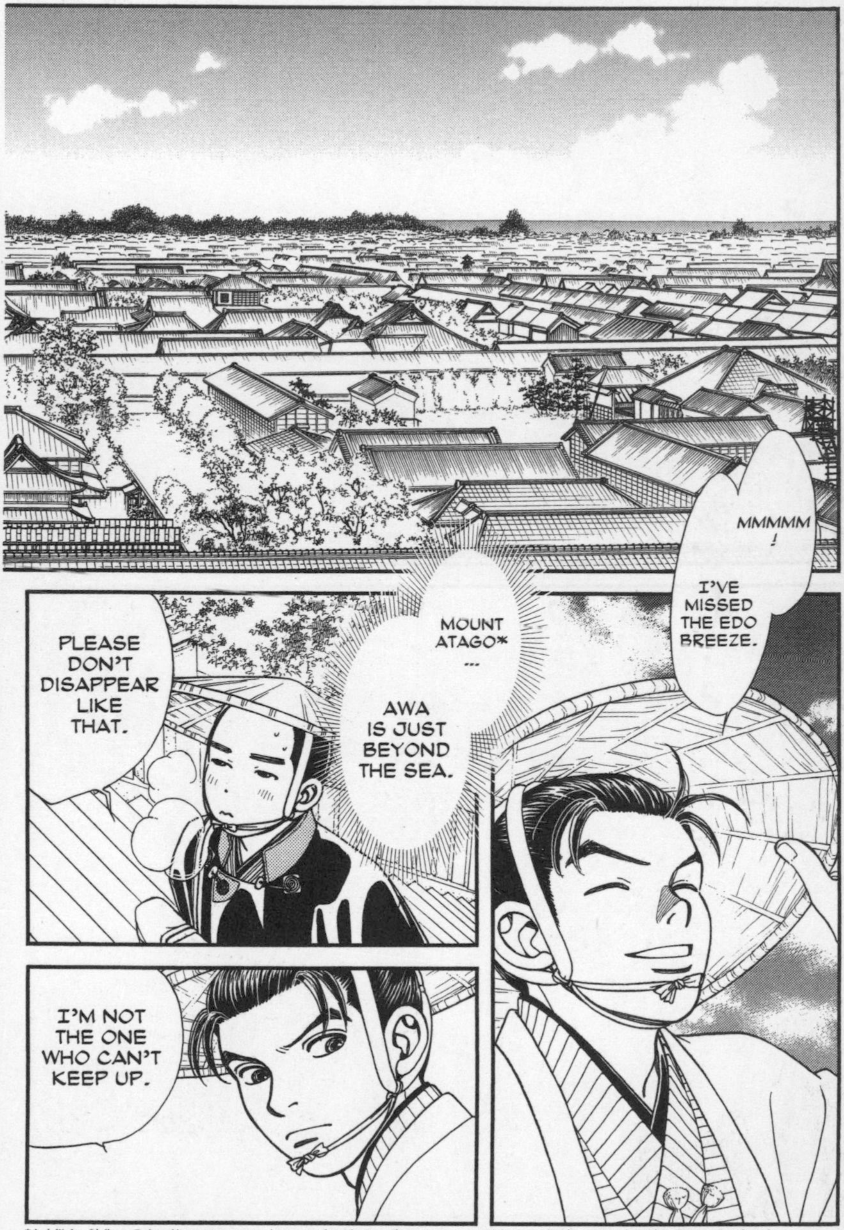
MMMMM!
I'VE MISSED THE EDO BREEZE.
MOUNT ATAGO*...
AWA IS JUST BEYOND THE SEA.
PLEASE DON'T DISAPPEAR LIKE THAT.
I'M NOT THE ONE WHO CAN'T KEEP UP.

*A hill in Shiba, Edo. It was a popular scenic view, where one could see all the way to the Boso Peninsula.

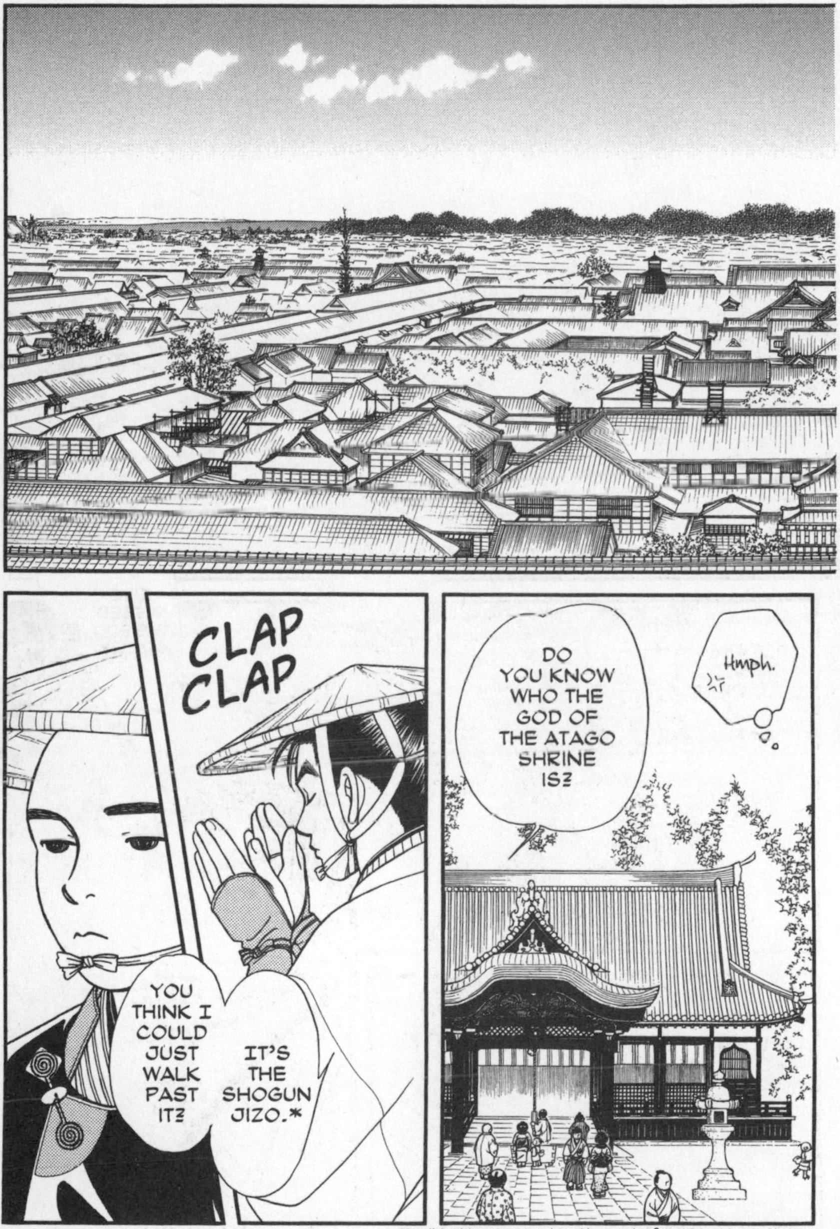
Hmph.
DO YOU KNOW WHO THE GOD OF THE ATAGO SHRINE IS?
CLAP CLAP
IT'S THE SHOGUN JIZO.*
YOU THINK I COULD JUST WALK PAST IT?

*Bodhisattva revered as the god of armies. Atago Shrine was erected by the first Tokugawa Shogunate, Ieyasu.

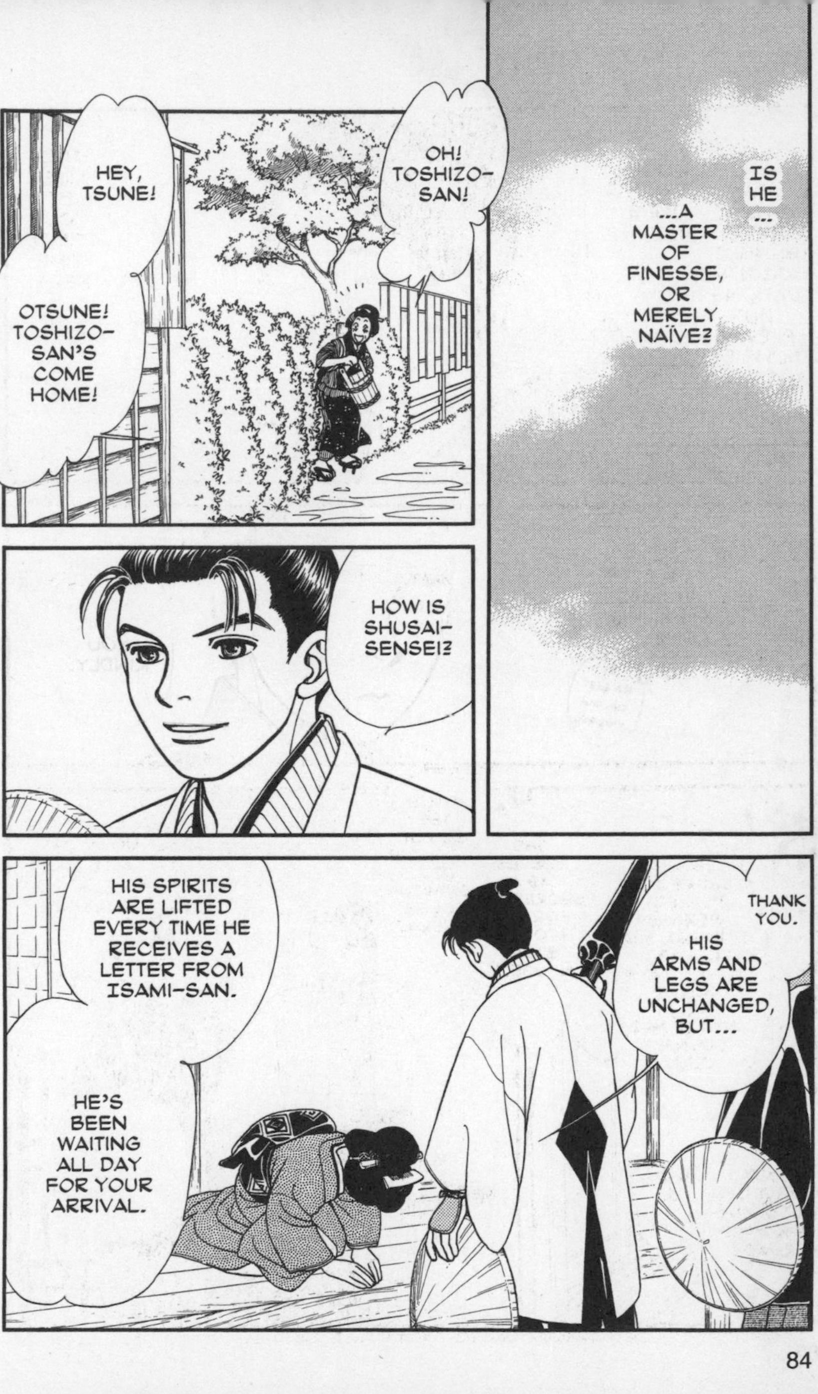
IS HE ...
...A MASTER OF FINESSE, OR MERELY NAÏVE?
OH! TOSHIZO-SAN!
HEY, TSUNE!
OTSUNE! TOSHIZO-SAN'S COME HOME!
HOW IS SHUSAI-SENSEI!?
THANK YOU.
HIS ARMS AND LEGS ARE UNCHANGED, BUT...
HIS SPIRITS ARE LIFTED EVERY TIME HE RECEIVES A LETTER FROM ISAMI-SAN.
HE'S BEEN WAITING ALL DAY FOR YOUR ARRIVAL.

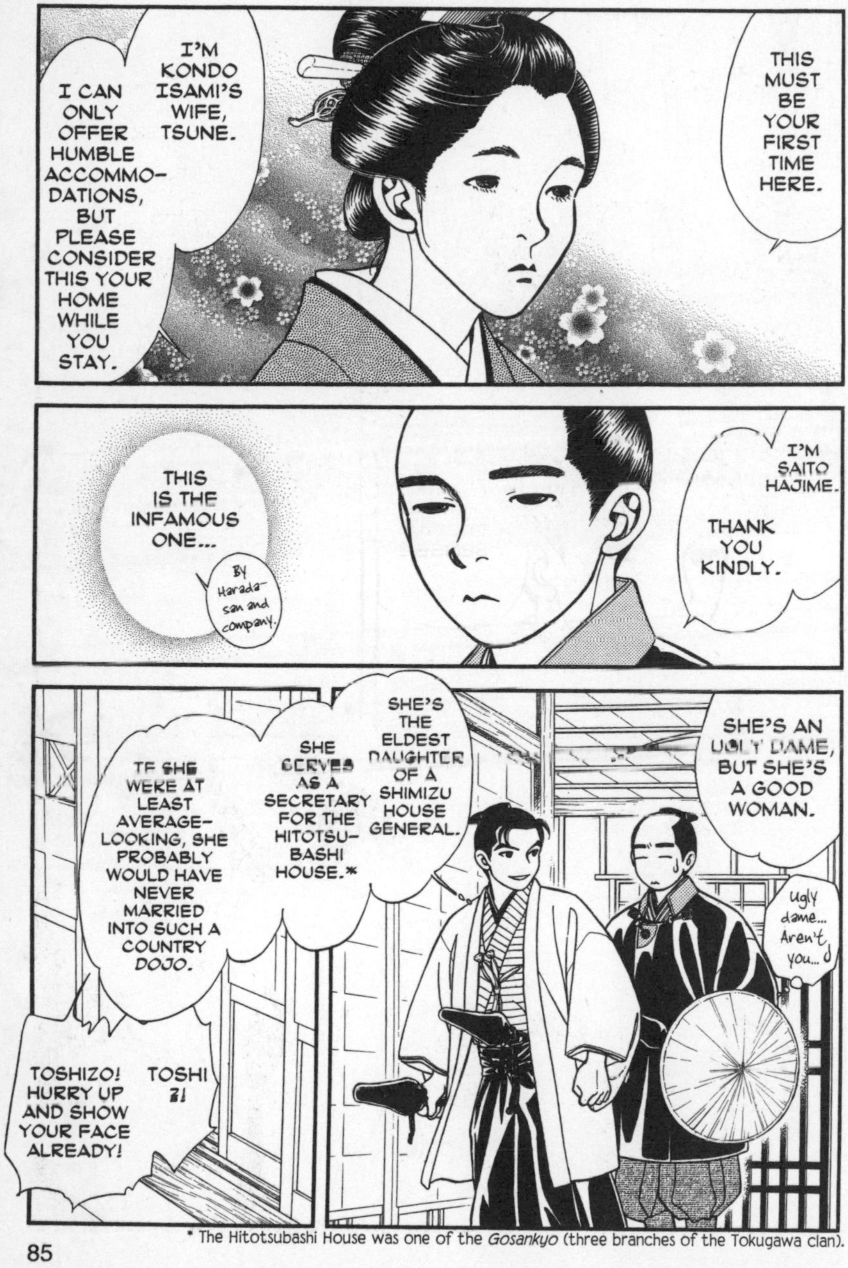
THIS MUST BE YOUR FIRST TIME HERE.
I'M KONDO ISAMI'S WIFE, TSUNE.
I CAN ONLY OFFER HUMBLE ACCOMMODATIONS, BUT PLEASE CONSIDER THIS YOUR HOME WHILE YOU STAY.
I'M SAITO HAJIME.
THANK YOU KINDLY.
THIS IS THE INFAMOUS ONE...
By Harada-san and company.
SHE'S AN UGLY DAME, BUT SHE'S A GOOD WOMAN.
Ugly dame... Aren't you...
SHE'S THE ELDEST DAUGHTER OF A SHIMIZU HOUSE GENERAL.
SHE SERVES AS A SECRETARY FOR THE HITOTSUBASHI HOUSE.*
IF SHE WERE AT LEAST AVERAGE-LOOKING, SHE PROBABLY WOULD HAVE NEVER MARRIED INTO SUCH A COUNTRY *DOJO*.
TOSHI ZI
TOSHIZO! HURRY UP AND SHOW YOUR FACE ALREADY!

* The Hitotsubashi House was one of the *Gosankyo* (three branches of the Tokugawa clan).

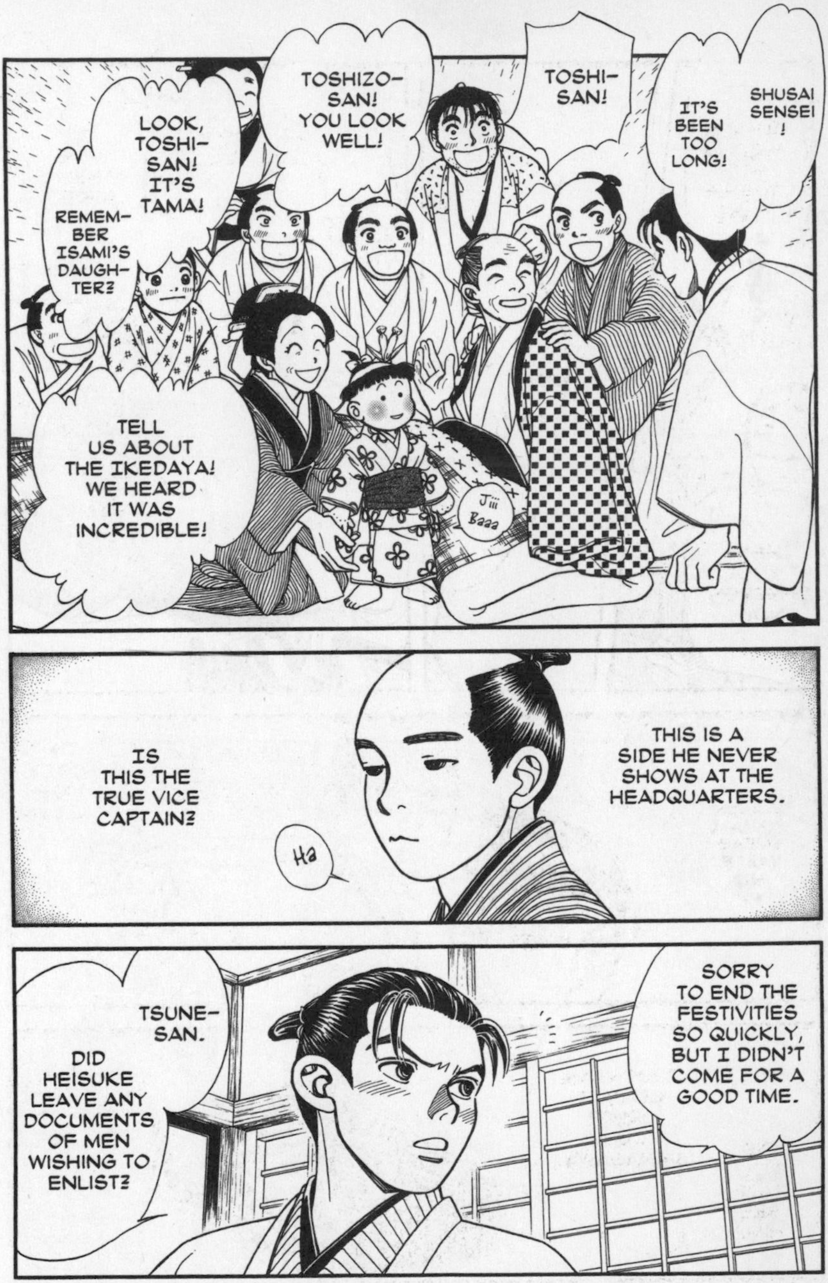
SHUSAI SENSEI!
IT'S BEEN TOO LONG!
TOSHI-SAN!
TOSHIZO-SAN! YOU LOOK WELL!
LOOK, TOSHI-SAN! IT'S TAMA!
REMEMBER ISAMI'S DAUGHTER?
Jiii Baaa
TELL US ABOUT THE IKEDAYA! WE HEARD IT WAS INCREDIBLE!
THIS IS A SIDE HE NEVER SHOWS AT THE HEADQUARTERS.
IS THIS THE TRUE VICE CAPTAIN?
Ha
SORRY TO END THE FESTIVITIES SO QUICKLY, BUT I DIDN'T COME FOR A GOOD TIME.
TSUNE-SAN.
DID HEISUKE LEAVE ANY DOCUMENTS OF MEN WISHING TO ENLIST?

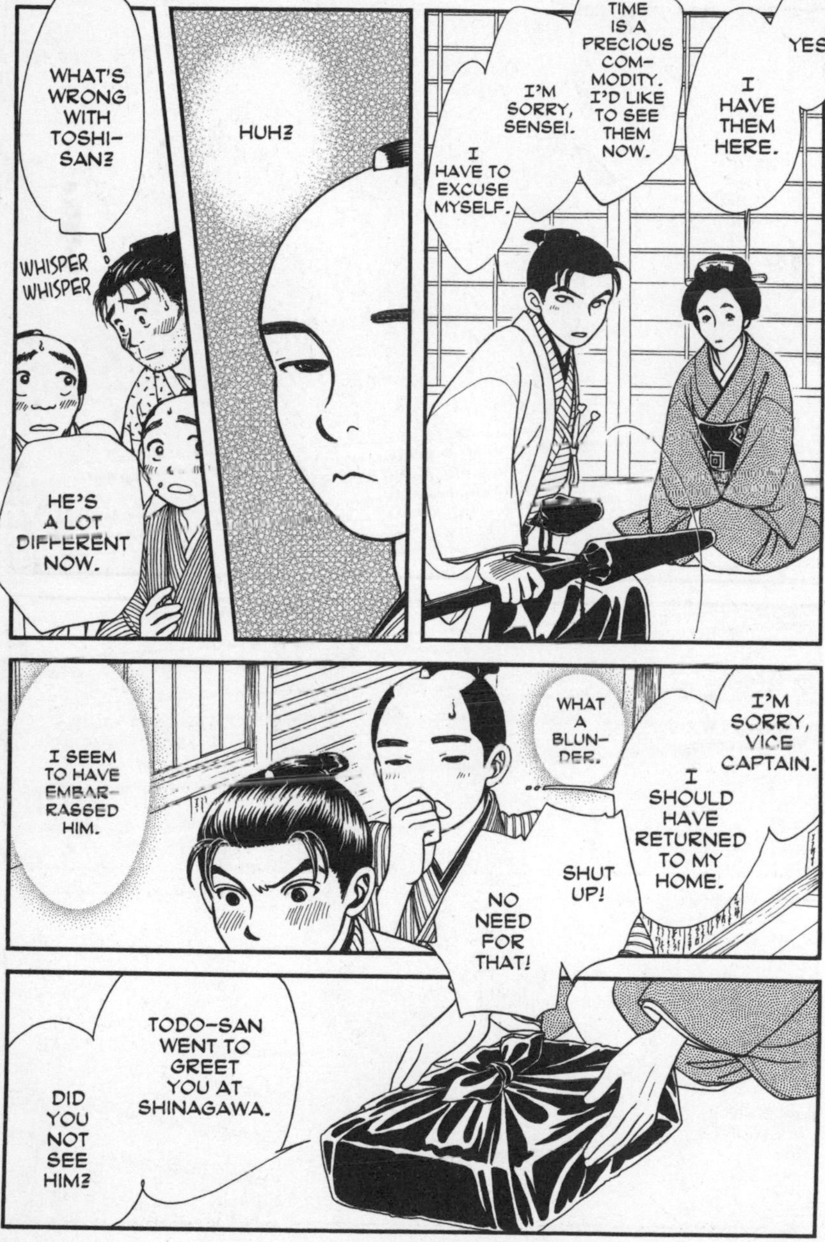
YES.
I HAVE THEM HERE.
TIME IS A PRECIOUS COMMODITY. I'D LIKE TO SEE THEM NOW.
I'M SORRY, SENSEI.
I HAVE TO EXCUSE MYSELF.
HUH?
WHAT'S WRONG WITH TOSHI-SAN?
WHISPER WHISPER
HE'S A LOT DIFFERENT NOW.
I'M SORRY, VICE CAPTAIN.
I SHOULD HAVE RETURNED TO MY HOME.
WHAT A BLUNDER.
...
SHUT UP!
NO NEED FOR THAT!
I SEEM TO HAVE EMBARRASSED HIM.
TODO-SAN WENT TO GREET YOU AT SHINAGAWA.
DID YOU NOT SEE HIM?

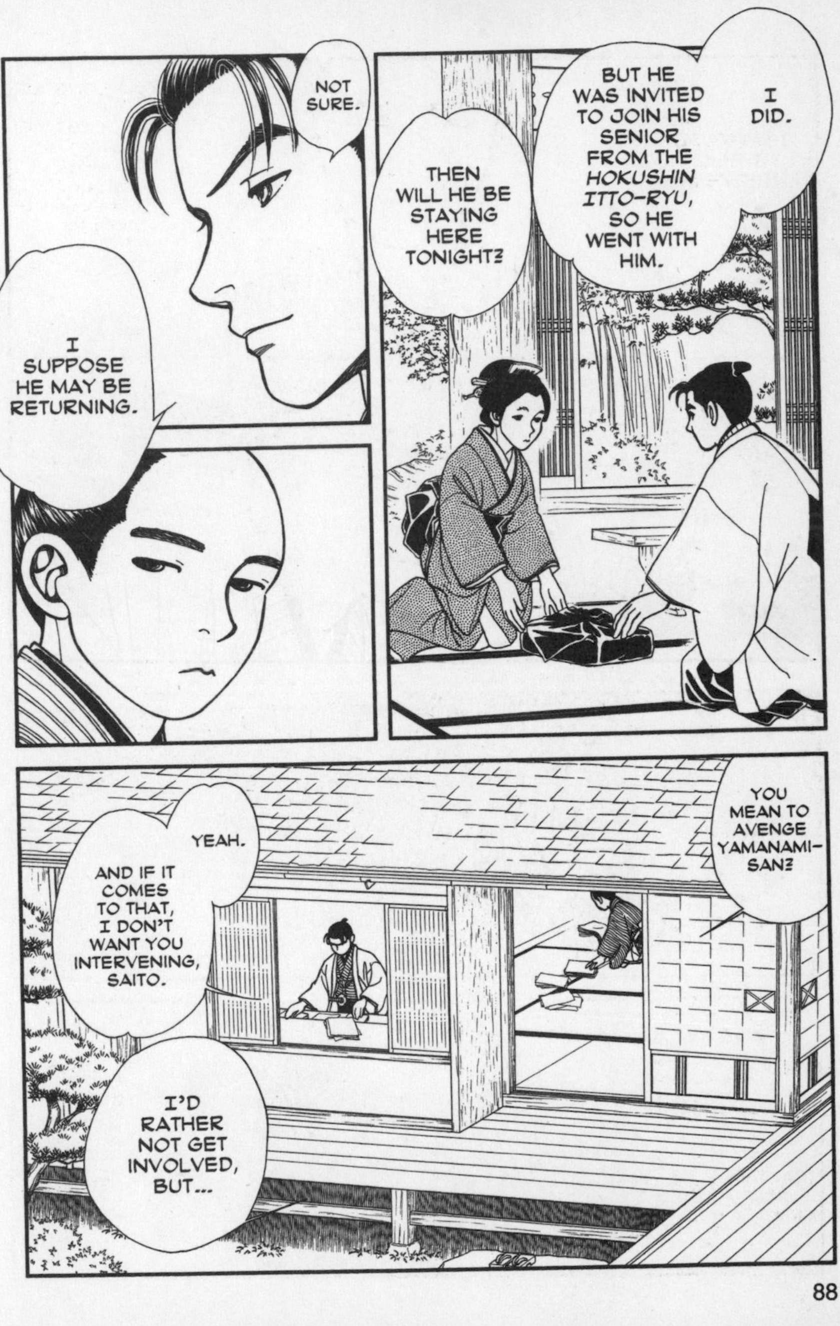
I DID.
BUT HE WAS INVITED TO JOIN HIS SENIOR FROM THE *HOKUSHIN ITTO-RYU*, SO HE WENT WITH HIM.
THEN WILL HE BE STAYING HERE TONIGHT?
NOT SURE.
I SUPPOSE HE MAY BE RETURNING.
YOU MEAN TO AVENGE YAMANAMI-SAN?
YEAH.
AND IF IT COMES TO THAT, I DON'T WANT YOU INTERVENING, SAITO.
I'D RATHER NOT GET INVOLVED, BUT...

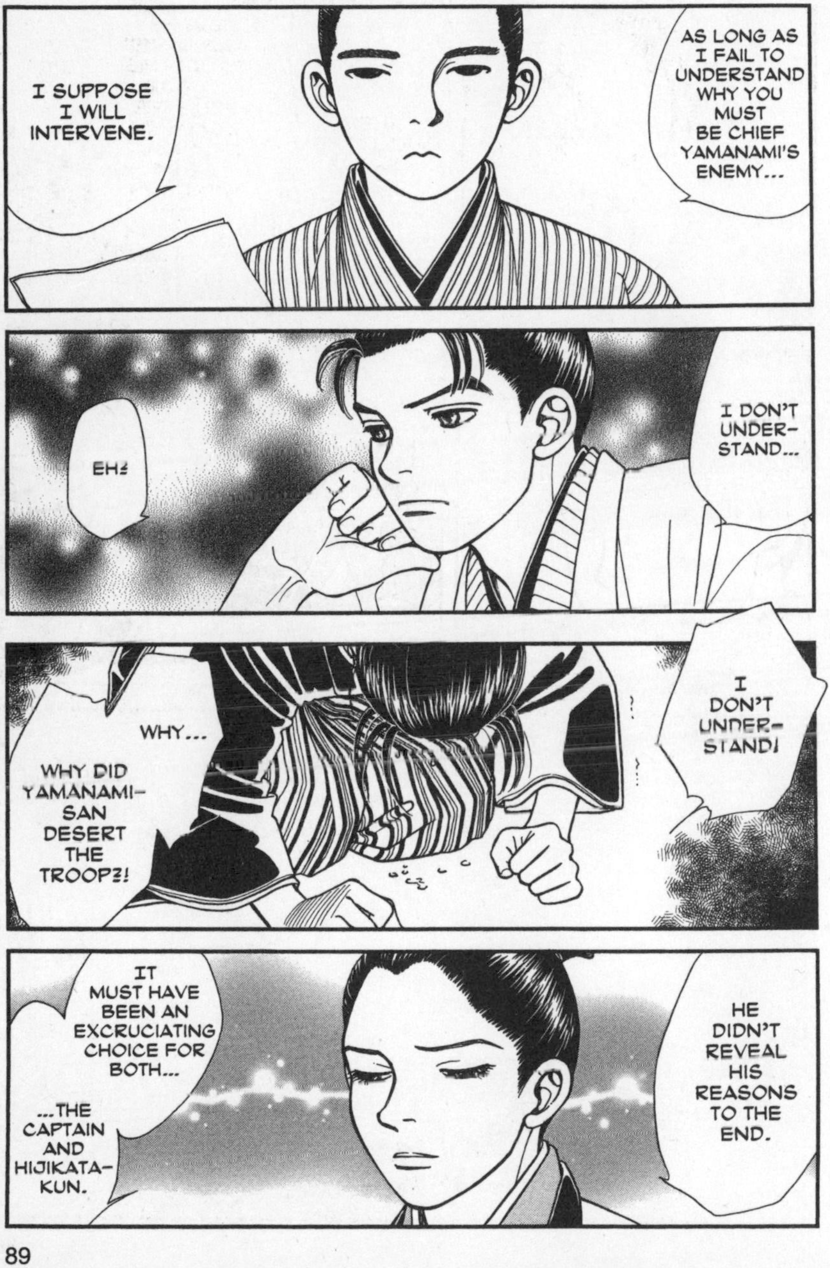
AS LONG AS I FAIL TO UNDERSTAND WHY YOU MUST BE CHIEF YAMANAMI'S ENEMY...
I SUPPOSE I WILL INTERVENE.
I DON'T UNDERSTAND...
EH?
I DON'T UNDERSTAND!
WHY...
WHY DID YAMANAMI-SAN DESERT THE TROOP?!
HE DIDN'T REVEAL HIS REASONS TO THE END.
IT MUST HAVE BEEN AN EXCRUCIATING CHOICE FOR BOTH...
...THE CAPTAIN AND HIJIKATA-KUN.

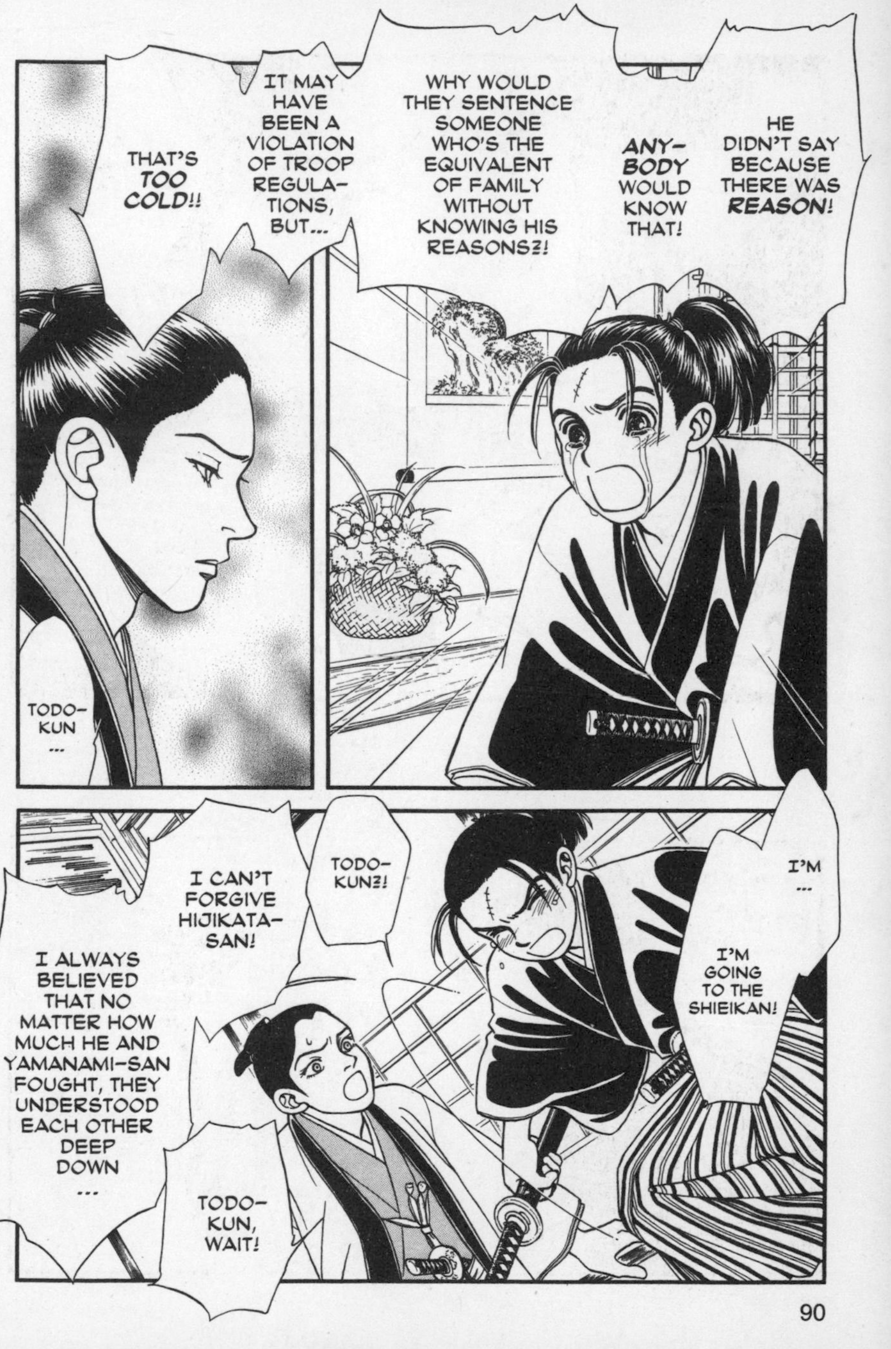
HE DIDN'T SAY BECAUSE THERE WAS **REASON**!
ANY-BODY WOULD KNOW THAT!
WHY WOULD THEY SENTENCE SOMEONE WHO'S THE EQUIVALENT OF FAMILY WITHOUT KNOWING HIS REASONS?!
IT MAY HAVE BEEN A VIOLATION OF TROOP REGULA-TIONS, BUT...
THAT'S ***TOO COLD***!!
TODO-KUN ...
I'M ...
I'M GOING TO THE SHIEIKAN!
TODO-KUN?!
I CAN'T FORGIVE HIJIKATA-SAN!
I ALWAYS BELIEVED THAT NO MATTER HOW MUCH HE AND YAMANAMI-SAN FOUGHT, THEY UNDERSTOOD EACH OTHER DEEP DOWN ...
TODO-KUN, WAIT!

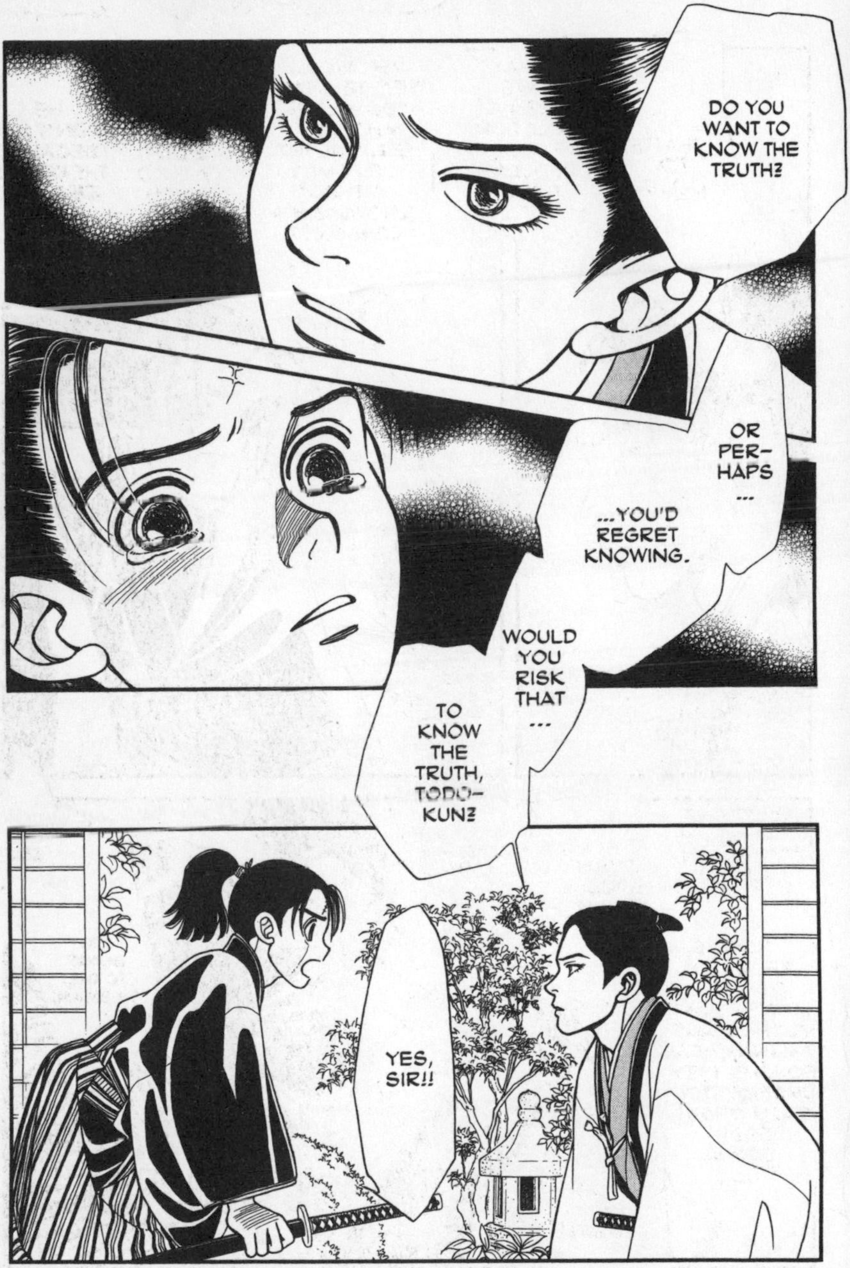
DO YOU WANT TO KNOW THE TRUTH?
OR PER-HAPS...
...YOU'D REGRET KNOWING.
WOULD YOU RISK THAT...
TO KNOW THE TRUTH, TODO-KUN?
YES, SIR!!

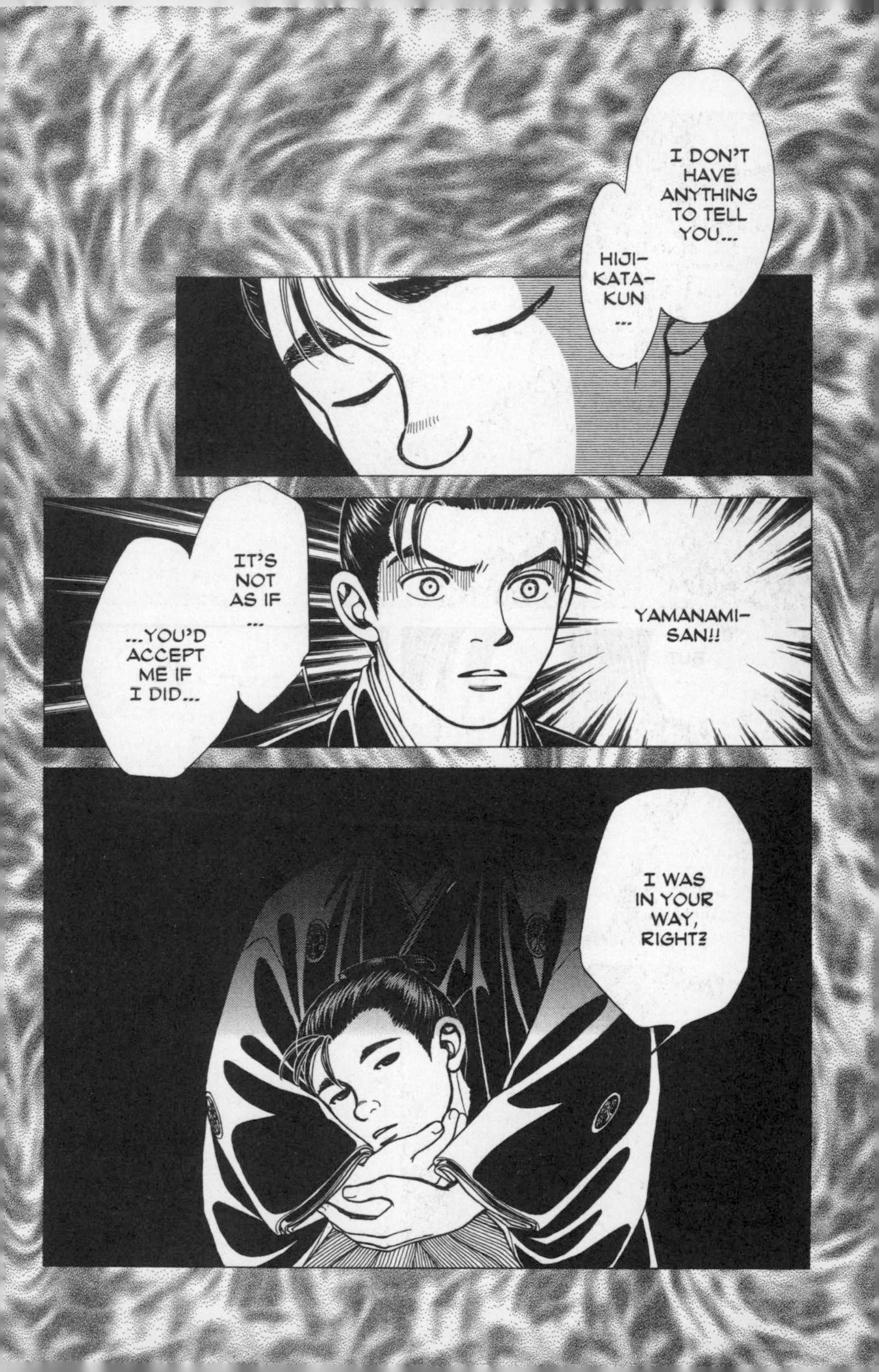
I DON'T HAVE ANYTHING TO TELL YOU...
HIJI-KATA-KUN ...
YAMANAMI-SAN!!
IT'S NOT AS IF ...
...YOU'D ACCEPT ME IF I DID...
I WAS IN YOUR WAY, RIGHT?

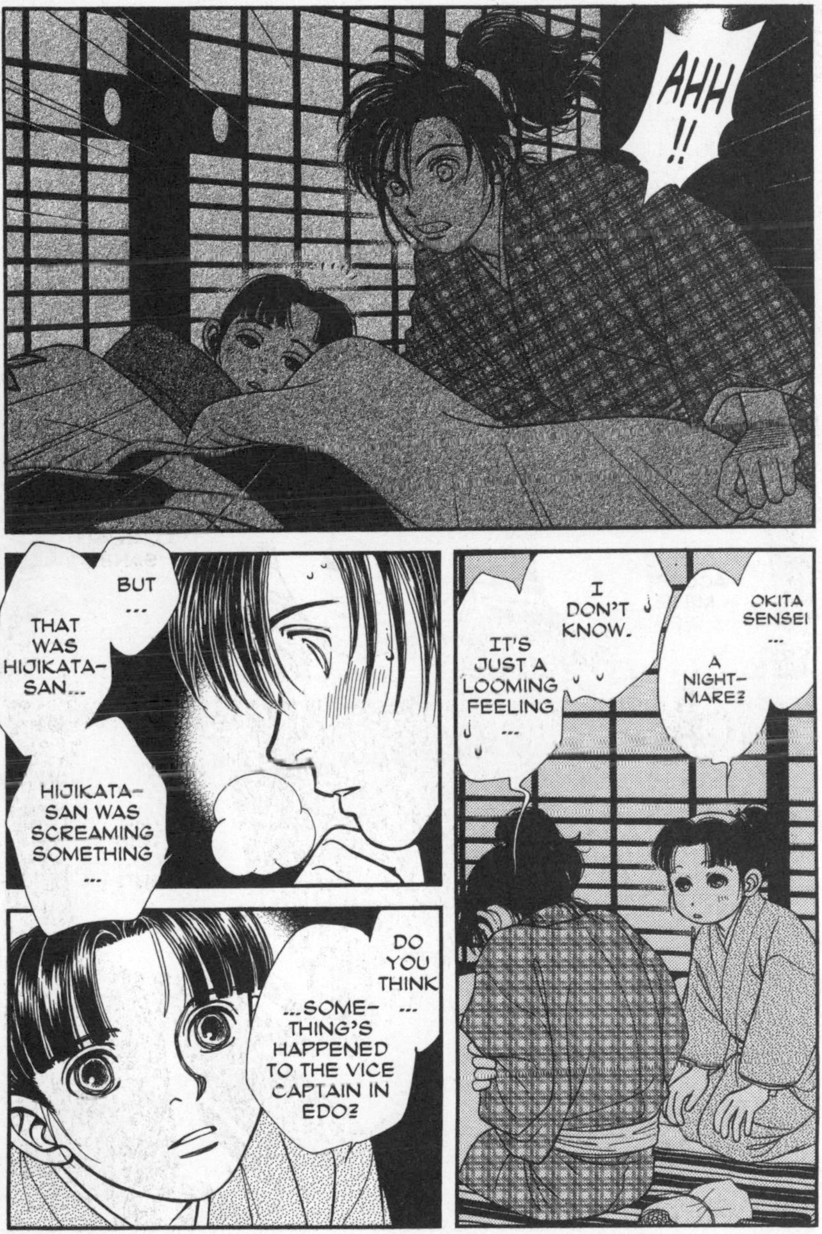
AHH!!
OKITA SENSEI... A NIGHTMARE?
I DON'T KNOW.
IT'S JUST A LOOMING FEELING...
BUT... THAT WAS HIJIKATA-SAN...
HIJIKATA-SAN WAS SCREAMING SOMETHING...
DO YOU THINK...
...SOMETHING'S HAPPENED TO THE VICE CAPTAIN IN EDO?

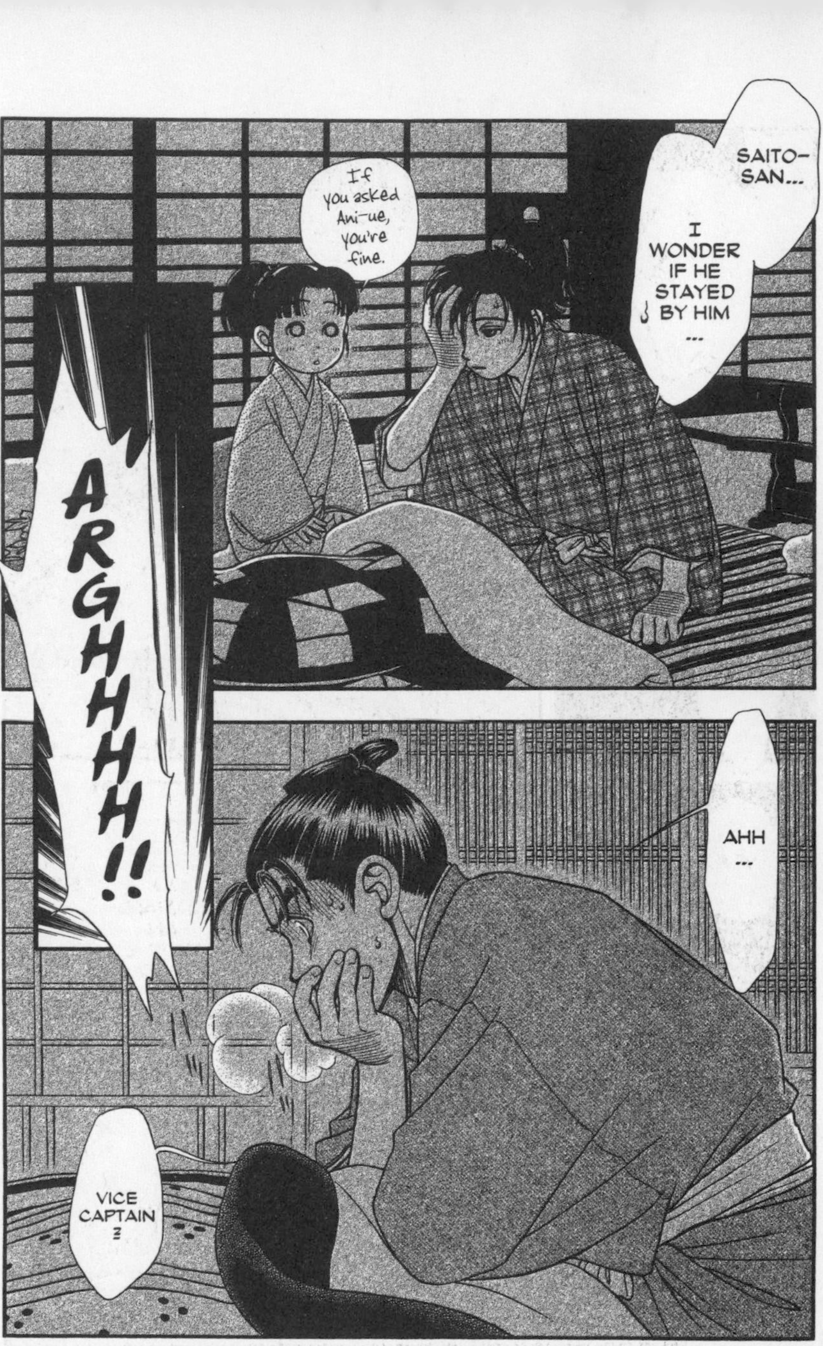
SAITO-SAN...
I WONDER IF HE STAYED BY HIM ...
If you asked Ani-ue, you're fine.
ARGHHHH!!
AHH ...
VICE CAPTAIN

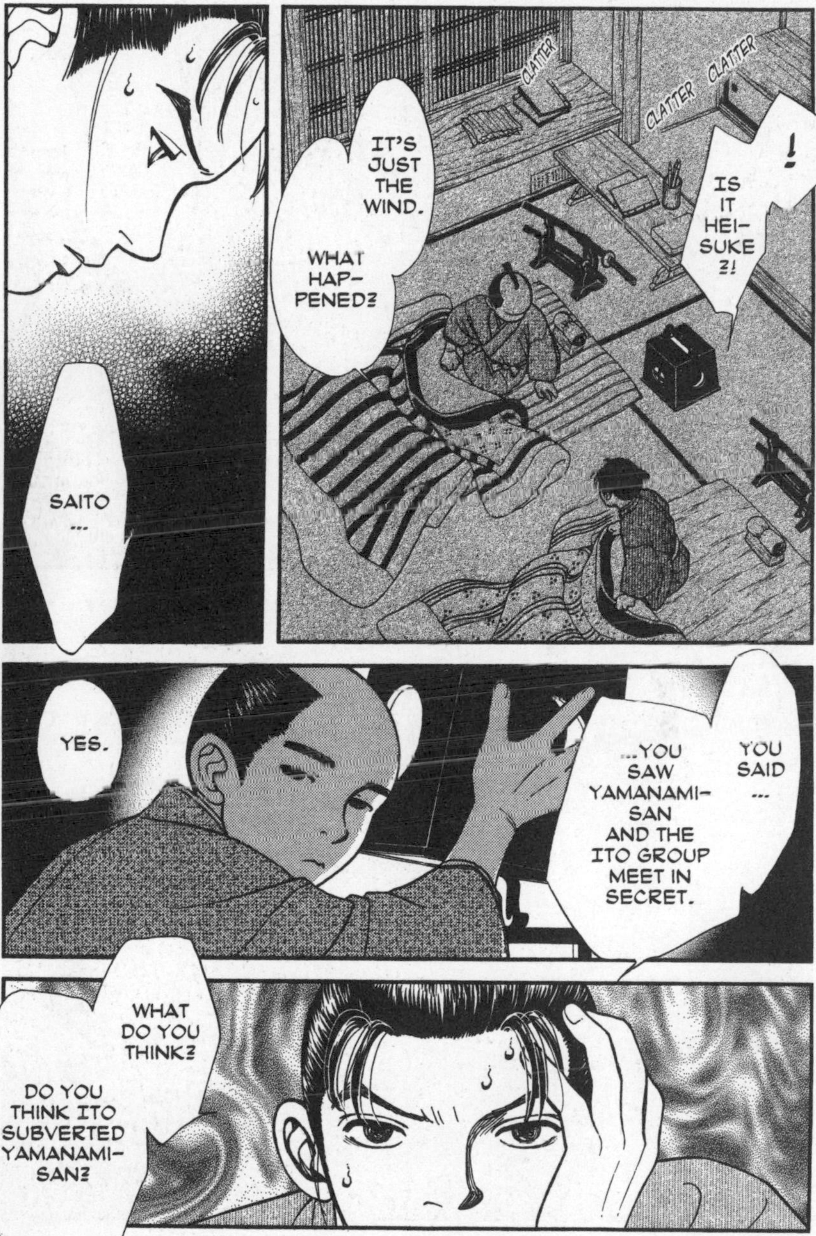
CLATTER
CLATTER CLATTER
!
IS IT HEI-SUKE?!
IT'S JUST THE WIND.
WHAT HAP-PENED?
SAITO ...
YOU SAID ...
...YOU SAW YAMANAMI-SAN AND THE ITO GROUP MEET IN SECRET.
YES.
WHAT DO YOU THINK?
DO YOU THINK ITO SUBVERTED YAMANAMI-SAN?

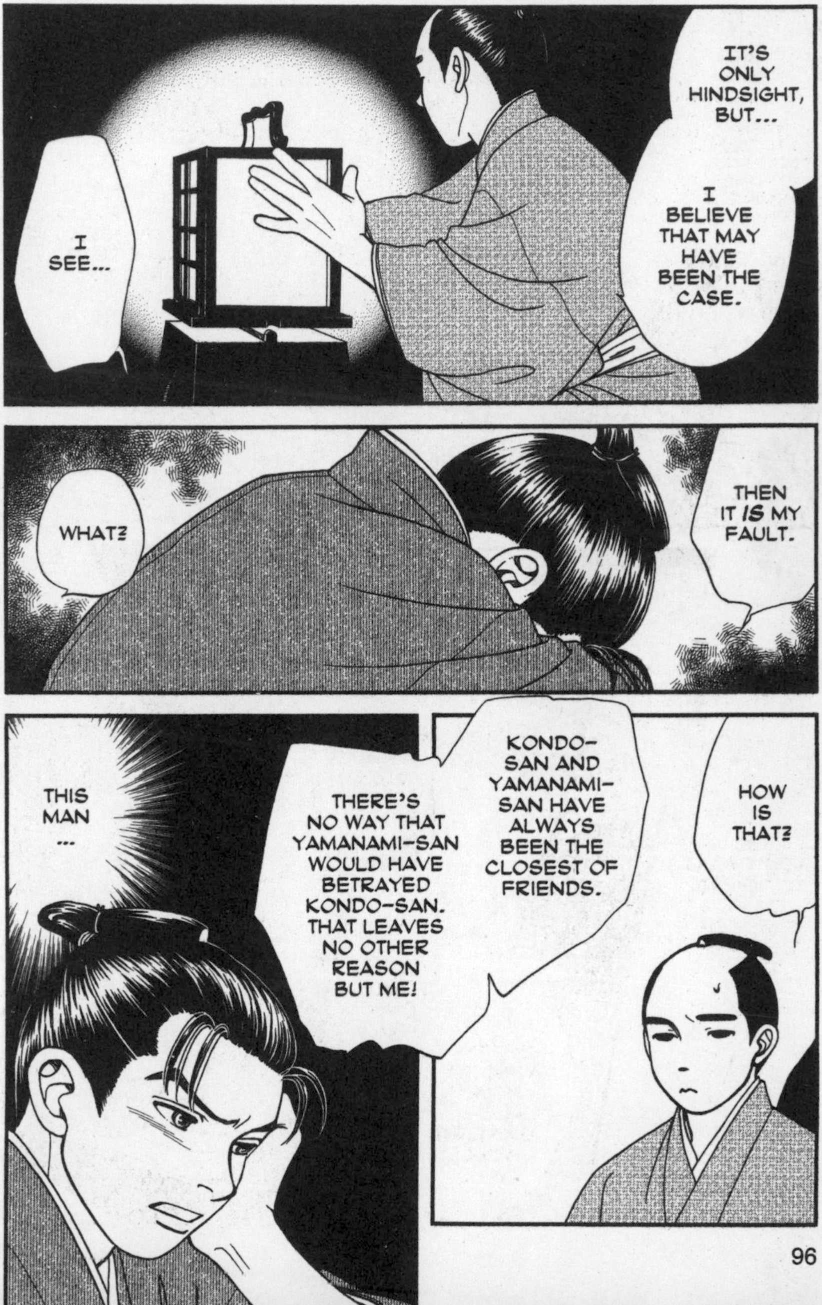
IT'S ONLY HINDSIGHT, BUT...
I BELIEVE THAT MAY HAVE BEEN THE CASE.
I SEE...
THEN IT *IS* MY FAULT.
WHAT?
HOW IS THAT?
KONDO-SAN AND YAMANAMI-SAN HAVE ALWAYS BEEN THE CLOSEST OF FRIENDS.
THERE'S NO WAY THAT YAMANAMI-SAN WOULD HAVE BETRAYED KONDO-SAN. THAT LEAVES NO OTHER REASON BUT ME!
THIS MAN ...

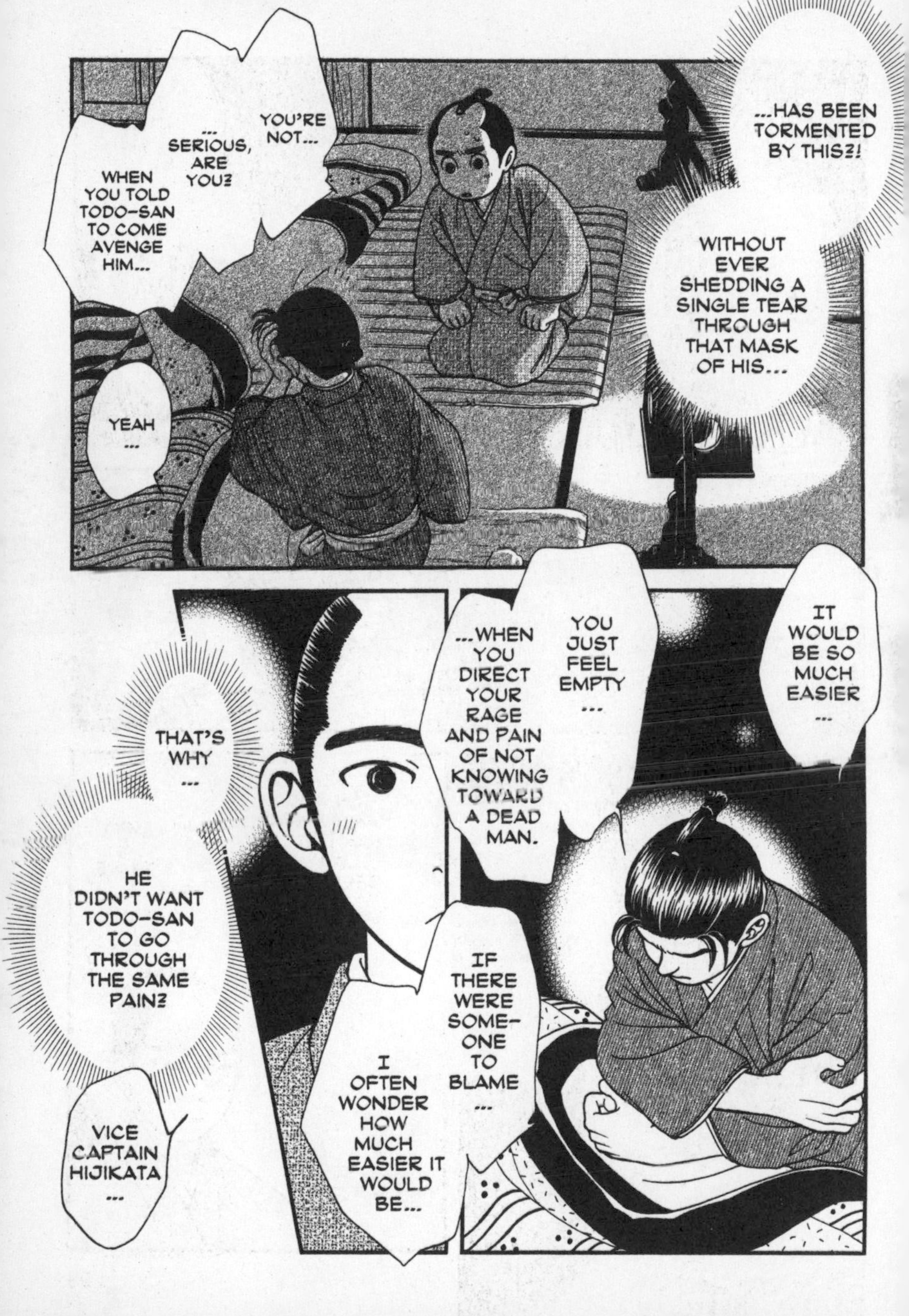
...HAS BEEN TORMENTED BY THIS?!
WITHOUT EVER SHEDDING A SINGLE TEAR THROUGH THAT MASK OF HIS...
YOU'RE NOT...
...SERIOUS, ARE YOU?
WHEN YOU TOLD TODO-SAN TO COME AVENGE HIM...
YEAH...
IT WOULD BE SO MUCH EASIER...
YOU JUST FEEL EMPTY...
...WHEN YOU DIRECT YOUR RAGE AND PAIN OF NOT KNOWING TOWARD A DEAD MAN.
IF THERE WERE SOMEONE TO BLAME...
I OFTEN WONDER HOW MUCH EASIER IT WOULD BE...
THAT'S WHY...
HE DIDN'T WANT TODO-SAN TO GO THROUGH THE SAME PAIN?
VICE CAPTAIN HIJIKATA...

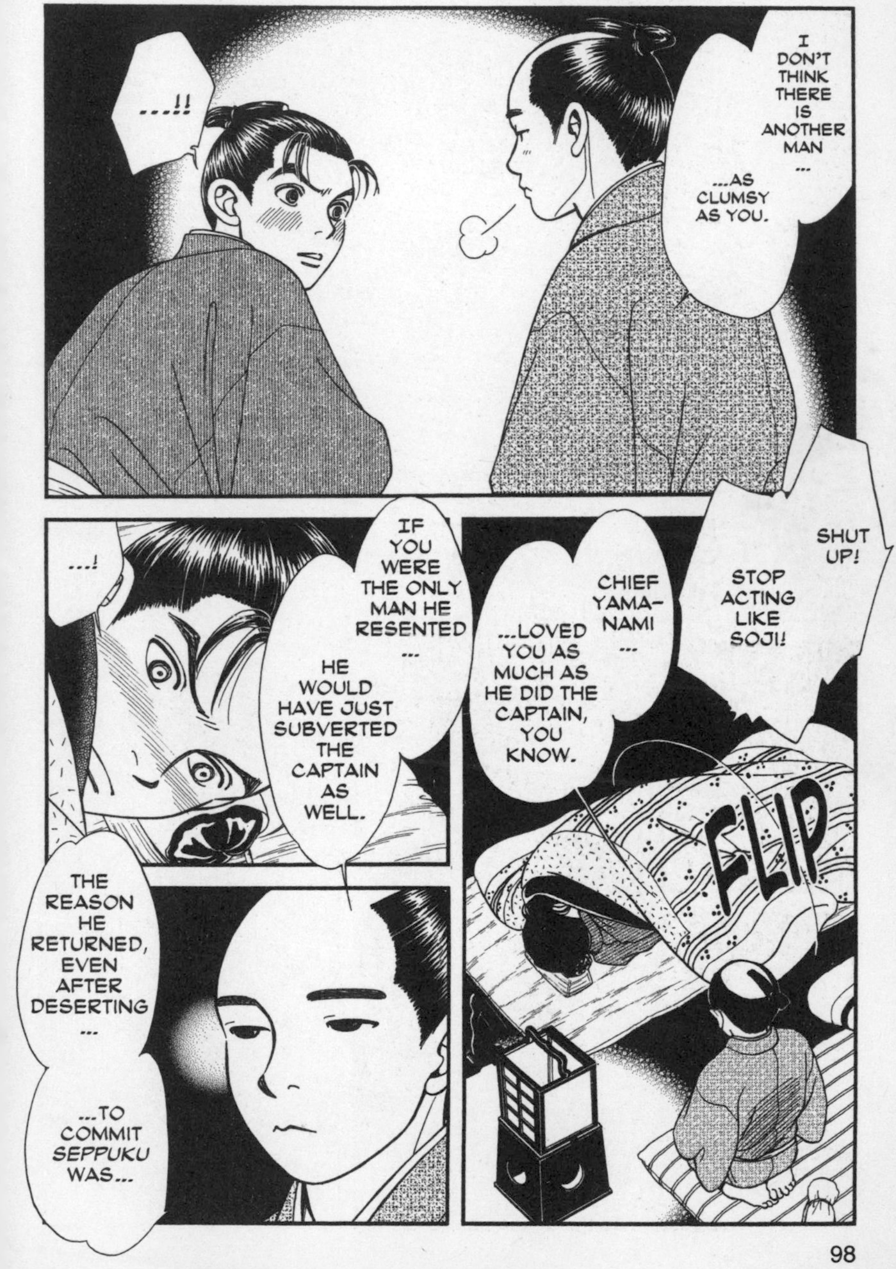
I DON'T THINK THERE IS ANOTHER MAN ...
...AS CLUMSY AS YOU.
...!!
SHUT UP!
STOP ACTING LIKE SOJI!
CHIEF YAMA-NAMI ...
...LOVED YOU AS MUCH AS HE DID THE CAPTAIN, YOU KNOW.
FLIP
IF YOU WERE THE ONLY MAN HE RESENTED ...
HE WOULD HAVE JUST SUBVERTED THE CAPTAIN AS WELL.
...!
THE REASON HE RETURNED, EVEN AFTER DESERTING ...
...TO COMMIT SEPPUKU WAS...

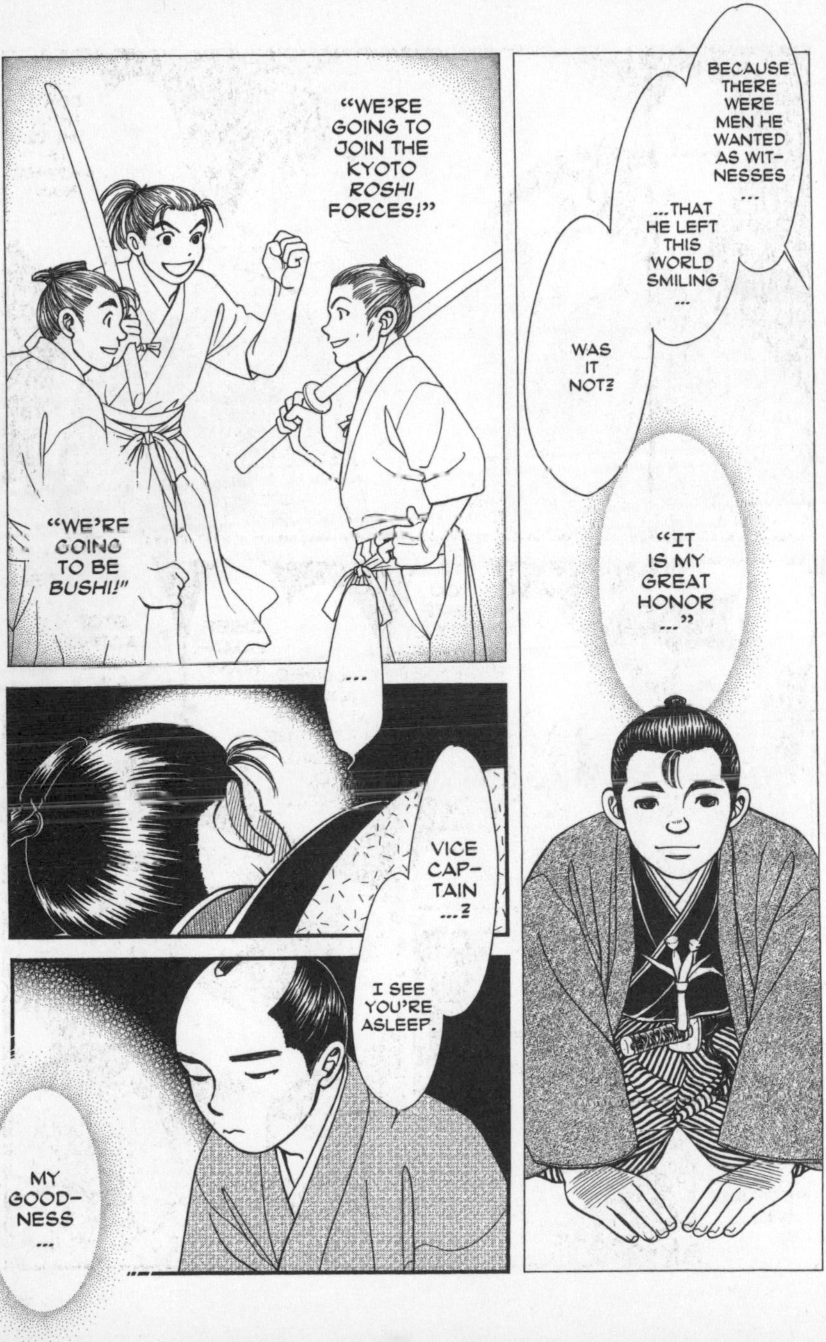
BECAUSE THERE WERE MEN HE WANTED AS WITNESSES ...
...THAT HE LEFT THIS WORLD SMILING ...
WAS IT NOT?
“IT IS MY GREAT HONOR ...”
“WE'RE GOING TO JOIN THE KYOTO *ROSHI* FORCES!”
“WE'RE GOING TO BE *BUSHI!*”
...
VICE CAPTAIN ...?
I SEE YOU'RE ASLEEP.
MY GOODNESS ...

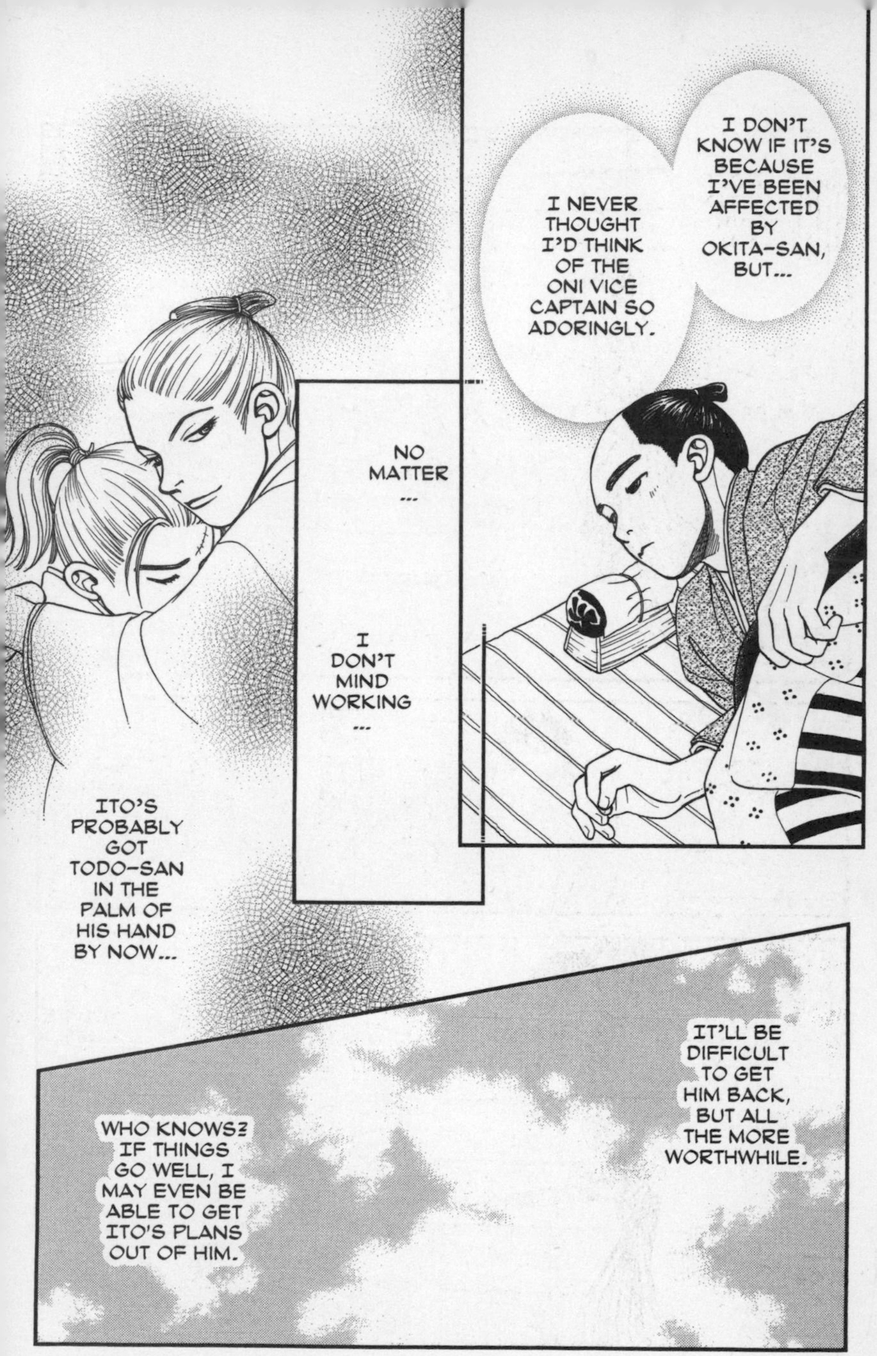
I DON'T KNOW IF IT'S BECAUSE I'VE BEEN AFFECTED BY OKITA-SAN, BUT...
I NEVER THOUGHT I'D THINK OF THE ONI VICE CAPTAIN SO ADORINGLY.
NO MATTER...
I DON'T MIND WORKING...
ITO'S PROBABLY GOT TODO-SAN IN THE PALM OF HIS HAND BY NOW...
IT'LL BE DIFFICULT TO GET HIM BACK, BUT ALL THE MORE WORTHWHILE.
WHO KNOWS? IF THINGS GO WELL, I MAY EVEN BE ABLE TO GET ITO'S PLANS OUT OF HIM.

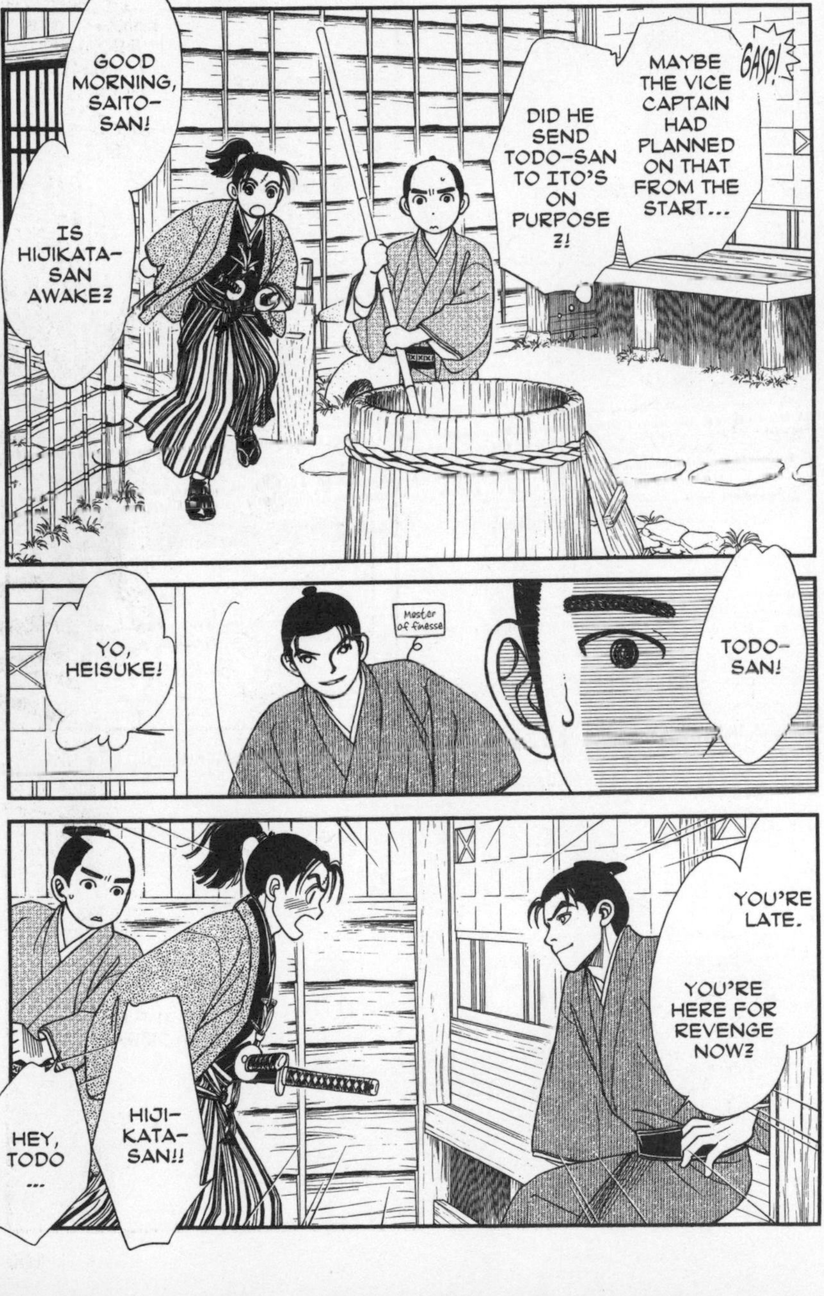
GASP!
MAYBE THE VICE CAPTAIN HAD PLANNED ON THAT FROM THE START...
DID HE SEND TODO-SAN TO ITO'S ON PURPOSE?!
GOOD MORNING, SAITO-SAN!
IS HIJIKATA-SAN AWAKE?
TODO-SAN!
Master of finesse
YO, HEISUKE!
YOU'RE LATE.
YOU'RE HERE FOR REVENGE NOW?
HIJI-KATA-SAN!!
HEY, TODO...

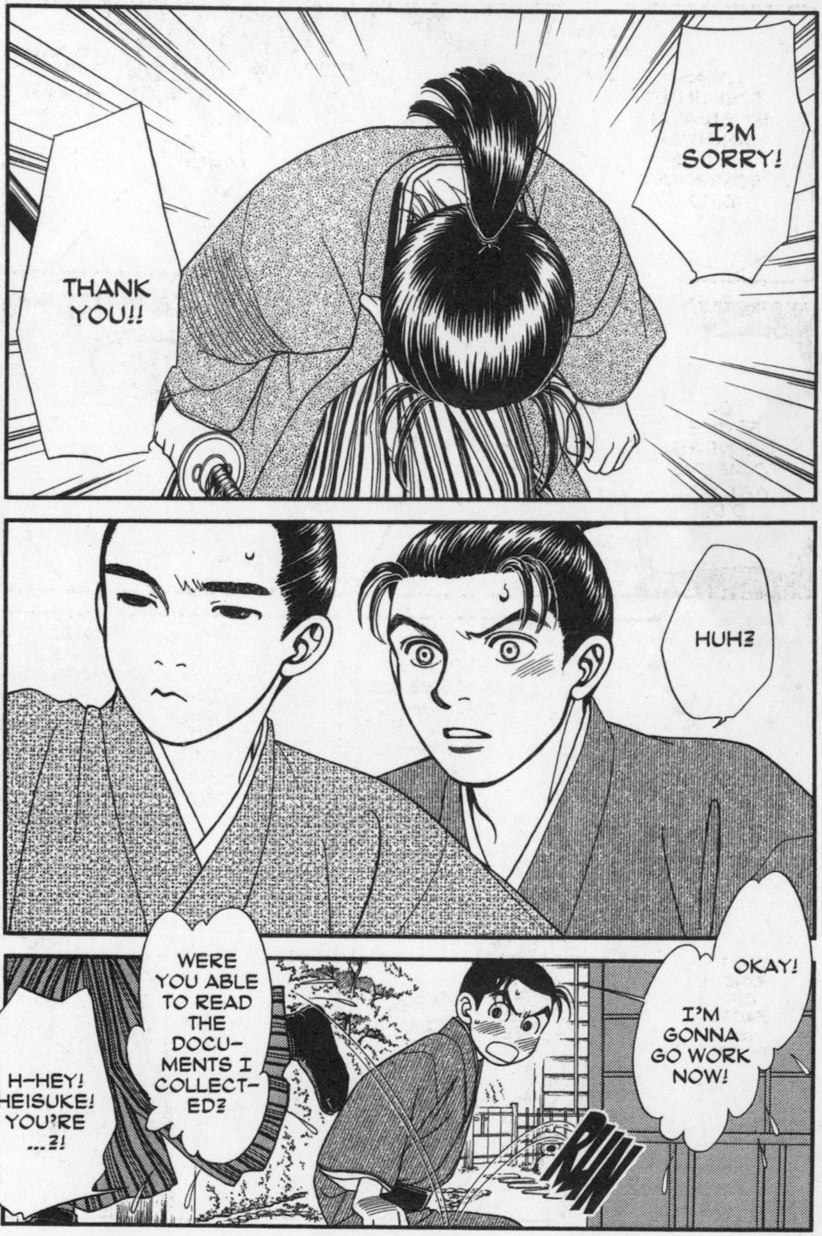
I'M SORRY!
THANK YOU!!
HUH?
OKAY! I'M GONNA GO WORK NOW!
RUN
WERE YOU ABLE TO READ THE DOCUMENTS I COLLECTED?
H-HEY! HEISUKE! YOU'RE ...?!

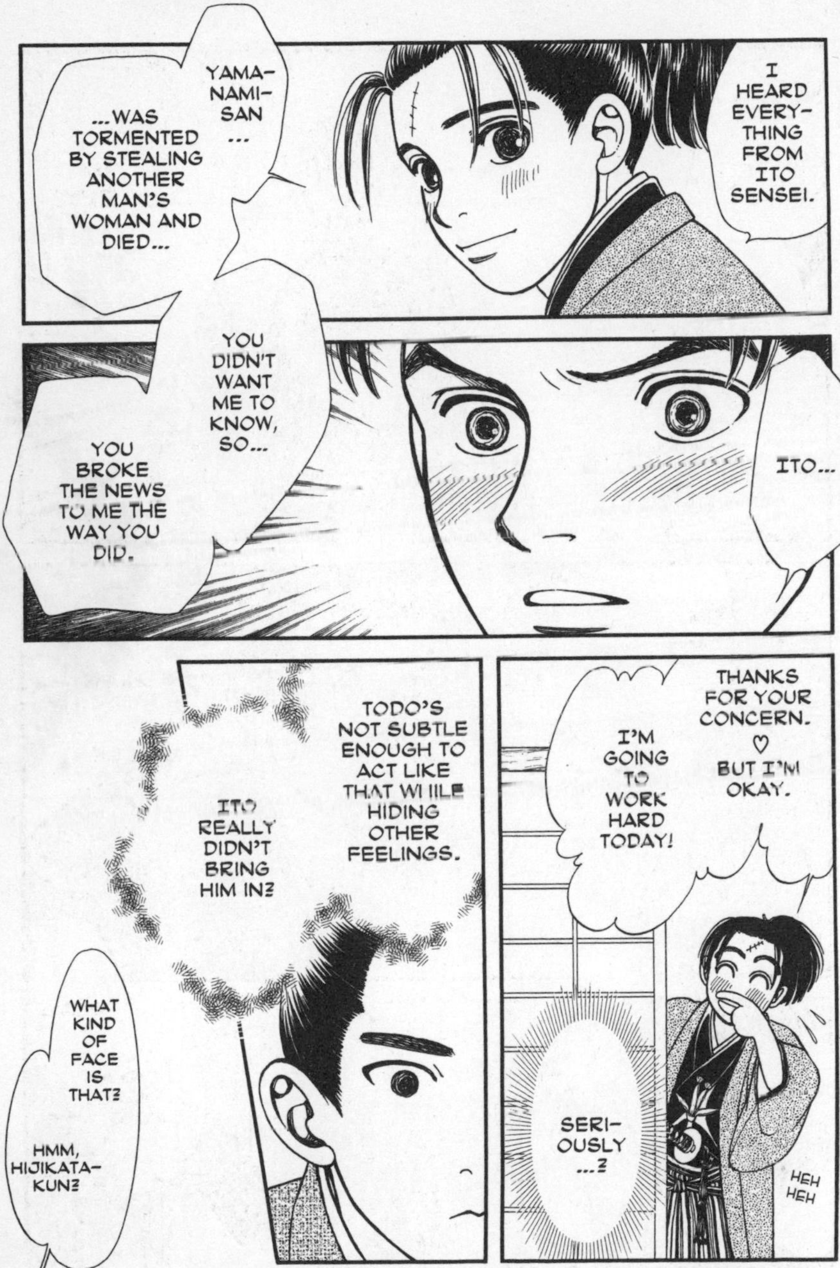

I HEARD EVERYTHING FROM ITO SENSEI.
YAMANAMI-SAN...
...WAS TORMENTED BY STEALING ANOTHER MAN'S WOMAN AND DIED...
ITO...
YOU DIDN'T WANT ME TO KNOW, SO...
YOU BROKE THE NEWS TO ME THE WAY YOU DID.
THANKS FOR YOUR CONCERN. ♡ BUT I'M OKAY.
I'M GOING TO WORK HARD TODAY!
SERIOUSLY...?
HEH HEH
TODO'S NOT SUBTLE ENOUGH TO ACT LIKE THAT WHILE HIDING OTHER FEELINGS.
ITO REALLY DIDN'T BRING HIM IN?
WHAT KIND OF FACE IS THAT?
HMM, HIJIKATA-KUN?

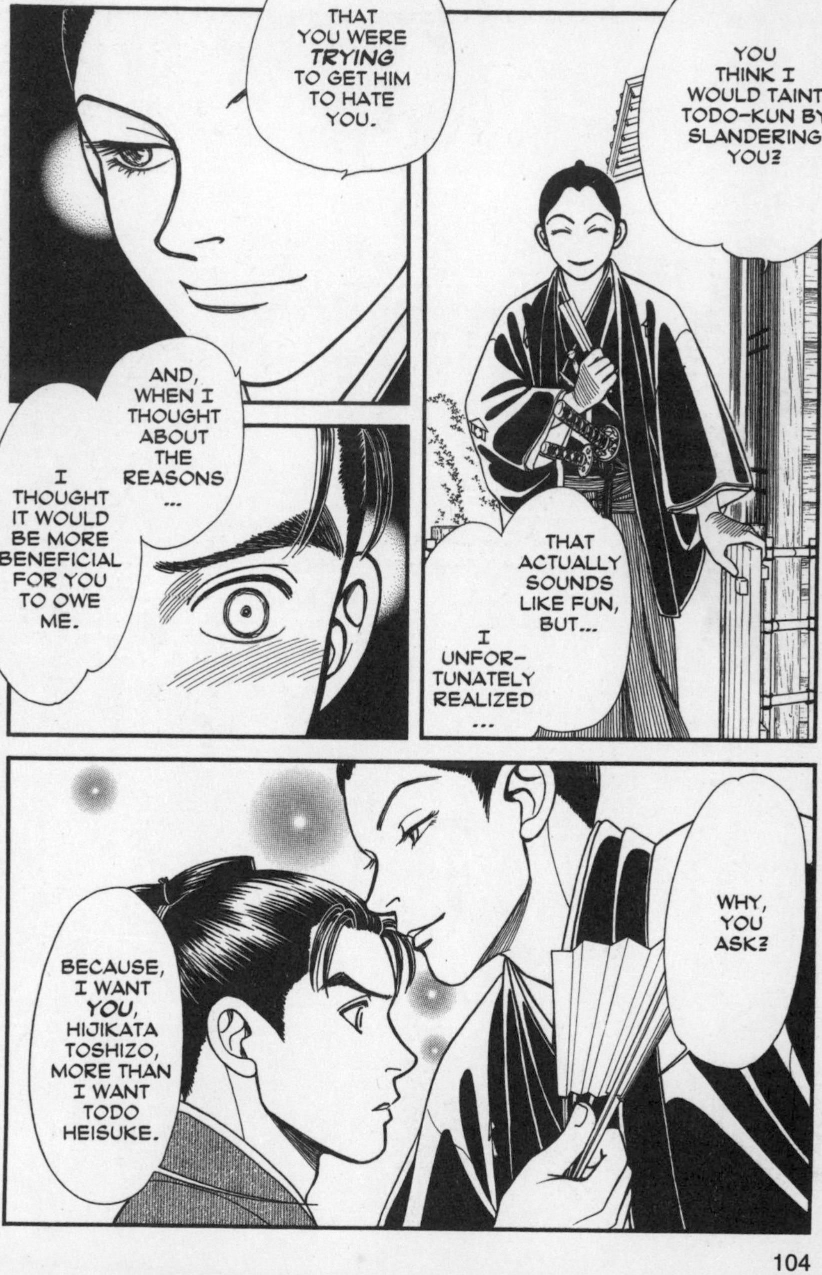
YOU THINK I WOULD TAINT TODO-KUN BY SLANDERING YOU?
THAT ACTUALLY SOUNDS LIKE FUN, BUT...
I UNFORTUNATELY REALIZED...
THAT YOU WERE *TRYING* TO GET HIM TO HATE YOU.
AND, WHEN I THOUGHT ABOUT THE REASONS...
I THOUGHT IT WOULD BE MORE BENEFICIAL FOR YOU TO OWE ME.
WHY, YOU ASK?
BECAUSE, I WANT *YOU*, HIJIKATA TOSHIZO, MORE THAN I WANT TODO HEISUKE.

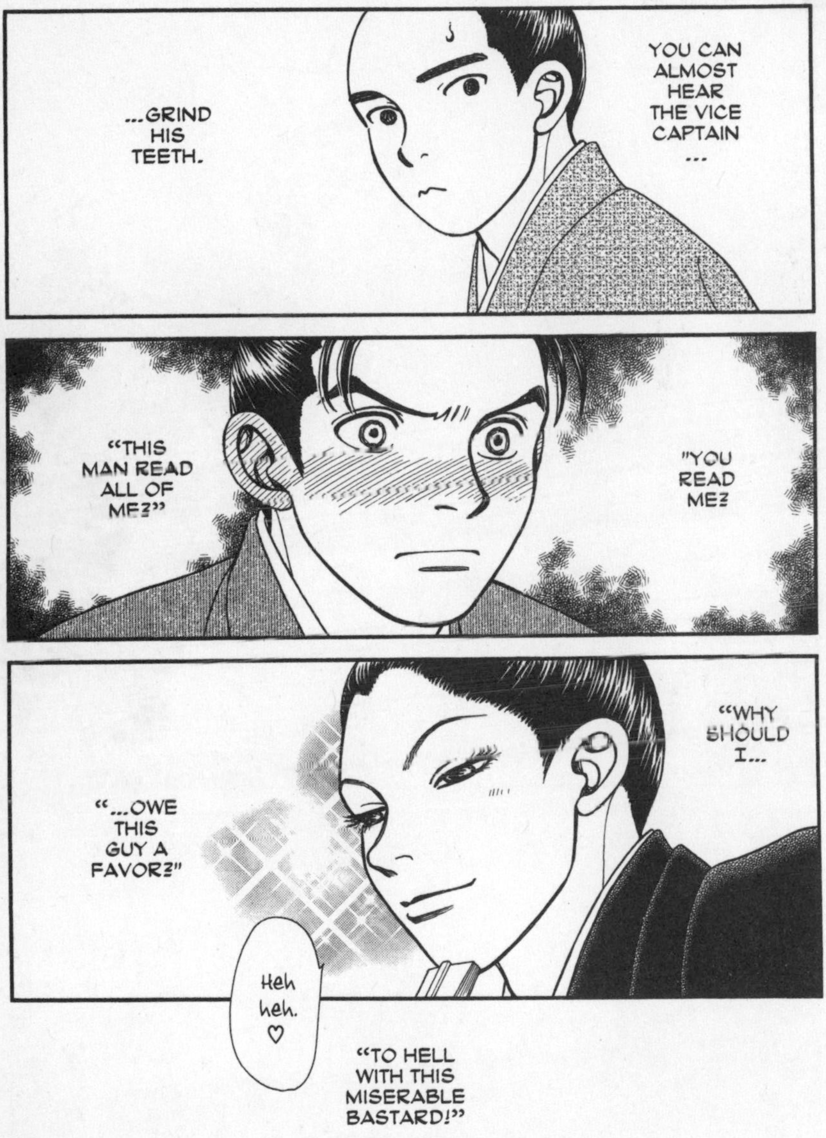
YOU CAN ALMOST HEAR THE VICE CAPTAIN ...
...GRIND HIS TEETH.
"YOU READ ME?
"THIS MAN READ ALL OF ME?"
"WHY SHOULD I...
"...OWE THIS GUY A FAVOR?"
"TO HELL WITH THIS MISERABLE BASTARD!"
Heh heh. ♡

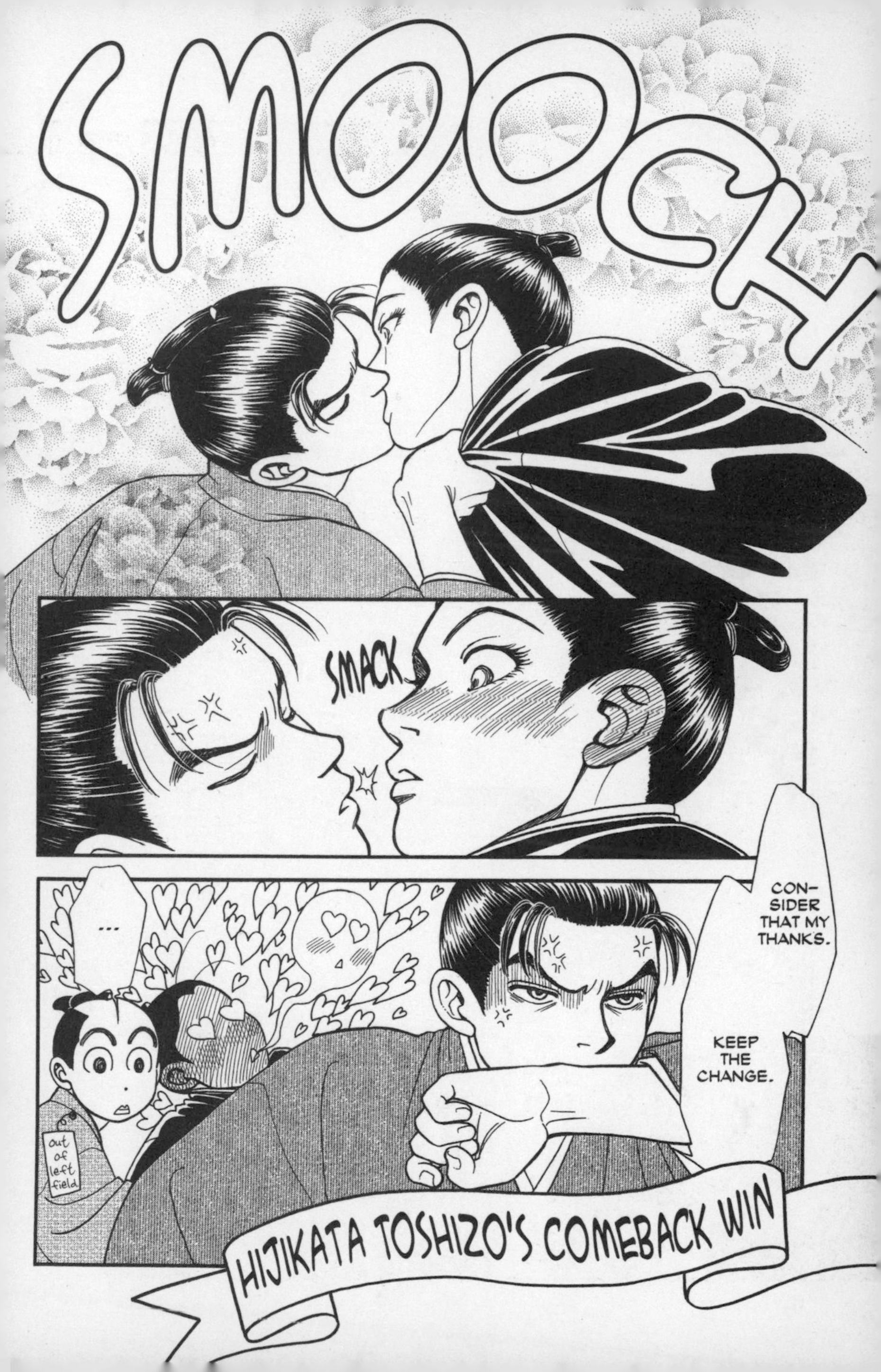
SMOOCH
SMACK
CON-SIDER THAT MY THANKS.
KEEP THE CHANGE.
...
out of left field
HIJIKATA TOSHIZO'S COMEBACK WIN

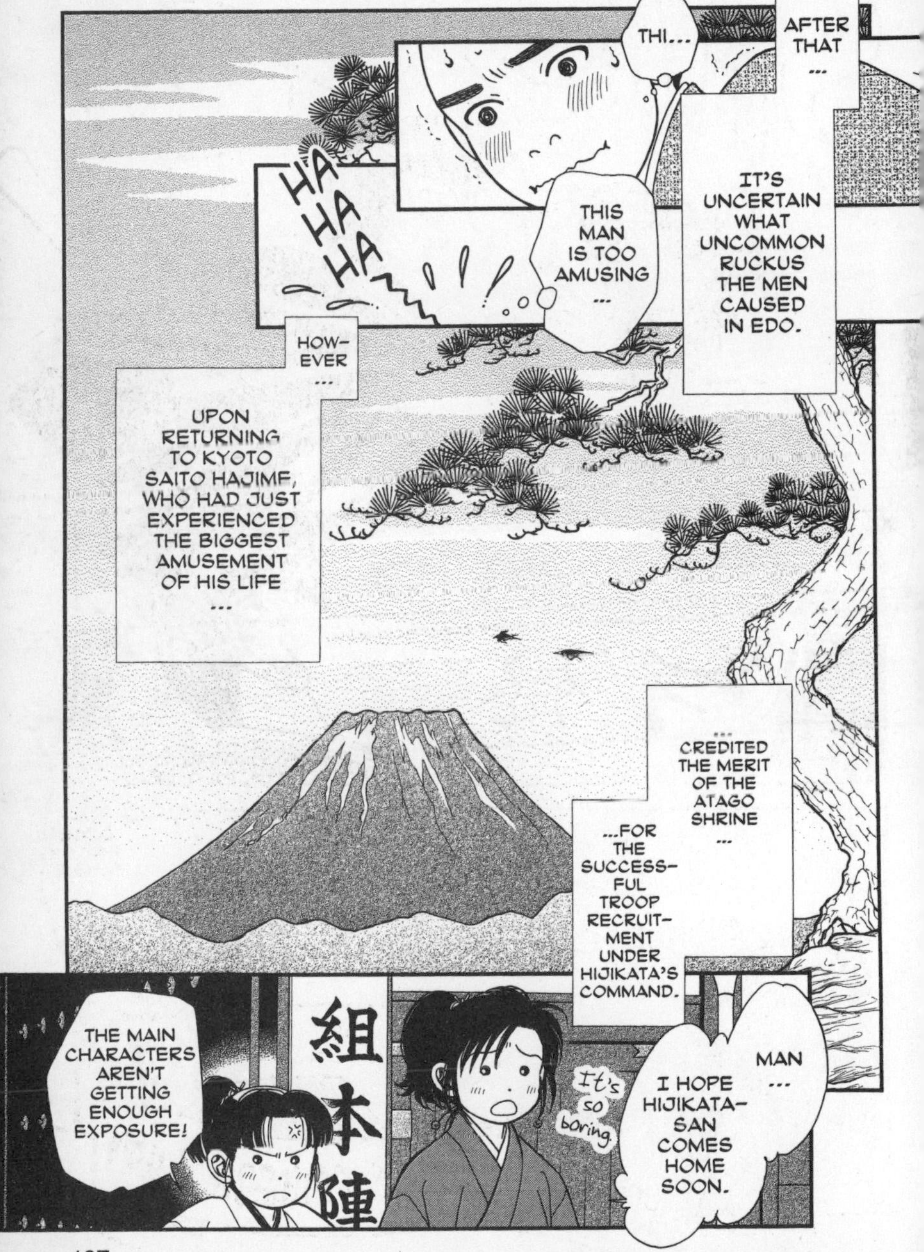
AFTER THAT ...
THI...
IT'S UNCERTAIN WHAT UNCOMMON RUCKUS THE MEN CAUSED IN EDO.
THIS MAN IS TOO AMUSING ...
HA HA HA
HOW-EVER ...
UPON RETURNING TO KYOTO SAITO HAJIME, WHO HAD JUST EXPERIENCED THE BIGGEST AMUSEMENT OF HIS LIFE ...
... CREDITED THE MERIT OF THE ATAGO SHRINE ...
...FOR THE SUCCESSFUL TROOP RECRUITMENT UNDER HIJIKATA'S COMMAND.
MAN ... I HOPE HIJIKATA-SAN COMES HOME SOON.
It's so boring.
組本陣
THE MAIN CHARACTERS AREN'T GETTING ENOUGH EXPOSURE!

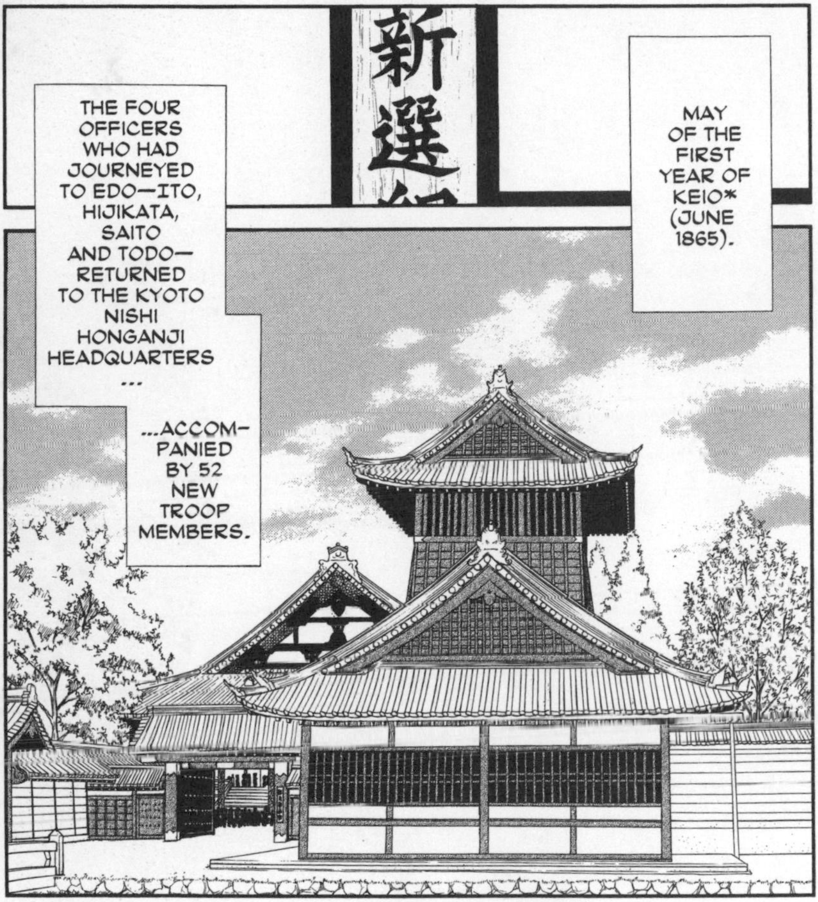
新選
MAY OF THE FIRST YEAR OF KEIO* (JUNE 1865).
THE FOUR OFFICERS WHO HAD JOURNEYED TO EDO—ITO, HIJIKATA, SAITO AND TODO—RETURNED TO THE KYOTO NISHI HONGANJI HEADQUARTERS ...
...ACCOMPANIED BY 52 NEW TROOP MEMBERS.

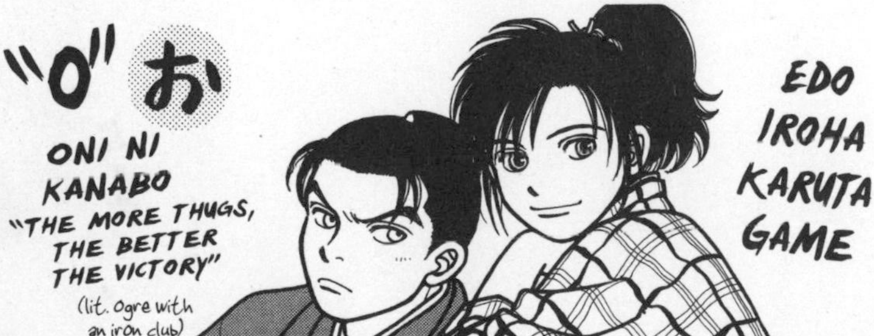
EDO IROHA KARUTA GAME
"O" お
ONI NI KANABO
"THE MORE THUGS, THE BETTER THE VICTORY"
(lit. Ogre with an iron club)

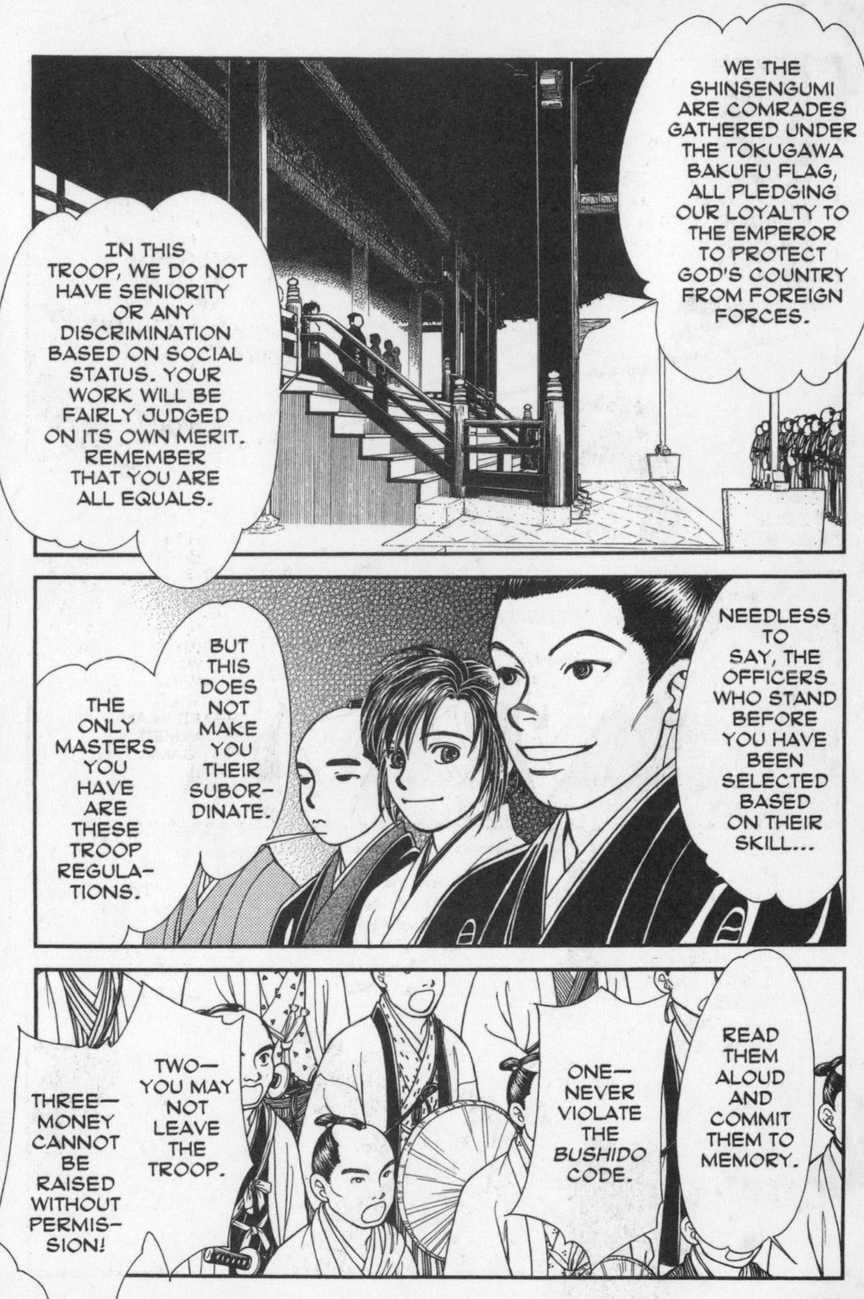
WE THE SHINSENGUMI ARE COMRADES GATHERED UNDER THE TOKUGAWA BAKUFU FLAG, ALL PLEDGING OUR LOYALTY TO THE EMPEROR TO PROTECT GOD'S COUNTRY FROM FOREIGN FORCES.
IN THIS TROOP, WE DO NOT HAVE SENIORITY OR ANY DISCRIMINATION BASED ON SOCIAL STATUS. YOUR WORK WILL BE FAIRLY JUDGED ON ITS OWN MERIT. REMEMBER THAT YOU ARE ALL EQUALS.
NEEDLESS TO SAY, THE OFFICERS WHO STAND BEFORE YOU HAVE BEEN SELECTED BASED ON THEIR SKILL...
BUT THIS DOES NOT MAKE YOU THEIR SUBOR-DINATE.
THE ONLY MASTERS YOU HAVE ARE THESE TROOP REGULA-TIONS.
READ THEM ALOUD AND COMMIT THEM TO MEMORY.
ONE—NEVER VIOLATE THE *BUSHIDO* CODE.
TWO—YOU MAY NOT LEAVE THE TROOP.
THREE—MONEY CANNOT BE RAISED WITHOUT PERMIS-SION!

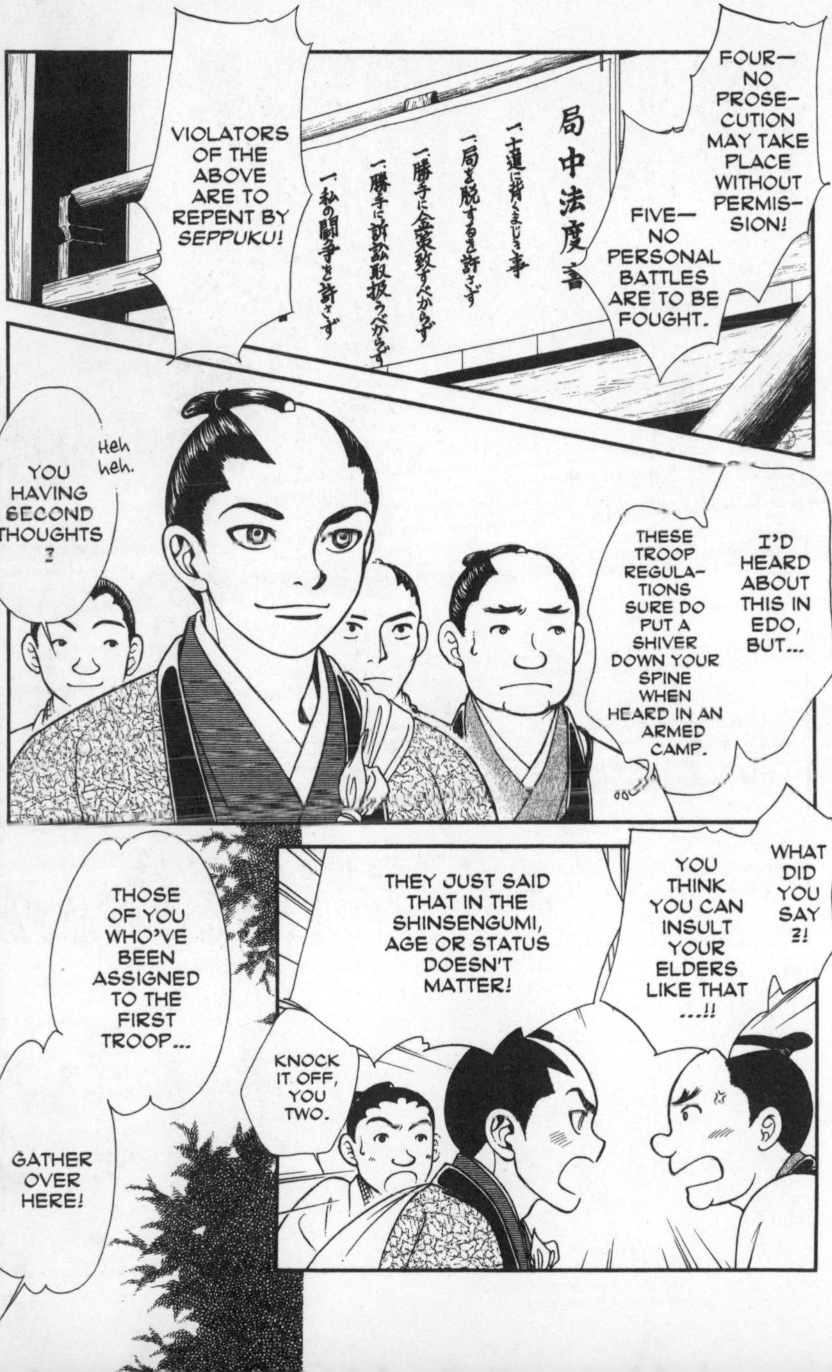
FOUR—NO PROSECUTION MAY TAKE PLACE WITHOUT PERMISSION!
FIVE—NO PERSONAL BATTLES ARE TO BE FOUGHT.
局中法度書
一、士道に背くまじき事
一、局を脱するを許さず
一、勝手に金策致すべからず
一、勝手に訴訟取扱うべからず
一、私の闘争を許さず
VIOLATORS OF THE ABOVE ARE TO REPENT BY *SEPPUKU*!
I'D HEARD ABOUT THIS IN EDO, BUT...
THESE TROOP REGULATIONS SURE DO PUT A SHIVER DOWN YOUR SPINE WHEN HEARD IN AN ARMED CAMP.
Heh heh.
YOU HAVING SECOND THOUGHTS?
WHAT DID YOU SAY?!
YOU THINK YOU CAN INSULT YOUR ELDERS LIKE THAT...!!
THEY JUST SAID THAT IN THE SHINSENGUMI, AGE OR STATUS DOESN'T MATTER!
KNOCK IT OFF, YOU TWO.
THOSE OF YOU WHO'VE BEEN ASSIGNED TO THE FIRST TROOP...
GATHER OVER HERE!

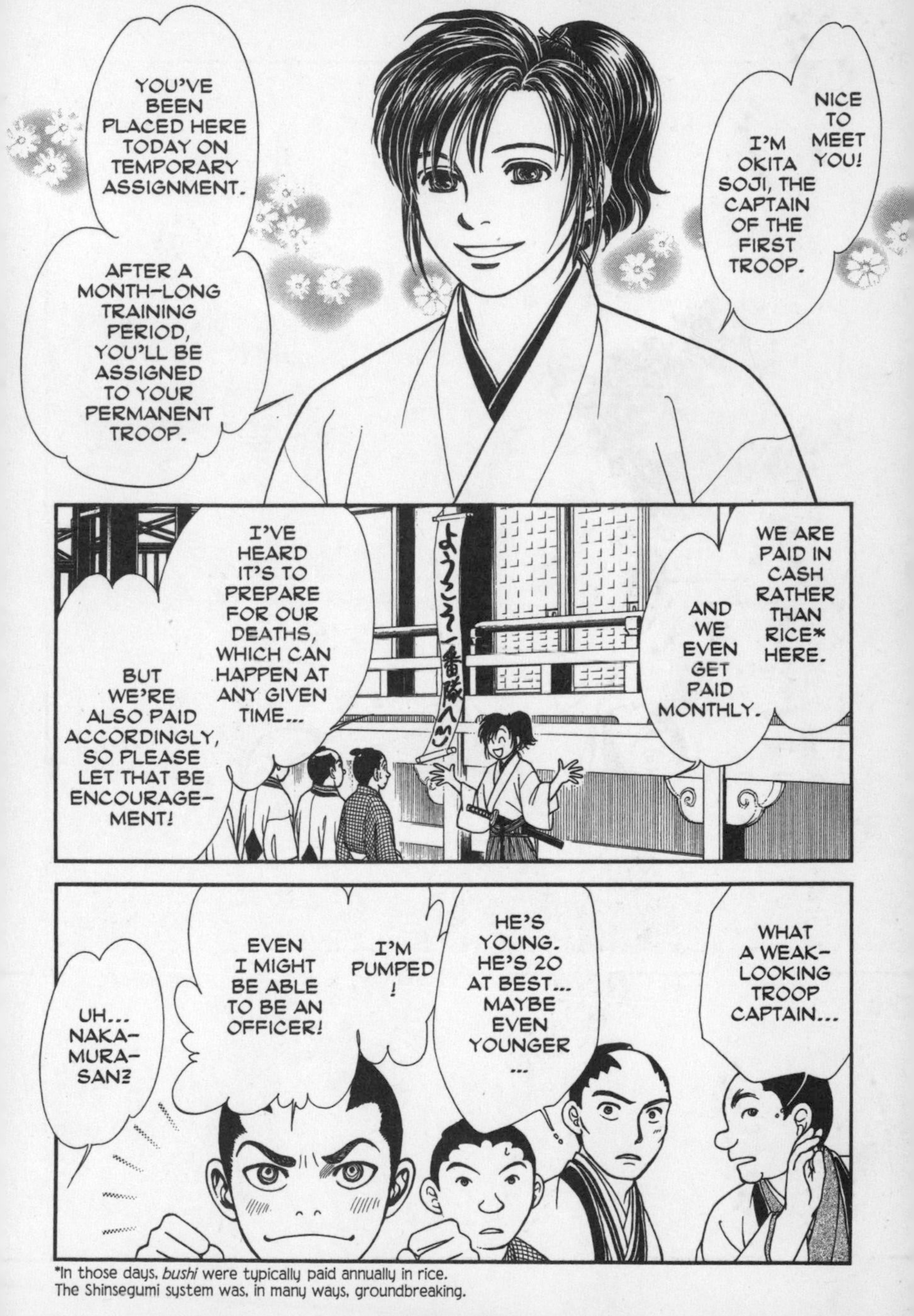
NICE TO MEET YOU!
I'M OKITA SOJI, THE CAPTAIN OF THE FIRST TROOP.
YOU'VE BEEN PLACED HERE TODAY ON TEMPORARY ASSIGNMENT.
AFTER A MONTH-LONG TRAINING PERIOD, YOU'LL BE ASSIGNED TO YOUR PERMANENT TROOP.
WE ARE PAID IN CASH RATHER THAN RICE* HERE.
AND WE EVEN GET PAID MONTHLY.
ようこそ一番隊へ
I'VE HEARD IT'S TO PREPARE FOR OUR DEATHS, WHICH CAN HAPPEN AT ANY GIVEN TIME...
BUT WE'RE ALSO PAID ACCORDINGLY, SO PLEASE LET THAT BE ENCOURAGE-MENT!
WHAT A WEAK-LOOKING TROOP CAPTAIN...
HE'S YOUNG. HE'S 20 AT BEST... MAYBE EVEN YOUNGER ...
I'M PUMPED!
EVEN I MIGHT BE ABLE TO BE AN OFFICER!
UH... NAKA-MURA-SAN?

*In those days, *bushi* were typically paid annually in rice. The Shinsegumi system was, in many ways, groundbreaking.

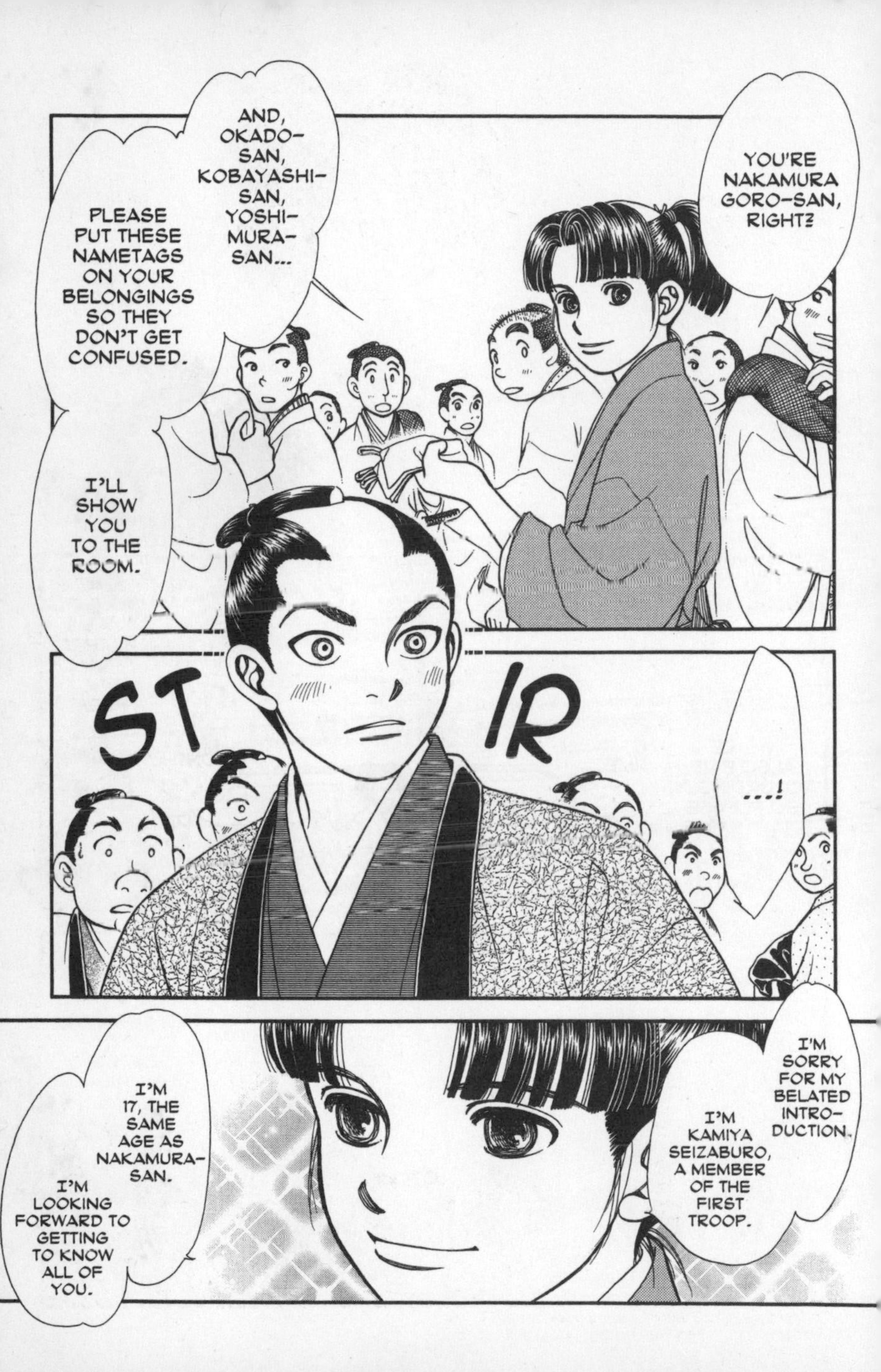
YOU'RE NAKAMURA GORO-SAN, RIGHT?
AND, OKADO-SAN, KOBAYASHI-SAN, YOSHIMURA-SAN...
PLEASE PUT THESE NAMETAGS ON YOUR BELONGINGS SO THEY DON'T GET CONFUSED.
I'LL SHOW YOU TO THE ROOM.
...!
ST IR
I'M SORRY FOR MY BELATED INTRODUCTION.
I'M KAMIYA SEIZABURO, A MEMBER OF THE FIRST TROOP.
I'M 17, THE SAME AGE AS NAKAMURA-SAN.
I'M LOOKING FORWARD TO GETTING TO KNOW ALL OF YOU.

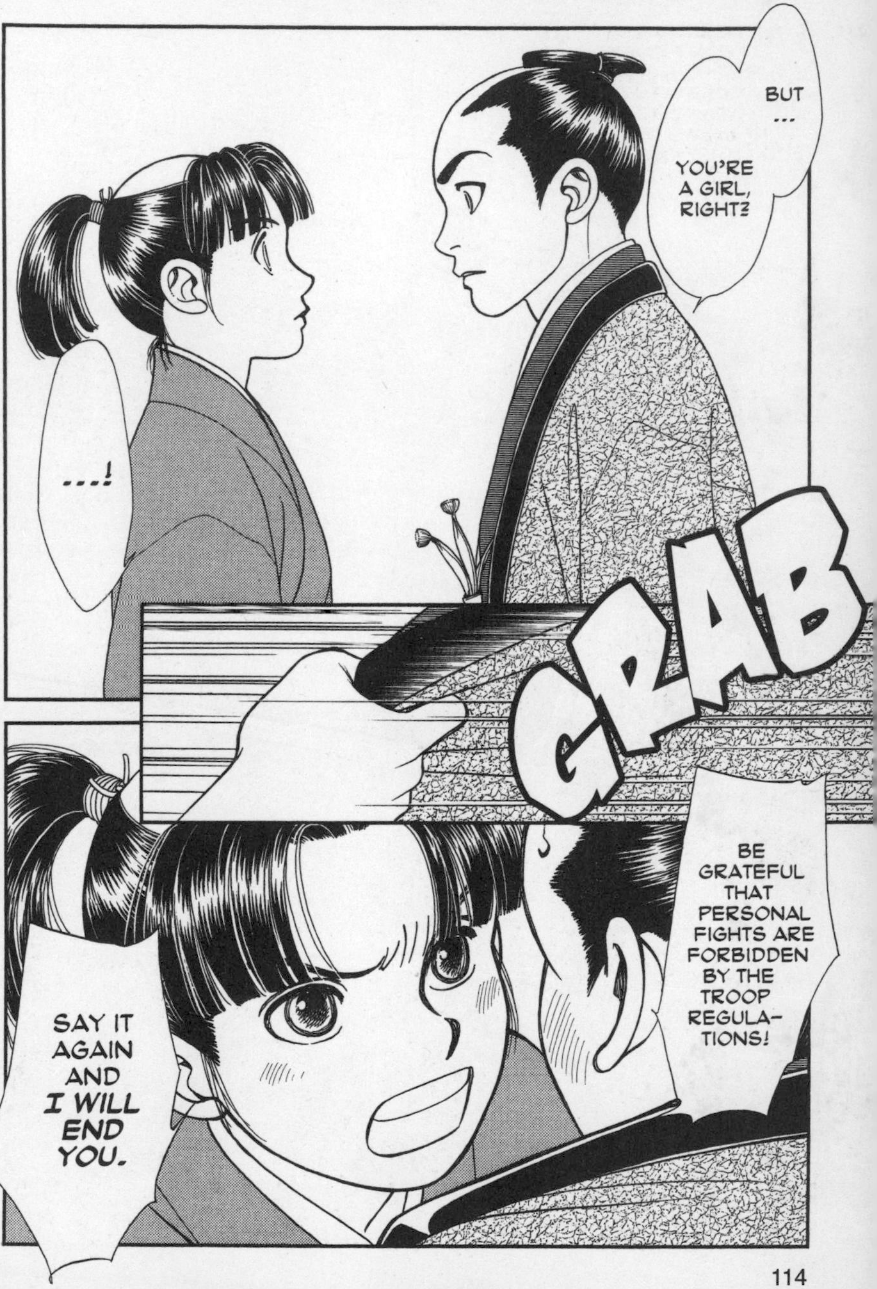
BUT... YOU'RE A GIRL, RIGHT?
...!
GRAB
BE GRATEFUL THAT PERSONAL FIGHTS ARE FORBIDDEN BY THE TROOP REGULATIONS!
SAY IT AGAIN AND I WILL END YOU.

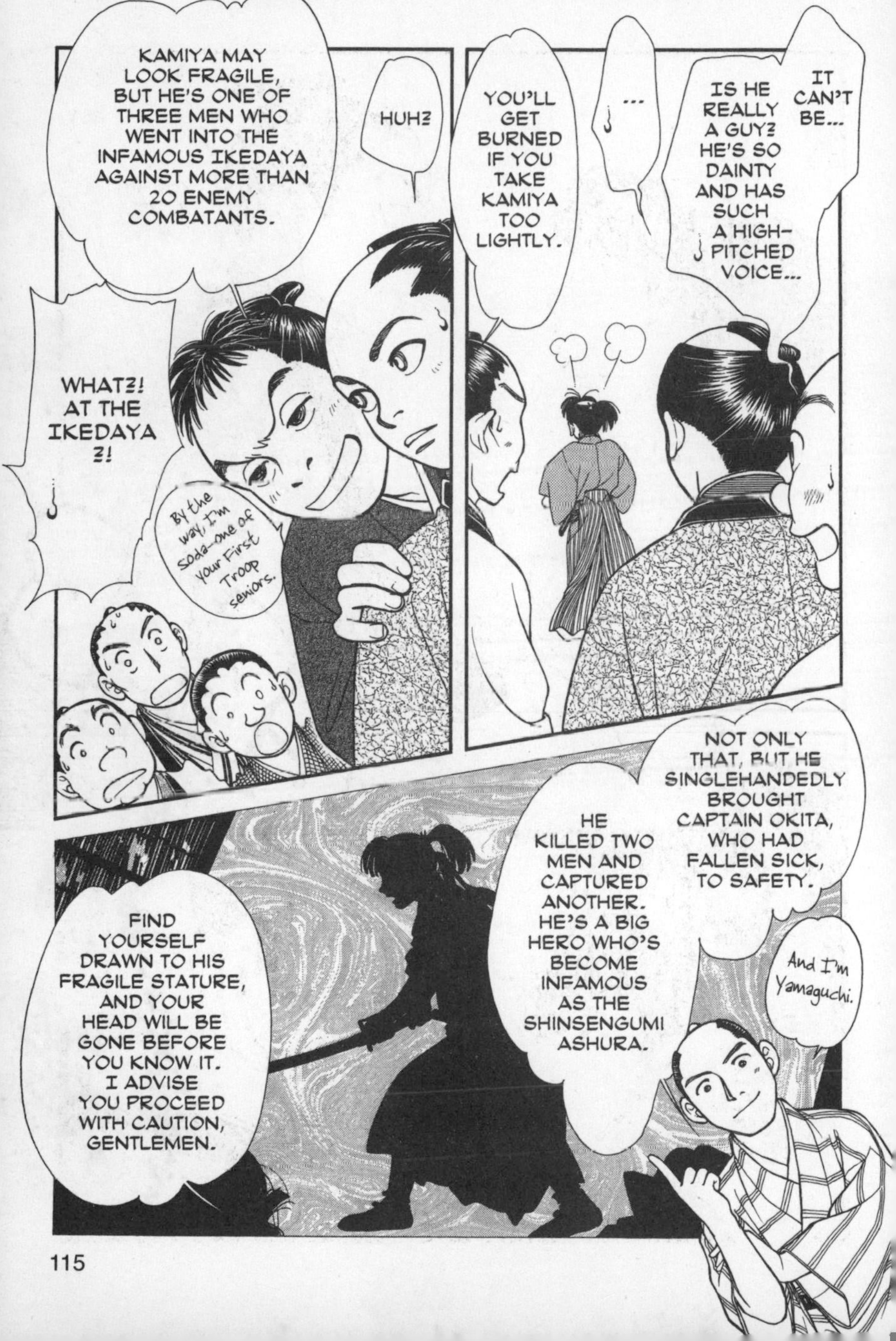
IT CAN'T BE...
IS HE REALLY A GUY? HE'S SO DAINTY AND HAS SUCH A HIGH-PITCHED VOICE...
...
YOU'LL GET BURNED IF YOU TAKE KAMIYA TOO LIGHTLY.
HUH?
KAMIYA MAY LOOK FRAGILE, BUT HE'S ONE OF THREE MEN WHO WENT INTO THE INFAMOUS IKEDAYA AGAINST MORE THAN 20 ENEMY COMBATANTS.
WHAT?! AT THE IKEDAYA?!
By the way, I'm Soda—one of your First Troop seniors.
NOT ONLY THAT, BUT HE SINGLEHANDEDLY BROUGHT CAPTAIN OKITA, WHO HAD FALLEN SICK, TO SAFETY.
HE KILLED TWO MEN AND CAPTURED ANOTHER. HE'S A BIG HERO WHO'S BECOME INFAMOUS AS THE SHINSENGUMI ASHURA.
And I'm Yamaguchi.
FIND YOURSELF DRAWN TO HIS FRAGILE STATURE, AND YOUR HEAD WILL BE GONE BEFORE YOU KNOW IT. I ADVISE YOU PROCEED WITH CAUTION, GENTLEMEN.

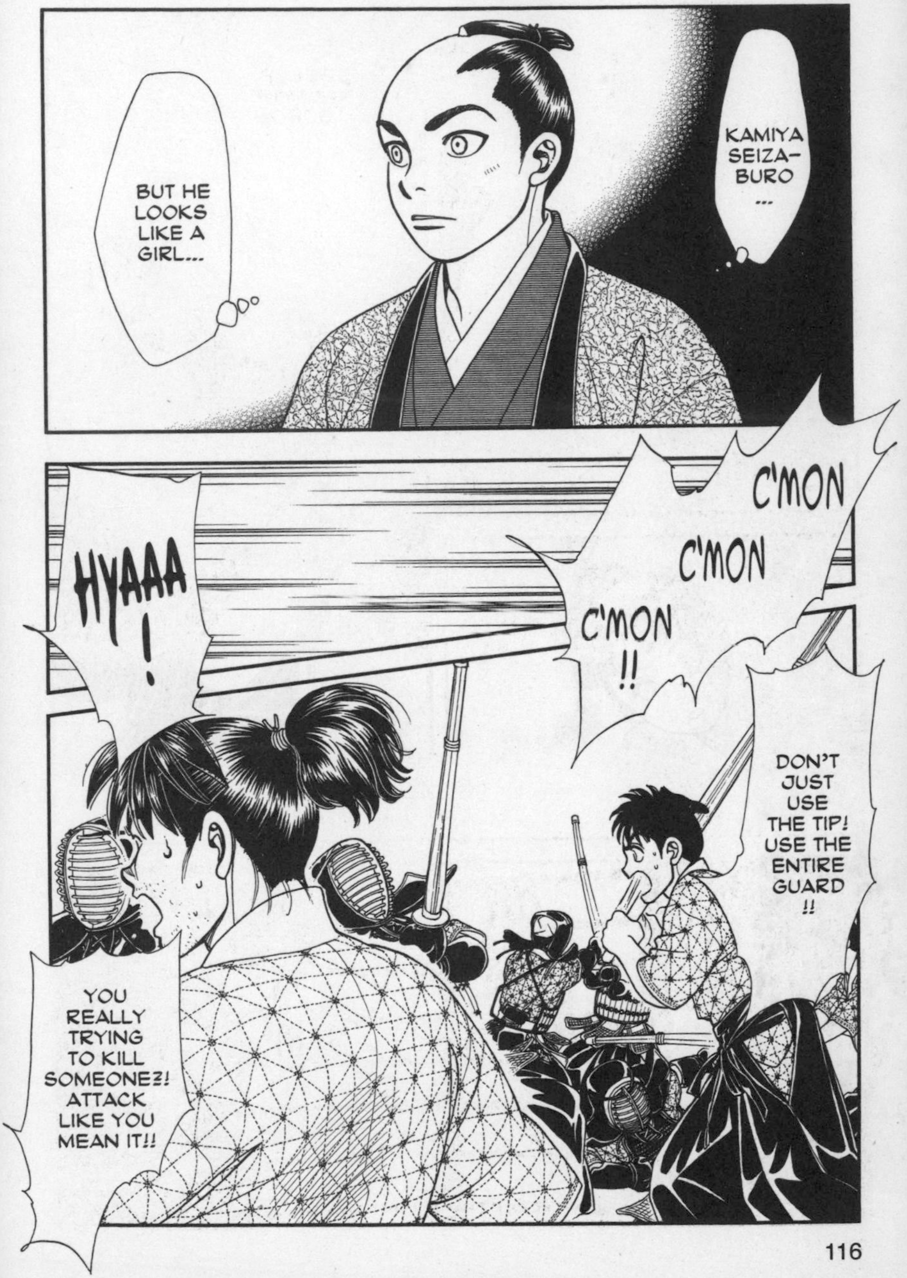
KAMIYA SEIZA-BURO ...
BUT HE LOOKS LIKE A GIRL...
C'MON C'MON C'MON !!
HYAAA !
DON'T JUST USE THE TIP! USE THE ENTIRE GUARD !!
YOU REALLY TRYING TO KILL SOMEONE?! ATTACK LIKE YOU MEAN IT!!

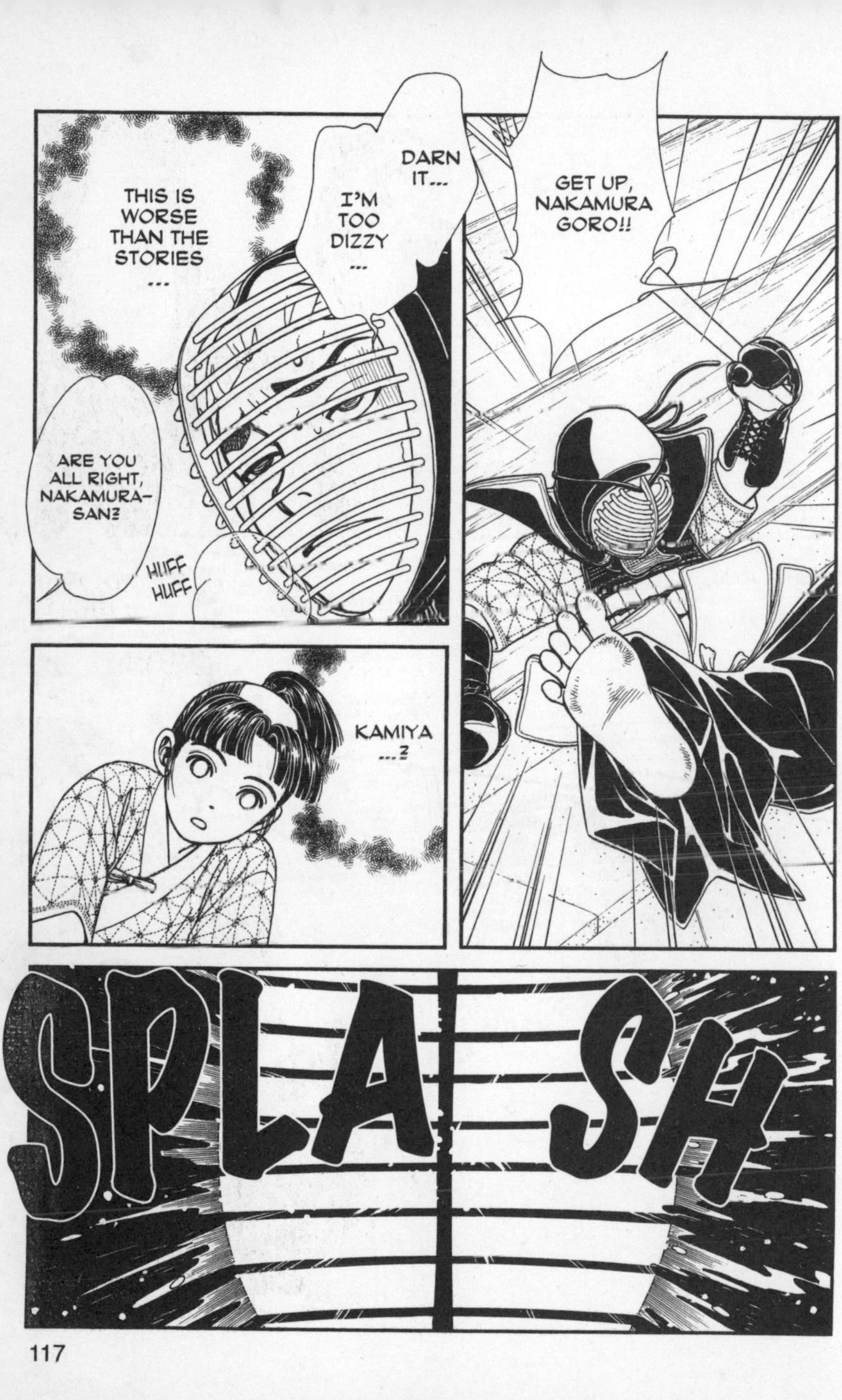
GET UP, NAKAMURA GORO!!
DARN IT...
I'M TOO DIZZY...
THIS IS WORSE THAN THE STORIES...
HUFF HUFF
ARE YOU ALL RIGHT, NAKAMURA-SAN?
KAMIYA...?
SPLASH

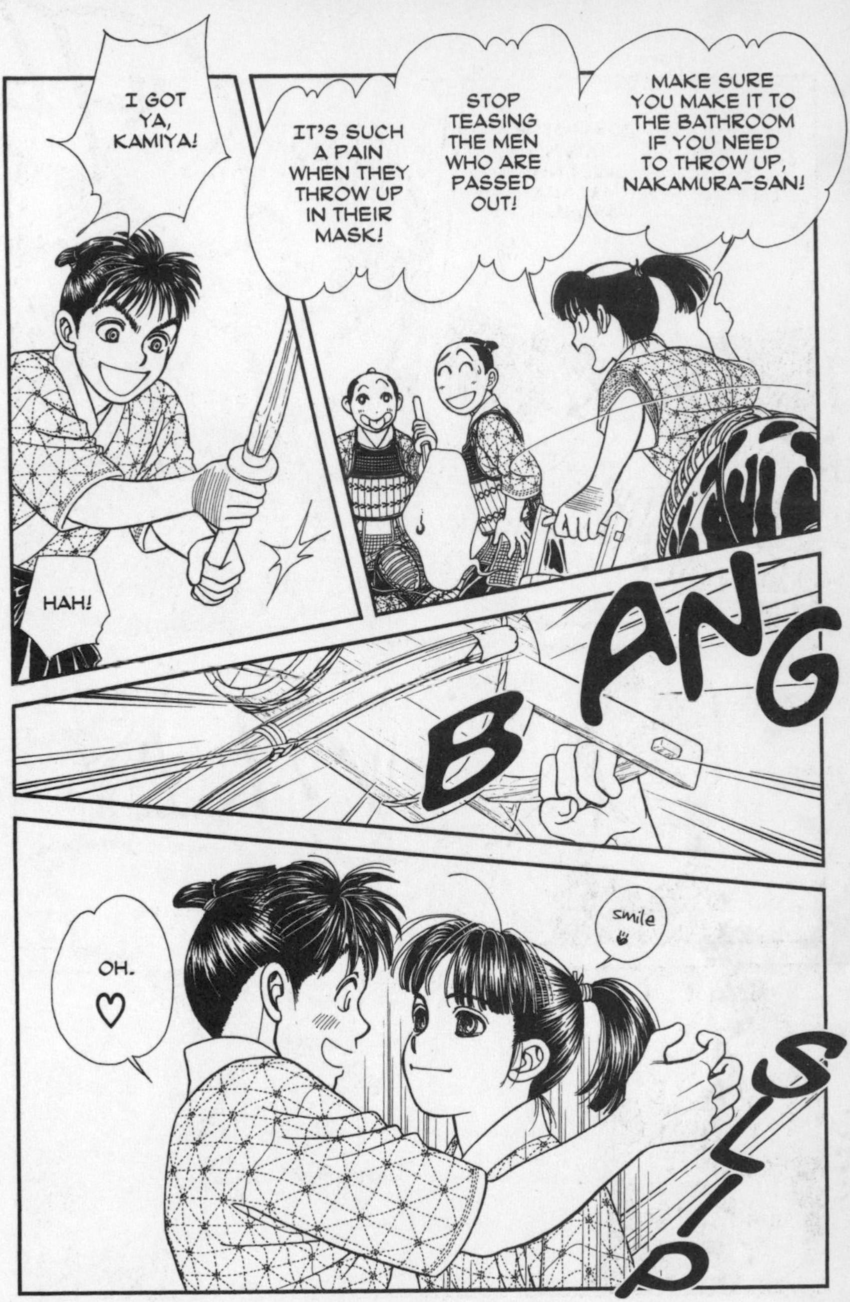
MAKE SURE YOU MAKE IT TO THE BATHROOM IF YOU NEED TO THROW UP, NAKAMURA-SAN!
STOP TEASING THE MEN WHO ARE PASSED OUT!
IT'S SUCH A PAIN WHEN THEY THROW UP IN THEIR MASK!
I GOT YA, KAMIYA!
HAH!
BANG
smile
OH. ♡
SLIP

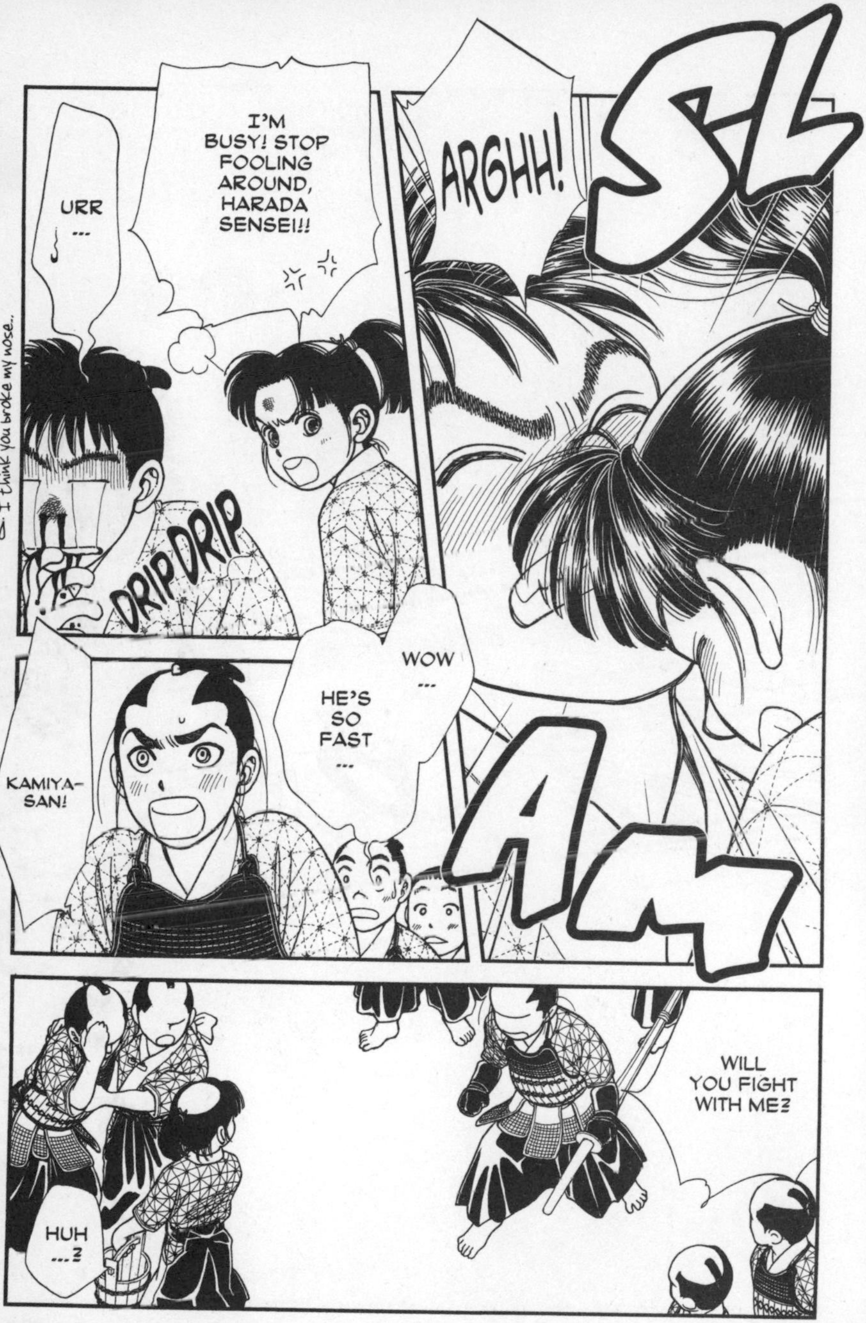
ARGHH!
SLAM
I'M BUSY! STOP FOOLING AROUND, HARADA SENSEI!!
URR ...
DRIP DRIP
I think you broke my nose...
WOW ...
HE'S SO FAST ...
KAMIYA-SAN!
WILL YOU FIGHT WITH ME?
HUH ...?

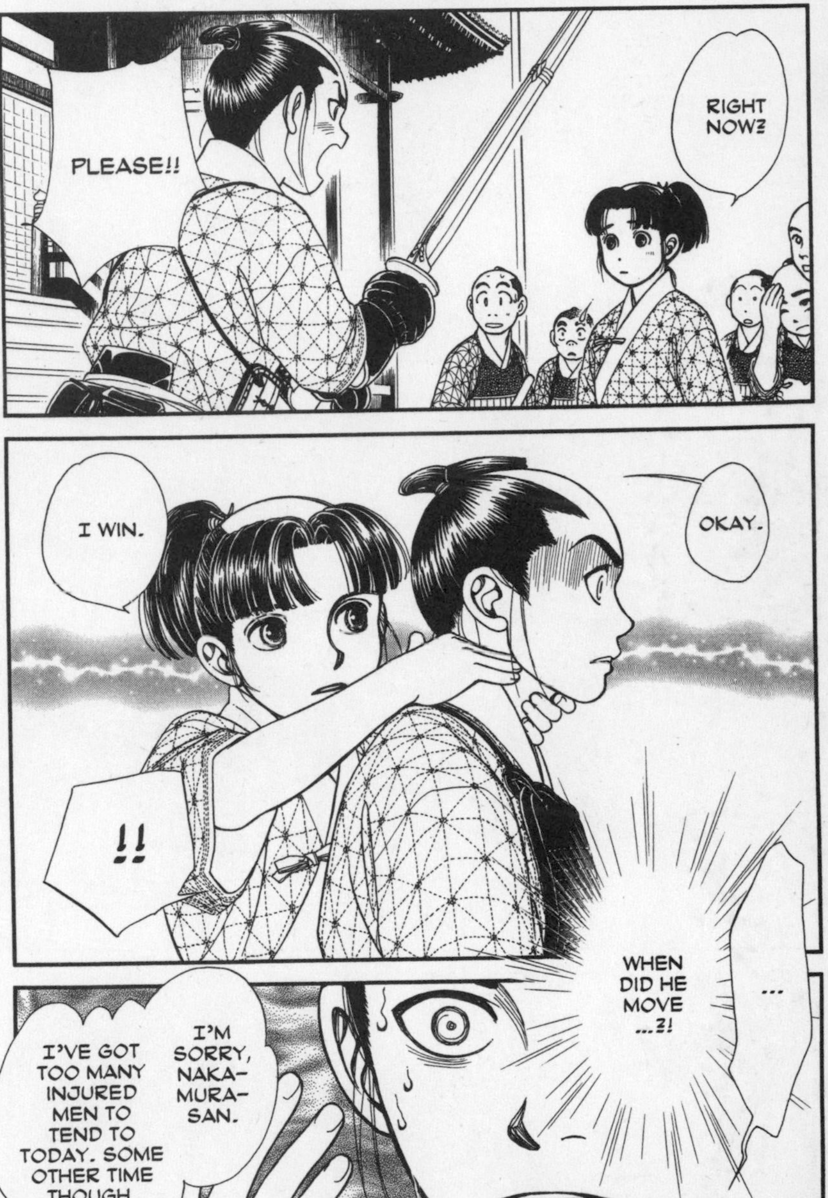
RIGHT NOW?
PLEASE!!
OKAY.
I WIN.
!!
...
WHEN DID HE MOVE ...?!
I'M SORRY, NAKAMURA-SAN.
I'VE GOT TOO MANY INJURED MEN TO TEND TO TODAY. SOME OTHER TIME THOUGH.

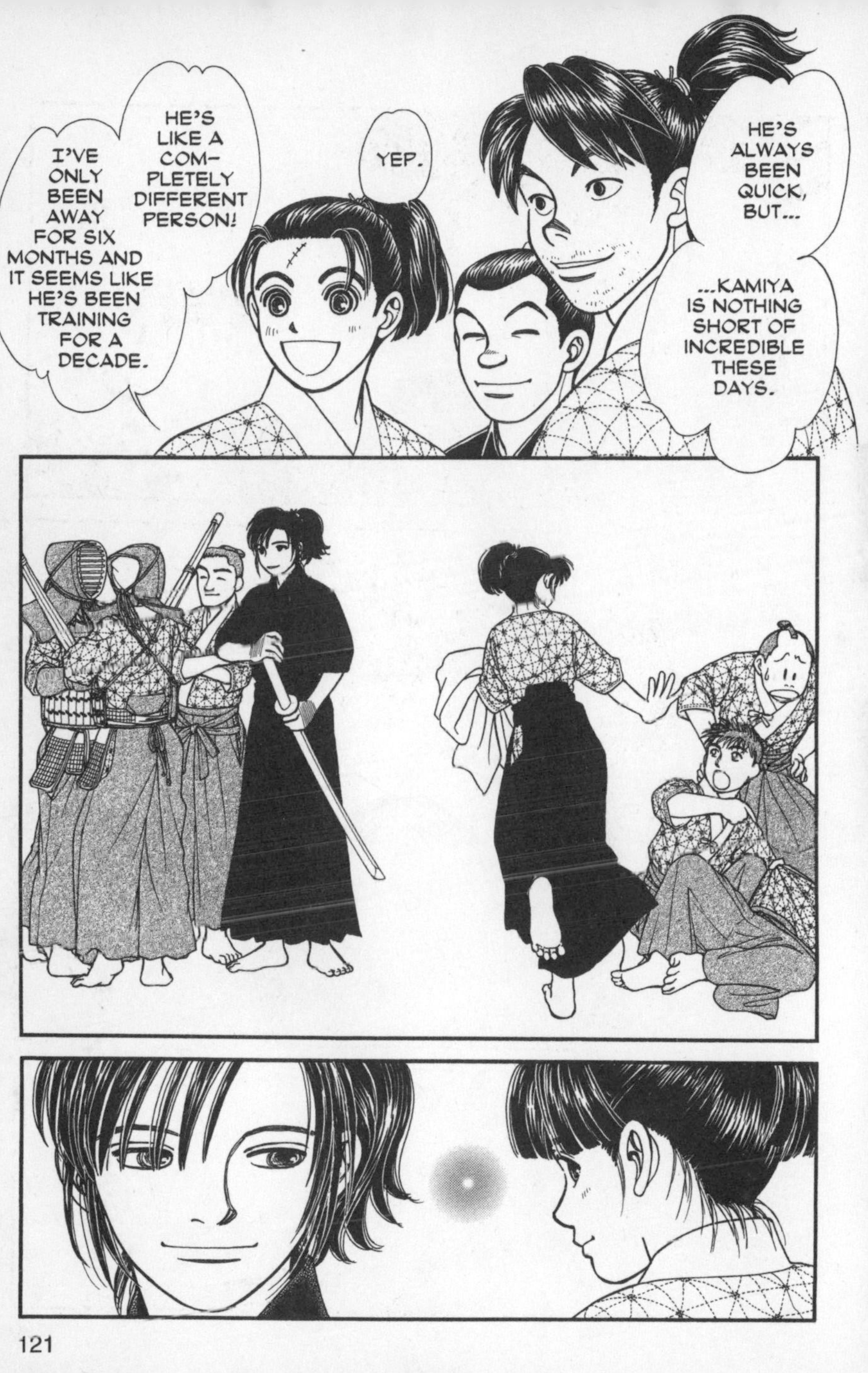
HE'S ALWAYS BEEN QUICK, BUT...
...KAMIYA IS NOTHING SHORT OF INCREDIBLE THESE DAYS.
YEP.
HE'S LIKE A COM-PLETELY DIFFERENT PERSON!
I'VE ONLY BEEN AWAY FOR SIX MONTHS AND IT SEEMS LIKE HE'S BEEN TRAINING FOR A DECADE.

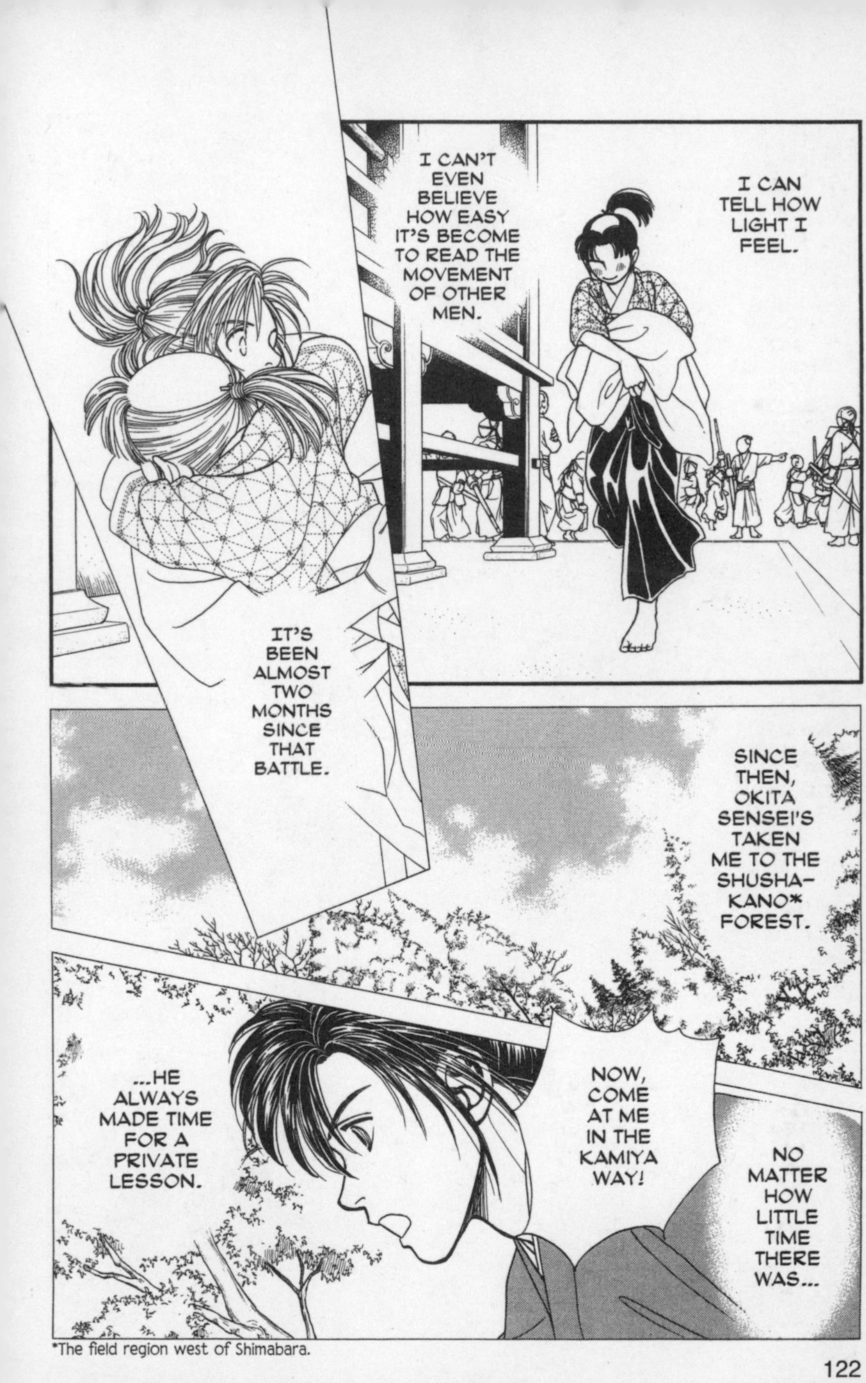
I CAN TELL HOW LIGHT I FEEL.
I CAN'T EVEN BELIEVE HOW EASY IT'S BECOME TO READ THE MOVEMENT OF OTHER MEN.
IT'S BEEN ALMOST TWO MONTHS SINCE THAT BATTLE.
SINCE THEN, OKITA SENSEI'S TAKEN ME TO THE SHUSHA-KANO* FOREST.
NO MATTER HOW LITTLE TIME THERE WAS...
NOW, COME AT ME IN THE KAMIYA WAY!
...HE ALWAYS MADE TIME FOR A PRIVATE LESSON.

*The field region west of Shimabara.

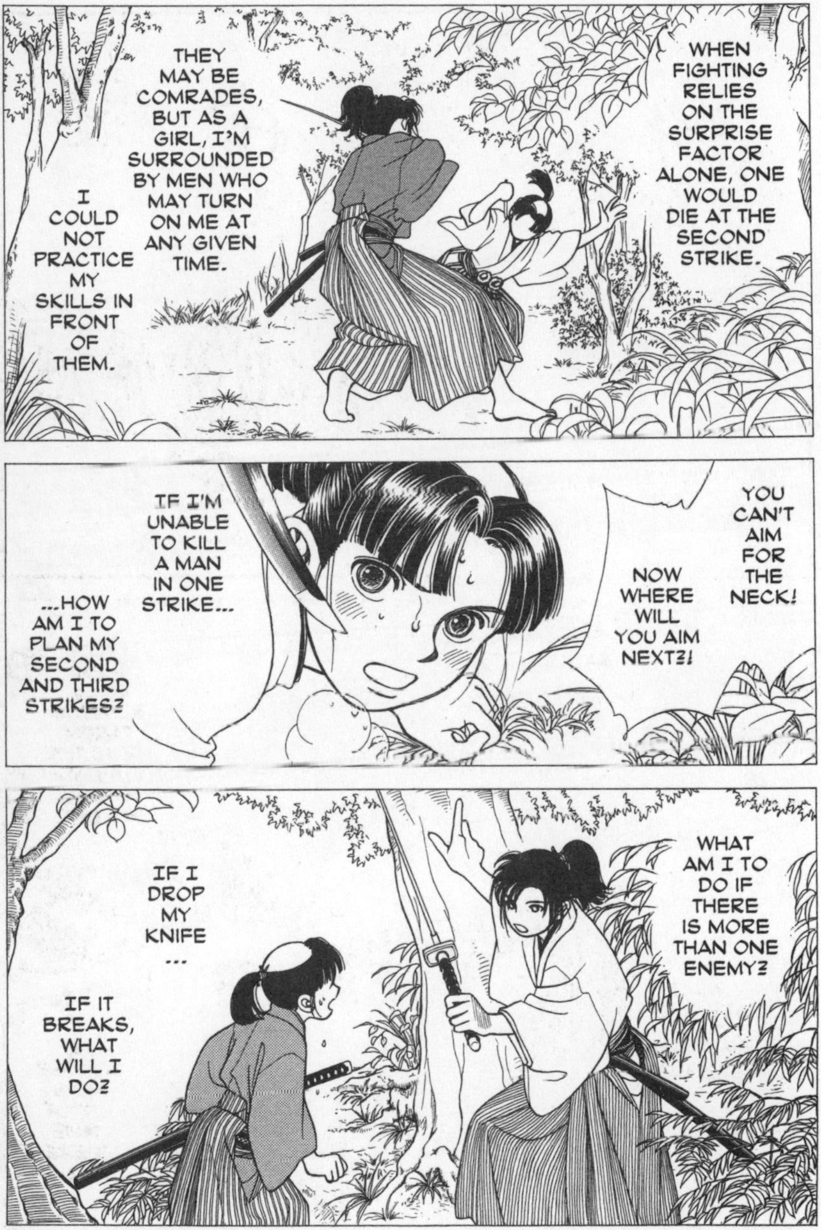
WHEN FIGHTING RELIES ON THE SURPRISE FACTOR ALONE, ONE WOULD DIE AT THE SECOND STRIKE.
THEY MAY BE COMRADES, BUT AS A GIRL, I'M SURROUNDED BY MEN WHO MAY TURN ON ME AT ANY GIVEN TIME.
I COULD NOT PRACTICE MY SKILLS IN FRONT OF THEM.
YOU CAN'T AIM FOR THE NECK!
NOW WHERE WILL YOU AIM NEXT?!
IF I'M UNABLE TO KILL A MAN IN ONE STRIKE...
...HOW AM I TO PLAN MY SECOND AND THIRD STRIKES?
WHAT AM I TO DO IF THERE IS MORE THAN ONE ENEMY?
IF I DROP MY KNIFE...
IF IT BREAKS, WHAT WILL I DO?

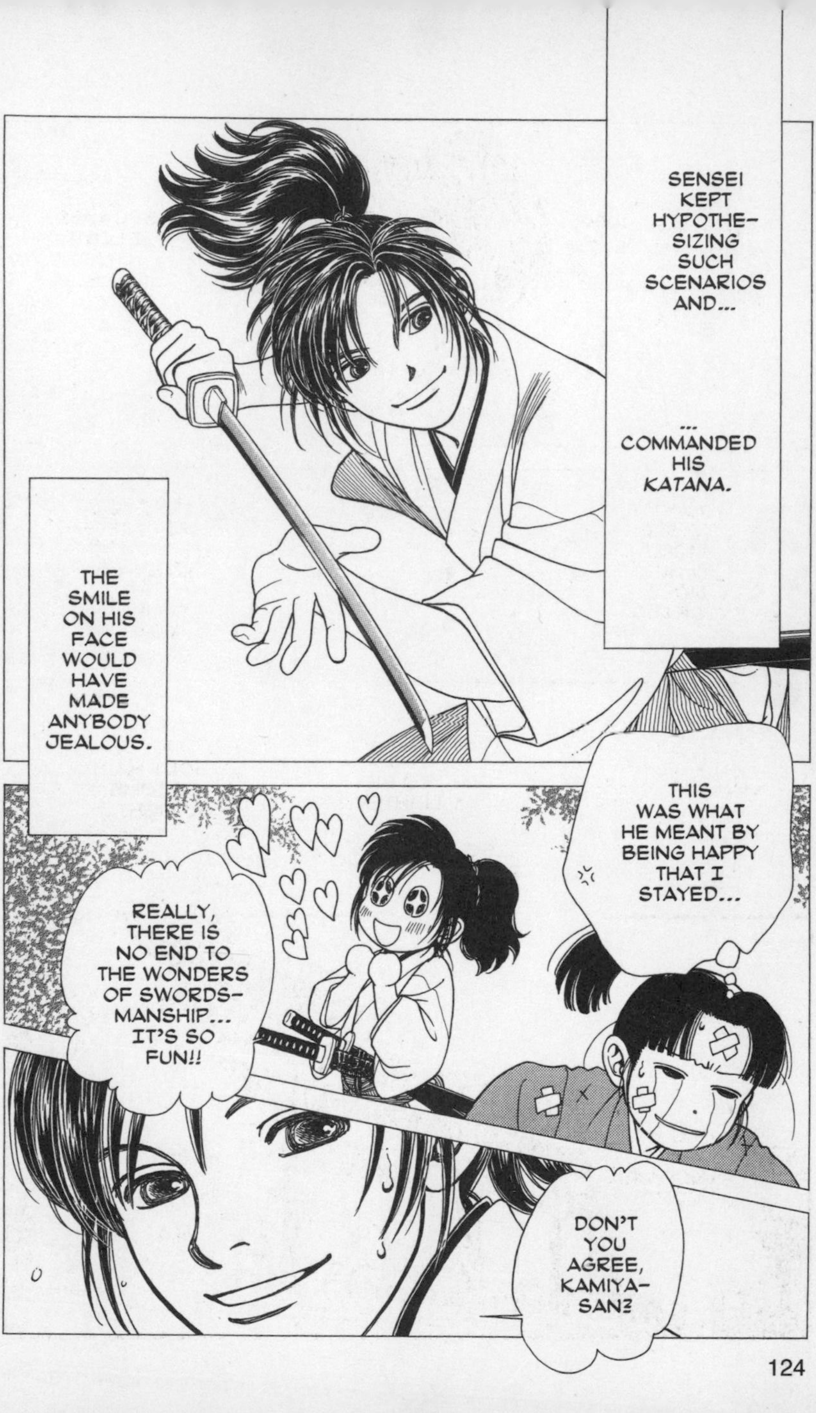
SENSEI KEPT HYPOTHE-SIZING SUCH SCENARIOS AND...
...COMMANDED HIS *KATANA.*
THE SMILE ON HIS FACE WOULD HAVE MADE ANYBODY JEALOUS.
THIS WAS WHAT HE MEANT BY BEING HAPPY THAT I STAYED...
REALLY, THERE IS NO END TO THE WONDERS OF SWORDS-MANSHIP... IT'S SO FUN!!
DON'T YOU AGREE, KAMIYA-SAN?

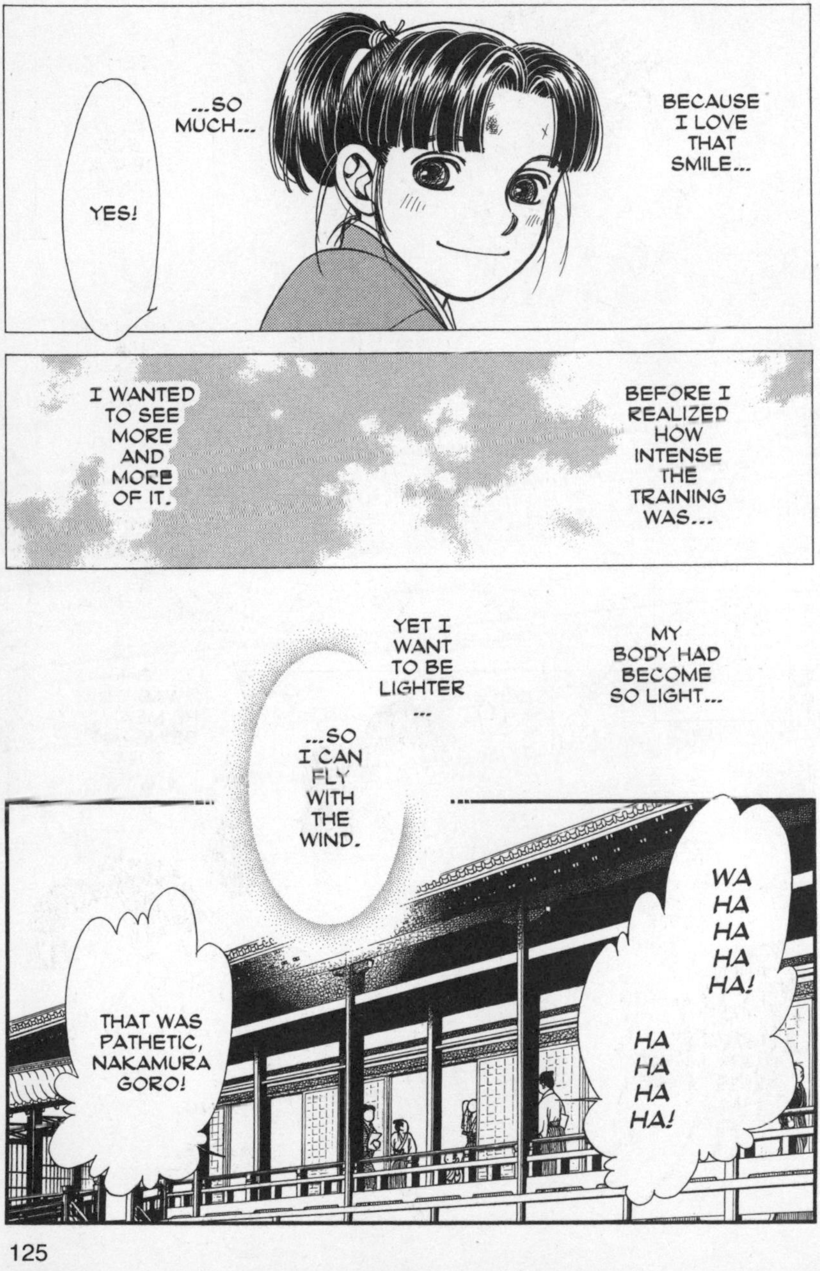
BECAUSE I LOVE THAT SMILE...
...SO MUCH...
YES!
BEFORE I REALIZED HOW INTENSE THE TRAINING WAS...
I WANTED TO SEE MORE AND MORE OF IT.
MY BODY HAD BECOME SO LIGHT...
YET I WANT TO BE LIGHTER...
...SO I CAN FLY WITH THE WIND.
WA HA HA HA HA!
HA HA HA HA!
THAT WAS PATHETIC, NAKAMURA GORO!

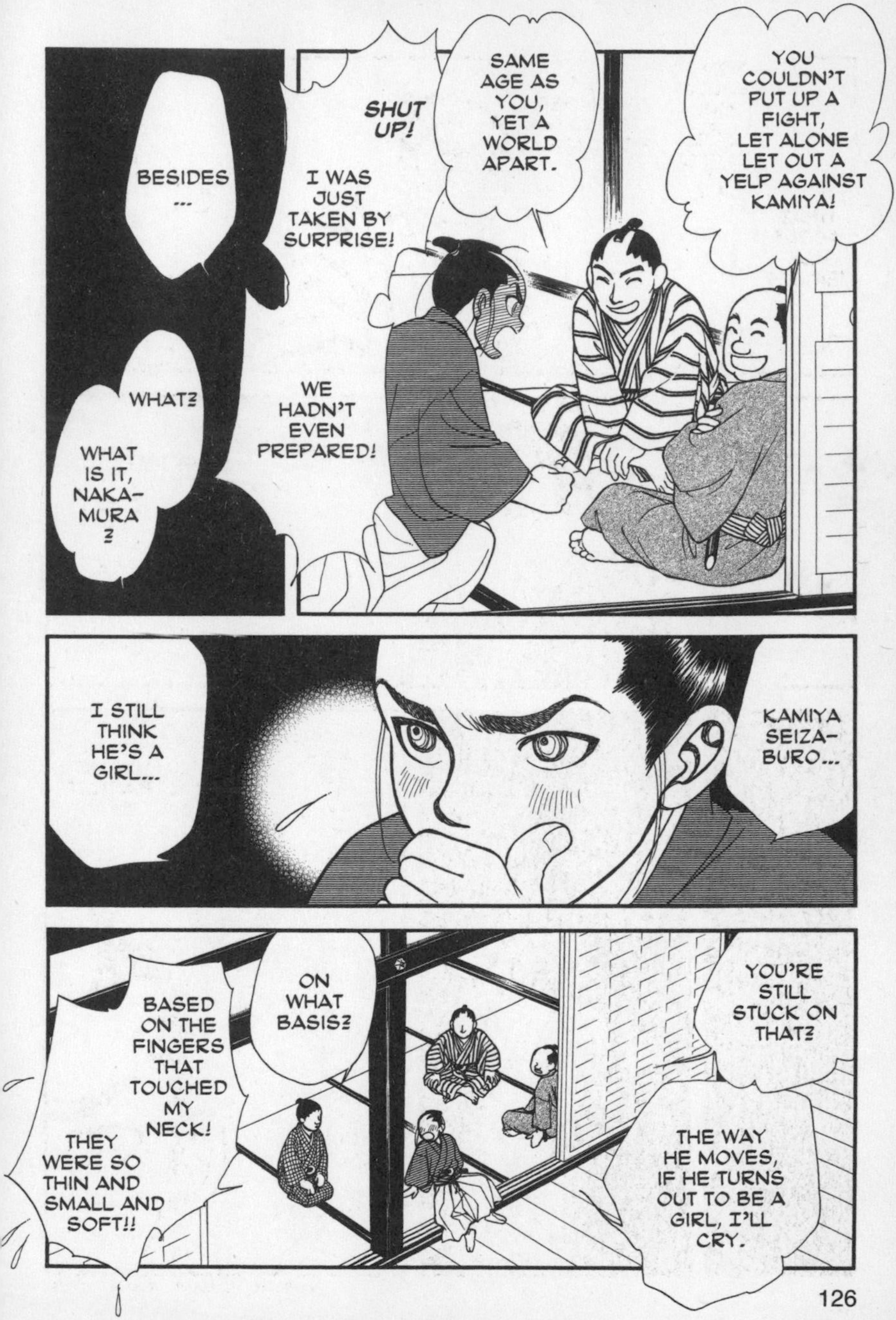
YOU COULDN'T PUT UP A FIGHT, LET ALONE LET OUT A YELP AGAINST KAMIYA!
SAME AGE AS YOU, YET A WORLD APART.
SHUT UP!
I WAS JUST TAKEN BY SURPRISE!
WE HADN'T EVEN PREPARED!
BESIDES...
WHAT?
WHAT IS IT, NAKAMURA?
KAMIYA SEIZABURO...
I STILL THINK HE'S A GIRL...
YOU'RE STILL STUCK ON THAT?
THE WAY HE MOVES, IF HE TURNS OUT TO BE A GIRL, I'LL CRY.
ON WHAT BASIS?
BASED ON THE FINGERS THAT TOUCHED MY NECK!
THEY WERE SO THIN AND SMALL AND SOFT!!

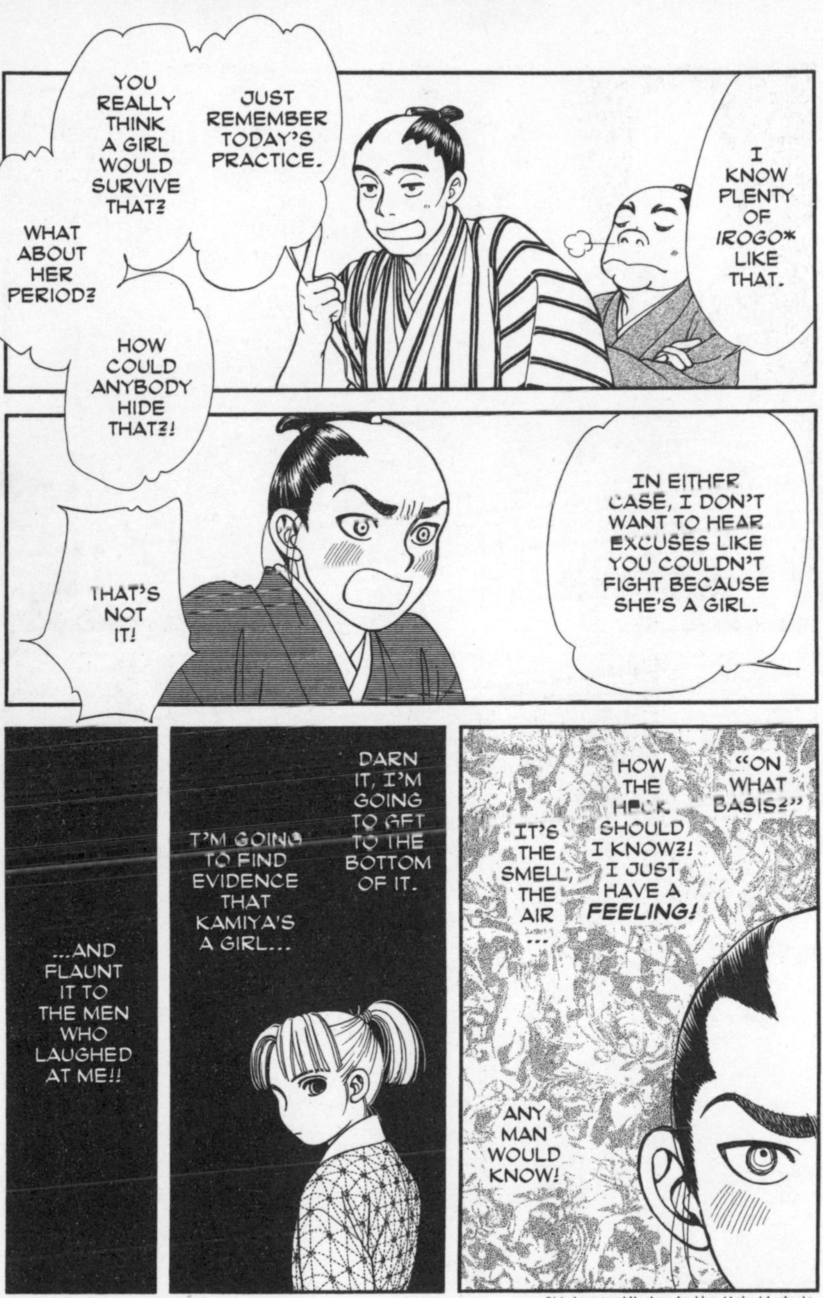
I KNOW PLENTY OF *IROGO** LIKE THAT.
JUST REMEMBER TODAY'S PRACTICE.
YOU REALLY THINK A GIRL WOULD SURVIVE THAT?
WHAT ABOUT HER PERIOD?
HOW COULD ANYBODY HIDE THAT?!
IN EITHER CASE, I DON'T WANT TO HEAR EXCUSES LIKE YOU COULDN'T FIGHT BECAUSE SHE'S A GIRL.
THAT'S NOT IT!
"ON WHAT BASIS?"
HOW THE HECK SHOULD I KNOW?! I JUST HAVE A ***FEELING!***
IT'S THE SMELL, THE AIR...
ANY MAN WOULD KNOW!
DARN IT, I'M GOING TO GET TO THE BOTTOM OF IT.
I'M GOING TO FIND EVIDENCE THAT KAMIYA'S A GIRL...
...AND FLAUNT IT TO THE MEN WHO LAUGHED AT ME!!

*Male prostitutes in the Kabuki circle.

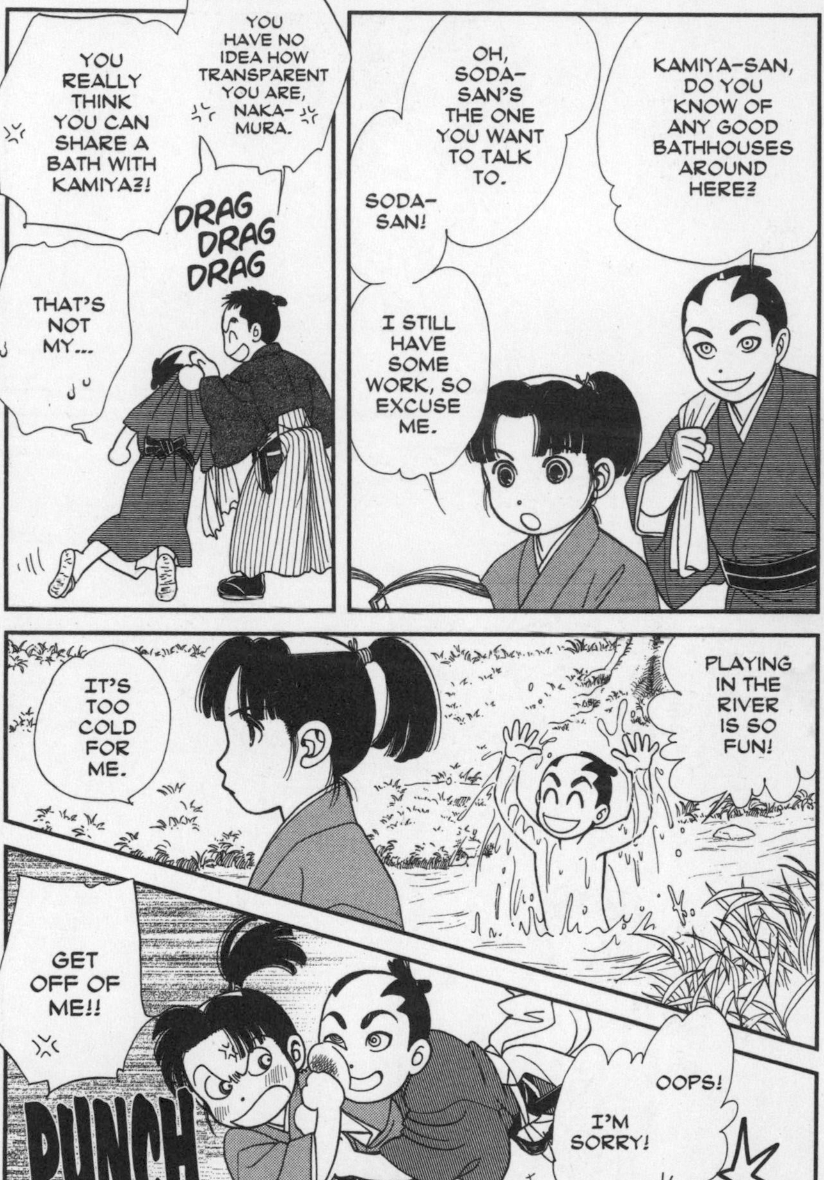
KAMIYA-SAN, DO YOU KNOW OF ANY GOOD BATHHOUSES AROUND HERE?
OH, SODA-SAN'S THE ONE YOU WANT TO TALK TO.
SODA-SAN!
I STILL HAVE SOME WORK, SO EXCUSE ME.
YOU HAVE NO IDEA HOW TRANSPARENT YOU ARE, NAKAMURA.
YOU REALLY THINK YOU CAN SHARE A BATH WITH KAMIYA?!
DRAG DRAG DRAG
THAT'S NOT MY...
PLAYING IN THE RIVER IS SO FUN!
IT'S TOO COLD FOR ME.
OOPS!
I'M SORRY!
I tripped...
GET OFF OF ME!!
PUNCH

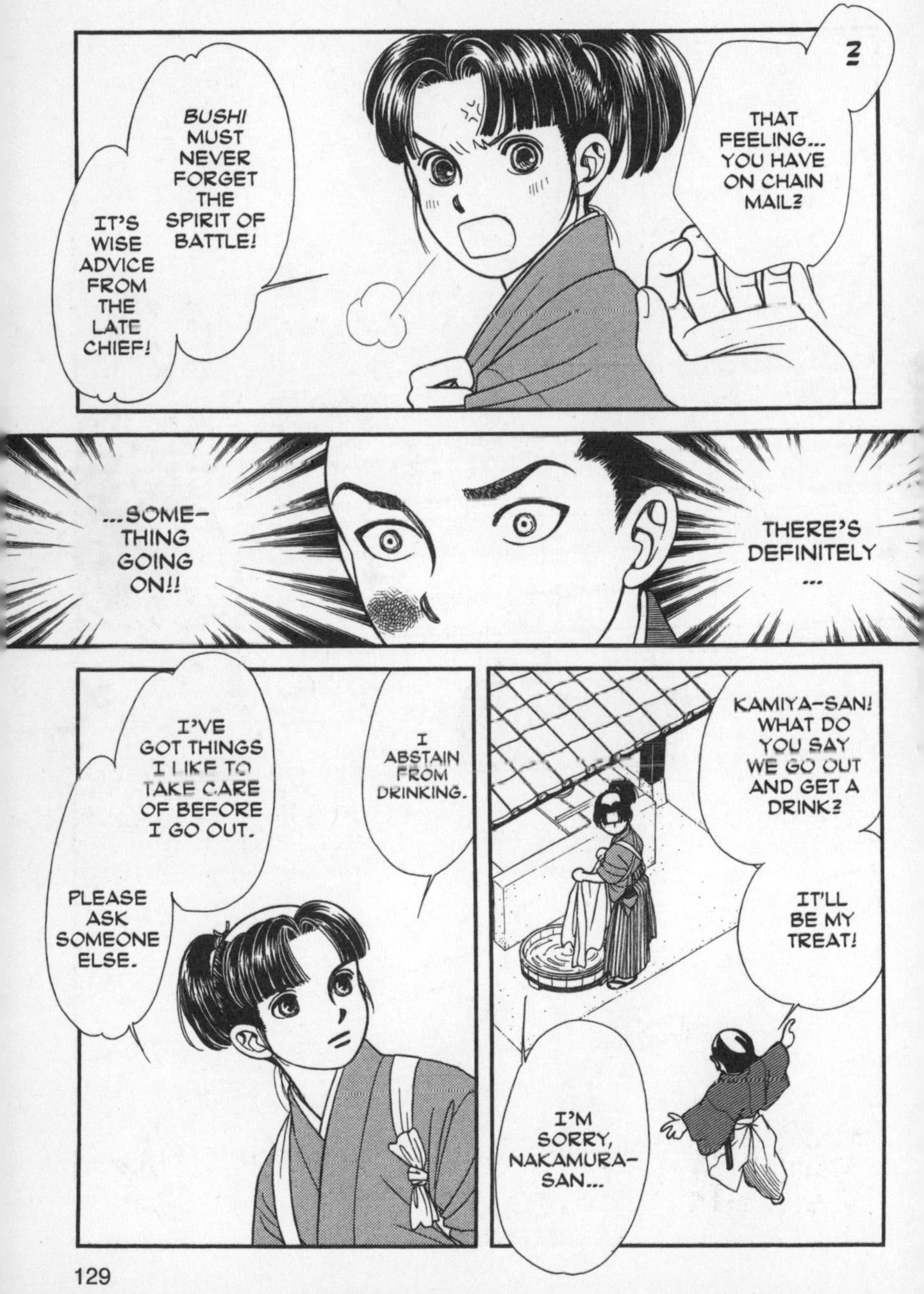
THAT FEELING... YOU HAVE ON CHAIN MAIL?
BUSHI MUST NEVER FORGET THE SPIRIT OF BATTLE!
IT'S WISE ADVICE FROM THE LATE CHIEF!
THERE'S DEFINITELY ...
...SOMETHING GOING ON!!
KAMIYA-SAN! WHAT DO YOU SAY WE GO OUT AND GET A DRINK?
IT'LL BE MY TREAT!
I'M SORRY, NAKAMURA-SAN...
I ABSTAIN FROM DRINKING.
I'VE GOT THINGS I LIKE TO TAKE CARE OF BEFORE I GO OUT.
PLEASE ASK SOMEONE ELSE.

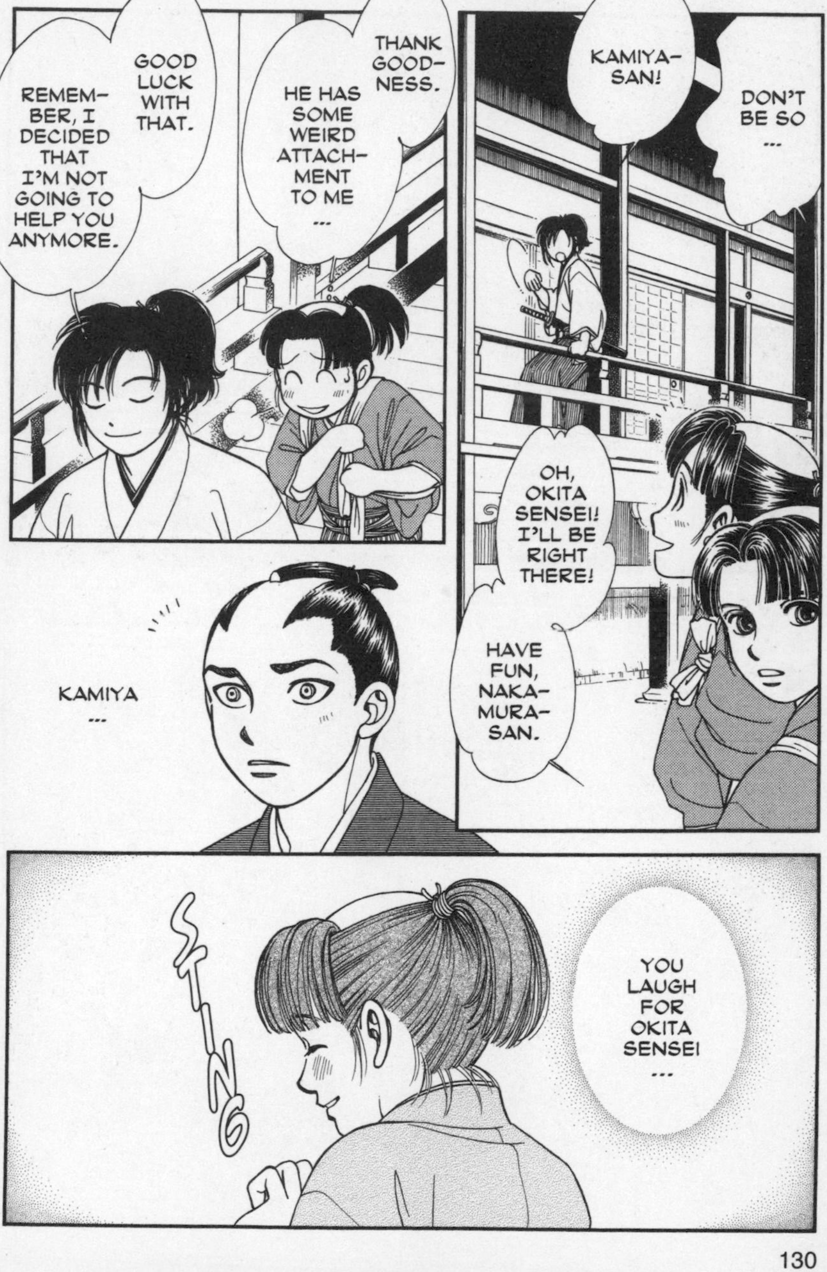
DON'T BE SO ...
KAMIYA-SAN!
OH, OKITA SENSEI! I'LL BE RIGHT THERE!
HAVE FUN, NAKAMURA-SAN.
THANK GOODNESS.
HE HAS SOME WEIRD ATTACHMENT TO ME ...
GOOD LUCK WITH THAT.
REMEMBER, I DECIDED THAT I'M NOT GOING TO HELP YOU ANYMORE.
KAMIYA ...
YOU LAUGH FOR OKITA SENSEI ...
STING

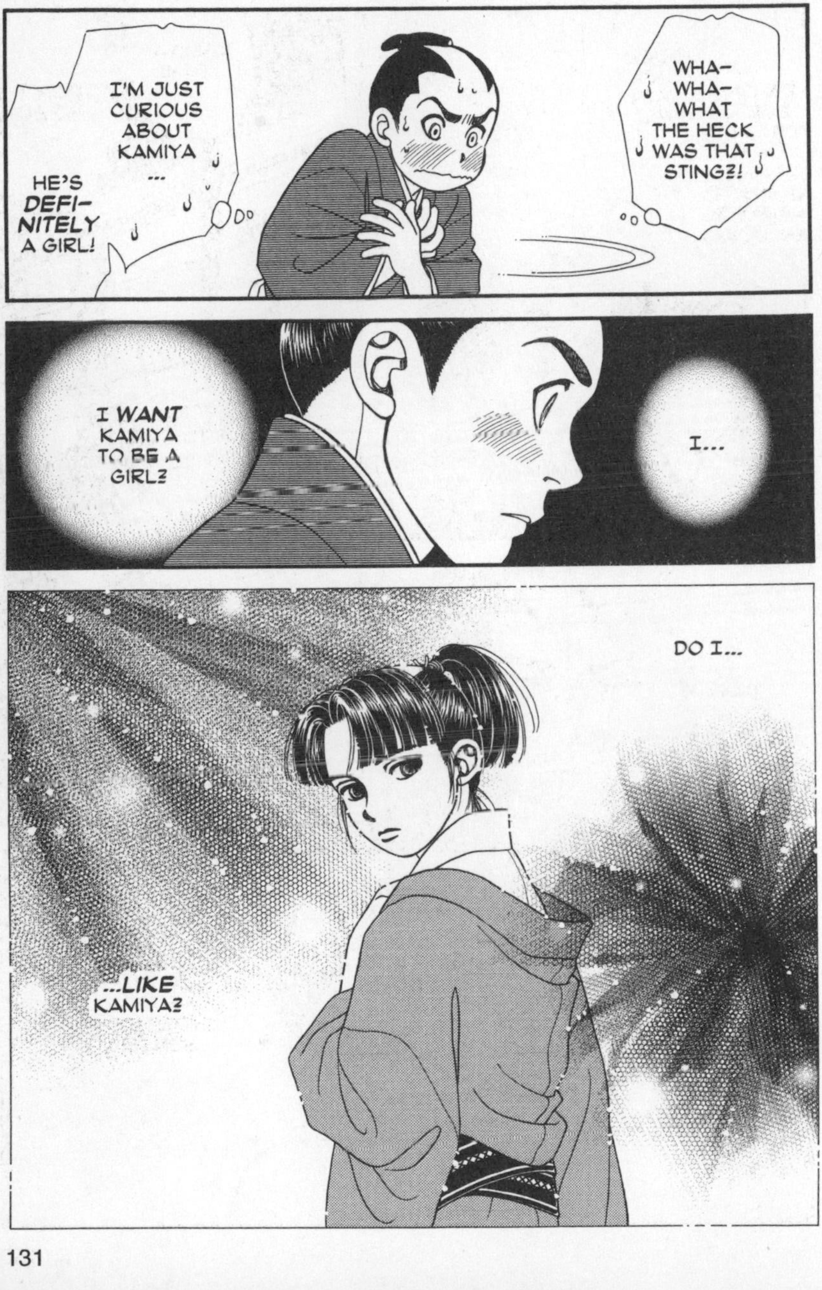
WHA-WHA-WHAT THE HECK WAS THAT STING?!
I'M JUST CURIOUS ABOUT KAMIYA ...
HE'S DEFINITELY A GIRL!
I...
I WANT KAMIYA TO BE A GIRL?
DO I...
...LIKE KAMIYA?

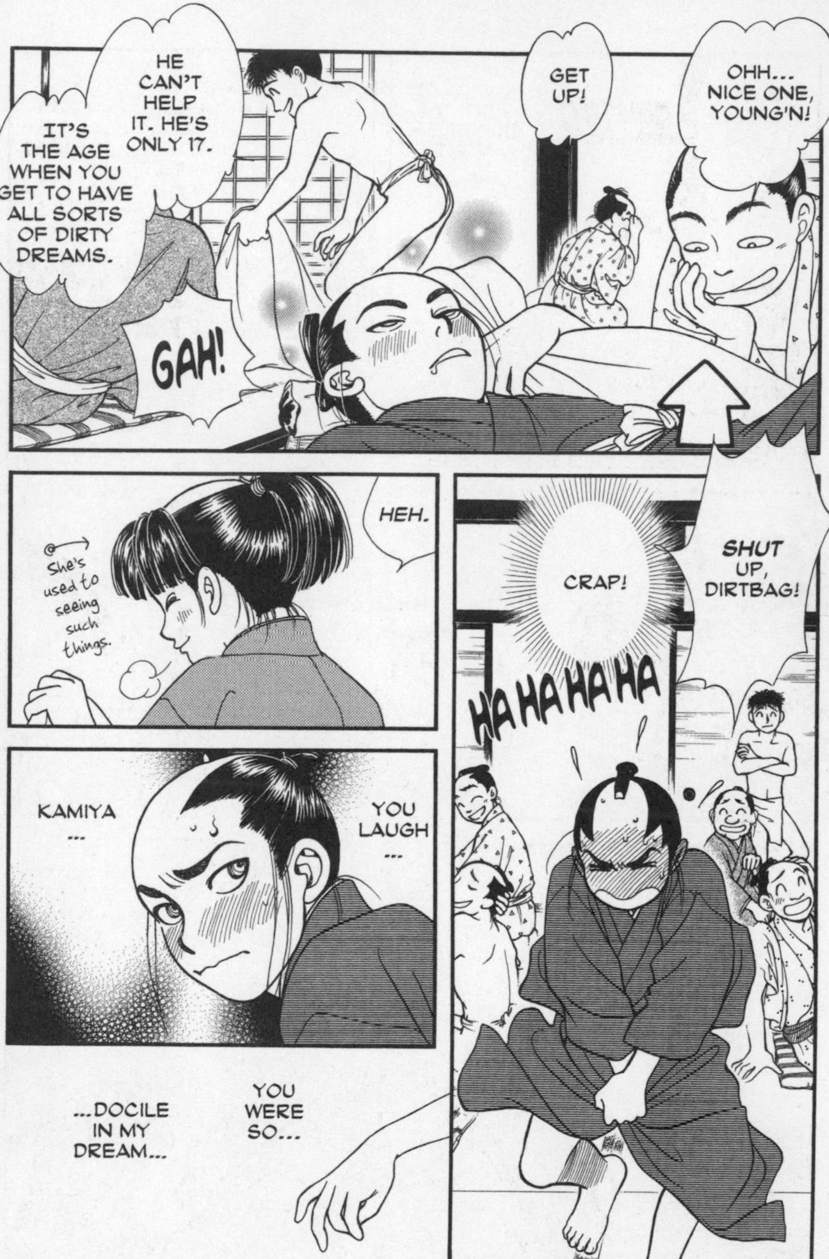
OHH... NICE ONE, YOUNG'N!
GET UP!
HE CAN'T HELP IT. HE'S ONLY 17.
IT'S THE AGE WHEN YOU GET TO HAVE ALL SORTS OF DIRTY DREAMS.
GAH!
SHUT UP, DIRTBAG!
CRAP!
HA HA HA HA
HEH.
She's used to seeing such things.
YOU LAUGH ...
KAMIYA ...
YOU WERE SO...
...DOCILE IN MY DREAM...

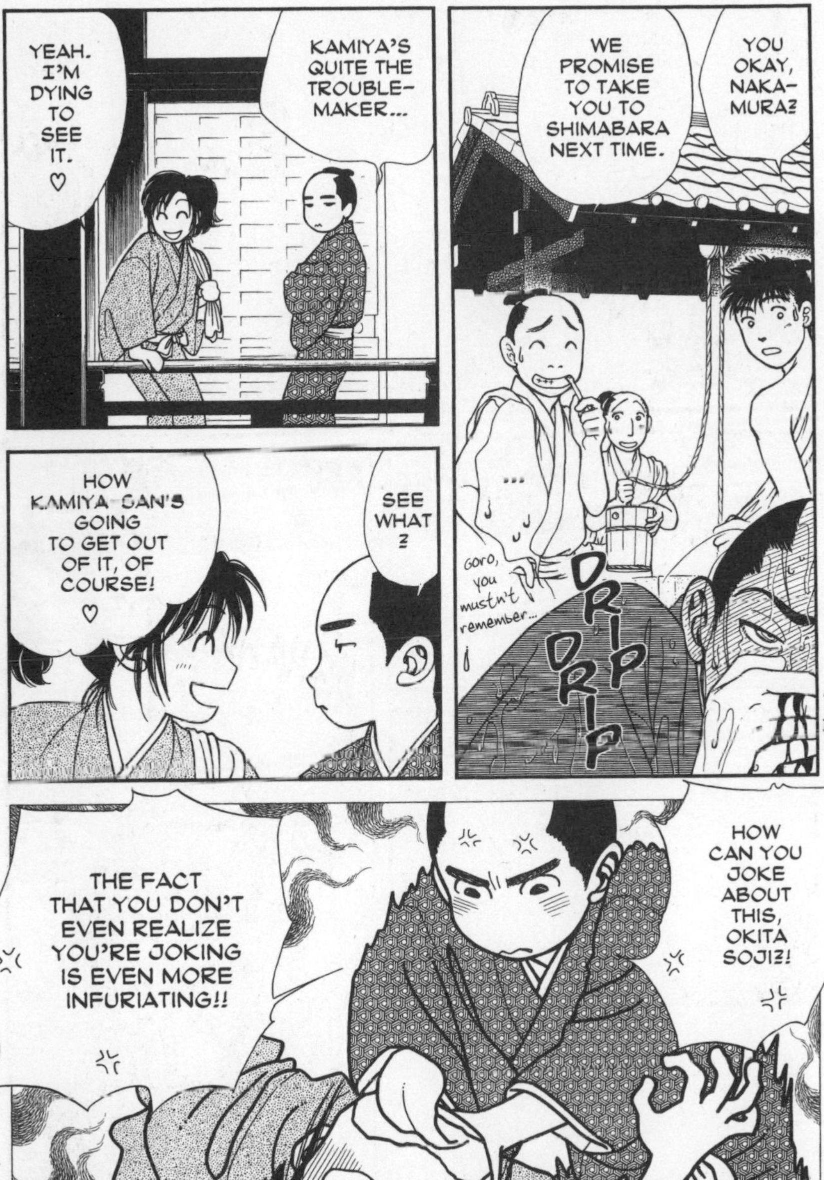
YOU OKAY, NAKA-MURA?
WE PROMISE TO TAKE YOU TO SHIMABARA NEXT TIME.
...
Goro, you mustn't remember...
DRIP DRIP
Bloo nos
KAMIYA'S QUITE THE TROUBLE-MAKER...
YEAH. I'M DYING TO SEE IT. ♡
SEE WHAT?
HOW KAMIYA-SAN'S GOING TO GET OUT OF IT, OF COURSE! ♡
HOW CAN YOU JOKE ABOUT THIS, OKITA SOJI?!
THE FACT THAT YOU DON'T EVEN REALIZE YOU'RE JOKING IS EVEN MORE INFURIATING!!

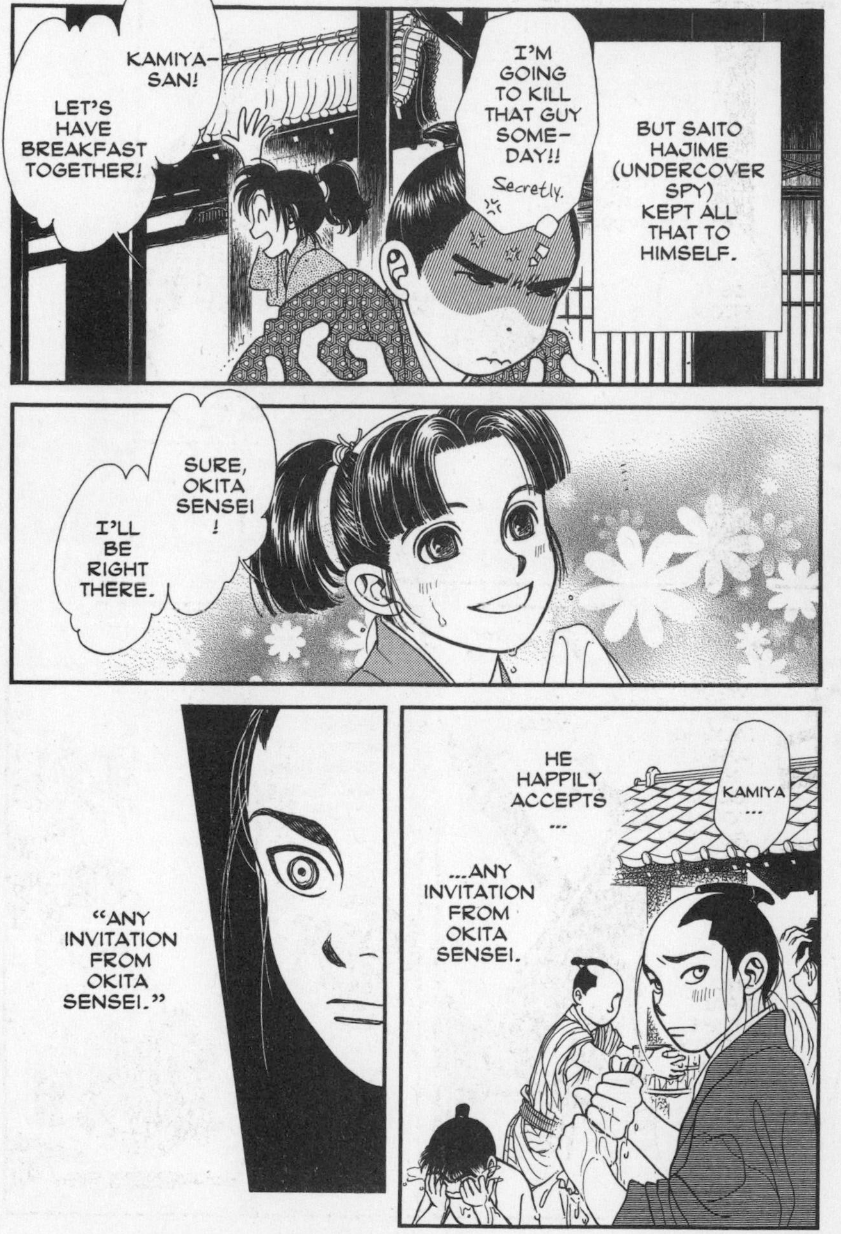
BUT SAITO HAJIME (UNDERCOVER SPY) KEPT ALL THAT TO HIMSELF.
I'M GOING TO KILL THAT GUY SOME-DAY!!
Secretly.
KAMIYA-SAN!
LET'S HAVE BREAKFAST TOGETHER!
SURE, OKITA SENSEI!
I'LL BE RIGHT THERE.
KAMIYA...
HE HAPPILY ACCEPTS...
...ANY INVITATION FROM OKITA SENSEI.
"ANY INVITATION FROM OKITA SENSEI."

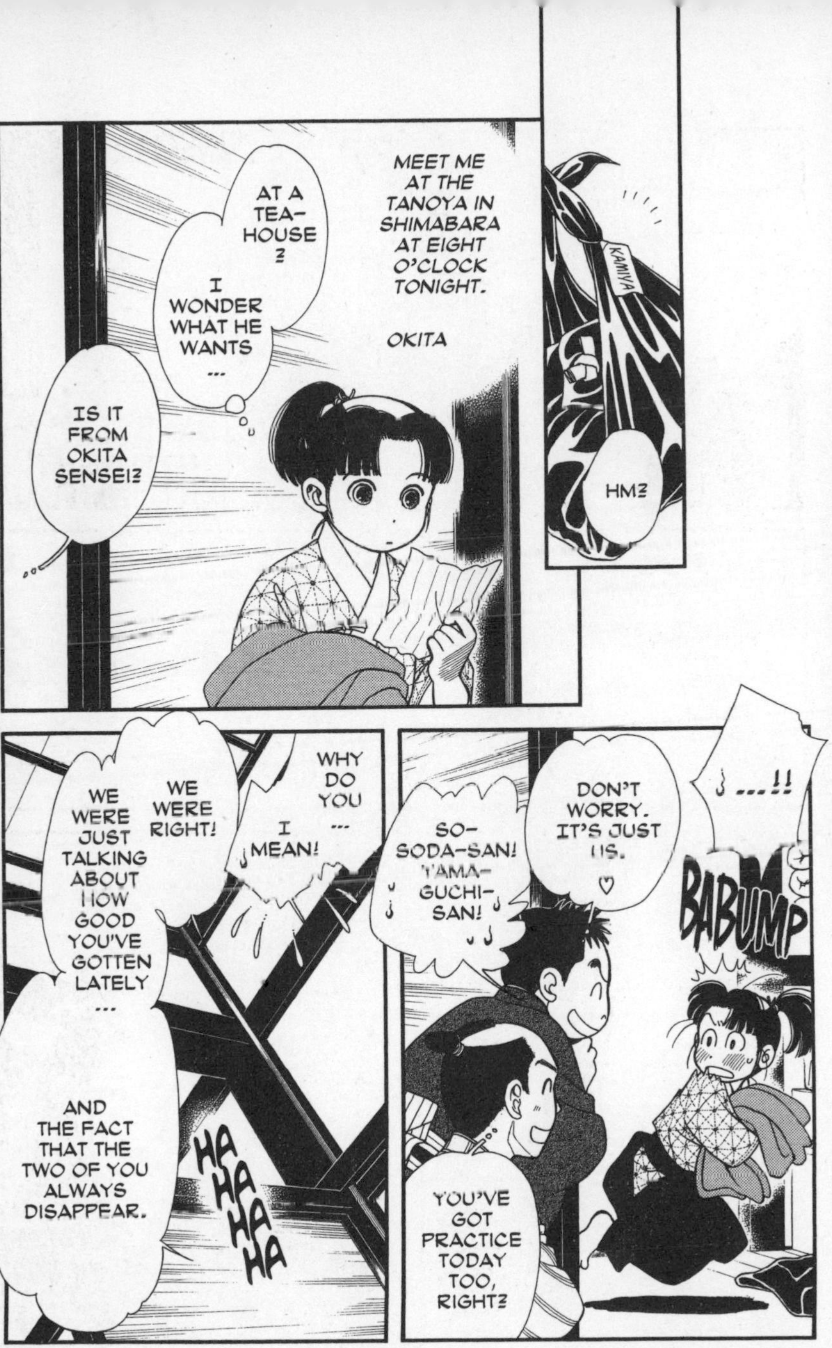
KAMIYA
HM?
MEET ME AT THE TANOYA IN SHIMABARA AT EIGHT O'CLOCK TONIGHT.
OKITA
AT A TEA-HOUSE?
I WONDER WHAT HE WANTS...
IS IT FROM OKITA SENSEI?
...!!
BABUMP
DON'T WORRY. IT'S JUST US. ♡
SO-SODA-SAN! YAMA-GUCHI-SAN!
YOU'VE GOT PRACTICE TODAY TOO, RIGHT?
WHY DO YOU...
I MEAN!
WE WERE RIGHT!
WE WERE JUST TALKING ABOUT HOW GOOD YOU'VE GOTTEN LATELY...
AND THE FACT THAT THE TWO OF YOU ALWAYS DISAPPEAR.
HAHAHAHA

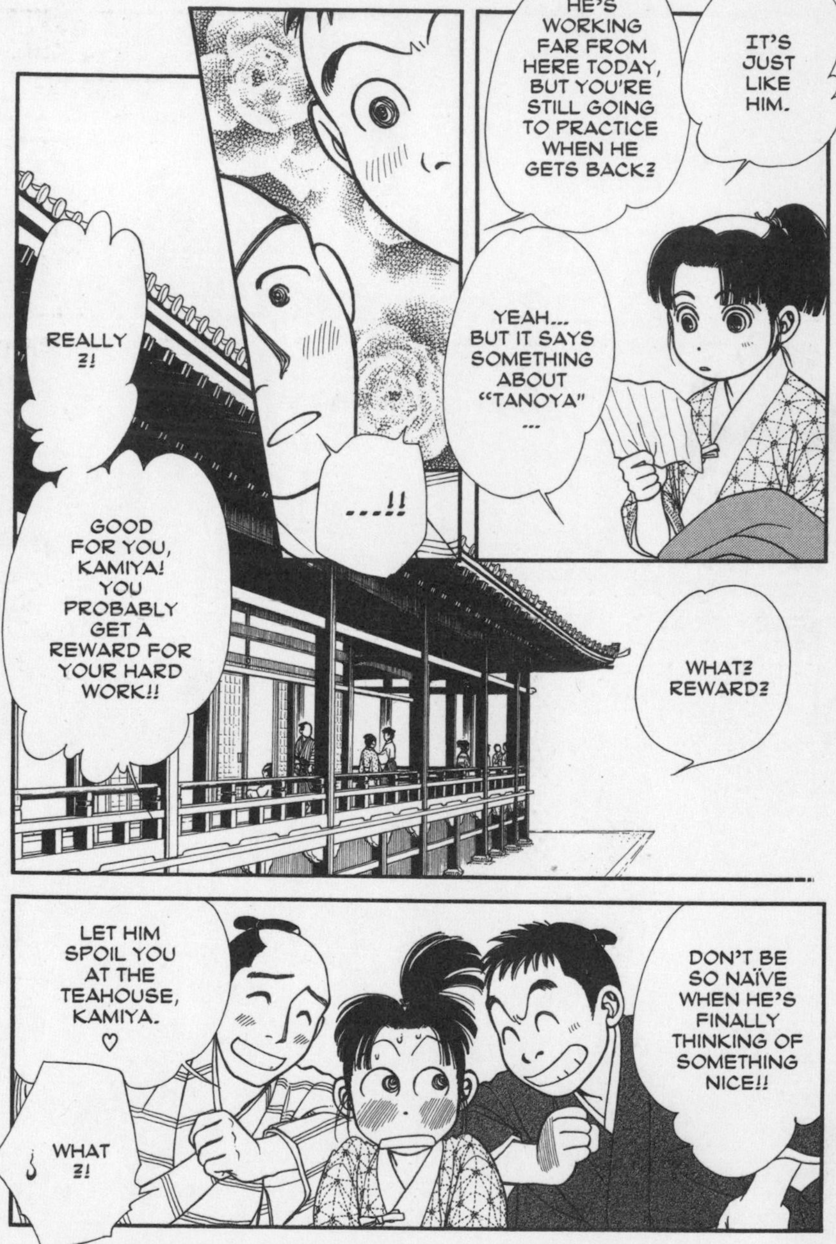
IT'S JUST LIKE HIM.
HE'S WORKING FAR FROM HERE TODAY, BUT YOU'RE STILL GOING TO PRACTICE WHEN HE GETS BACK?
YEAH... BUT IT SAYS SOMETHING ABOUT "TANOYA" ...
...!!
REALLY ?!
GOOD FOR YOU, KAMIYA! YOU PROBABLY GET A REWARD FOR YOUR HARD WORK!!
WHAT? REWARD?
DON'T BE SO NAÏVE WHEN HE'S FINALLY THINKING OF SOMETHING NICE!!
LET HIM SPOIL YOU AT THE TEAHOUSE, KAMIYA. ♡
WHAT ?!

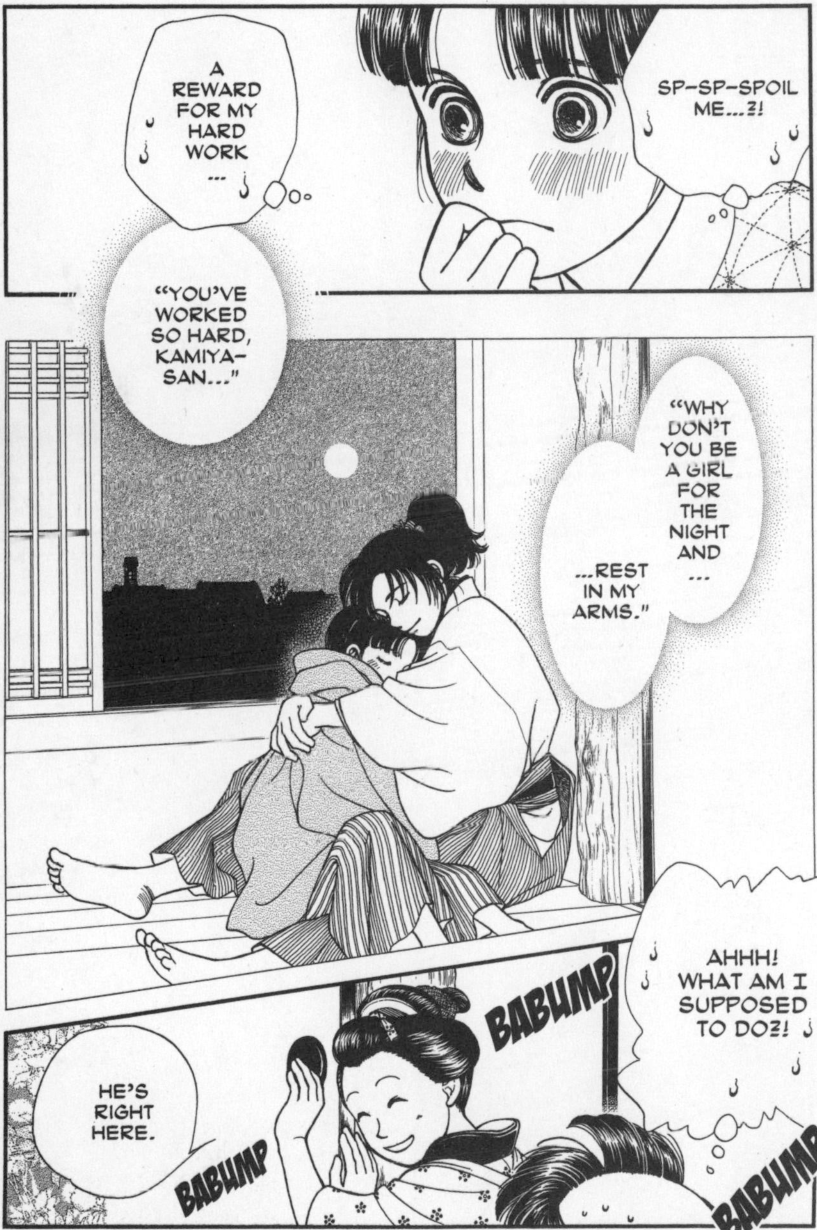
SP-SP-SPOIL ME...?!
A REWARD FOR MY HARD WORK ...
"YOU'VE WORKED SO HARD, KAMIYA-SAN..."
"WHY DON'T YOU BE A GIRL FOR THE NIGHT AND ...
...REST IN MY ARMS."
AHHH! WHAT AM I SUPPOSED TO DO?!
BABUMP
BABUMP
HE'S RIGHT HERE.
BABUMP

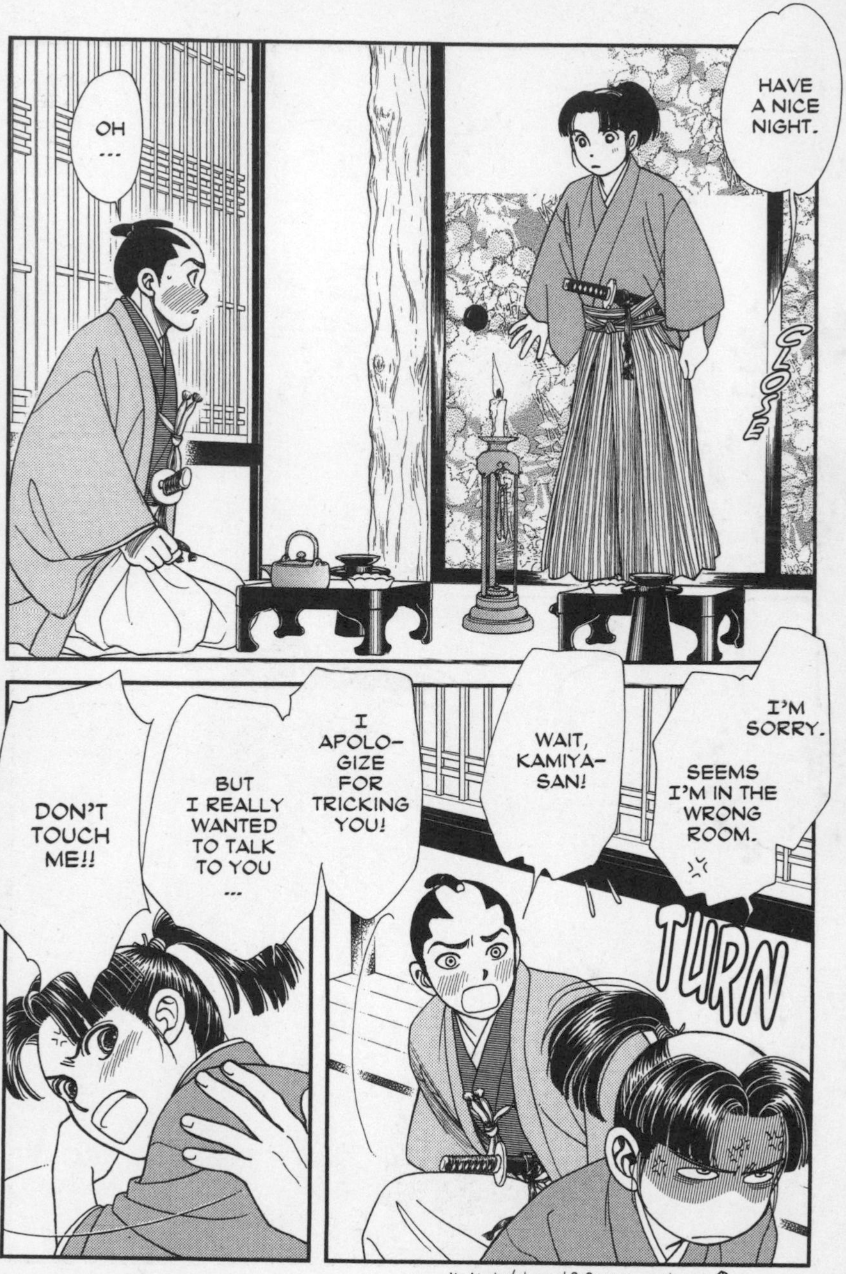
HAVE A NICE NIGHT.
CLOSE
OH ...
I'M SORRY.
SEEMS I'M IN THE WRONG ROOM.
TURN
WAIT, KAMIYA-SAN!
I APOLOGIZE FOR TRICKING YOU!
BUT I REALLY WANTED TO TALK TO YOU ...
DON'T TOUCH ME!!
Mad at herself for being so happy.

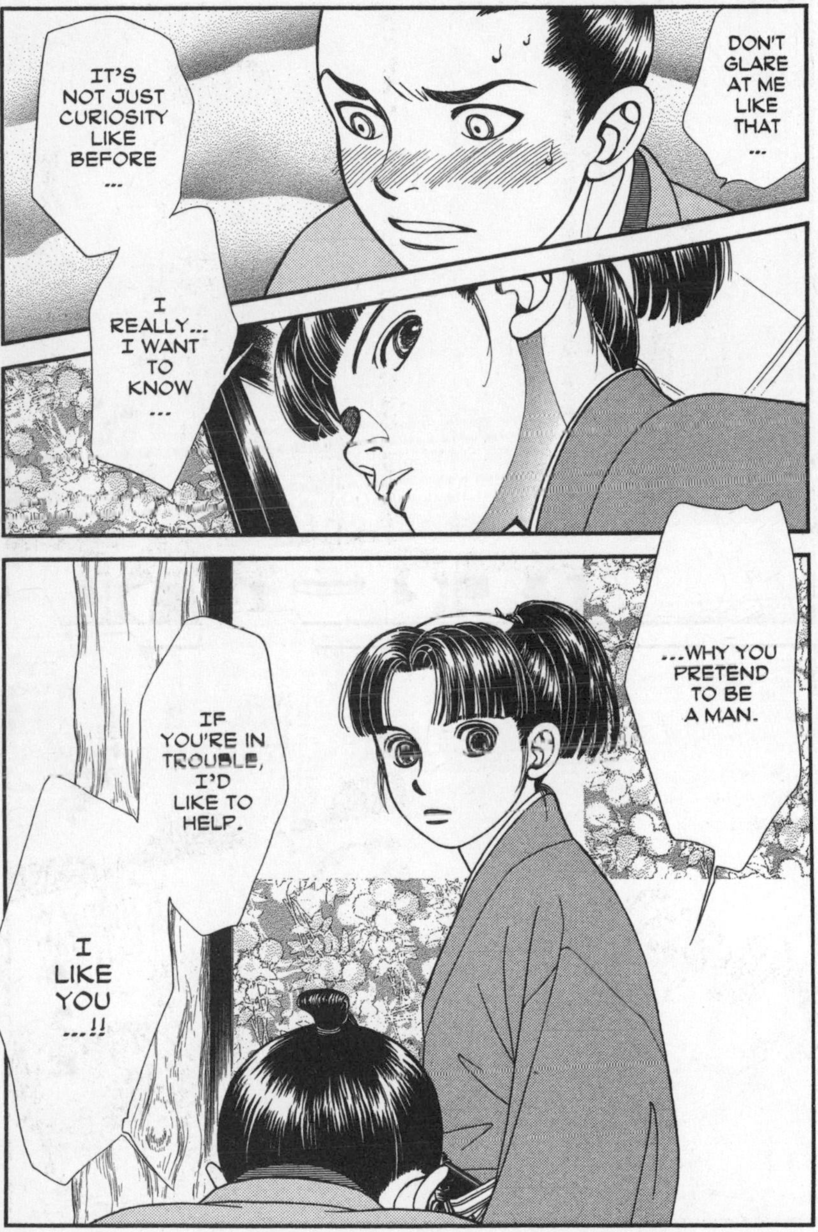
DON'T GLARE AT ME LIKE THAT ...
IT'S NOT JUST CURIOSITY LIKE BEFORE ...
I REALLY... I WANT TO KNOW ...
...WHY YOU PRETEND TO BE A MAN.
IF YOU'RE IN TROUBLE, I'D LIKE TO HELP.
I LIKE YOU ...!!

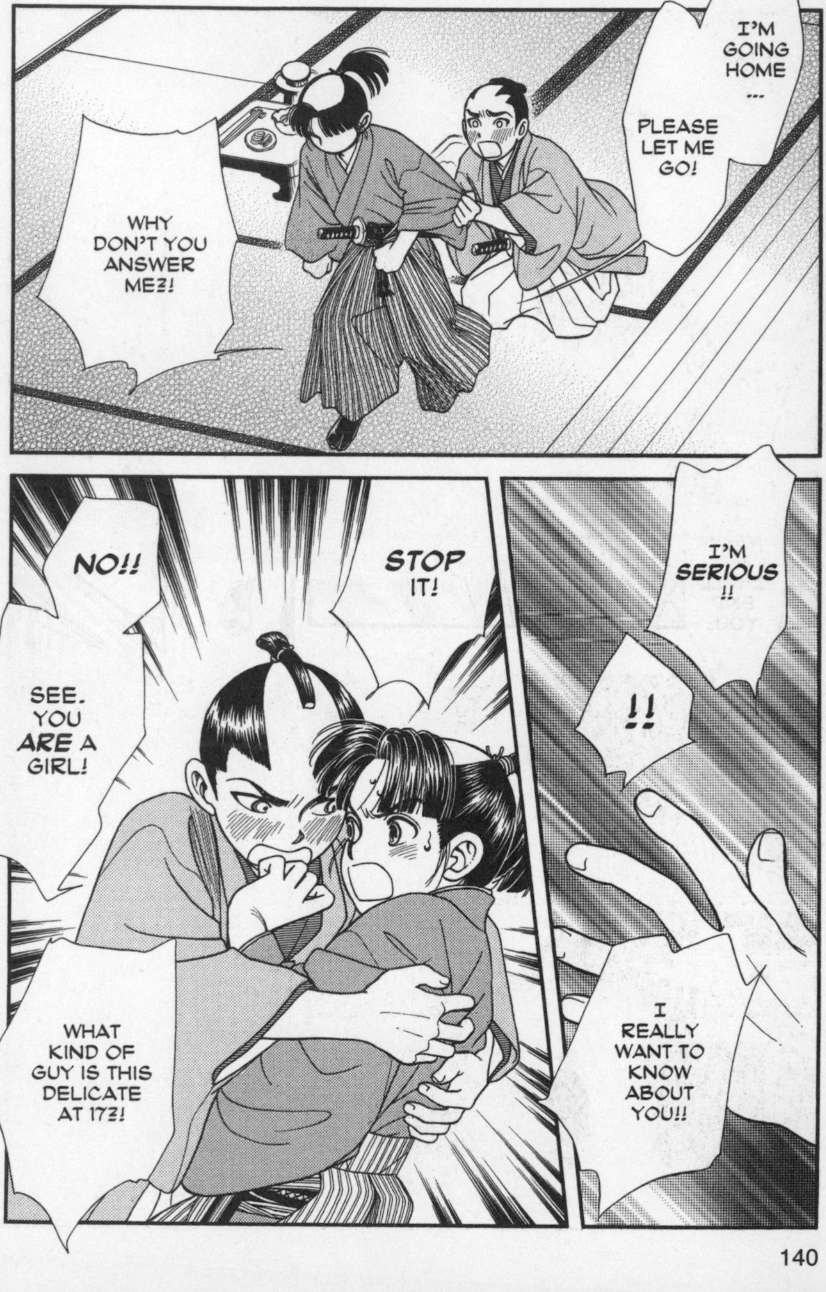
I'M GOING HOME ...
PLEASE LET ME GO!
WHY DON'T YOU ANSWER ME?!
I'M SERIOUS !!
!!
I REALLY WANT TO KNOW ABOUT YOU!!
STOP IT!
NO!!
SEE. YOU ARE A GIRL!
WHAT KIND OF GUY IS THIS DELICATE AT 17?!

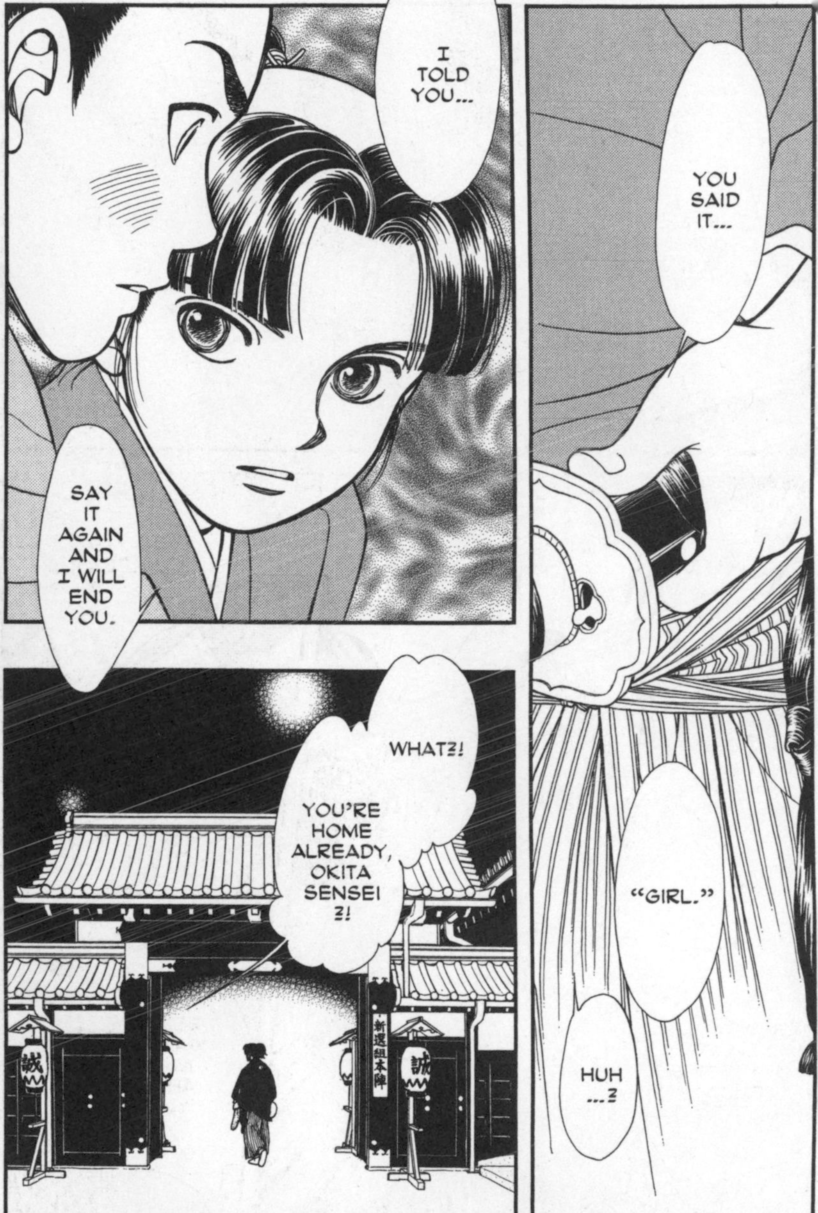
YOU SAID IT...
"GIRL."
HUH ...?
I TOLD YOU...
SAY IT AGAIN AND I WILL END YOU.
WHAT?!
YOU'RE HOME ALREADY, OKITA SENSEI ?!
新選組本陣
誠
誠

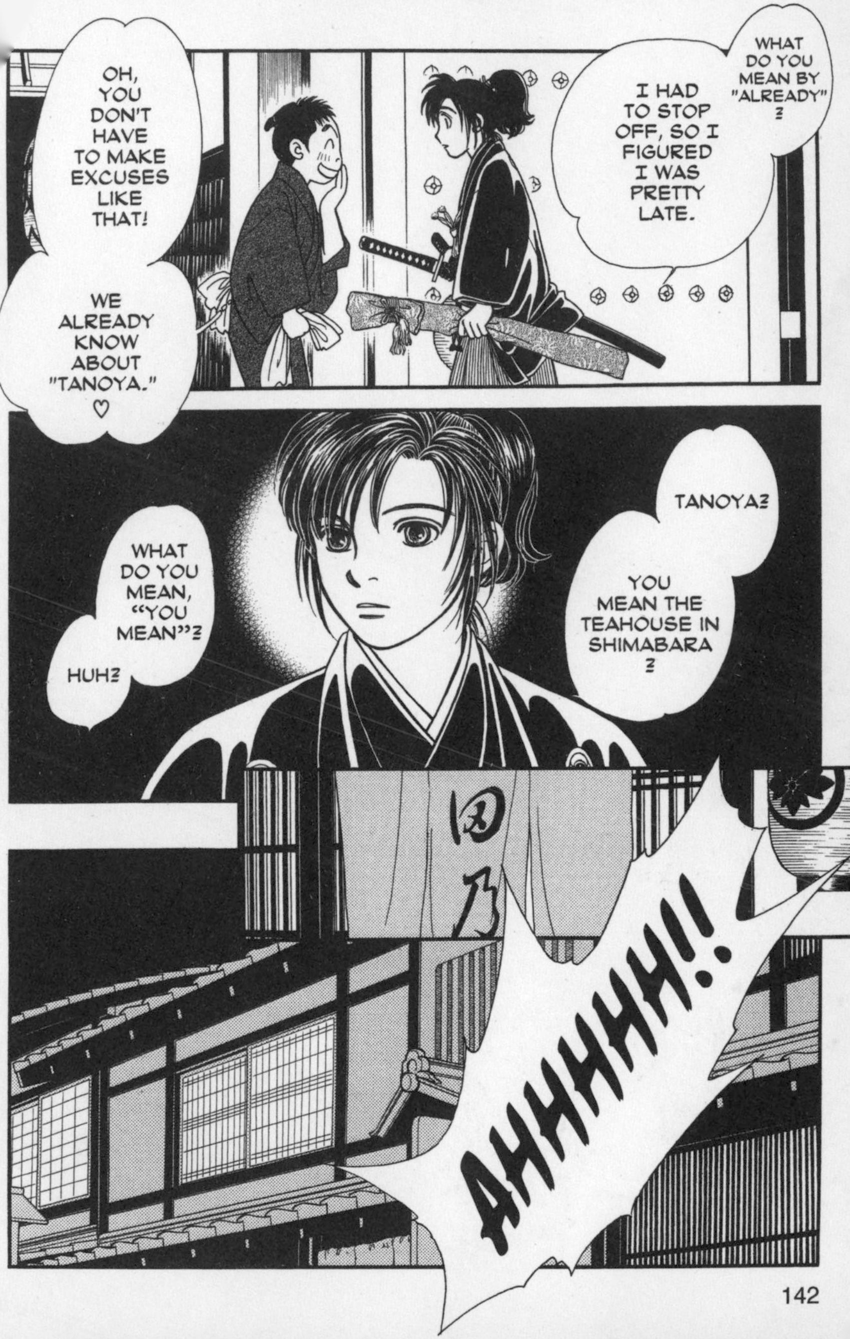
I HAD TO STOP OFF, SO I FIGURED I WAS PRETTY LATE.
OH, YOU DON'T HAVE TO MAKE EXCUSES LIKE THAT!
WE ALREADY KNOW ABOUT "TANOYA." ♡
WHAT DO YOU MEAN BY "ALREADY"?
TANOYA?
YOU MEAN THE TEAHOUSE IN SHIMABARA?
WHAT DO YOU MEAN, "YOU MEAN"?
HUH?
AHHHHH!!

EDO IROHA KARUTA GAME

"KU" く

KUSAIMONO NI FUTA WO SURU
"FIND A TEMPORARY SOLUTION"
(lit. Place a lid on odorous objects)

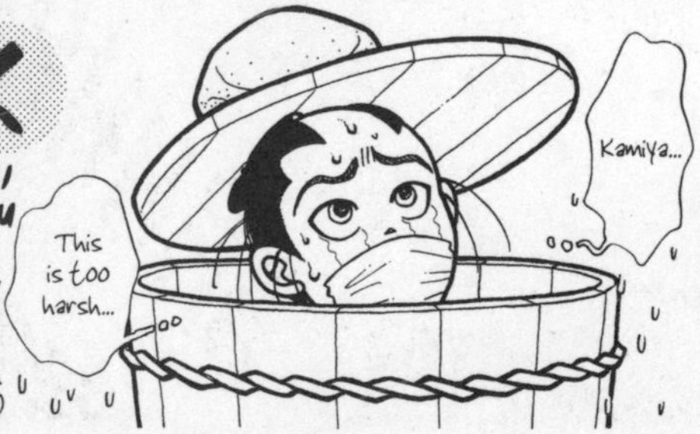
Kamiya...
This is too harsh...

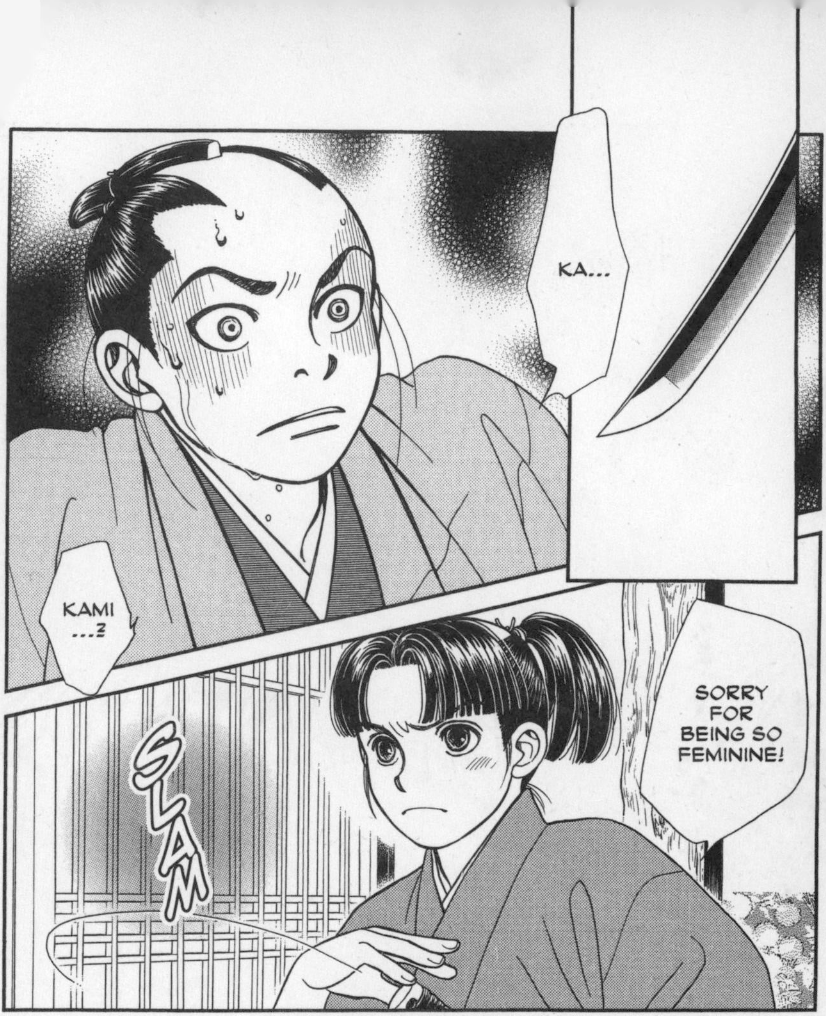
KA...
KAMI ...?
SORRY FOR BEING SO FEMININE!
SLAM

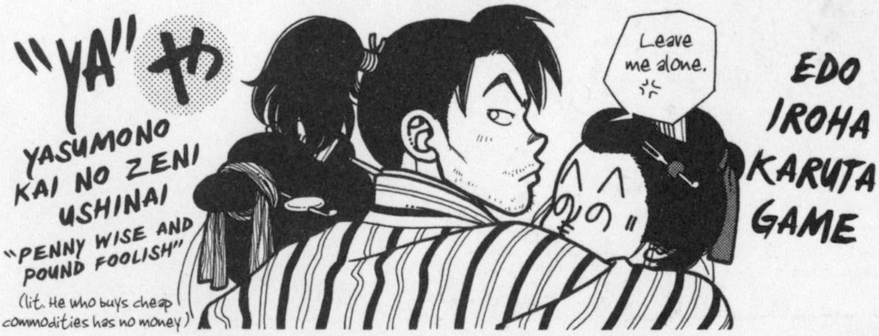
EDO IROHA KARUTA GAME
Leave me alone.
"YA" や
YASUMONO KAI NO ZENI USHINAI
"PENNY WISE AND POUND FOOLISH"
(lit. He who buys cheap commodities has no money)

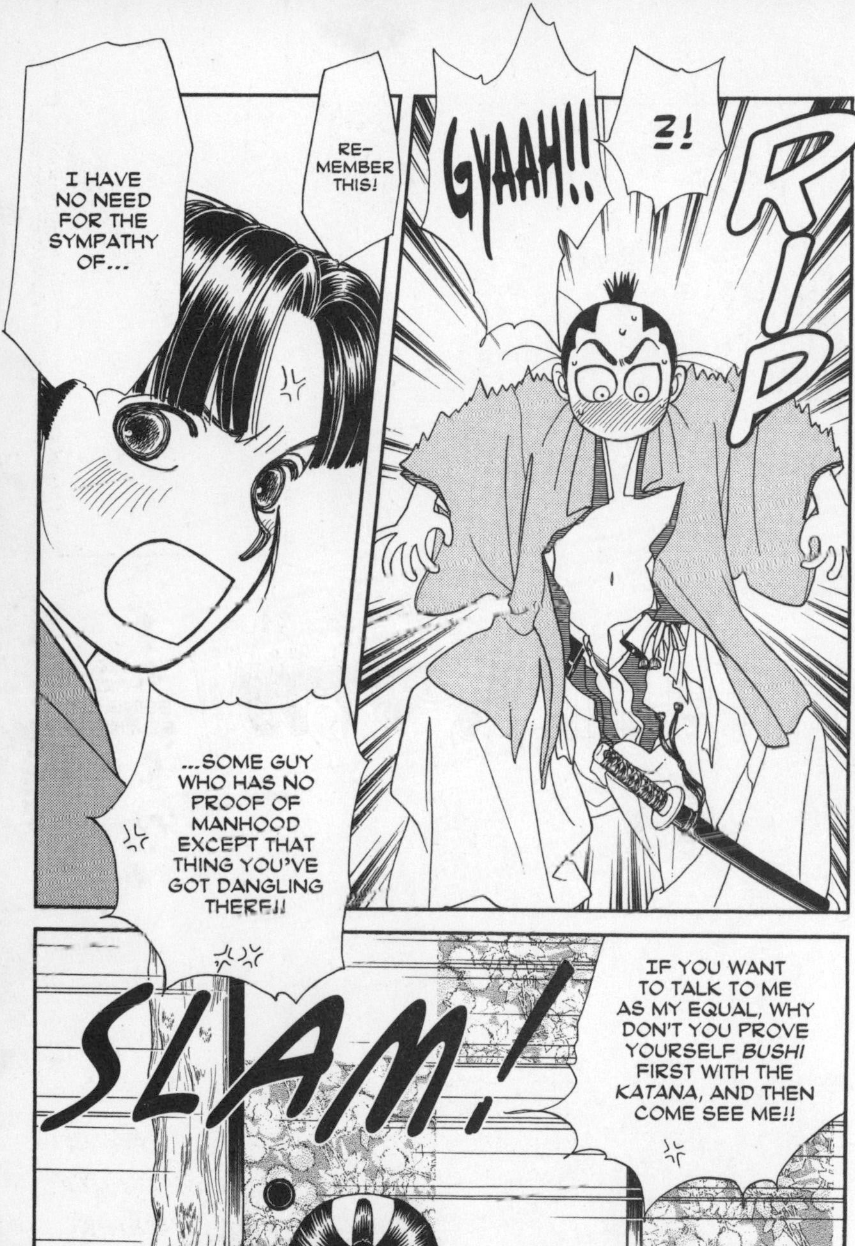
RIP
GYAAH!!
RE-MEMBER THIS!
I HAVE NO NEED FOR THE SYMPATHY OF...
...SOME GUY WHO HAS NO PROOF OF MANHOOD EXCEPT THAT THING YOU'VE GOT DANGLING THERE!!
IF YOU WANT TO TALK TO ME AS MY EQUAL, WHY DON'T YOU PROVE YOURSELF *BUSHI* FIRST WITH THE *KATANA*, AND THEN COME SEE ME!!
SLAM!

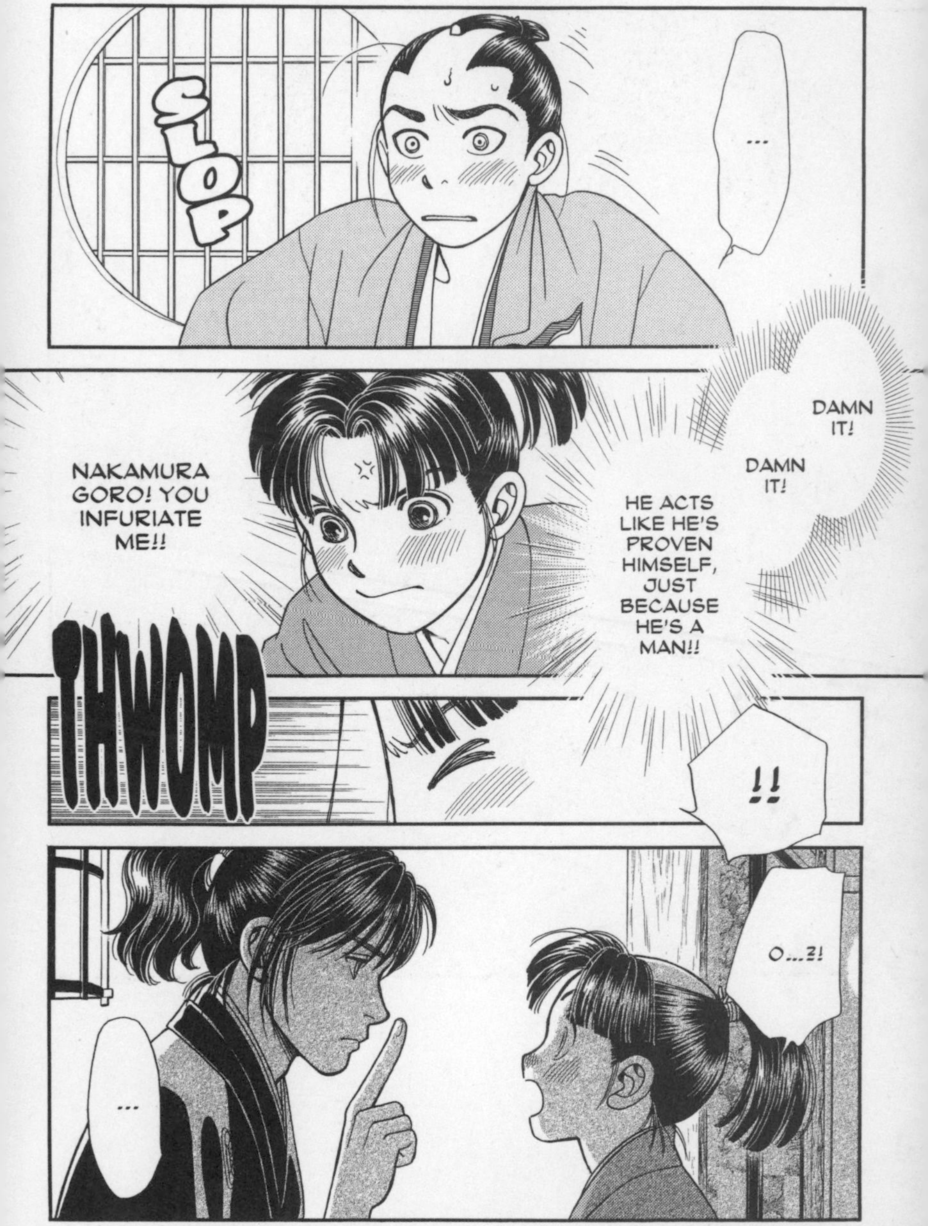
...
SLOP
DAMN IT!
DAMN IT!
HE ACTS LIKE HE'S PROVEN HIMSELF, JUST BECAUSE HE'S A MAN!!
NAKAMURA GORO! YOU INFURIATE ME!!
!!
THWOMP
O...?!
...

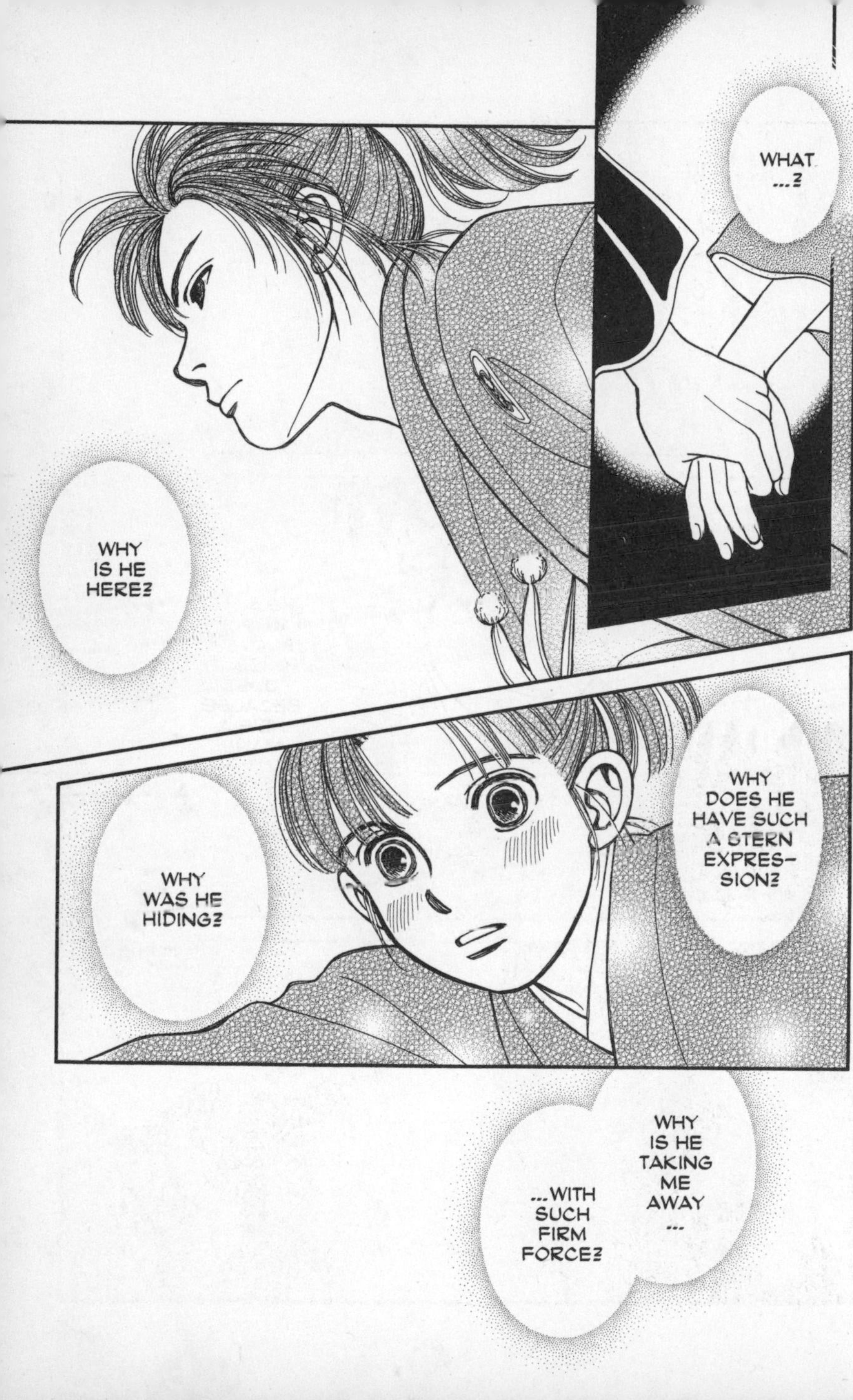
WHAT ...?
WHY IS HE HERE?
WHY DOES HE HAVE SUCH A STERN EXPRES- SION?
WHY WAS HE HIDING?
WHY IS HE TAKING ME AWAY ...
...WITH SUCH FIRM FORCE?

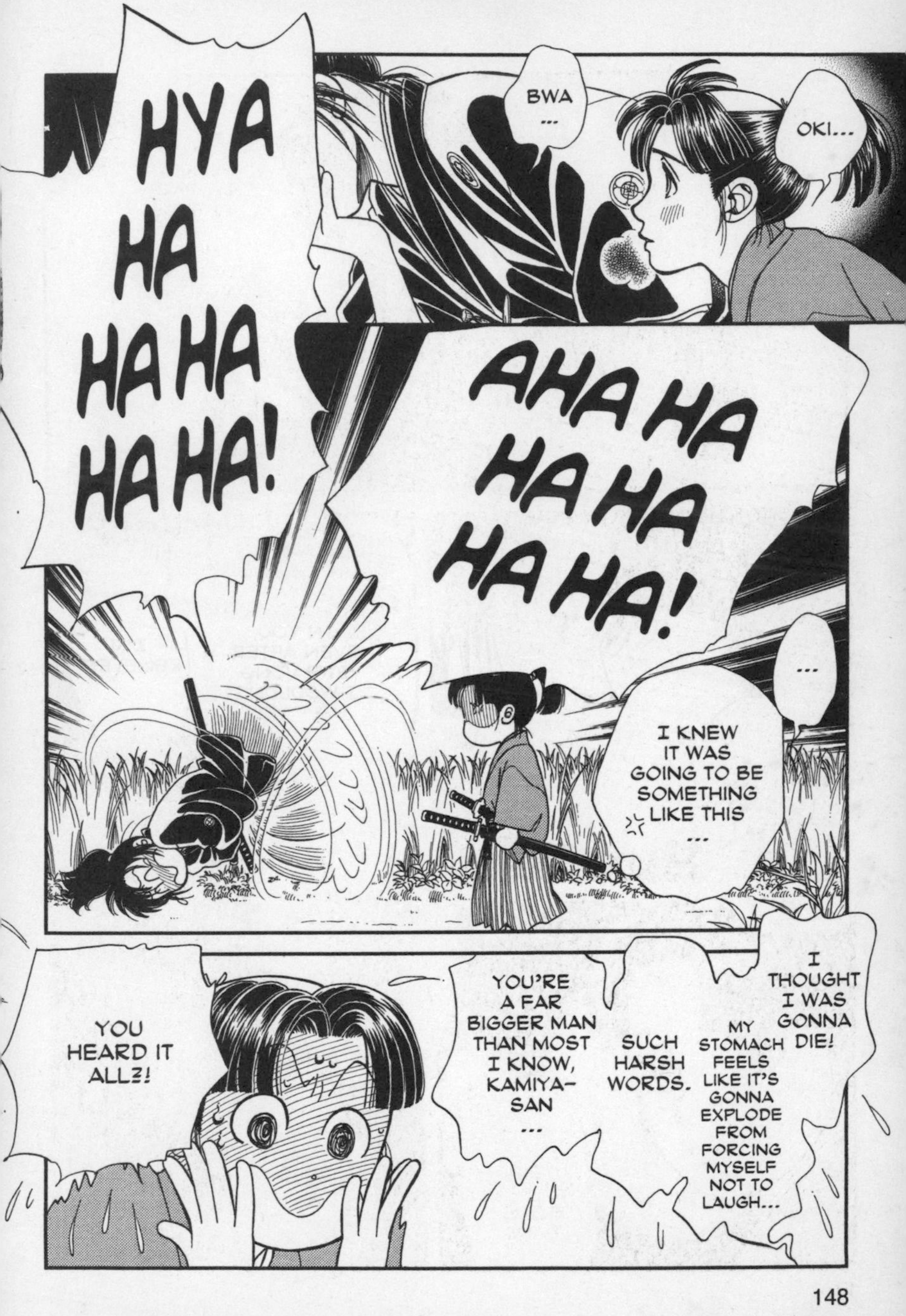
OKI...
BWA ...
HYA HA HA HA HA HA!
AHA HA HA HA HA HA HA HA!
...
I KNEW IT WAS GOING TO BE SOMETHING LIKE THIS ...
I THOUGHT I WAS GONNA DIE!
MY STOMACH FEELS LIKE IT'S GONNA EXPLODE FROM FORCING MYSELF NOT TO LAUGH...
SUCH HARSH WORDS.
YOU'RE A FAR BIGGER MAN THAN MOST I KNOW, KAMIYA-SAN ...
YOU HEARD IT ALL?!

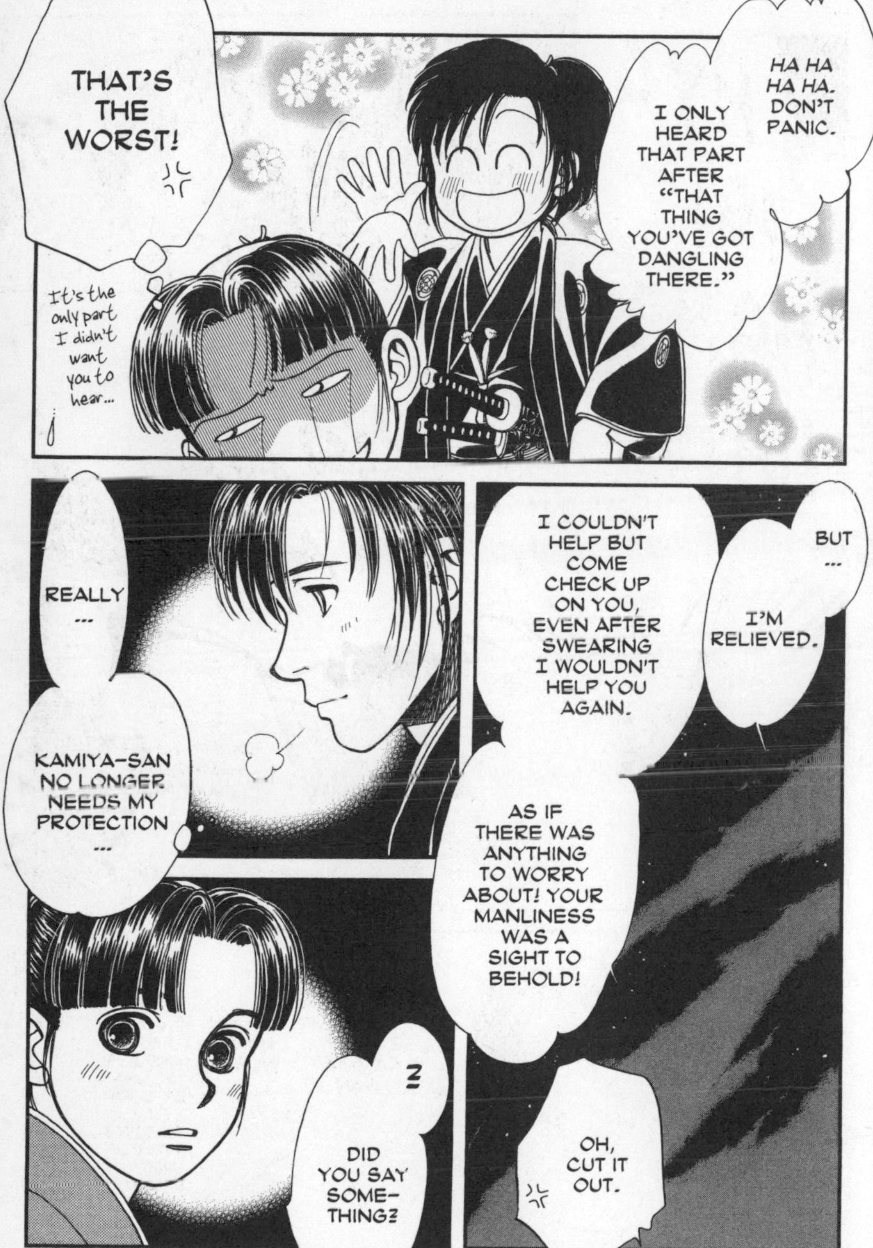
HA HA HA HA. DON'T PANIC.
I ONLY HEARD THAT PART AFTER "THAT THING YOU'VE GOT DANGLING THERE."
THAT'S THE WORST!
It's the only part I didn't want you to hear...
BUT ...
I'M RELIEVED.
I COULDN'T HELP BUT COME CHECK UP ON YOU, EVEN AFTER SWEARING I WOULDN'T HELP YOU AGAIN.
AS IF THERE WAS ANYTHING TO WORRY ABOUT! YOUR MANLINESS WAS A SIGHT TO BEHOLD!
OH, CUT IT OUT.
REALLY ...
KAMIYA-SAN NO LONGER NEEDS MY PROTECTION ...
DID YOU SAY SOME-THING?

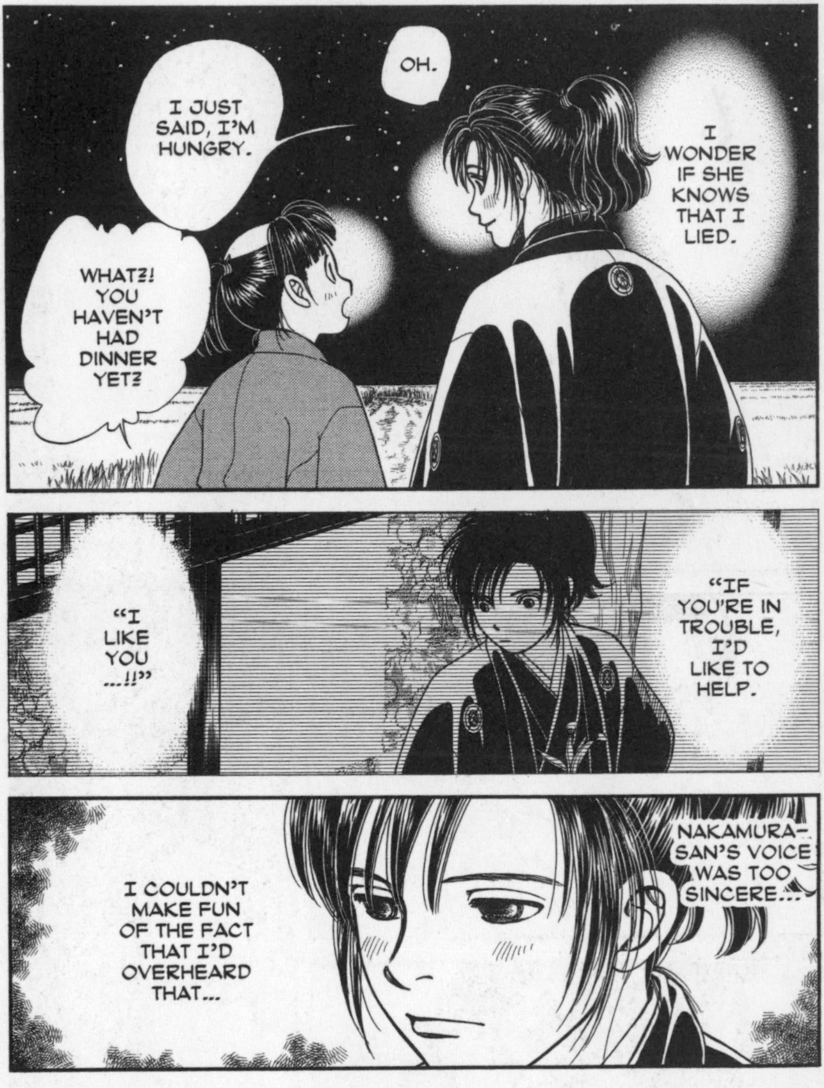
WHAT?! YOU HAVEN'T HAD DINNER YET?
I JUST SAID, I'M HUNGRY.
OH.
I WONDER IF SHE KNOWS THAT I LIED.
"IF YOU'RE IN TROUBLE, I'D LIKE TO HELP.
"I LIKE YOU ...!!"
NAKAMURA-SAN'S VOICE WAS TOO SINCERE...
I COULDN'T MAKE FUN OF THE FACT THAT I'D OVERHEARD THAT...
"WHY YOU PRETEND TO BE A MAN..."

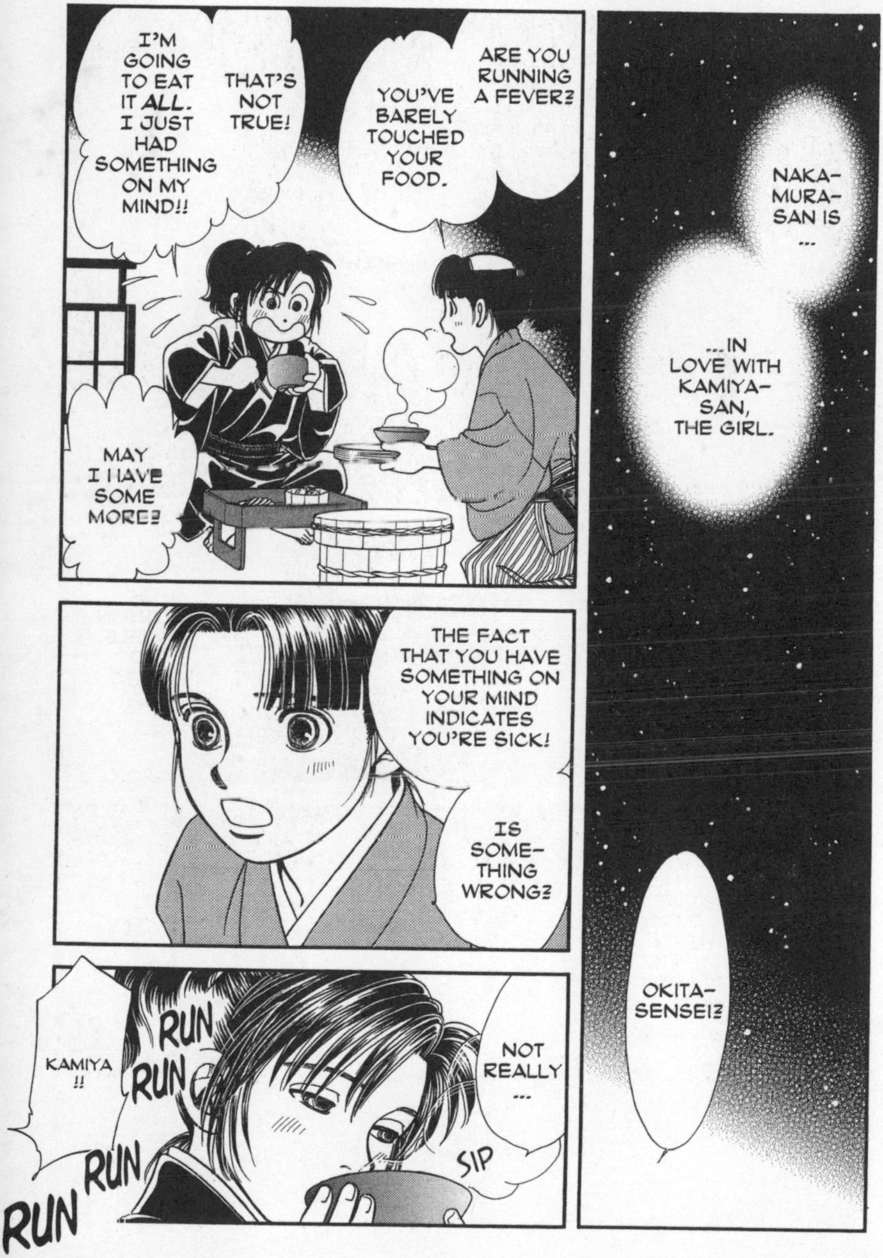
NAKA-MURA-SAN IS ...
...IN LOVE WITH KAMIYA-SAN, THE GIRL.
OKITA-SENSEI!?
ARE YOU RUNNING A FEVER?
YOU'VE BARELY TOUCHED YOUR FOOD.
THAT'S NOT TRUE!
I'M GOING TO EAT IT *ALL*. I JUST HAD SOMETHING ON MY MIND!!
MAY I HAVE SOME MORE?
THE FACT THAT YOU HAVE SOMETHING ON YOUR MIND INDICATES YOU'RE SICK!
IS SOME-THING WRONG?
NOT REALLY ...
SIP
RUN
RUN
KAMIYA !!
RUN
RUN
RUN

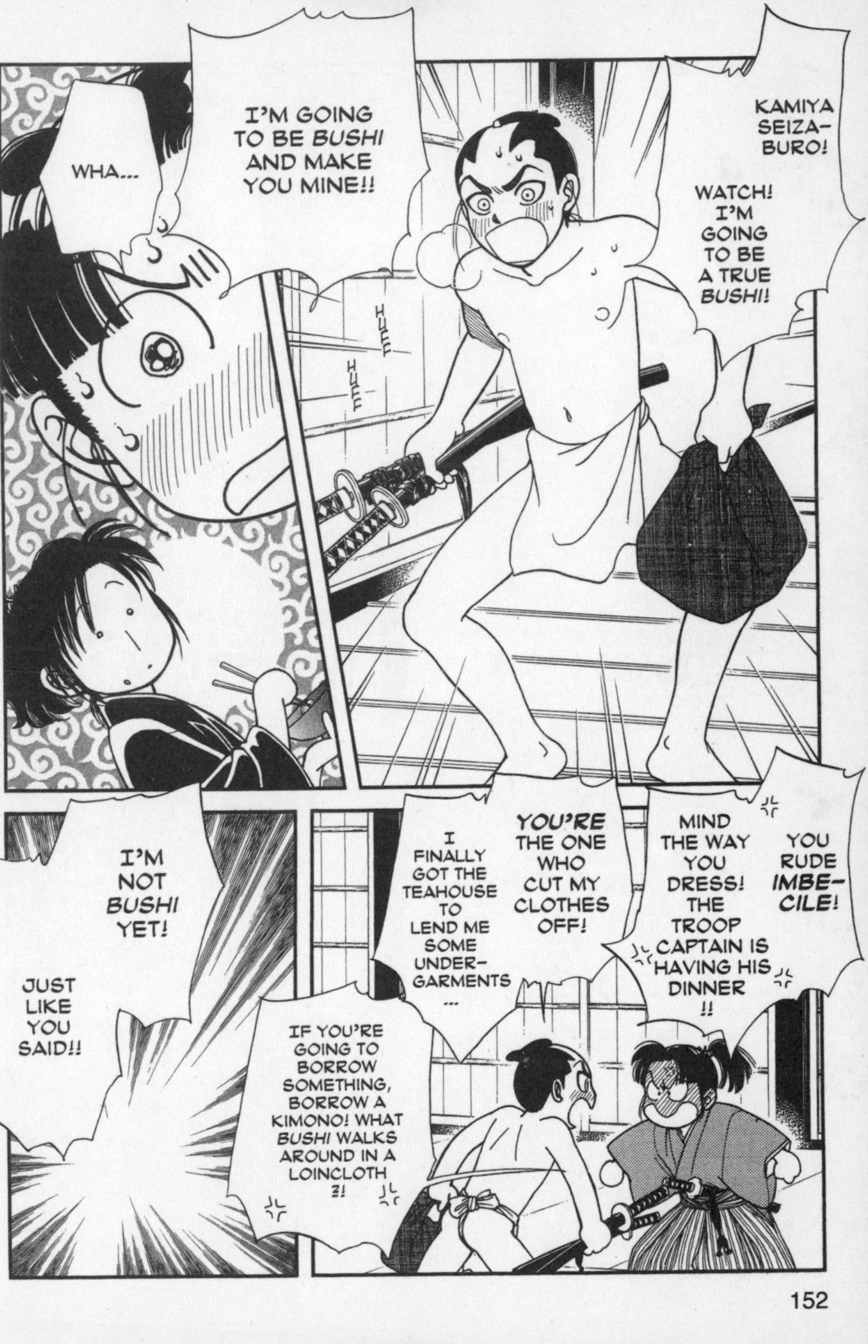
KAMIYA SEIZABURO!
WATCH! I'M GOING TO BE A TRUE *BUSHI*!
I'M GOING TO BE *BUSHI* AND MAKE YOU MINE!!
HUFF
HUFF
WHA...
YOU RUDE *IMBECILE*!
MIND THE WAY YOU DRESS! THE TROOP CAPTAIN IS HAVING HIS DINNER!!
YOU'RE THE ONE WHO CUT MY CLOTHES OFF!
I FINALLY GOT THE TEAHOUSE TO LEND ME SOME UNDERGARMENTS...
IF YOU'RE GOING TO BORROW SOMETHING, BORROW A KIMONO! WHAT *BUSHI* WALKS AROUND IN A LOINCLOTH?!
I'M NOT *BUSHI* YET!
JUST LIKE YOU SAID!!

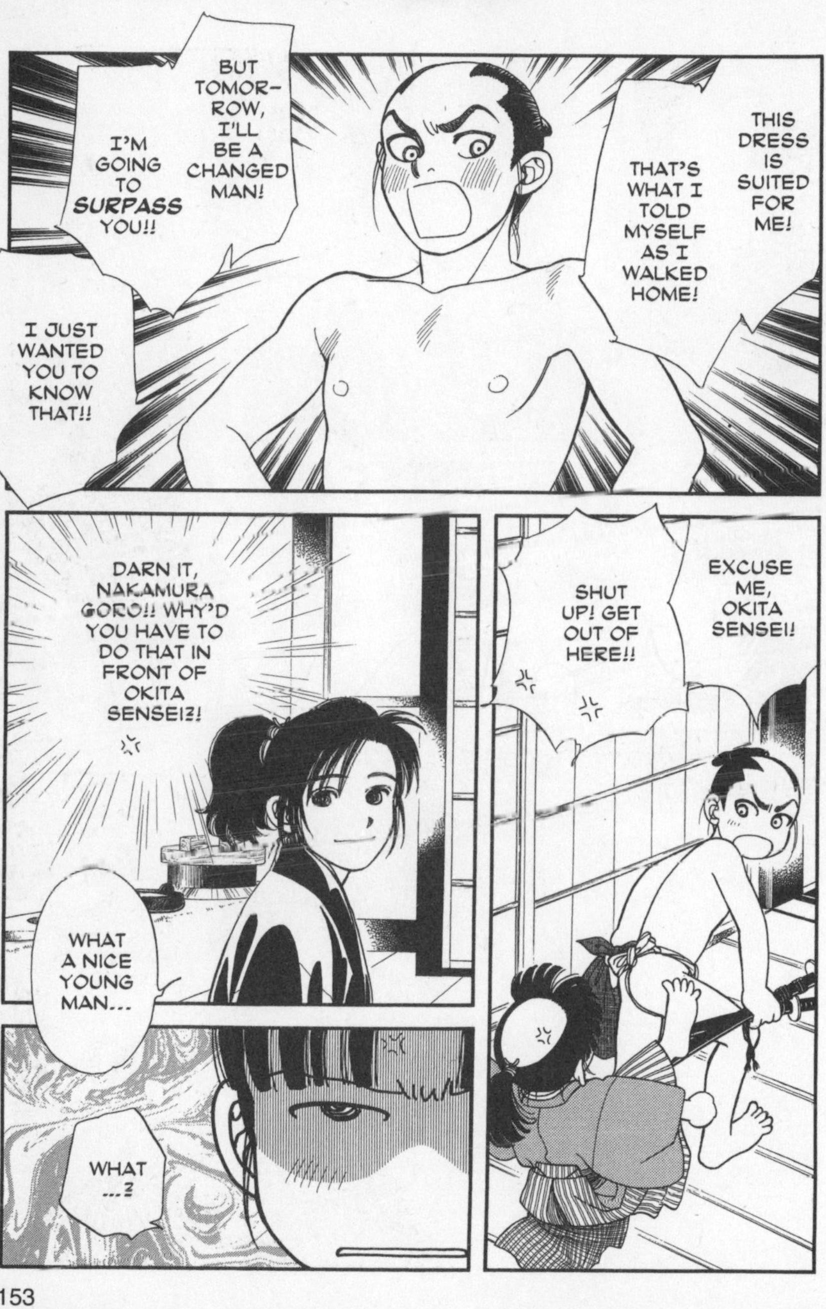
THIS DRESS IS SUITED FOR ME!
THAT'S WHAT I TOLD MYSELF AS I WALKED HOME!
BUT TOMORROW, I'LL BE A CHANGED MAN!
I'M GOING TO SURPASS YOU!!
I JUST WANTED YOU TO KNOW THAT!!
EXCUSE ME, OKITA SENSEI!
SHUT UP! GET OUT OF HERE!!
DARN IT, NAKAMURA GORO!! WHY'D YOU HAVE TO DO THAT IN FRONT OF OKITA SENSEI?!
WHAT A NICE YOUNG MAN...
WHAT ...?

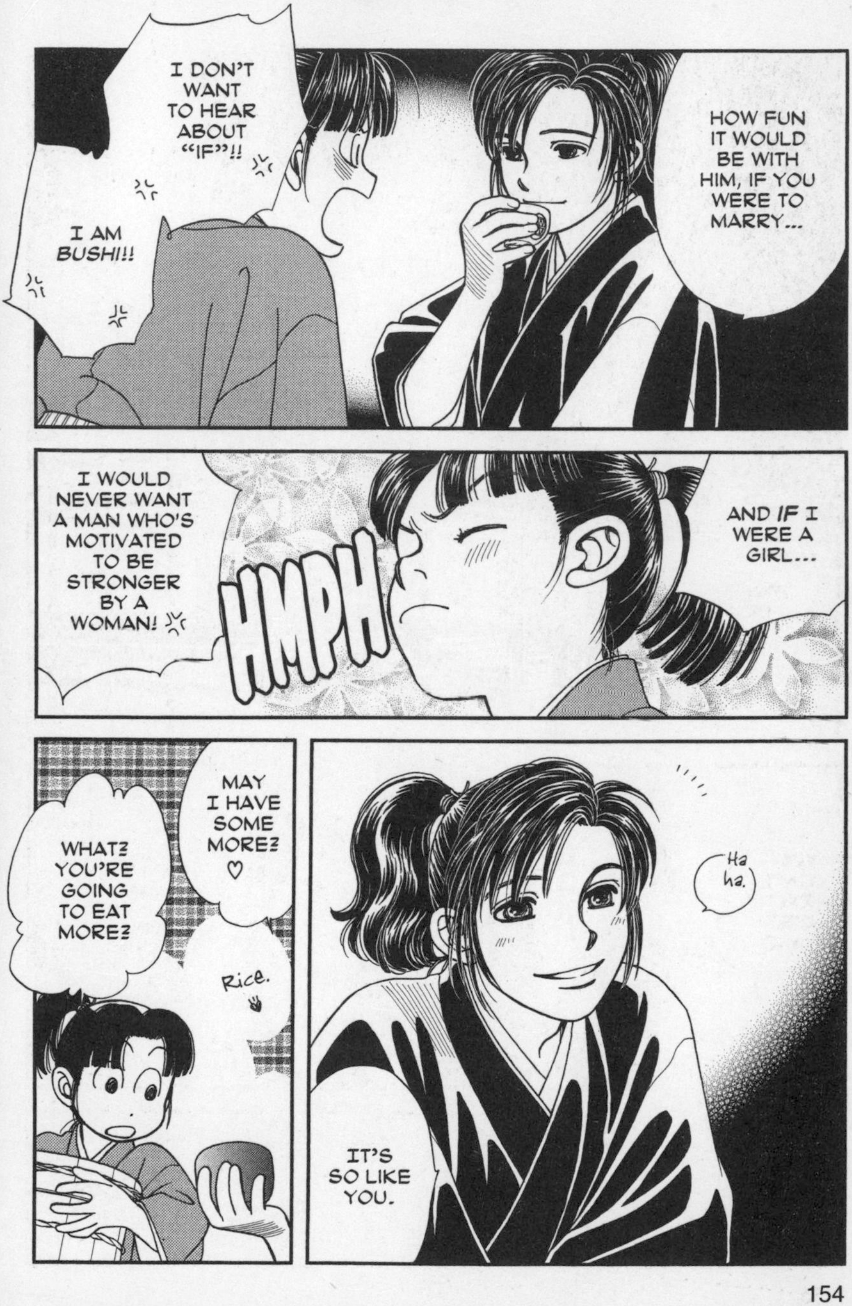
HOW FUN IT WOULD BE WITH HIM, IF YOU WERE TO MARRY...
I DON'T WANT TO HEAR ABOUT "IF"!!
I AM *BUSHI*!!!
AND *IF* I WERE A GIRL...
I WOULD NEVER WANT A MAN WHO'S MOTIVATED TO BE STRONGER BY A WOMAN!
HMPH
Ha ha.
IT'S SO LIKE YOU.
MAY I HAVE SOME MORE? ♡
WHAT? YOU'RE GOING TO EAT MORE?
Rice.

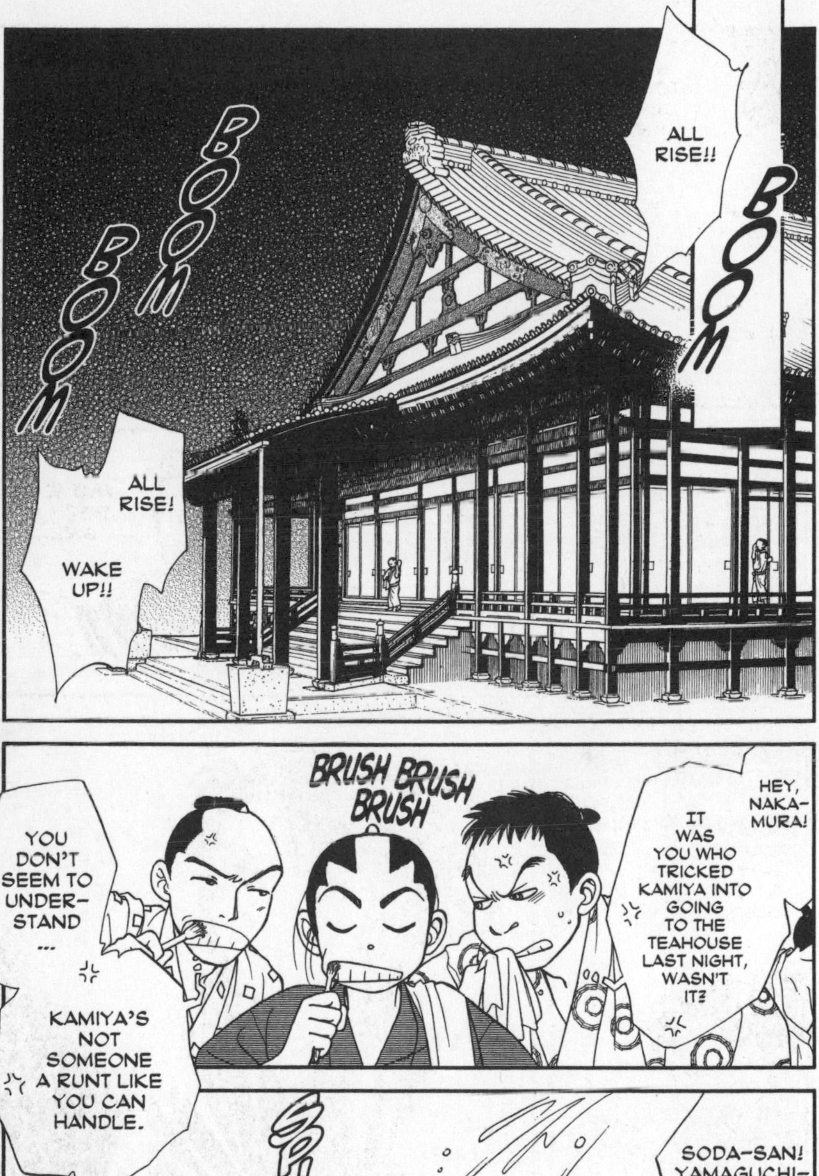
ALL RISE!!
BOOM
BOOM
BOOM
ALL RISE!
WAKE UP!!
BRUSH BRUSH BRUSH
HEY, NAKA-MURA!
IT WAS YOU WHO TRICKED KAMIYA INTO GOING TO THE TEAHOUSE LAST NIGHT, WASN'T IT?
YOU DON'T SEEM TO UNDER-STAND ...
KAMIYA'S NOT SOMEONE A RUNT LIKE YOU CAN HANDLE.
SODA-SAN! YAMAGUCHI-SAN!
SPIT

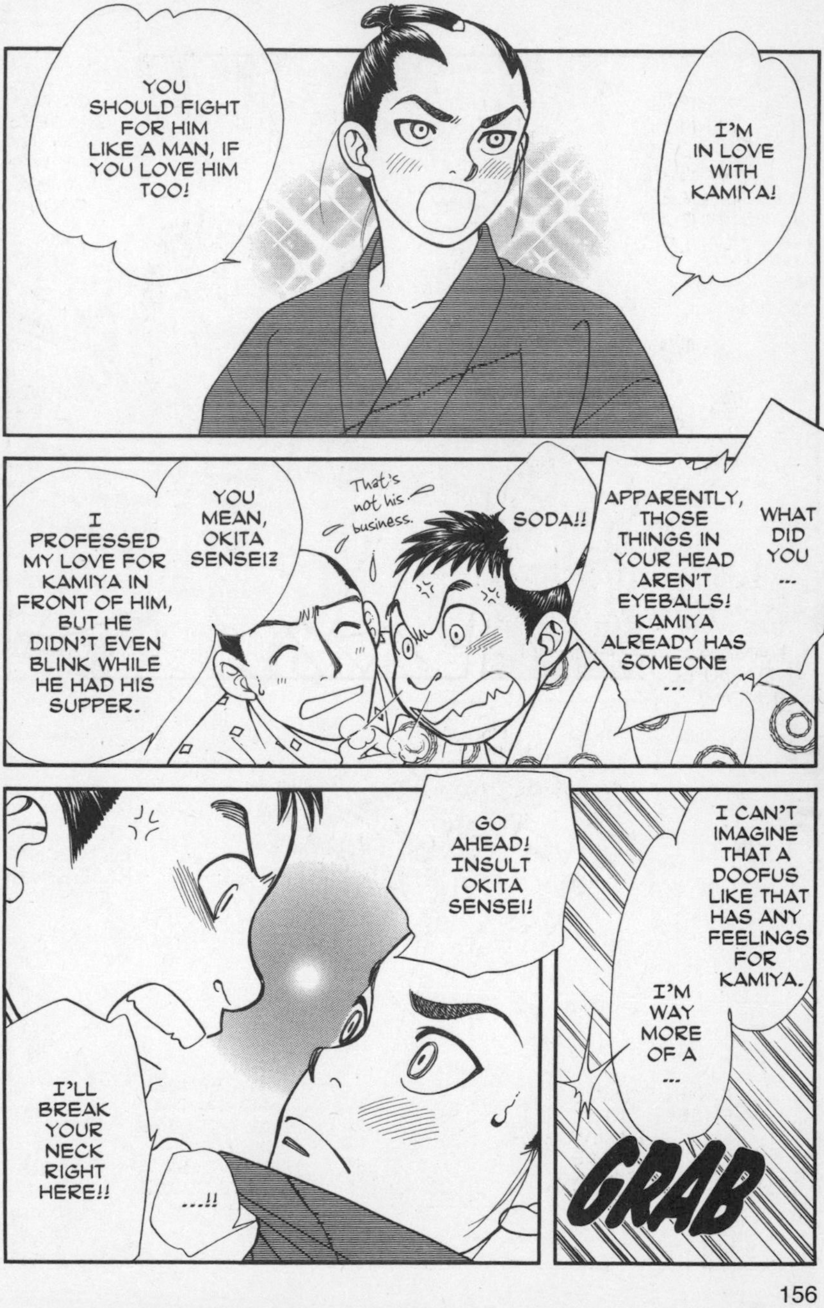
I'M IN LOVE WITH KAMIYA!
YOU SHOULD FIGHT FOR HIM LIKE A MAN, IF YOU LOVE HIM TOO!
WHAT DID YOU ...
APPARENTLY, THOSE THINGS IN YOUR HEAD AREN'T EYEBALLS! KAMIYA ALREADY HAS SOMEONE ...
SODA!!
That's not his business.
YOU MEAN, OKITA SENSEI!?
I PROFESSED MY LOVE FOR KAMIYA IN FRONT OF HIM, BUT HE DIDN'T EVEN BLINK WHILE HE HAD HIS SUPPER.
I CAN'T IMAGINE THAT A DOOFUS LIKE THAT HAS ANY FEELINGS FOR KAMIYA.
I'M WAY MORE OF A ...
GRAB
GO AHEAD! INSULT OKITA SENSEI!
I'LL BREAK YOUR NECK RIGHT HERE!!
...!!

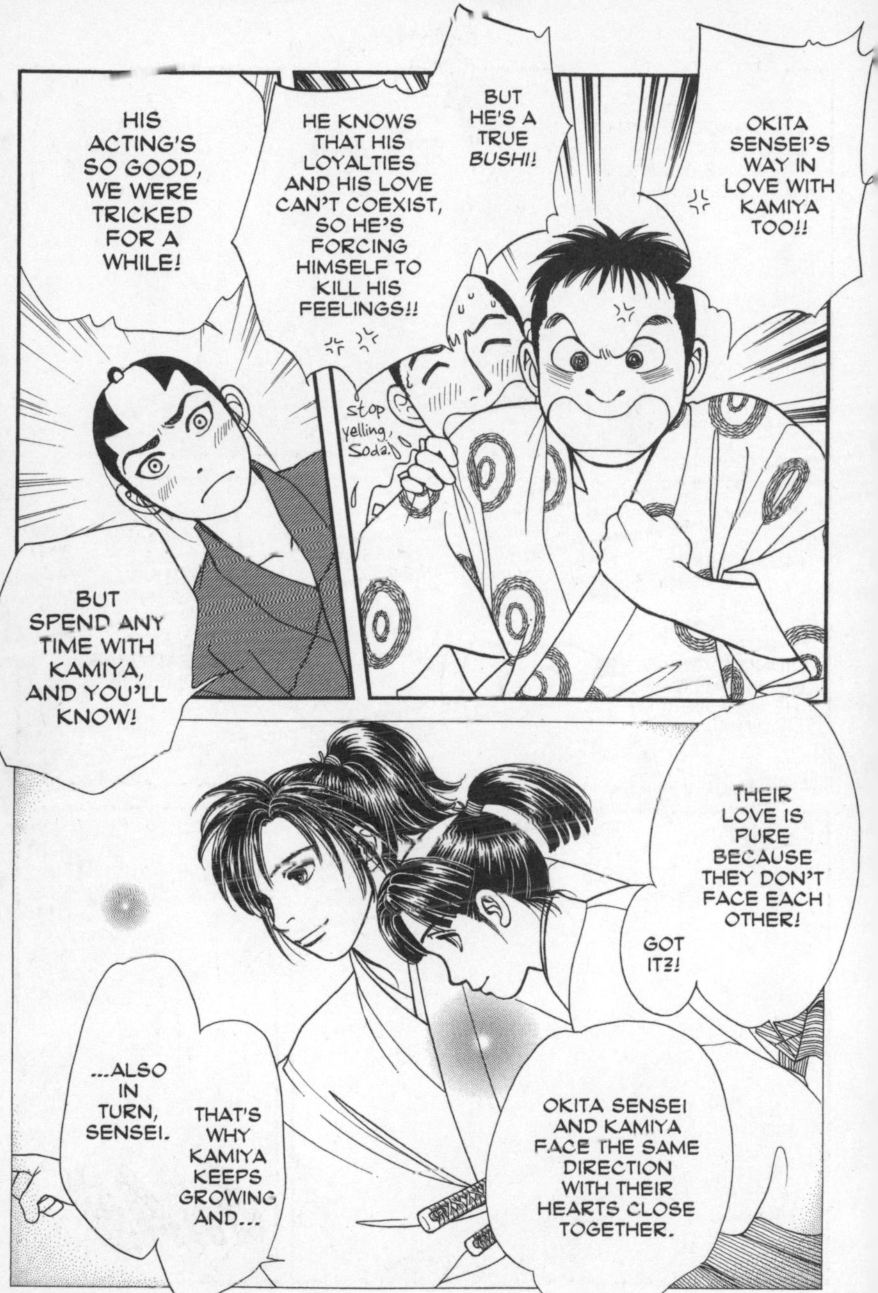
OKITA SENSEI'S WAY IN LOVE WITH KAMIYA TOO!!
BUT HE'S A TRUE *BUSHI*!
HE KNOWS THAT HIS LOYALTIES AND HIS LOVE CAN'T COEXIST, SO HE'S FORCING HIMSELF TO KILL HIS FEELINGS!!
HIS ACTING'S SO GOOD, WE WERE TRICKED FOR A WHILE!
stop yelling, Soda!
BUT SPEND ANY TIME WITH KAMIYA, AND YOU'LL KNOW!
THEIR LOVE IS PURE BECAUSE THEY DON'T FACE EACH OTHER!
GOT IT?!
OKITA SENSEI AND KAMIYA FACE THE SAME DIRECTION WITH THEIR HEARTS CLOSE TOGETHER.
THAT'S WHY KAMIYA KEEPS GROWING AND...
...ALSO IN TURN, SENSEI.

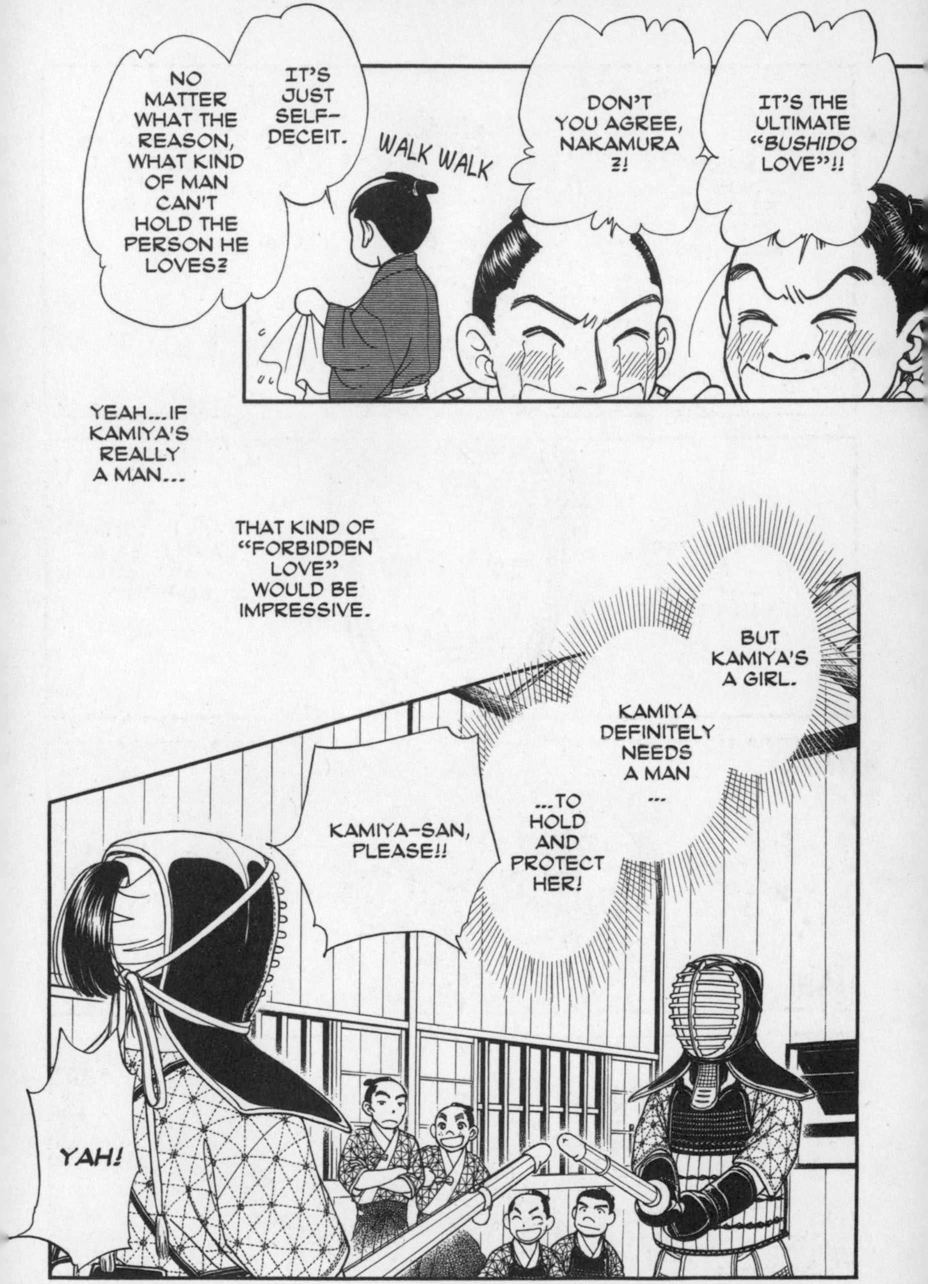
IT'S THE ULTIMATE "BUSHIDO LOVE"!!
DON'T YOU AGREE, NAKAMURA ?!
WALK WALK
IT'S JUST SELF-DECEIT.
NO MATTER WHAT THE REASON, WHAT KIND OF MAN CAN'T HOLD THE PERSON HE LOVES?
YEAH...IF KAMIYA'S REALLY A MAN...
THAT KIND OF "FORBIDDEN LOVE" WOULD BE IMPRESSIVE.
BUT KAMIYA'S A GIRL.
KAMIYA DEFINITELY NEEDS A MAN ...
...TO HOLD AND PROTECT HER!
KAMIYA-SAN, PLEASE!!
YAH!

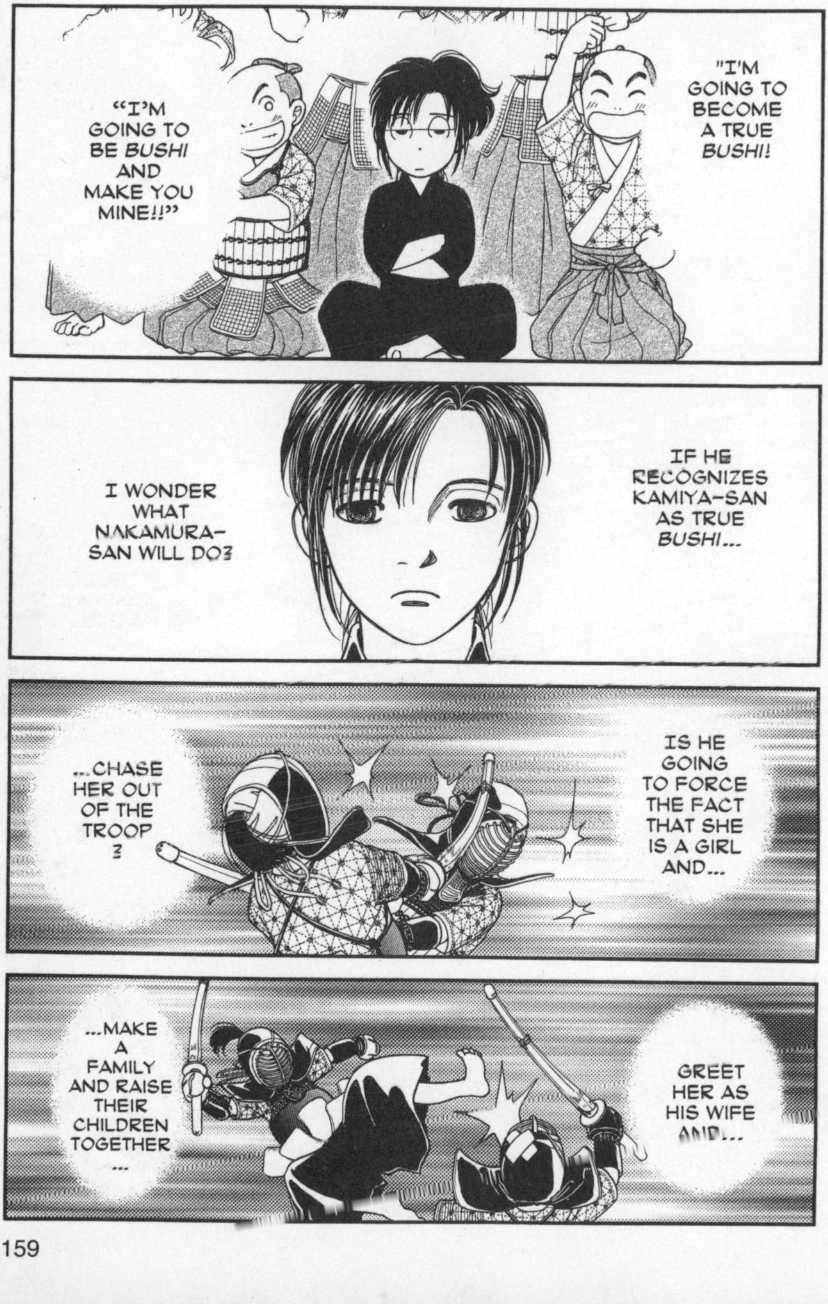
"I'M GOING TO BECOME A TRUE *BUSHI*!
"I'M GOING TO BE *BUSHI* AND MAKE YOU MINE!!"
IF HE RECOGNIZES KAMIYA-SAN AS TRUE *BUSHI*...
I WONDER WHAT NAKAMURA-SAN WILL DO?
IS HE GOING TO FORCE THE FACT THAT SHE IS A GIRL AND...
...CHASE HER OUT OF THE TROOP?
GREET HER AS HIS WIFE AND...
...MAKE A FAMILY AND RAISE THEIR CHILDREN TOGETHER...

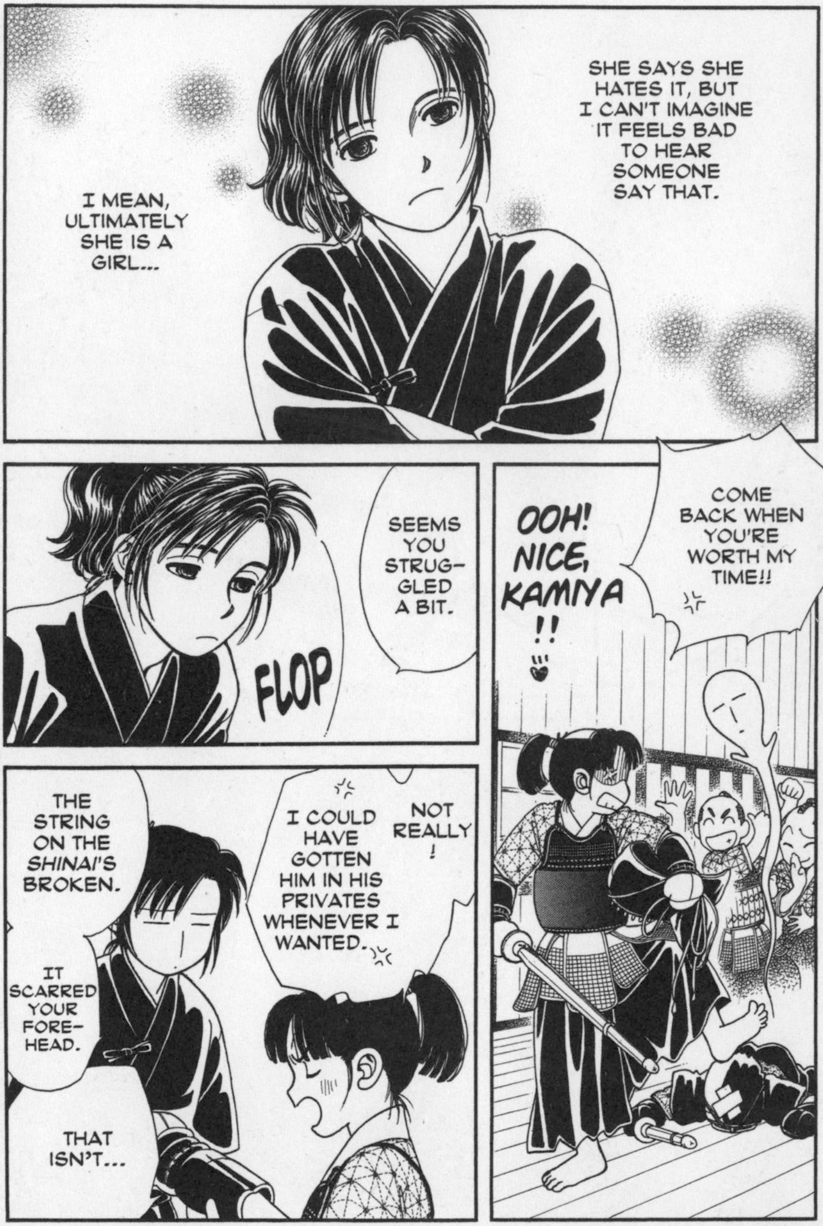
SHE SAYS SHE HATES IT, BUT I CAN'T IMAGINE IT FEELS BAD TO HEAR SOMEONE SAY THAT.
I MEAN, ULTIMATELY SHE IS A GIRL...
COME BACK WHEN YOU'RE WORTH MY TIME!!
OOH! NICE, KAMIYA!!
SEEMS YOU STRUG-GLED A BIT.
FLOP
NOT REALLY!
I COULD HAVE GOTTEN HIM IN HIS PRIVATES WHENEVER I WANTED.
THE STRING ON THE *SHINAI'S* BROKEN.
IT SCARRED YOUR FORE-HEAD.
THAT ISN'T...

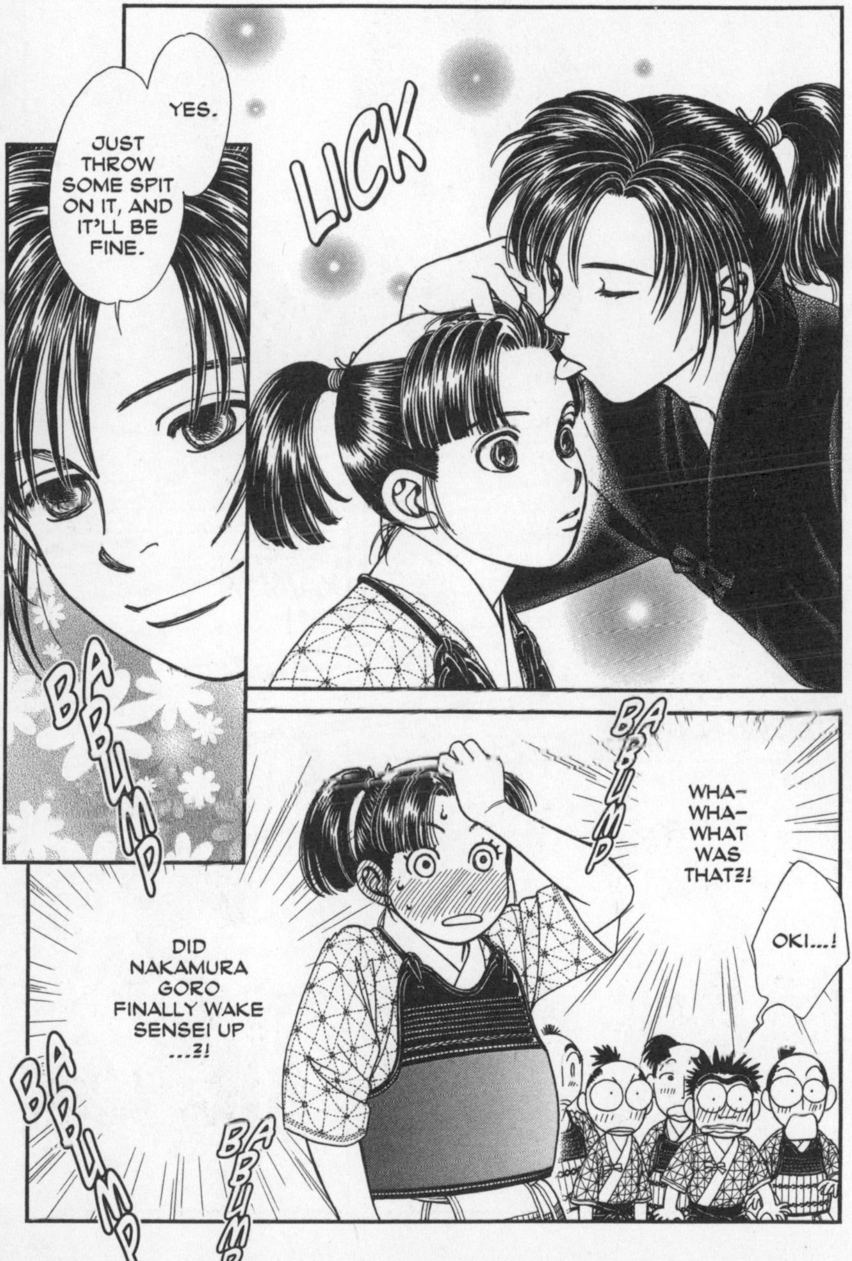
YES. JUST THROW SOME SPIT ON IT, AND IT'LL BE FINE.
LICK
BABUMP
BABUMP
WHA-WHA-WHAT WAS THAT?!
OKI...!
DID NAKAMURA GORO FINALLY WAKE SENSEI UP ...?!
BABUMP
BABUMP

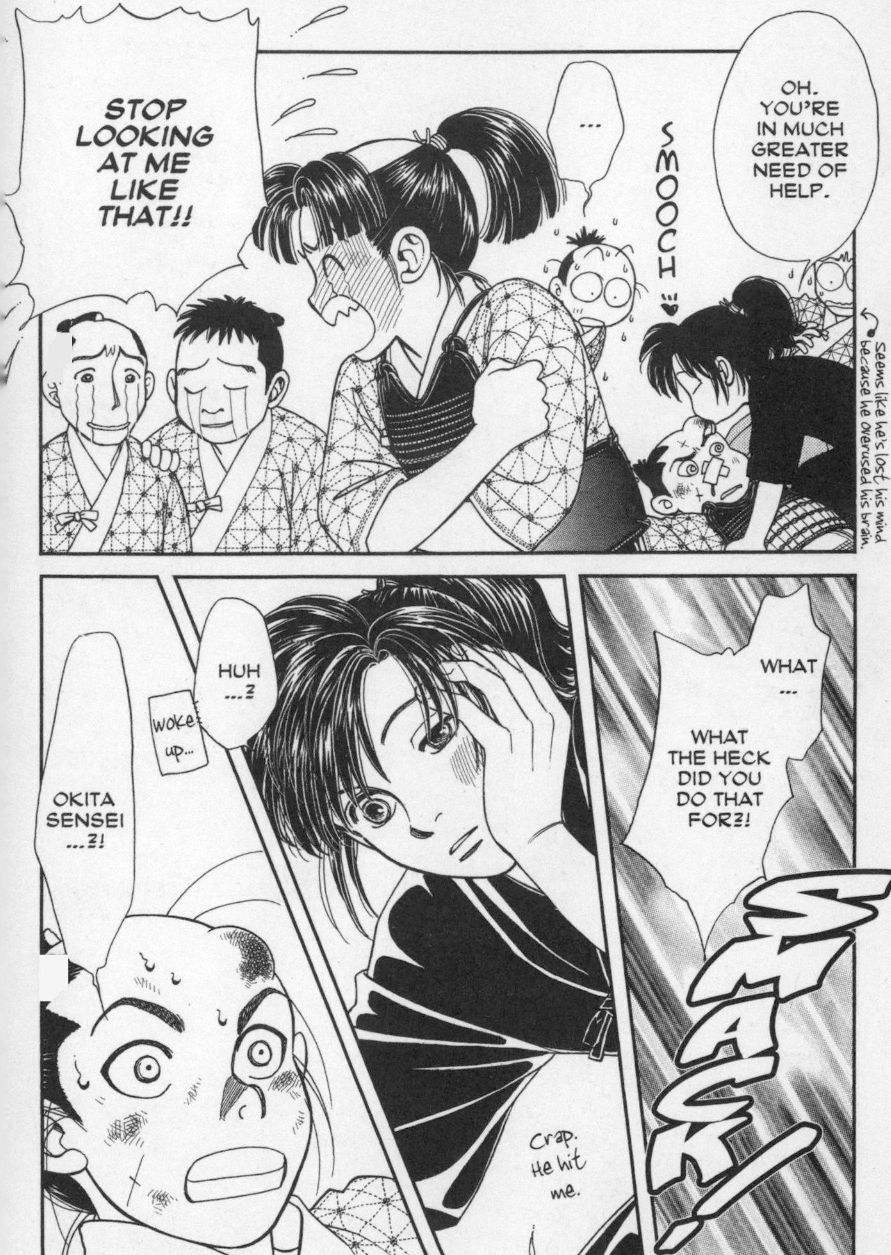
OH. YOU'RE IN MUCH GREATER NEED OF HELP.
Seems like he's lost his mind because he overused his brain.
SMOOCH
...
STOP LOOKING AT ME LIKE THAT!!
WHAT ...
WHAT THE HECK DID YOU DO THAT FOR?!
SMACK!
HUH ...?
Crap. He hit me.
woke up...
OKITA SENSEI ...?!

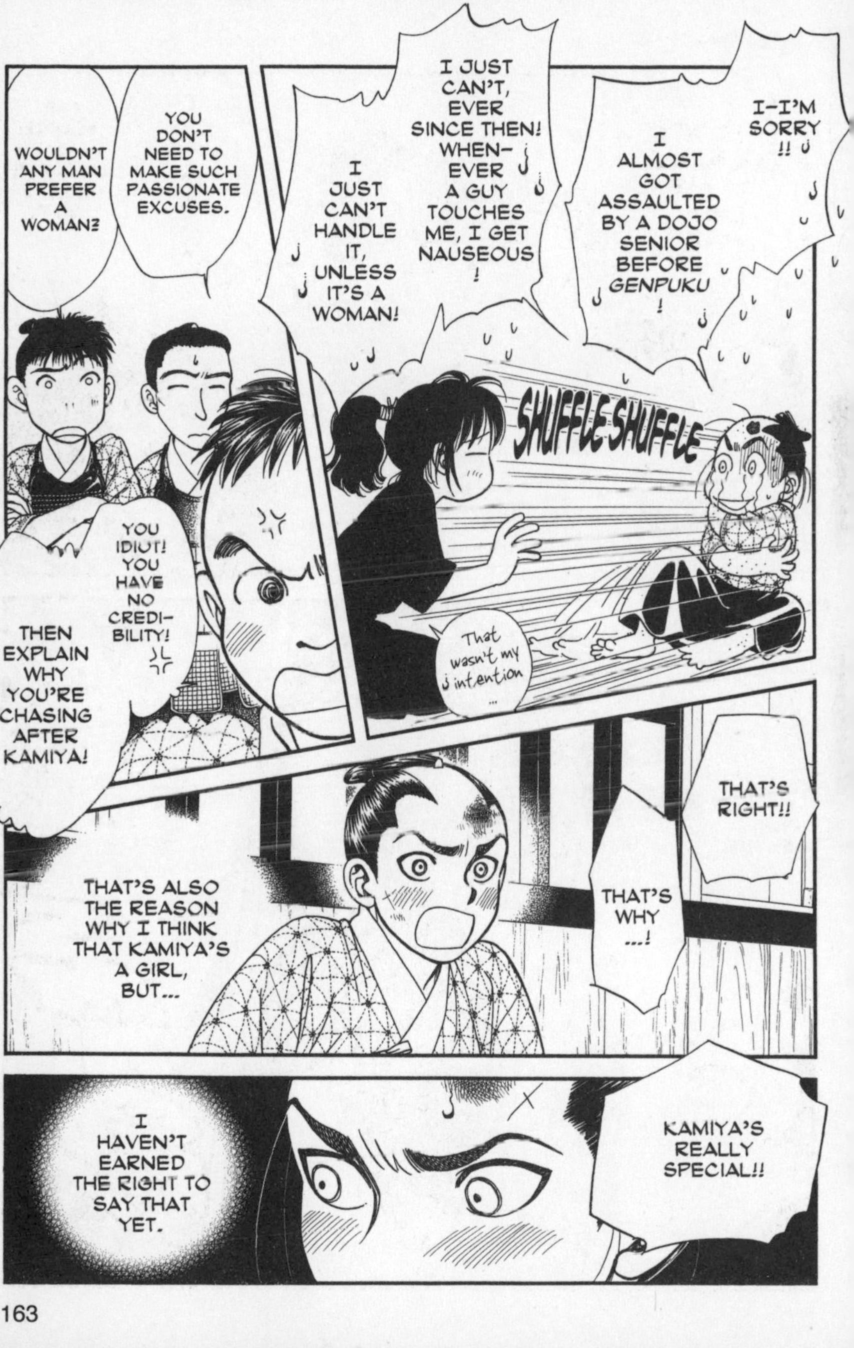
I-I'M SORRY!!
I ALMOST GOT ASSAULTED BY A DOJO SENIOR BEFORE GENPUKU!
I JUST CAN'T, EVER SINCE THEN! WHEN-EVER A GUY TOUCHES ME, I GET NAUSEOUS!
I JUST CAN'T HANDLE IT, UNLESS IT'S A WOMAN!
SHUFFLE SHUFFLE
That wasn't my intention...
YOU DON'T NEED TO MAKE SUCH PASSIONATE EXCUSES.
WOULDN'T ANY MAN PREFER A WOMAN?
YOU IDIOT! YOU HAVE NO CREDI-BILITY!
THEN EXPLAIN WHY YOU'RE CHASING AFTER KAMIYA!
THAT'S RIGHT!!
THAT'S WHY...!
THAT'S ALSO THE REASON WHY I THINK THAT KAMIYA'S A GIRL, BUT...
KAMIYA'S REALLY SPECIAL!!
I HAVEN'T EARNED THE RIGHT TO SAY THAT YET.

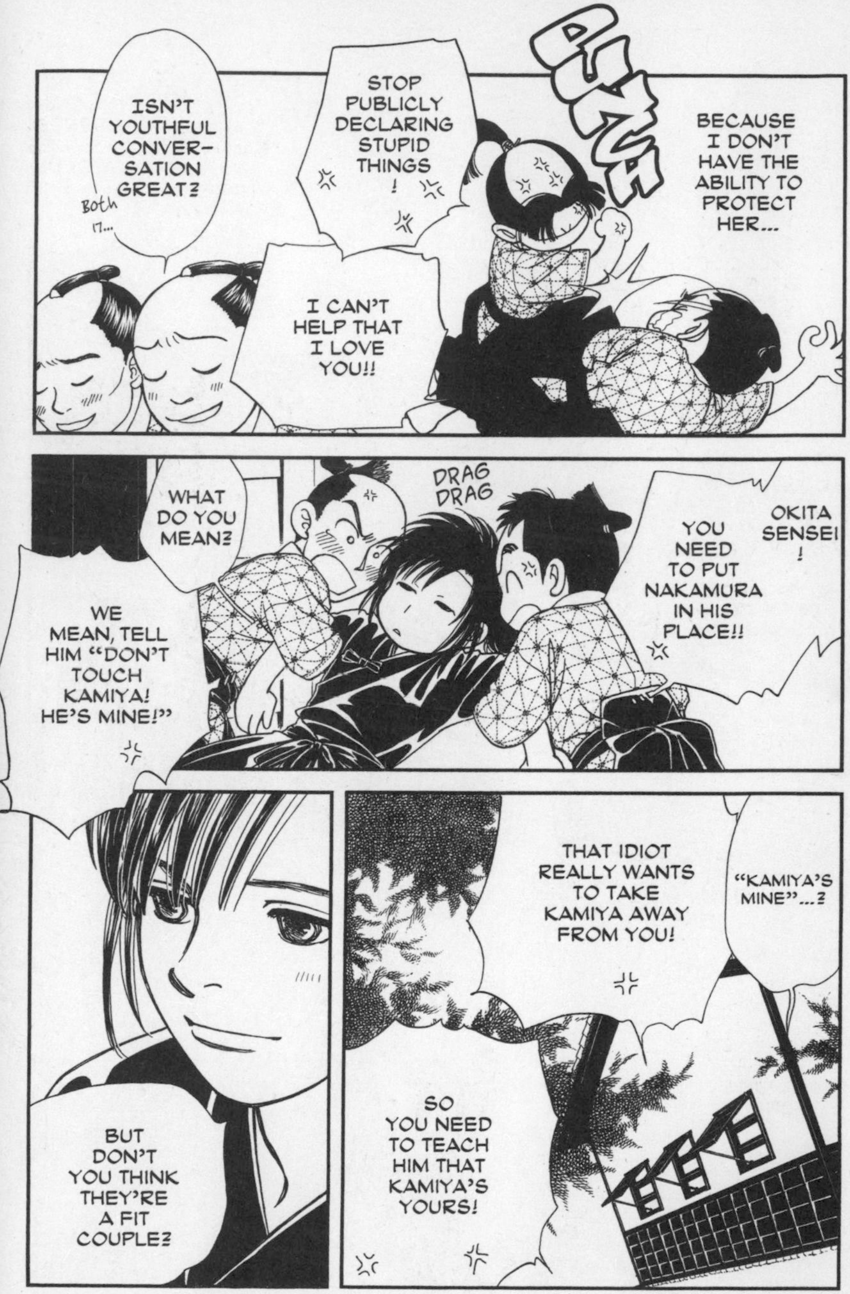
BECAUSE I DON'T HAVE THE ABILITY TO PROTECT HER...
STOP PUBLICLY DECLARING STUPID THINGS!
I CAN'T HELP THAT I LOVE YOU!!
ISN'T YOUTHFUL CONVER-SATION GREAT?
Both 17...
OKITA SENSEI!
YOU NEED TO PUT NAKAMURA IN HIS PLACE!!
DRAG DRAG
WHAT DO YOU MEAN?
WE MEAN, TELL HIM "DON'T TOUCH KAMIYA! HE'S MINE!"
"KAMIYA'S MINE"...?
THAT IDIOT REALLY WANTS TO TAKE KAMIYA AWAY FROM YOU!
SO YOU NEED TO TEACH HIM THAT KAMIYA'S YOURS!
BUT DON'T YOU THINK THEY'RE A FIT COUPLE?

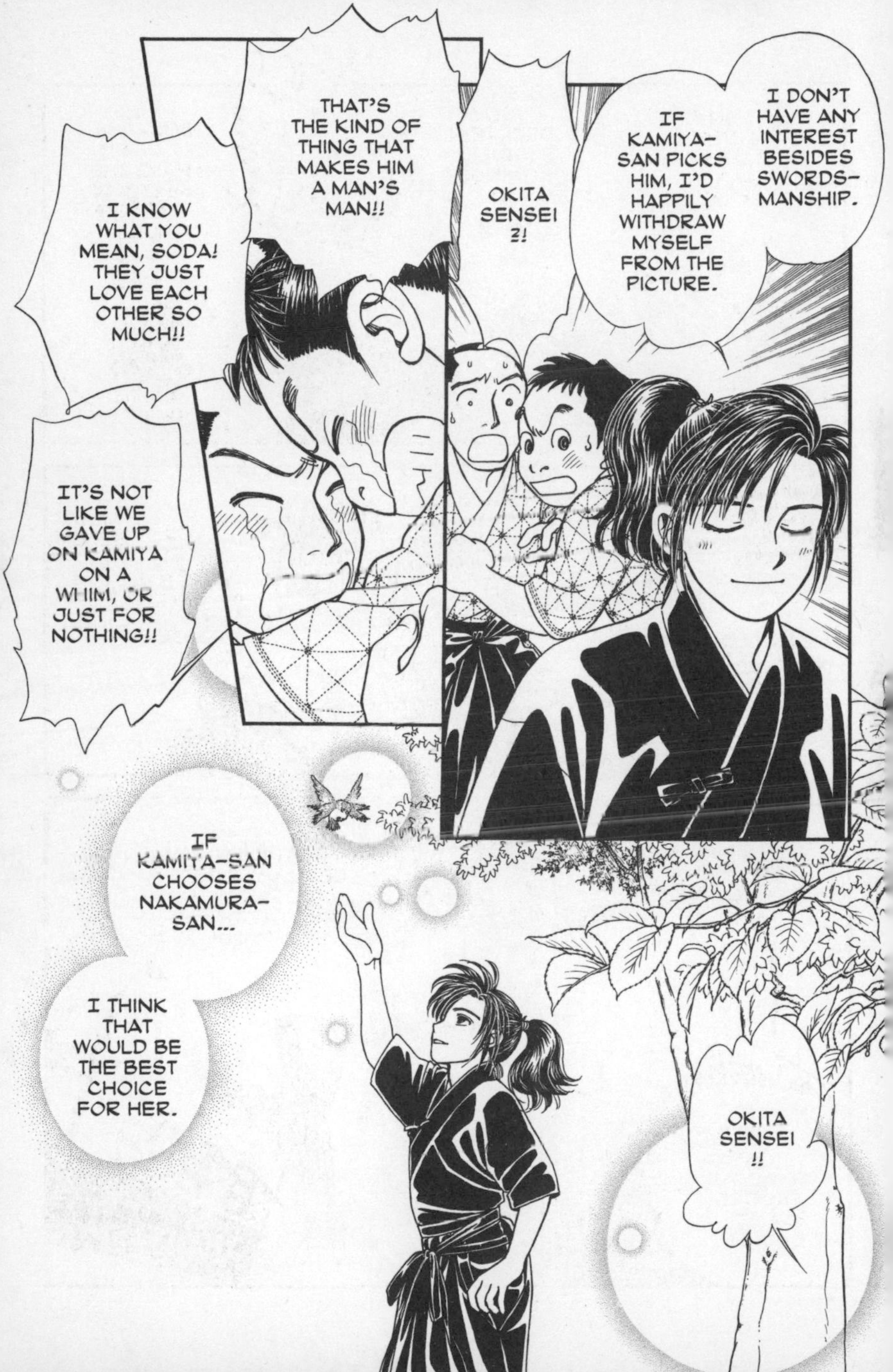
I DON'T HAVE ANY INTEREST BESIDES SWORDS-MANSHIP.
IF KAMIYA-SAN PICKS HIM, I'D HAPPILY WITHDRAW MYSELF FROM THE PICTURE.
OKITA SENSEI?!
THAT'S THE KIND OF THING THAT MAKES HIM A MAN'S MAN!!
I KNOW WHAT YOU MEAN, SODA! THEY JUST LOVE EACH OTHER SO MUCH!!
IT'S NOT LIKE WE GAVE UP ON KAMIYA ON A WHIM, OR JUST FOR NOTHING!!
OKITA SENSEI!!
IF KAMIYA-SAN CHOOSES NAKAMURA-SAN...
I THINK THAT WOULD BE THE BEST CHOICE FOR HER.

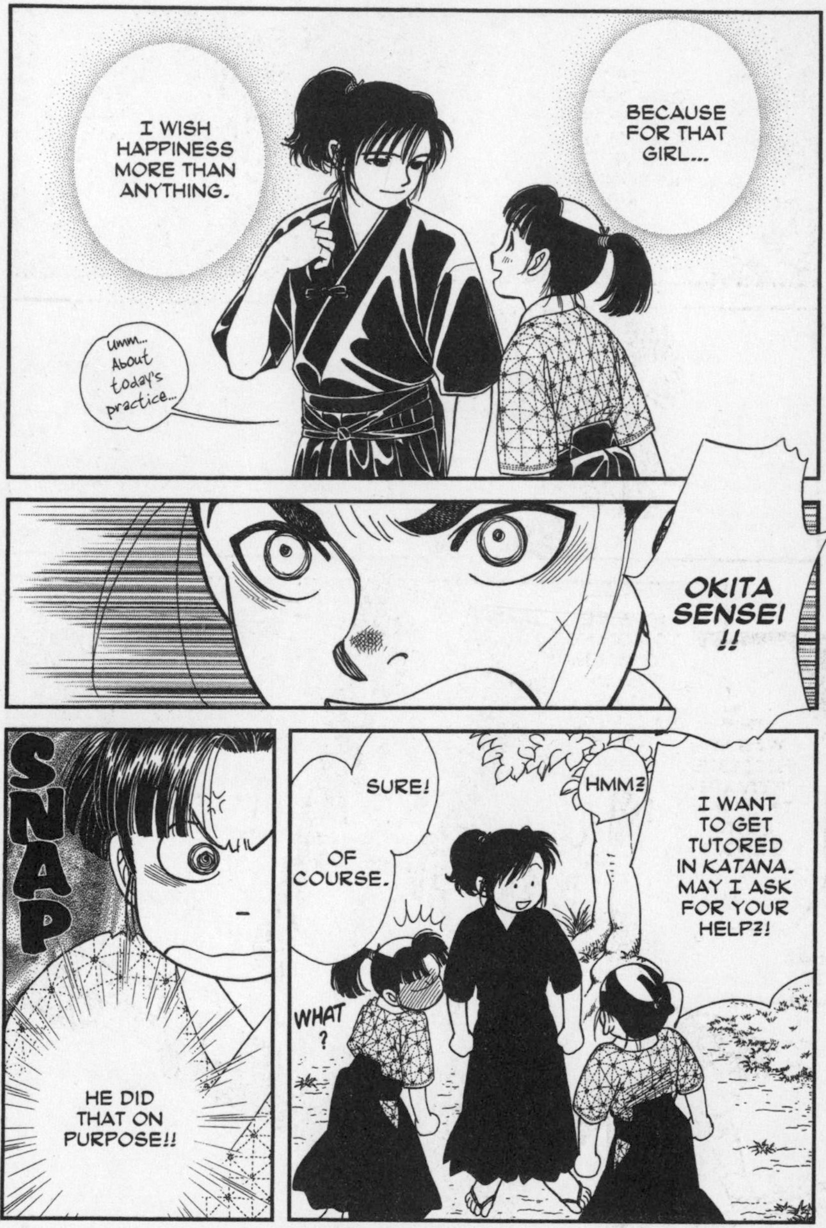
BECAUSE FOR THAT GIRL...
I WISH HAPPINESS MORE THAN ANYTHING.
Umm... About today's practice...
OKITA SENSEI !!
I WANT TO GET TUTORED IN KATANA. MAY I ASK FOR YOUR HELP?!
HMM?
SURE! OF COURSE.
WHAT ?
SNAP
HE DID THAT ON PURPOSE!!

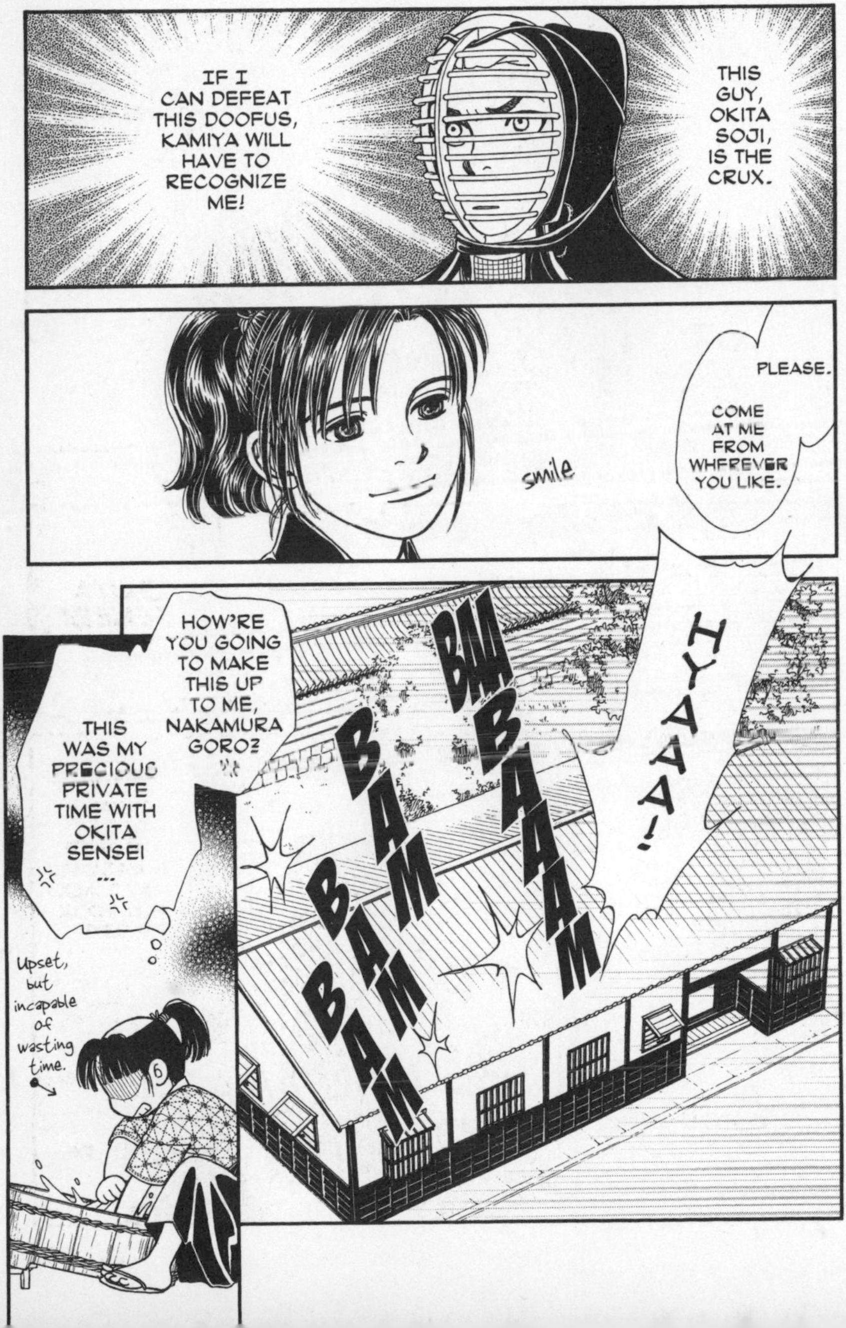
THIS GUY, OKITA SOJI, IS THE CRUX.
IF I CAN DEFEAT THIS DOOFUS, KAMIYA WILL HAVE TO RECOGNIZE ME!
PLEASE.
COME AT ME FROM WHEREVER YOU LIKE.
smile
HYAAAA!
BAM BAAAAM
BAM BAM BAM
HOW'RE YOU GOING TO MAKE THIS UP TO ME, NAKAMURA GORO?
THIS WAS MY PRECIOUS PRIVATE TIME WITH OKITA SENSEI ...
Upset, but incapable of wasting time.

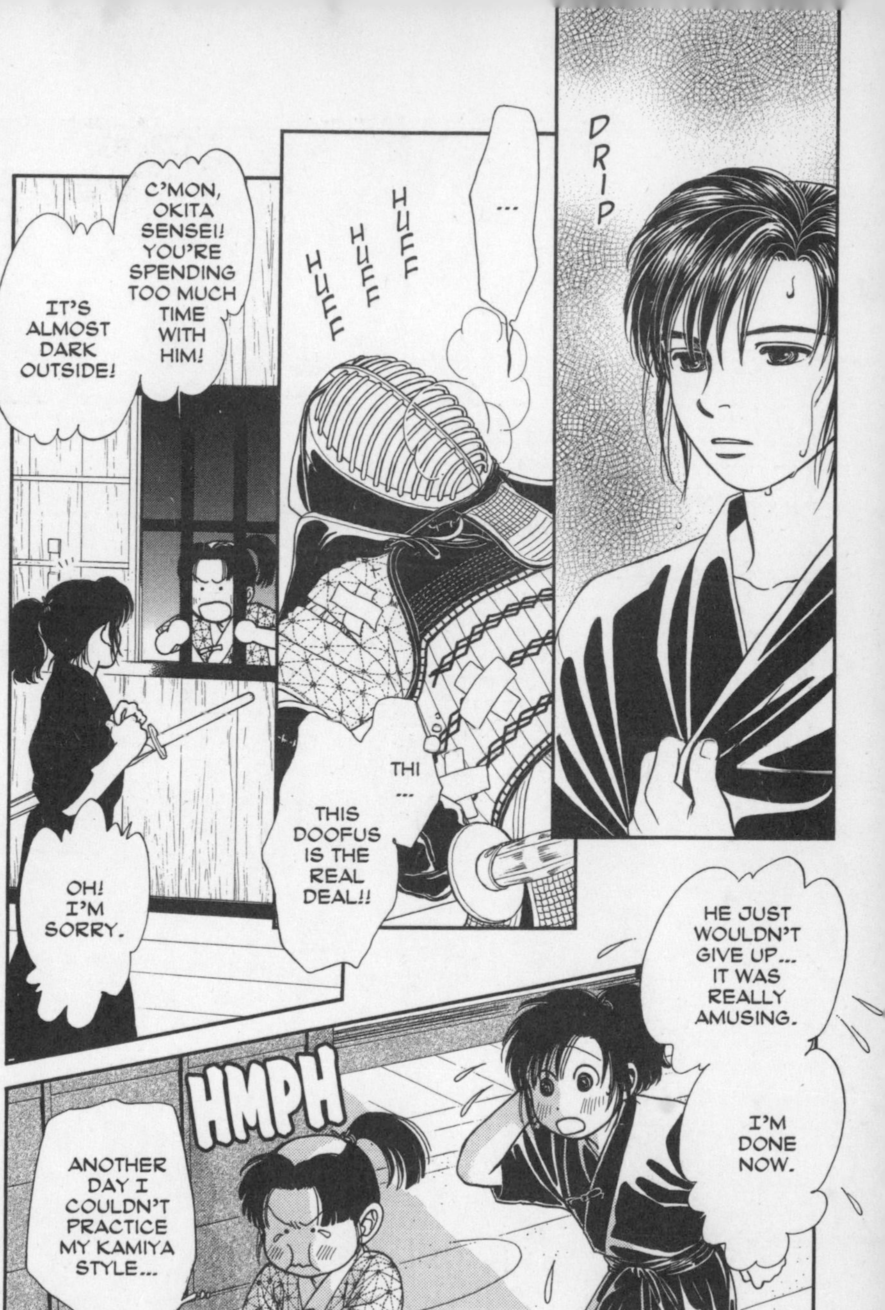
DRIP
...
HUFF HUFF HUFF
THI...
THIS DOOFUS IS THE REAL DEAL!!
C'MON, OKITA SENSEI! YOU'RE SPENDING TOO MUCH TIME WITH HIM!
IT'S ALMOST DARK OUTSIDE!
OH! I'M SORRY.
HE JUST WOULDN'T GIVE UP... IT WAS REALLY AMUSING.
I'M DONE NOW.
HMPH
ANOTHER DAY I COULDN'T PRACTICE MY KAMIYA STYLE...

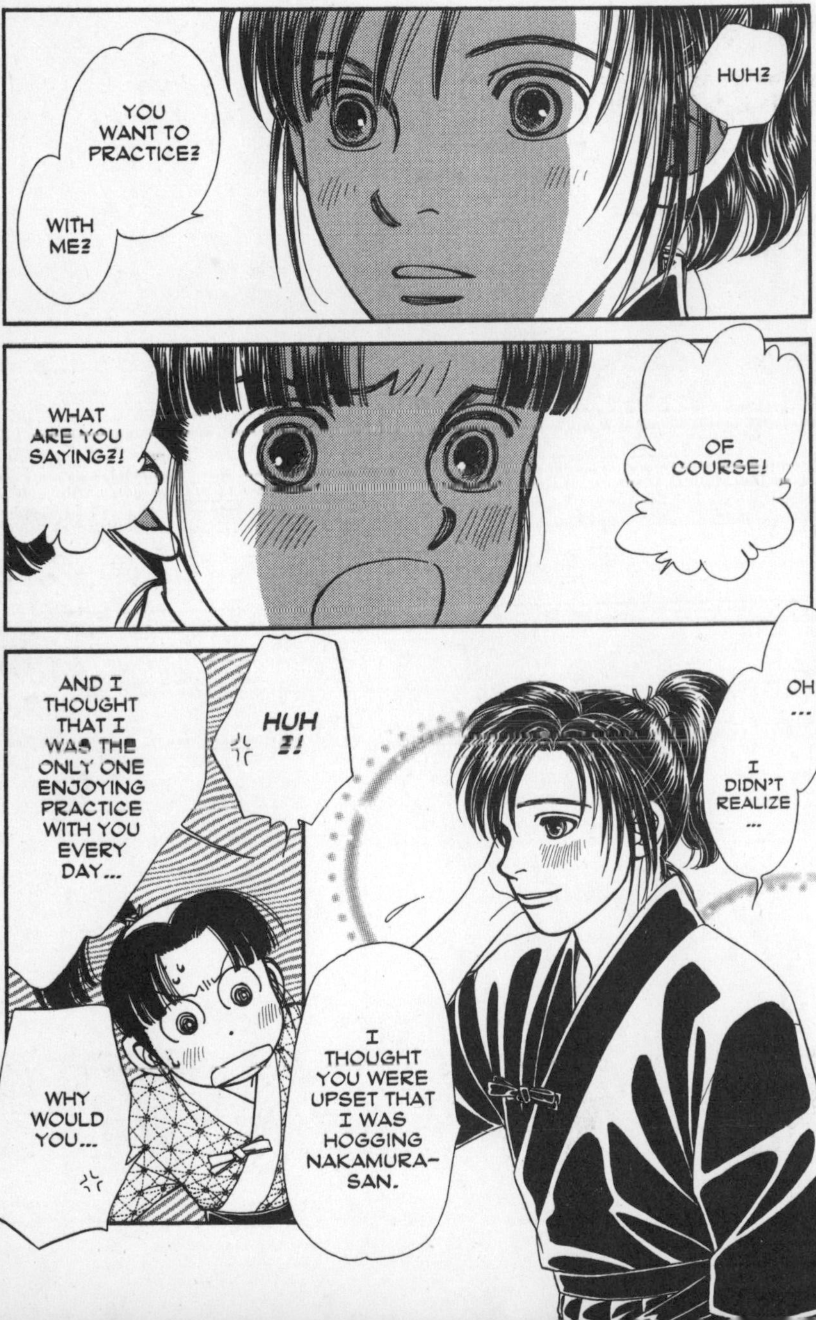
HUH?
YOU WANT TO PRACTICE? WITH ME?
OF COURSE!
WHAT ARE YOU SAYING?!
OH ... I DIDN'T REALIZE ...
I THOUGHT YOU WERE UPSET THAT I WAS HOGGING NAKAMURA-SAN.
HUH?!
AND I THOUGHT THAT I WAS THE ONLY ONE ENJOYING PRACTICE WITH YOU EVERY DAY...
WHY WOULD YOU...

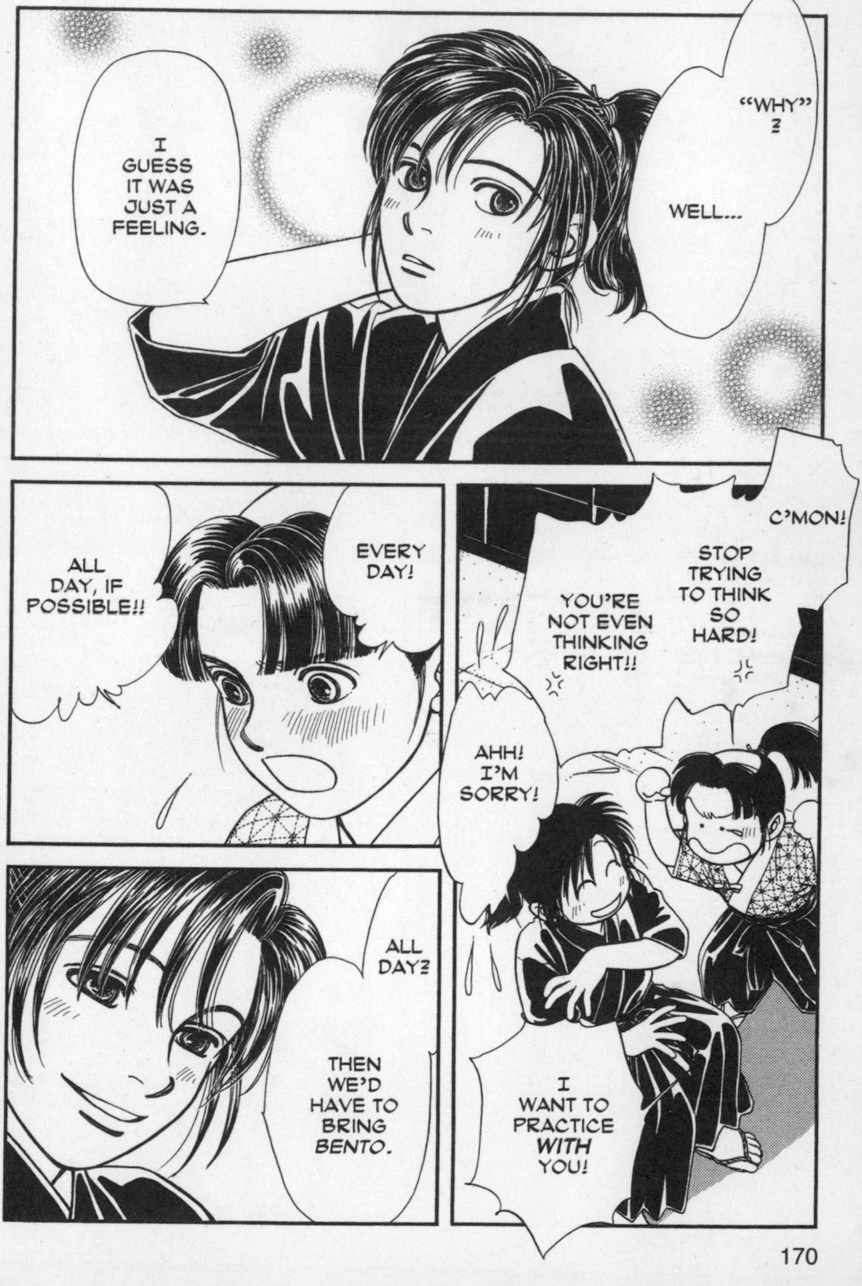
"WHY"?
WELL...
I GUESS IT WAS JUST A FEELING.
C'MON! STOP TRYING TO THINK SO HARD!
YOU'RE NOT EVEN THINKING RIGHT!!
AHH! I'M SORRY!
I WANT TO PRACTICE *WITH* YOU!
EVERY DAY!
ALL DAY, IF POSSIBLE!!
ALL DAY?
THEN WE'D HAVE TO BRING *BENTO*.

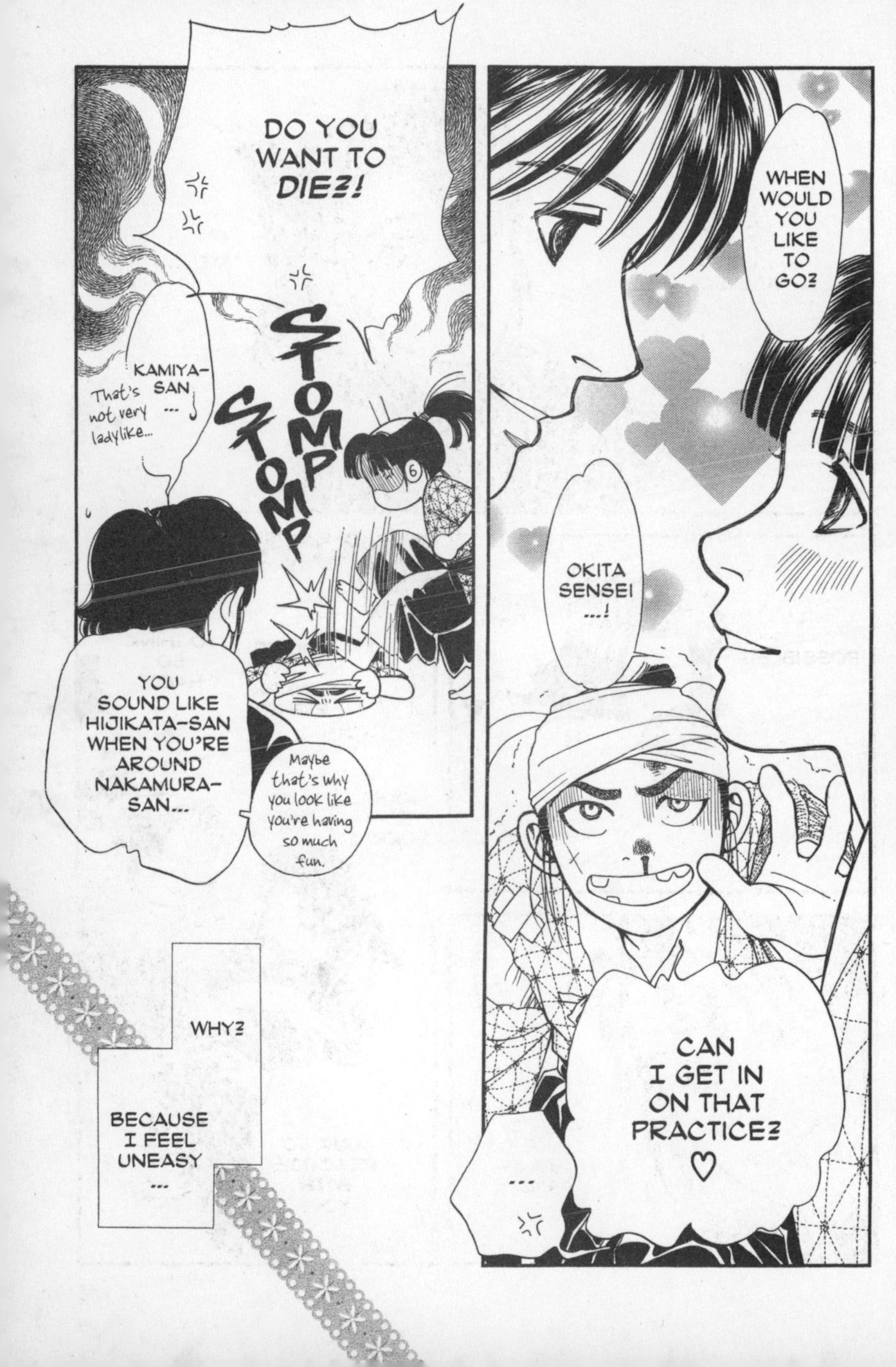
WHEN WOULD YOU LIKE TO GO?
OKITA SENSEI ...!
CAN I GET IN ON THAT PRACTICE? ♡
...
DO YOU WANT TO DIE?!
STOMP STOMP
KAMIYA-SAN ...
That's not very ladylike...
YOU SOUND LIKE HIJIKATA-SAN WHEN YOU'RE AROUND NAKAMURA-SAN...
Maybe that's why you look like you're having so much fun.
WHY?
BECAUSE I FEEL UNEASY ...

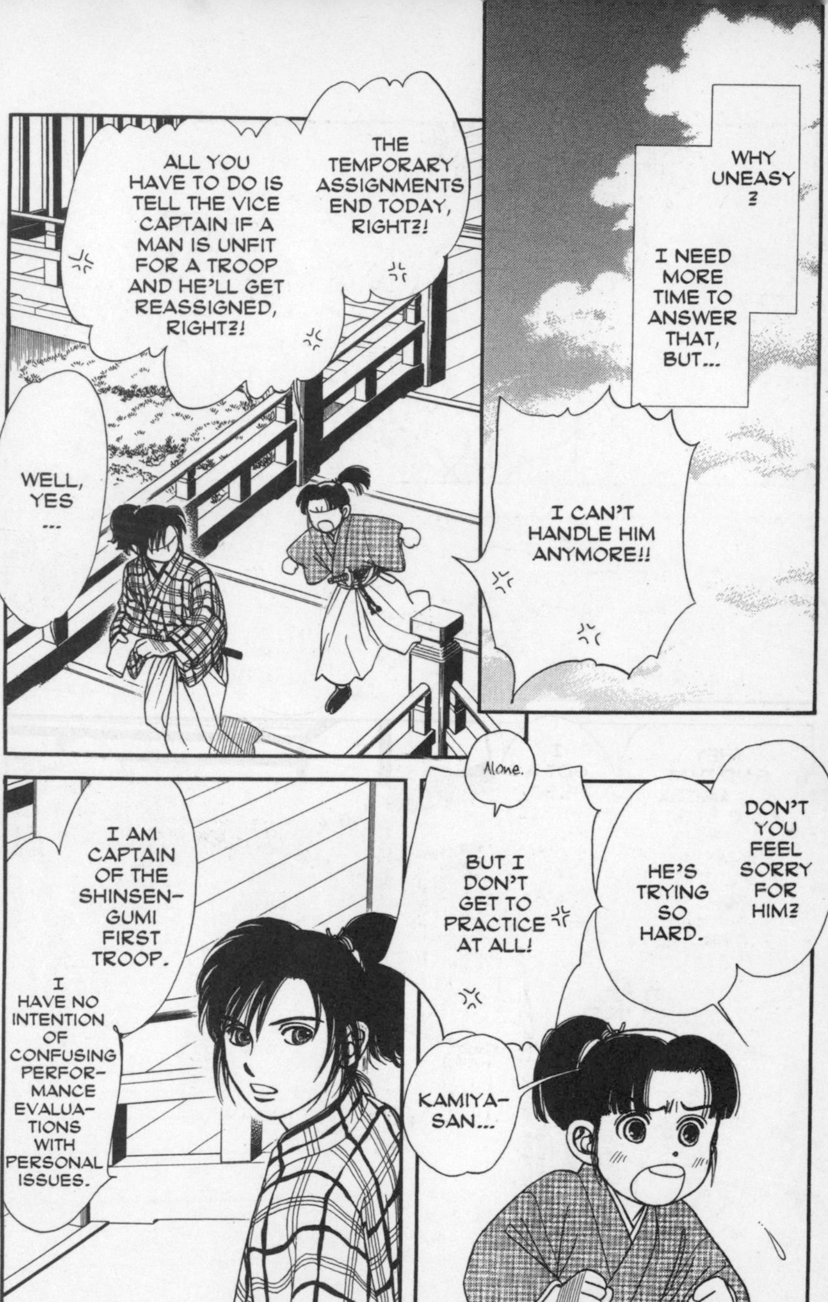
WHY UNEASY?
I NEED MORE TIME TO ANSWER THAT, BUT...
I CAN'T HANDLE HIM ANYMORE!!
THE TEMPORARY ASSIGNMENTS END TODAY, RIGHT?!
ALL YOU HAVE TO DO IS TELL THE VICE CAPTAIN IF A MAN IS UNFIT FOR A TROOP AND HE'LL GET REASSIGNED, RIGHT?!
WELL, YES...
DON'T YOU FEEL SORRY FOR HIM?
HE'S TRYING SO HARD.
Alone.
BUT I DON'T GET TO PRACTICE AT ALL!
KAMIYA-SAN...
I AM CAPTAIN OF THE SHINSEN-GUMI FIRST TROOP.
I HAVE NO INTENTION OF CONFUSING PERFORMANCE EVALUATIONS WITH PERSONAL ISSUES.

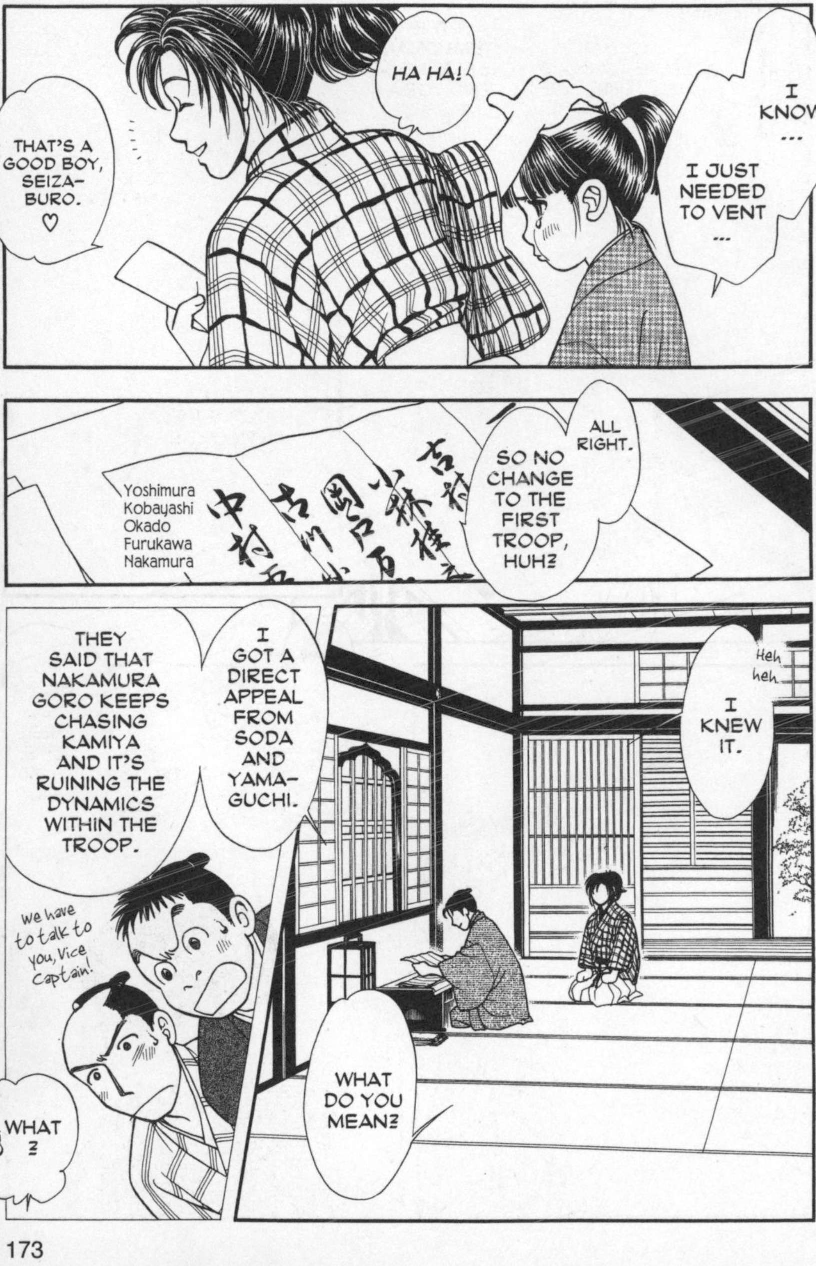
I KNOW ... I JUST NEEDED TO VENT ...
HA HA!
THAT'S A GOOD BOY, SEIZA-BURO. ♡
ALL RIGHT.
SO NO CHANGE TO THE FIRST TROOP, HUH?
Yoshimura
Kobayashi
Okado
Furukawa
Nakamura
Heh heh
I KNEW IT.
I GOT A DIRECT APPEAL FROM SODA AND YAMA-GUCHI.
THEY SAID THAT NAKAMURA GORO KEEPS CHASING KAMIYA AND IT'S RUINING THE DYNAMICS WITHIN THE TROOP.
WHAT DO YOU MEAN?
we have to talk to you, Vice Captain!
WHAT?

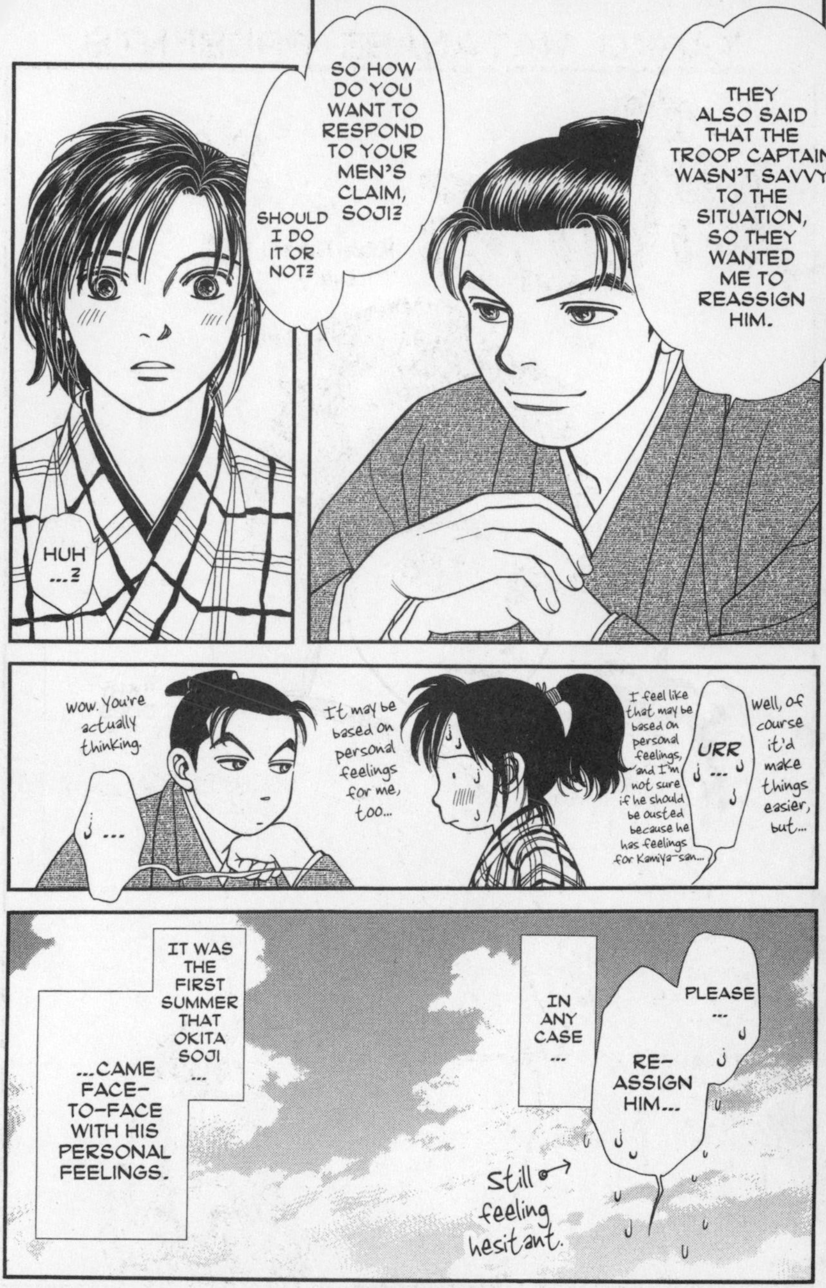
THEY ALSO SAID THAT THE TROOP CAPTAIN WASN'T SAVVY TO THE SITUATION, SO THEY WANTED ME TO REASSIGN HIM.
SO HOW DO YOU WANT TO RESPOND TO YOUR MEN'S CLAIM, SOJI?
SHOULD I DO IT OR NOT?
HUH ...?
Well, of course it'd make things easier, but...
URR ...
I feel like that may be based on personal feelings, and I'm not sure if he should be ousted because he has feelings for Kamiya-san...
It may be based on personal feelings for me, too...
Wow. You're actually thinking.
...
PLEASE ... RE-ASSIGN HIM...
IN ANY CASE ...
Still feeling hesitant.
IT WAS THE FIRST SUMMER THAT OKITA SOJI ...
...CAME FACE-TO-FACE WITH HIS PERSONAL FEELINGS.

To Be Continued!

TAEKO WATANABE PRESENTS

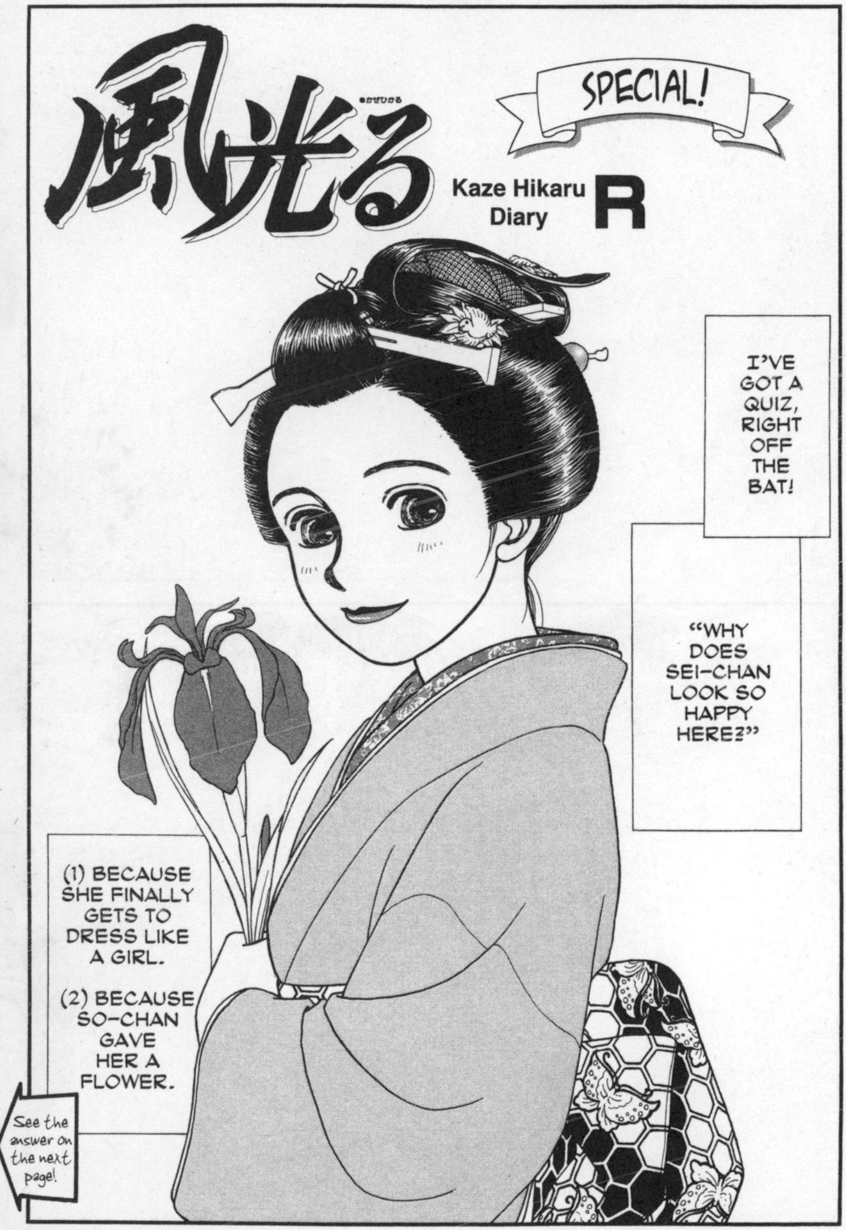
風光る
SPECIAL!
Kaze Hikaru Diary R
I'VE GOT A QUIZ, RIGHT OFF THE BAT!
"WHY DOES SEI-CHAN LOOK SO HAPPY HERE?"
(1) BECAUSE SHE FINALLY GETS TO DRESS LIKE A GIRL.
(2) BECAUSE SO-CHAN GAVE HER A FLOWER.
See the answer on the next page!

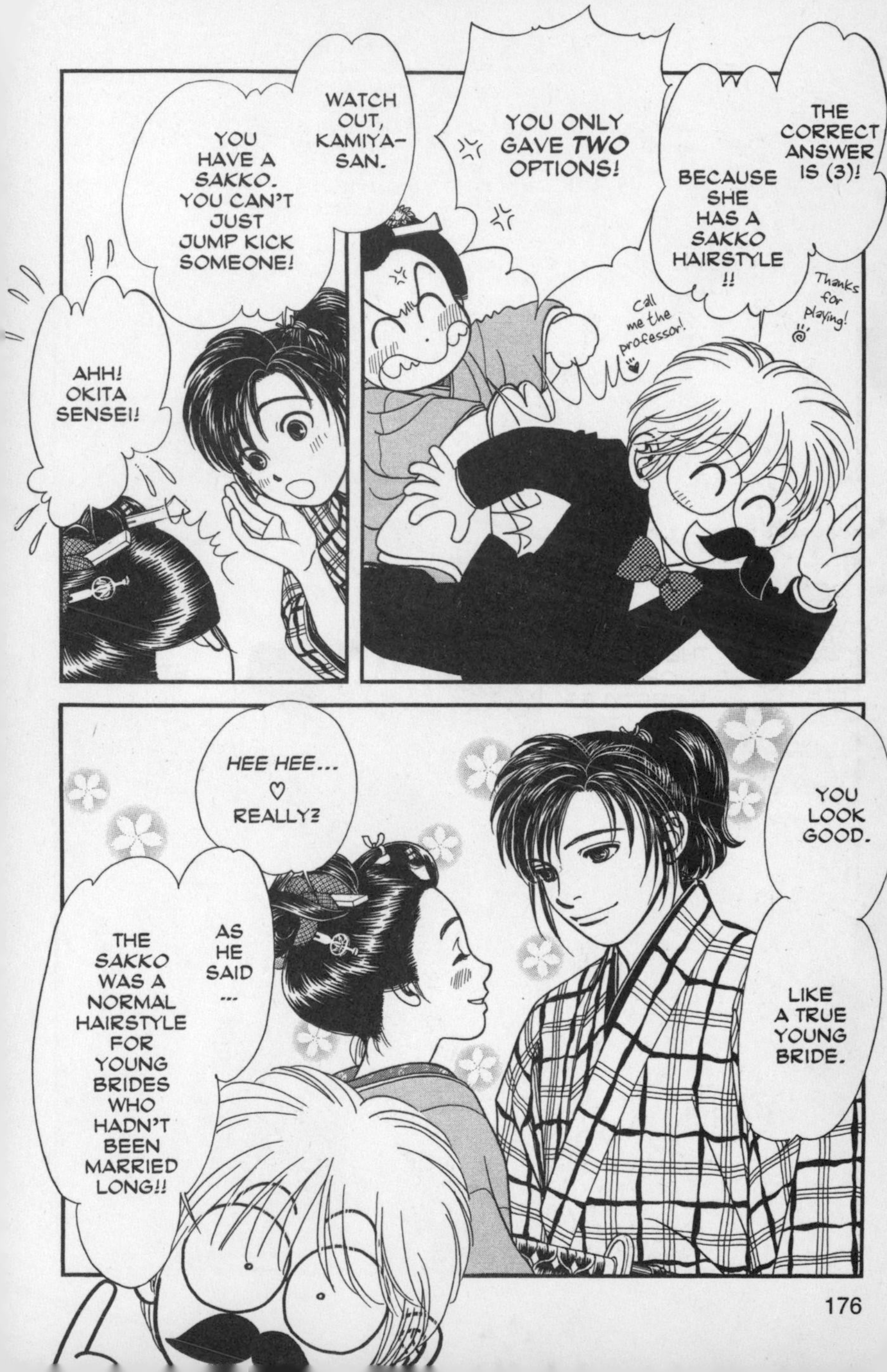
THE CORRECT ANSWER IS (3)!
BECAUSE SHE HAS A SAKKO HAIRSTYLE!!
Thanks for playing!
Call me the professor!
YOU ONLY GAVE TWO OPTIONS!
WATCH OUT, KAMIYA-SAN.
YOU HAVE A SAKKO. YOU CAN'T JUST JUMP KICK SOMEONE!
AHH! OKITA SENSEI!
YOU LOOK GOOD.
LIKE A TRUE YOUNG BRIDE.
HEE HEE... ♡ REALLY?
AS HE SAID...
THE SAKKO WAS A NORMAL HAIRSTYLE FOR YOUNG BRIDES WHO HADN'T BEEN MARRIED LONG!!

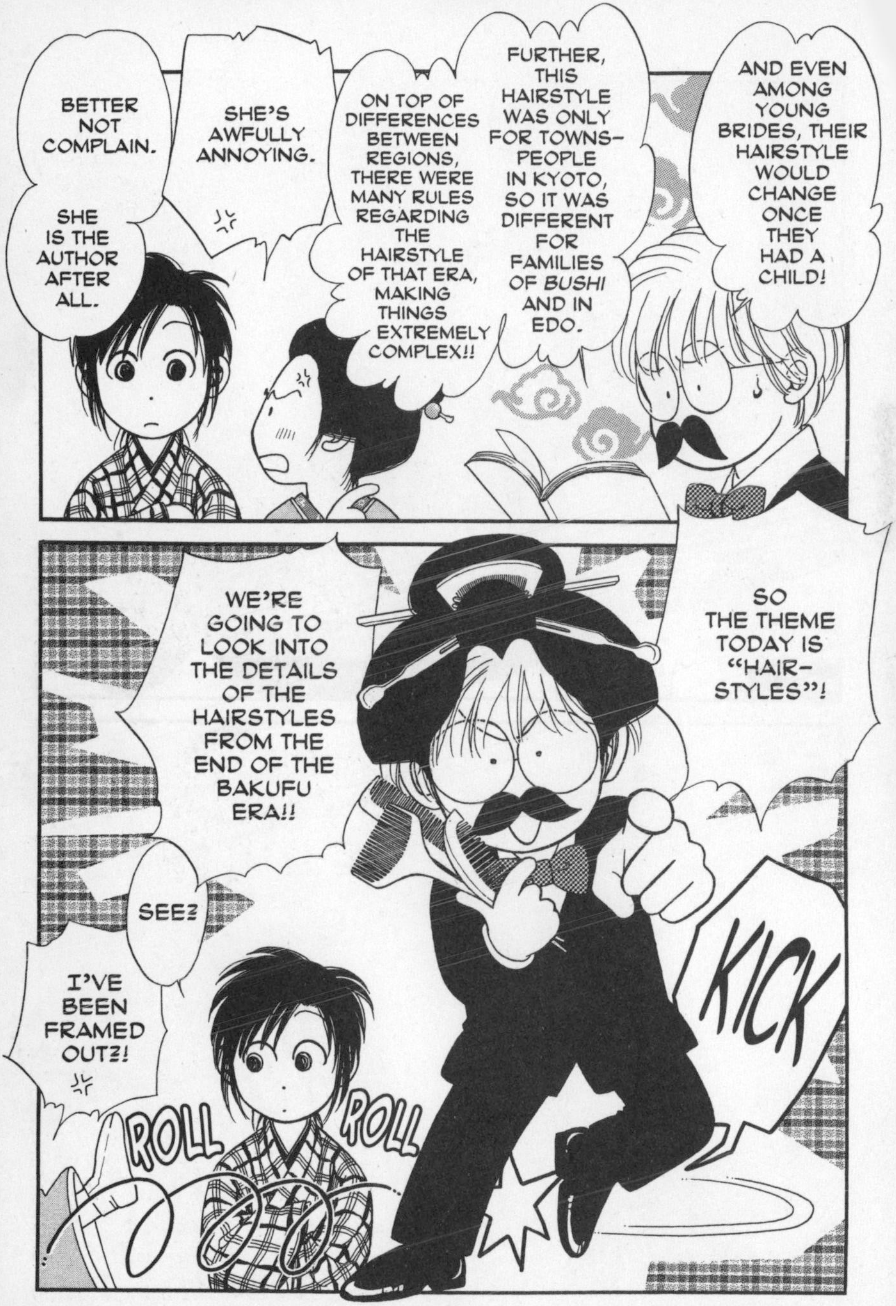
AND EVEN AMONG YOUNG BRIDES, THEIR HAIRSTYLE WOULD CHANGE ONCE THEY HAD A CHILD!
FURTHER, THIS HAIRSTYLE WAS ONLY FOR TOWNS-PEOPLE IN KYOTO, SO IT WAS DIFFERENT FOR FAMILIES OF *BUSHI* AND IN EDO.
ON TOP OF DIFFERENCES BETWEEN REGIONS, THERE WERE MANY RULES REGARDING THE HAIRSTYLE OF THAT ERA, MAKING THINGS EXTREMELY COMPLEX!!
SHE'S AWFULLY ANNOYING.
BETTER NOT COMPLAIN.
SHE IS THE AUTHOR AFTER ALL.
SO THE THEME TODAY IS "HAIR-STYLES"!
WE'RE GOING TO LOOK INTO THE DETAILS OF THE HAIRSTYLES FROM THE END OF THE BAKUFU ERA!!
KICK
SEE?
I'VE BEEN FRAMED OUT?!
ROLL
ROLL

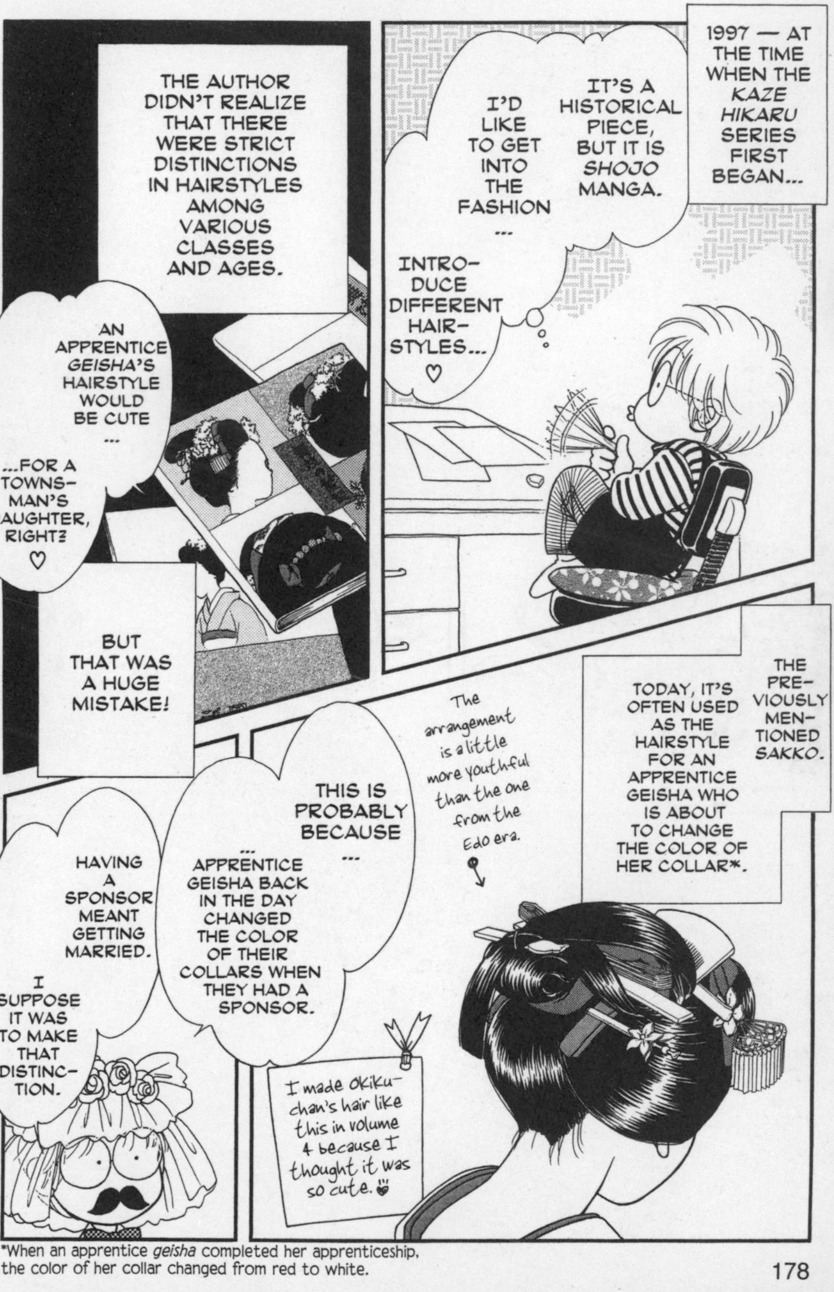
1997 — AT THE TIME WHEN THE *KAZE HIKARU* SERIES FIRST BEGAN...
IT'S A HISTORICAL PIECE, BUT IT IS *SHOJO* MANGA.
I'D LIKE TO GET INTO THE FASHION...
INTRODUCE DIFFERENT HAIRSTYLES... ♡
THE AUTHOR DIDN'T REALIZE THAT THERE WERE STRICT DISTINCTIONS IN HAIRSTYLES AMONG VARIOUS CLASSES AND AGES.
AN APPRENTICE *GEISHA*'S HAIRSTYLE WOULD BE CUTE...
...FOR A TOWNSMAN'S DAUGHTER, RIGHT? ♡
BUT THAT WAS A HUGE MISTAKE!
THE PREVIOUSLY MENTIONED *SAKKO*.
TODAY, IT'S OFTEN USED AS THE HAIRSTYLE FOR AN APPRENTICE GEISHA WHO IS ABOUT TO CHANGE THE COLOR OF HER COLLAR*.
The arrangement is a little more youthful than the one from the Edo era.
I made Okiku-chan's hair like this in volume 4 because I thought it was so cute.
THIS IS PROBABLY BECAUSE...
...APPRENTICE GEISHA BACK IN THE DAY CHANGED THE COLOR OF THEIR COLLARS WHEN THEY HAD A SPONSOR.
HAVING A SPONSOR MEANT GETTING MARRIED.
I SUPPOSE IT WAS TO MAKE THAT DISTINCTION.

*When an apprentice *geisha* completed her apprenticeship, the color of her collar changed from red to white.

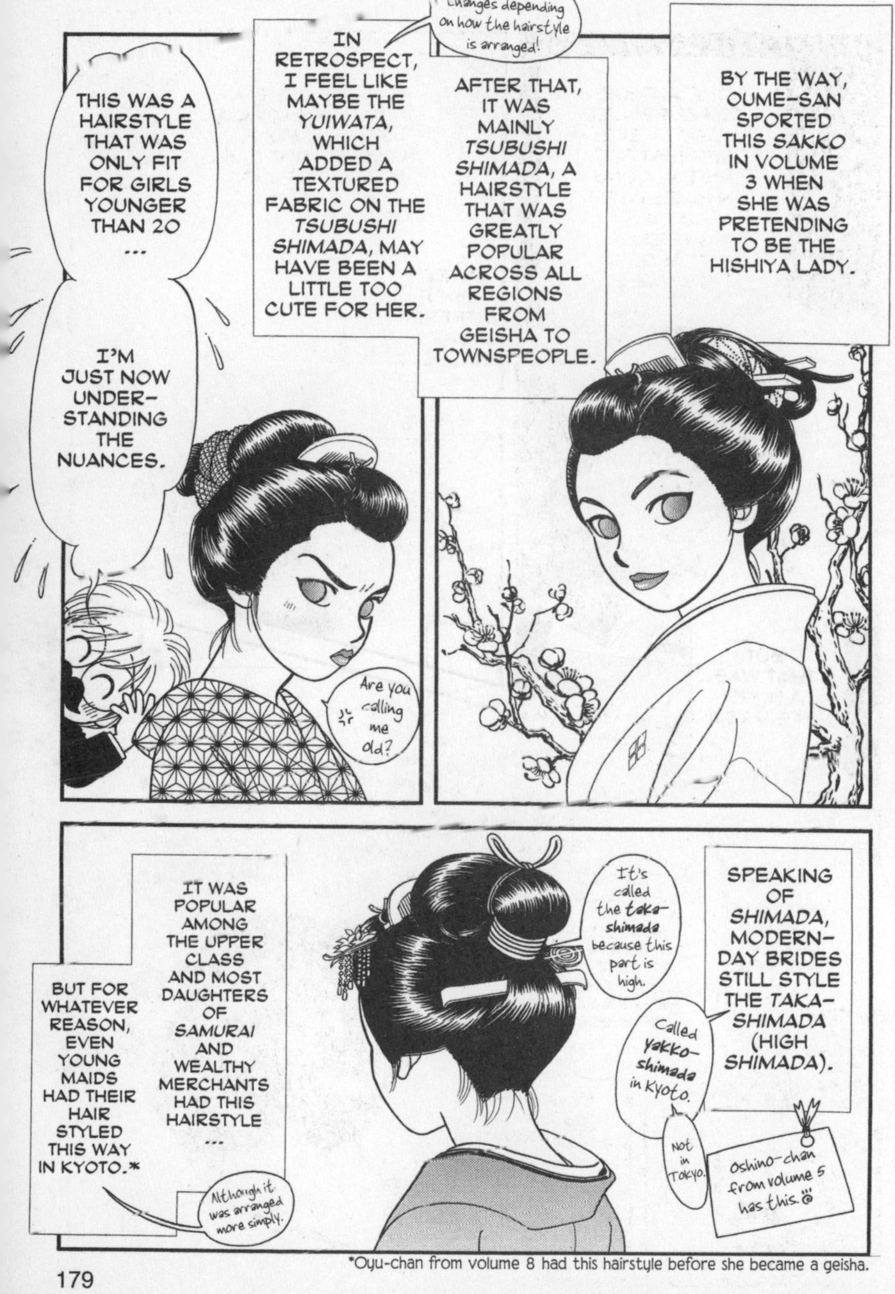
BY THE WAY, OUME-SAN SPORTED THIS *SAKKO* IN VOLUME 3 WHEN SHE WAS PRETENDING TO BE THE HISHIYA LADY.
AFTER THAT, IT WAS MAINLY *TSUBUSHI SHIMADA*, A HAIRSTYLE THAT WAS GREATLY POPULAR ACROSS ALL REGIONS FROM GEISHA TO TOWNSPEOPLE.
The
changes depending on how the hairstyle is arranged!
IN RETROSPECT, I FEEL LIKE MAYBE THE *YUIWATA*, WHICH ADDED A TEXTURED FABRIC ON THE *TSUBUSHI SHIMADA*, MAY HAVE BEEN A LITTLE TOO CUTE FOR HER.
THIS WAS A HAIRSTYLE THAT WAS ONLY FIT FOR GIRLS YOUNGER THAN 20 ...
I'M JUST NOW UNDER-STANDING THE NUANCES.
Are you calling me old?
SPEAKING OF *SHIMADA*, MODERN-DAY BRIDES STILL STYLE THE *TAKA-SHIMADA* (HIGH *SHIMADA*).
It's called the **taka-shimada** because this part is high.
Called **yakko-shimada** in Kyoto.
Not in Tokyo.
Oshino-chan from volume 5 has this.
IT WAS POPULAR AMONG THE UPPER CLASS AND MOST DAUGHTERS OF *SAMURAI* AND WEALTHY MERCHANTS HAD THIS HAIRSTYLE ...
BUT FOR WHATEVER REASON, EVEN YOUNG MAIDS HAD THEIR HAIR STYLED THIS WAY IN KYOTO.*
Although it was arranged more simply.

*Oyu-chan from volume 8 had this hairstyle before she became a geisha.

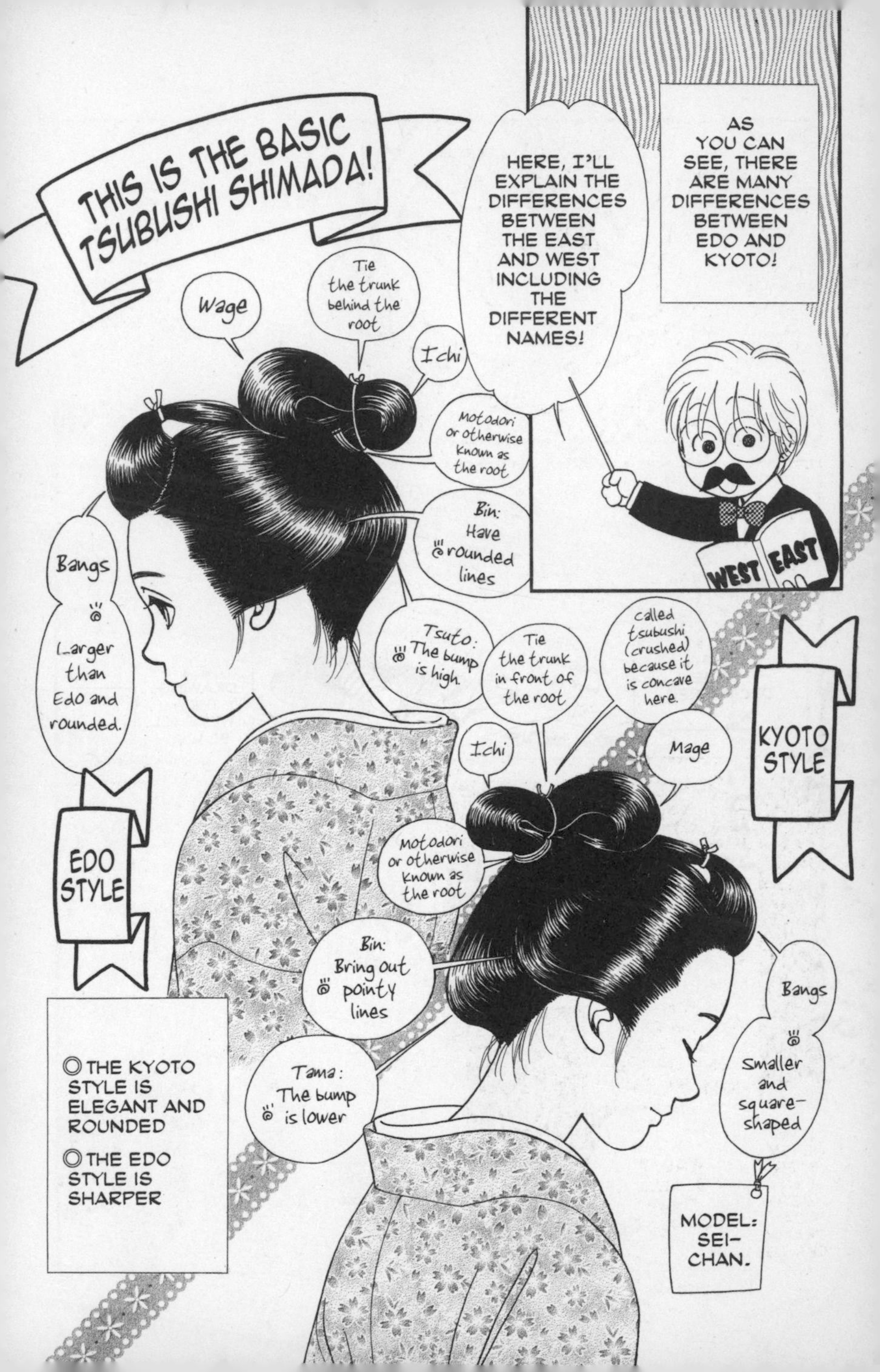
AS YOU CAN SEE, THERE ARE MANY DIFFERENCES BETWEEN EDO AND KYOTO!
HERE, I'LL EXPLAIN THE DIFFERENCES BETWEEN THE EAST AND WEST INCLUDING THE DIFFERENT NAMES!
WEST
EAST
THIS IS THE BASIC TSUBUSHI SHIMADA!
Tie the trunk behind the root
Wage
Ichi
Motodori or otherwise known as the root
Bin: Have ◎ rounded lines
Bangs ◎ Larger than Edo and rounded.
Tsuto: ◎ The bump is high.
EDO STYLE
KYOTO STYLE
called tsubushi (crushed) because it is concave here.
Tie the trunk in front of the root
Mage
Ichi
Motodori or otherwise known as the root
Bin: Bring out ◎ pointy lines
Tama: ◎ The bump is lower
Bangs ◎ Smaller and square-shaped
◎ THE KYOTO STYLE IS ELEGANT AND ROUNDED
◎ THE EDO STYLE IS SHARPER
MODEL: SEI-CHAN.

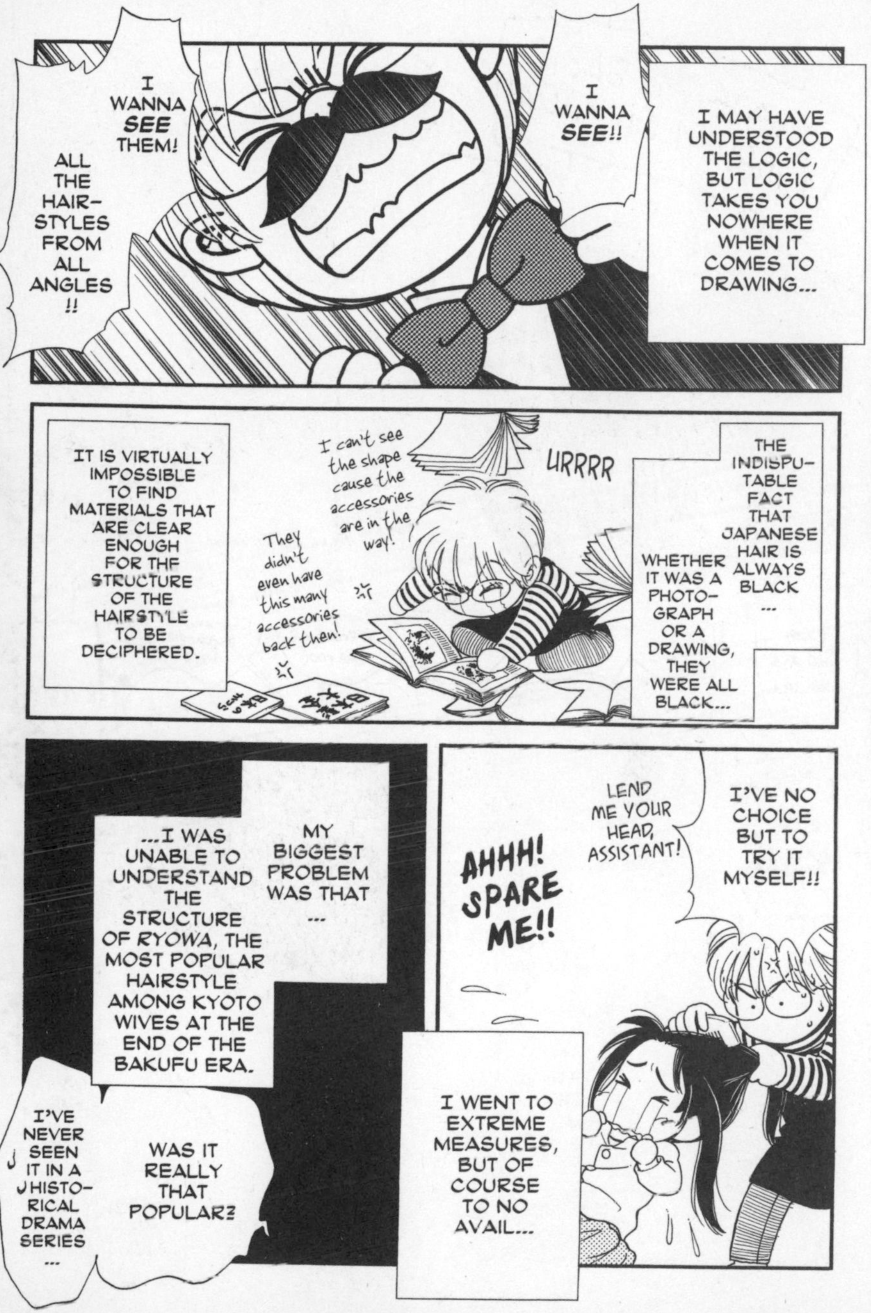
I MAY HAVE UNDERSTOOD THE LOGIC, BUT LOGIC TAKES YOU NOWHERE WHEN IT COMES TO DRAWING...
I WANNA SEE!!
I WANNA SEE THEM!
ALL THE HAIR-STYLES FROM ALL ANGLES!!
THE INDISPU-TABLE FACT THAT JAPANESE HAIR IS ALWAYS BLACK ...
WHETHER IT WAS A PHOTO-GRAPH OR A DRAWING, THEY WERE ALL BLACK...
URRRR
I can't see the shape cause the accessories are in the way!
They didn't even have this many accessories back then!
IT IS VIRTUALLY IMPOSSIBLE TO FIND MATERIALS THAT ARE CLEAR ENOUGH FOR THF STRUCTURE OF THE HAIRSTYLE TO BE DECIPHERED.
I'VE NO CHOICE BUT TO TRY IT MYSELF!!
LEND ME YOUR HEAD, ASSISTANT!
AHHH! SPARE ME!!
I WENT TO EXTREME MEASURES, BUT OF COURSE TO NO AVAIL...
MY BIGGEST PROBLEM WAS THAT ...
...I WAS UNABLE TO UNDERSTAND THE STRUCTURE OF RYOWA, THE MOST POPULAR HAIRSTYLE AMONG KYOTO WIVES AT THE END OF THE BAKUFU ERA.
WAS IT REALLY THAT POPULAR?
I'VE NEVER SEEN IT IN A HISTOR-ICAL DRAMA SERIES ...

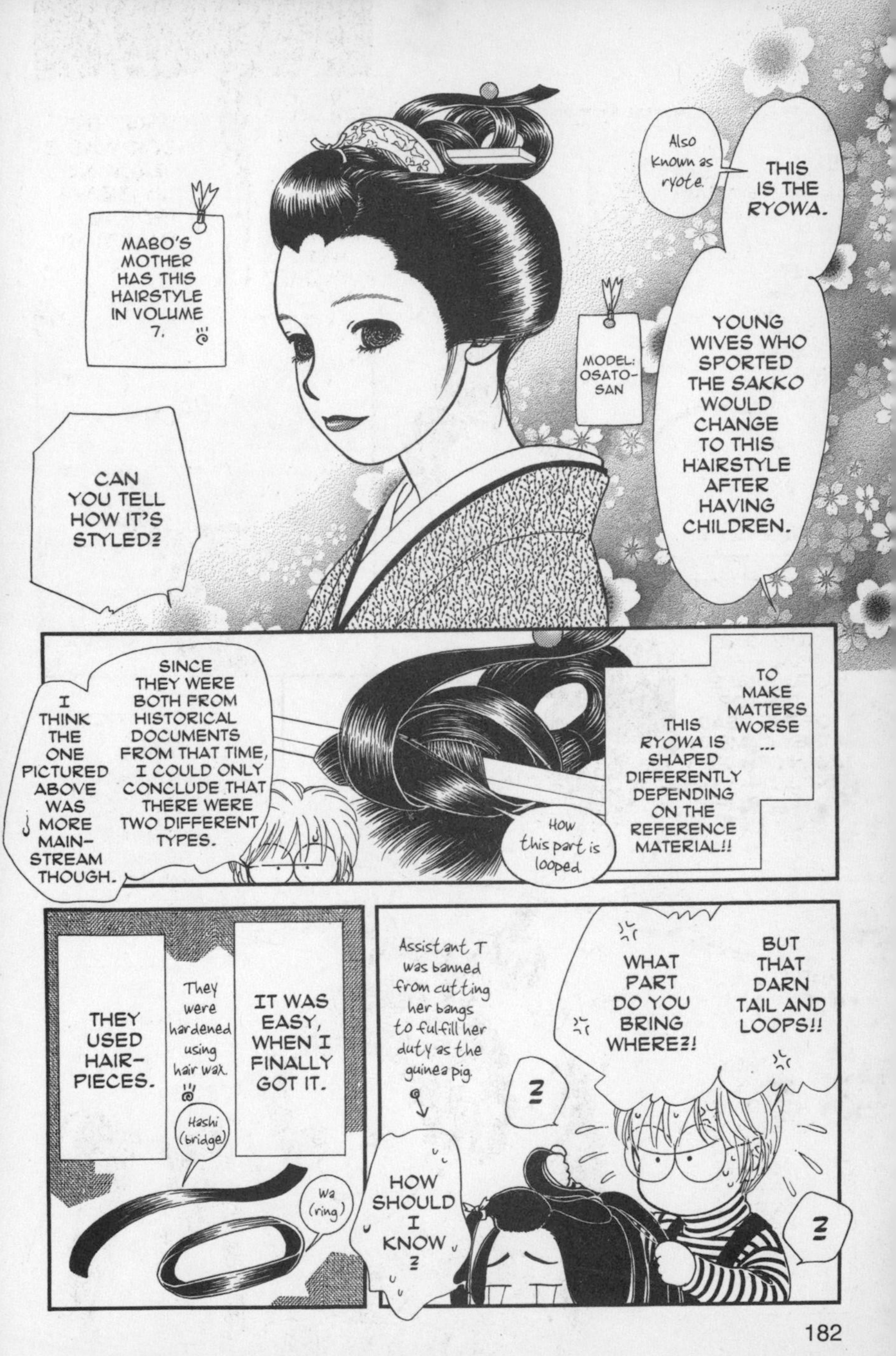
THIS IS THE RYOWA.
Also known as ryote.
YOUNG WIVES WHO SPORTED THE SAKKO WOULD CHANGE TO THIS HAIRSTYLE AFTER HAVING CHILDREN.
MODEL: OSATO-SAN
MABO'S MOTHER HAS THIS HAIRSTYLE IN VOLUME 7.
CAN YOU TELL HOW IT'S STYLED?
TO MAKE MATTERS WORSE...
THIS RYOWA IS SHAPED DIFFERENTLY DEPENDING ON THE REFERENCE MATERIAL!!
How this part is looped.
SINCE THEY WERE BOTH FROM HISTORICAL DOCUMENTS FROM THAT TIME, I COULD ONLY CONCLUDE THAT THERE WERE TWO DIFFERENT TYPES.
I THINK THE ONE PICTURED ABOVE WAS MORE MAIN-STREAM THOUGH.
BUT THAT DARN TAIL AND LOOPS!!
WHAT PART DO YOU BRING WHERE?!
?
?
Assistant T was banned from cutting her bangs to fulfill her duty as the guinea pig.
HOW SHOULD I KNOW?
IT WAS EASY, WHEN I FINALLY GOT IT.
They were hardened using hair wax.
THEY USED HAIR-PIECES.
Hashi (bridge)
Wa (ring)

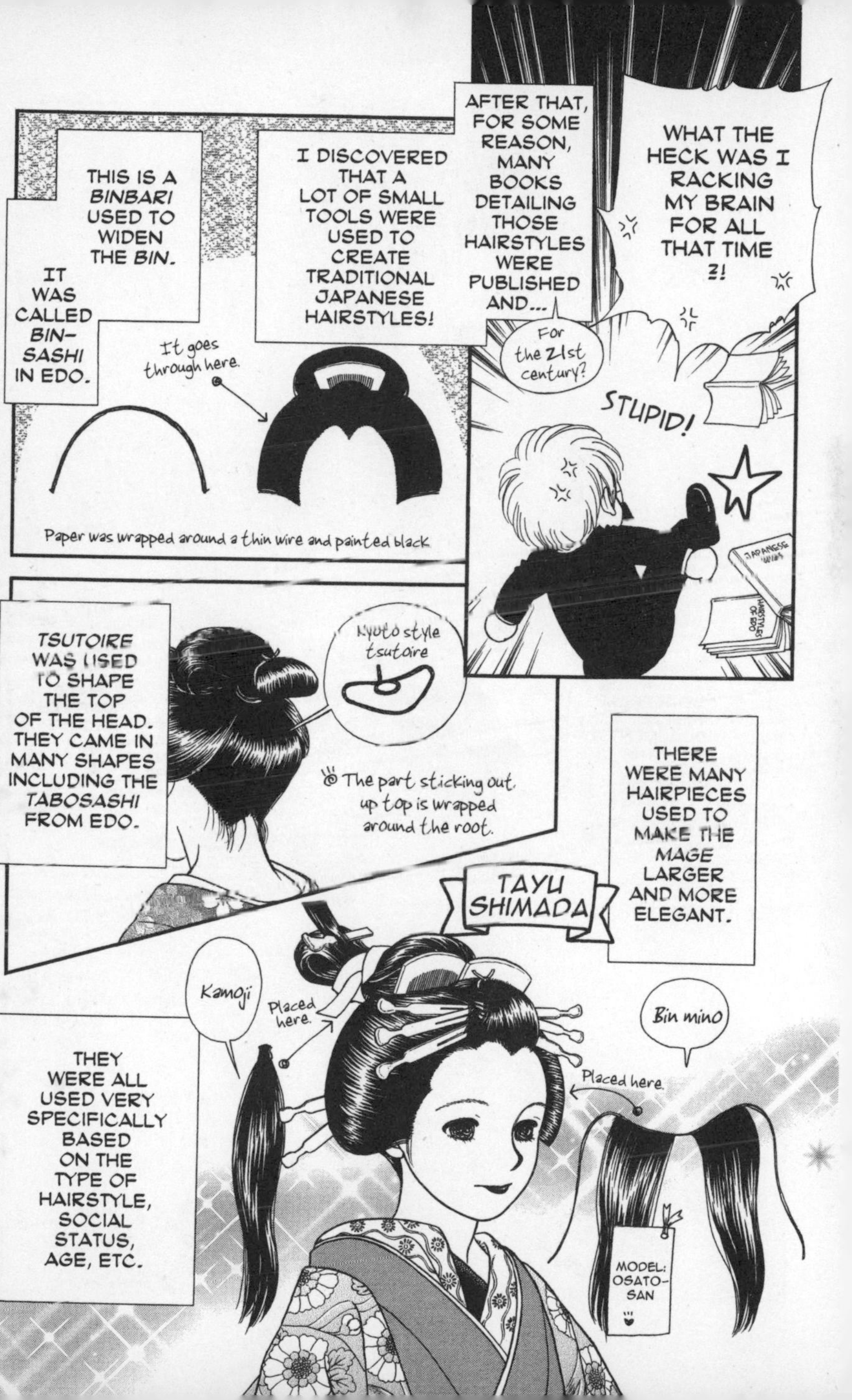
WHAT THE HECK WAS I RACKING MY BRAIN FOR ALL THAT TIME ?!
AFTER THAT, FOR SOME REASON, MANY BOOKS DETAILING THOSE HAIRSTYLES WERE PUBLISHED AND...
For the 21st century?
STUPID!
JAPANESE WIGS
HAIRSTYLES OF EDO
I DISCOVERED THAT A LOT OF SMALL TOOLS WERE USED TO CREATE TRADITIONAL JAPANESE HAIRSTYLES!
THIS IS A *BINBARI* USED TO WIDEN THE *BIN*.
IT WAS CALLED *BIN-SASHI* IN EDO.
It goes through here.
Paper was wrapped around a thin wire and painted black.
TSUTOIRE WAS USED TO SHAPE THE TOP OF THE HEAD. THEY CAME IN MANY SHAPES INCLUDING THE *TABOSASHI* FROM EDO.
Kyoto style tsutoire
The part sticking out up top is wrapped around the root.
THERE WERE MANY HAIRPIECES USED TO MAKE THE *MAGE* LARGER AND MORE ELEGANT.
TAYU SHIMADA
Bin mino
Placed here.
MODEL: OSATO-SAN
Kamoji
Placed here.
THEY WERE ALL USED VERY SPECIFICALLY BASED ON THE TYPE OF HAIRSTYLE, SOCIAL STATUS, AGE, ETC.

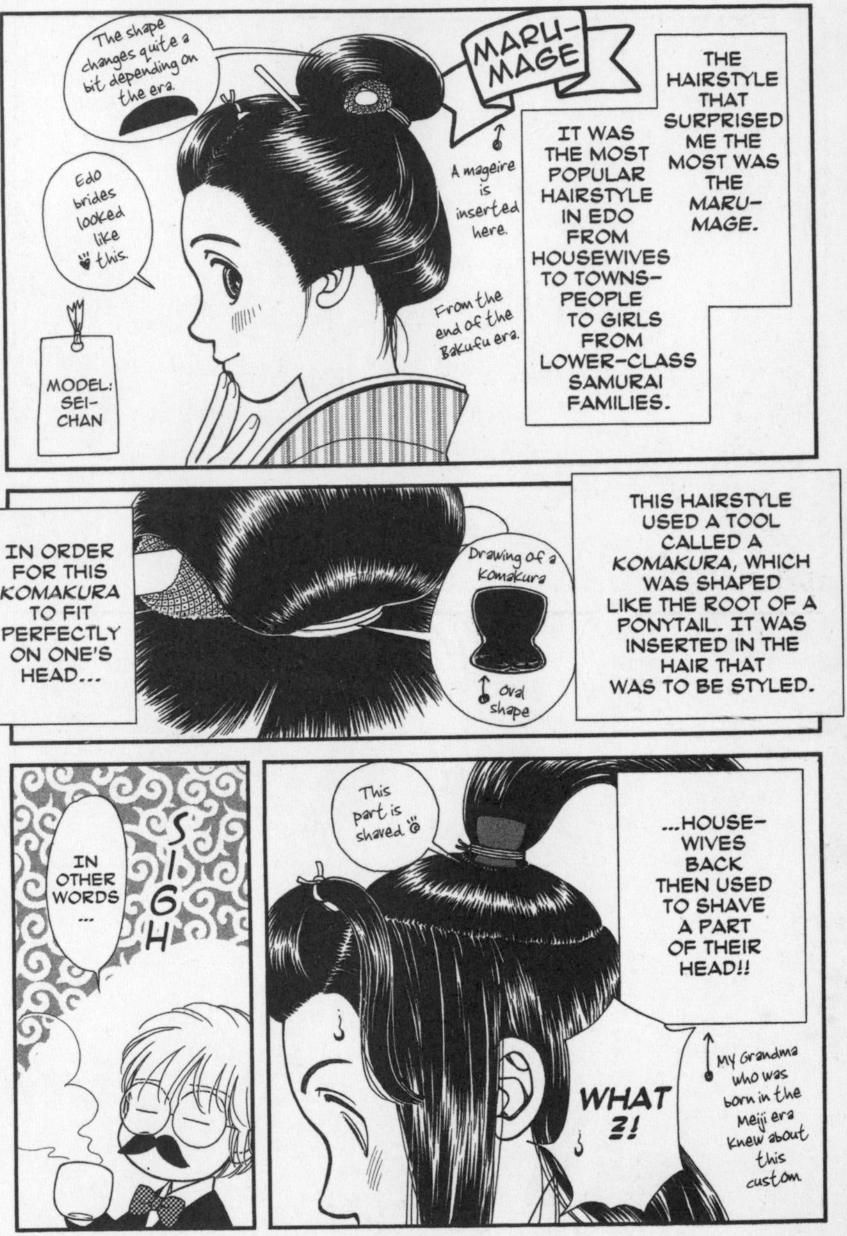
THE HAIRSTYLE THAT SURPRISED ME THE MOST WAS THE MARU-MAGE.
IT WAS THE MOST POPULAR HAIRSTYLE IN EDO FROM HOUSEWIVES TO TOWNS-PEOPLE TO GIRLS FROM LOWER-CLASS SAMURAI FAMILIES.
MARU-MAGE
A mageire is inserted here.
From the end of the Bakufu era.
The shape changes quite a bit depending on the era.
Edo brides looked like this.
MODEL: SEI-CHAN
THIS HAIRSTYLE USED A TOOL CALLED A KOMAKURA, WHICH WAS SHAPED LIKE THE ROOT OF A PONYTAIL. IT WAS INSERTED IN THE HAIR THAT WAS TO BE STYLED.
Drawing of a Komakura
Oval shape
IN ORDER FOR THIS KOMAKURA TO FIT PERFECTLY ON ONE'S HEAD...
...HOUSE-WIVES BACK THEN USED TO SHAVE A PART OF THEIR HEAD!!
My Grandma who was born in the Meiji era knew about this custom
WHAT?!
This part is shaved.
SIGH
IN OTHER WORDS...

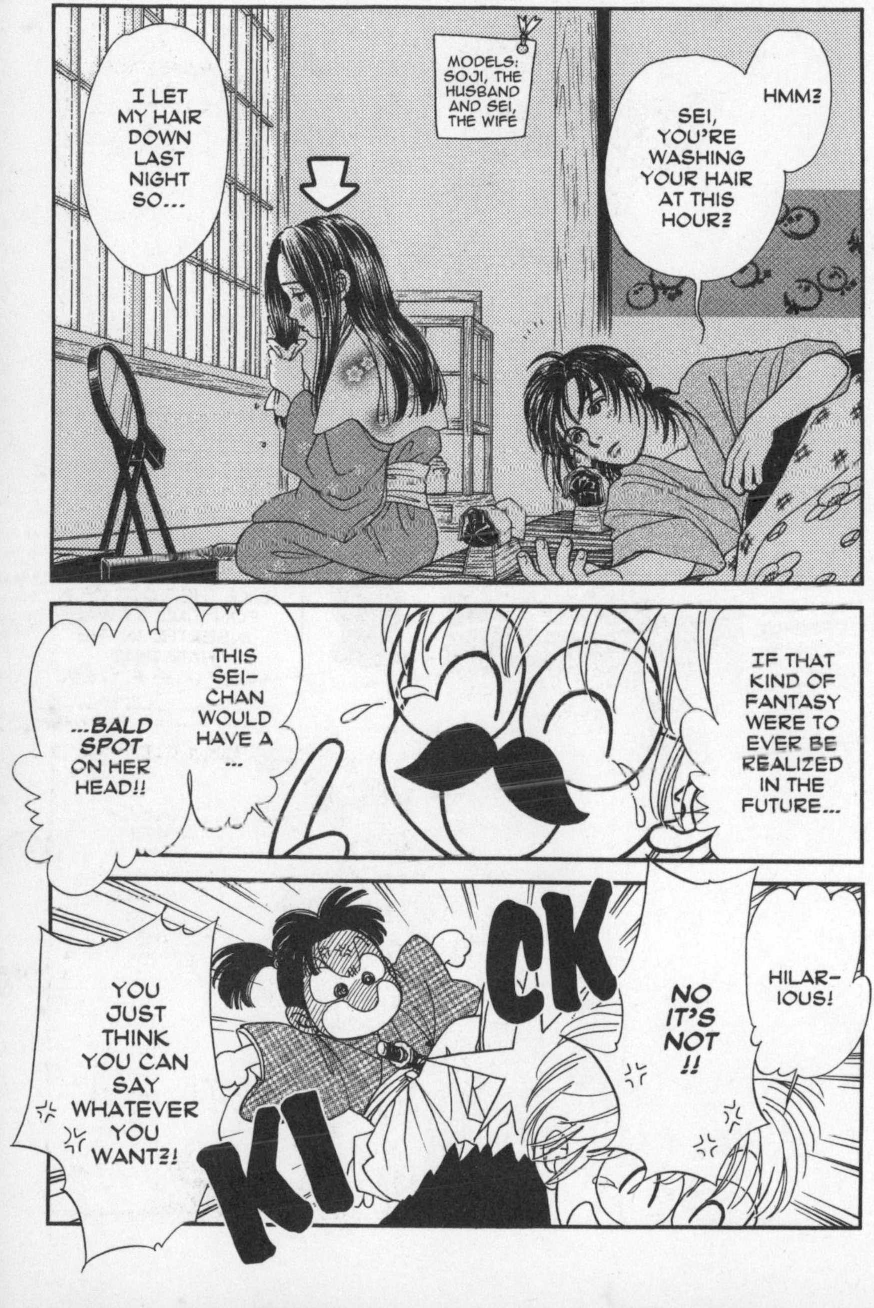
HMM?
SEI, YOU'RE WASHING YOUR HAIR AT THIS HOUR?
MODELS: SOJI, THE HUSBAND AND SEI, THE WIFE
I LET MY HAIR DOWN LAST NIGHT SO...
IF THAT KIND OF FANTASY WERE TO EVER BE REALIZED IN THE FUTURE...
THIS SEI-CHAN WOULD HAVE A ...
...BALD SPOT ON HER HEAD!!
HILAR-IOUS!
NO IT'S NOT!!
CK
KI
YOU JUST THINK YOU CAN SAY WHATEVER YOU WANT?!

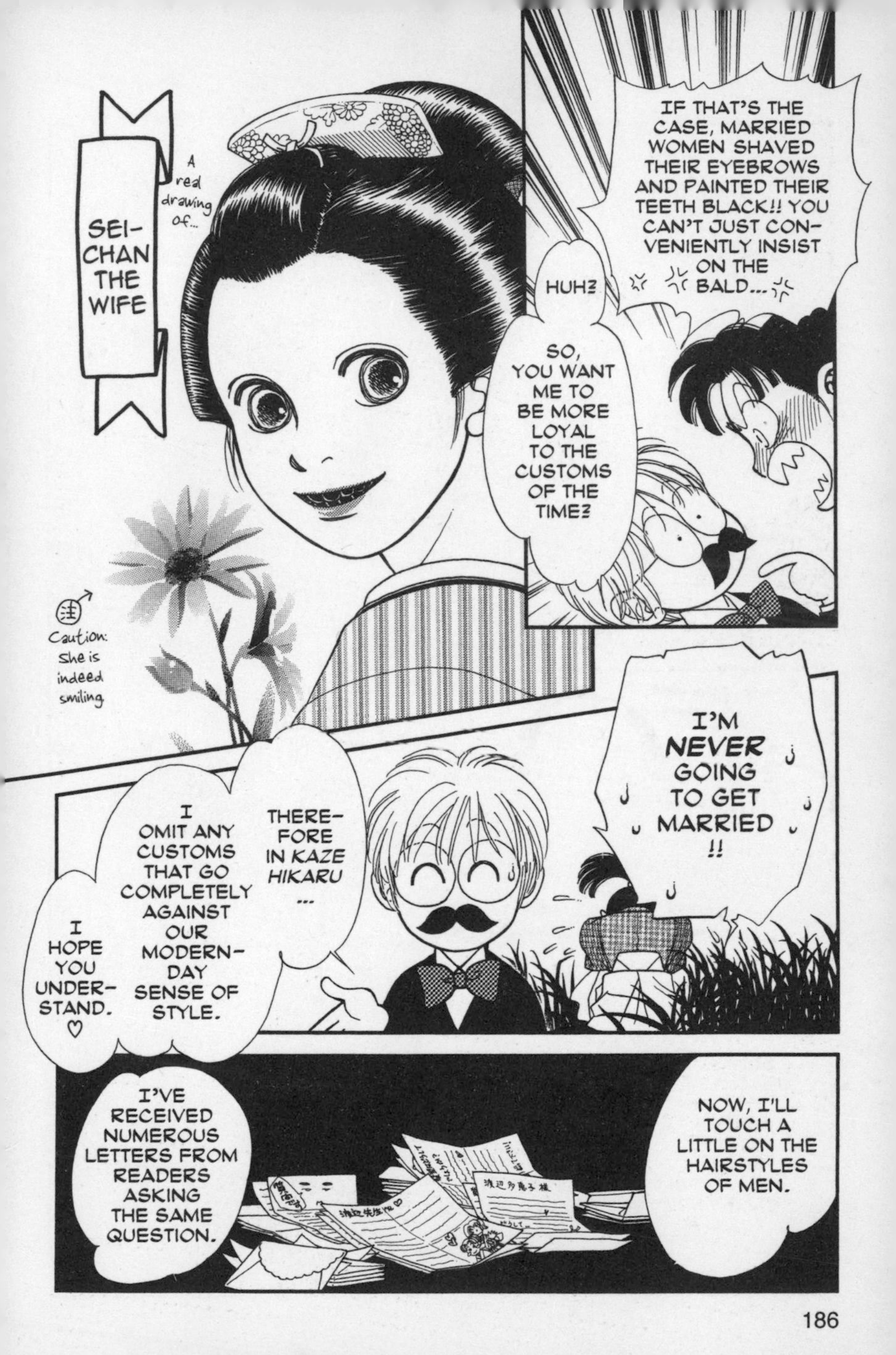
IF THAT'S THE CASE, MARRIED WOMEN SHAVED THEIR EYEBROWS AND PAINTED THEIR TEETH BLACK!! YOU CAN'T JUST CONVENIENTLY INSIST ON THE BALD...
HUH?
SO, YOU WANT ME TO BE MORE LOYAL TO THE CUSTOMS OF THE TIME?
SEI-CHAN THE WIFE
A red drawing of...
Caution: she is indeed smiling.
I'M NEVER GOING TO GET MARRIED!!
THEREFORE IN KAZE HIKARU ...
I OMIT ANY CUSTOMS THAT GO COMPLETELY AGAINST OUR MODERN-DAY SENSE OF STYLE.
I HOPE YOU UNDERSTAND. ♡
NOW, I'LL TOUCH A LITTLE ON THE HAIRSTYLES OF MEN.
I'VE RECEIVED NUMEROUS LETTERS FROM READERS ASKING THE SAME QUESTION.

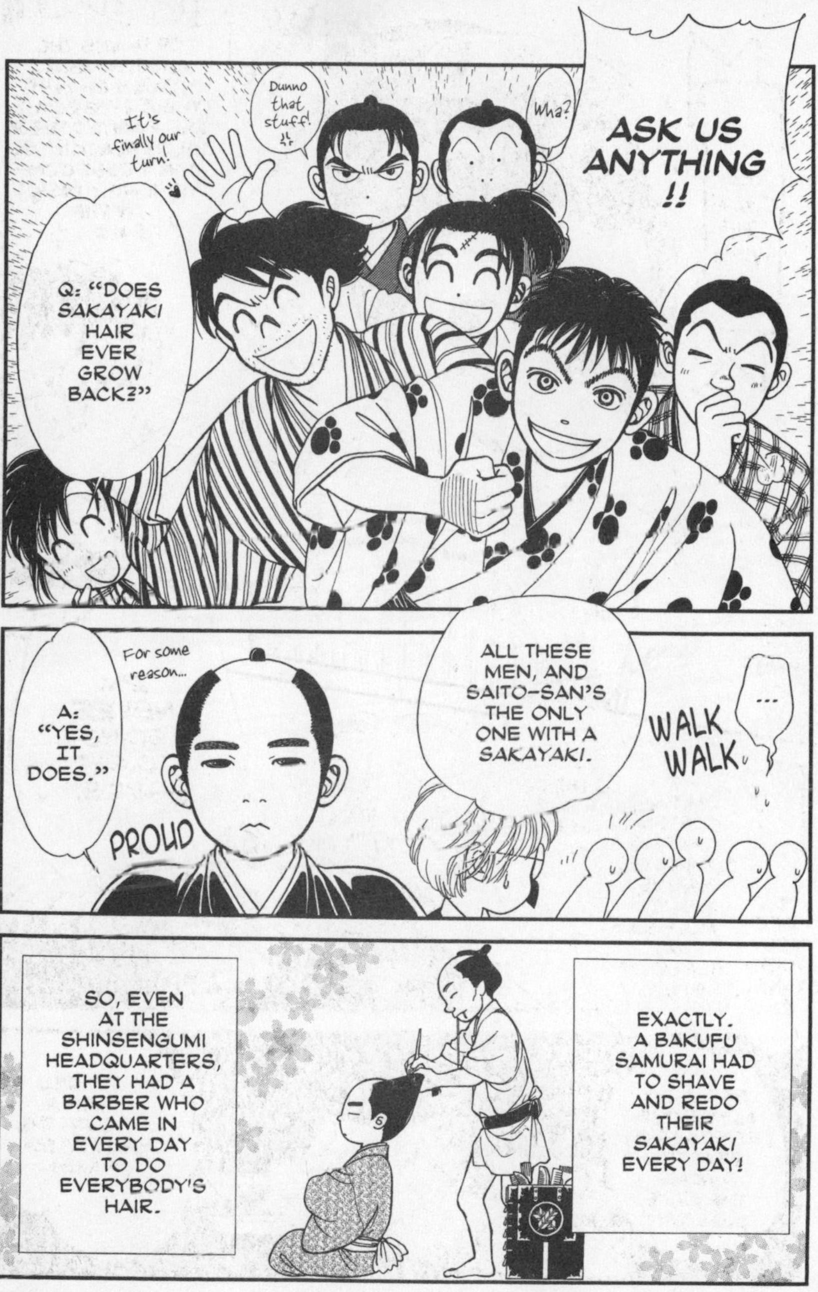
ASK US ANYTHING !!
Wha?
Dunno that stuff!
It's finally our turn!
Q: "DOES SAKAYAKI HAIR EVER GROW BACK?"
...
WALK WALK
ALL THESE MEN, AND SAITO-SAN'S THE ONLY ONE WITH A SAKAYAKI.
For some reason...
A: "YES, IT DOES."
PROUD
EXACTLY. A BAKUFU SAMURAI HAD TO SHAVE AND REDO THEIR SAKAYAKI EVERY DAY!
SO, EVEN AT THE SHINSENGUMI HEADQUARTERS, THEY HAD A BARBER WHO CAME IN EVERY DAY TO DO EVERYBODY'S HAIR.

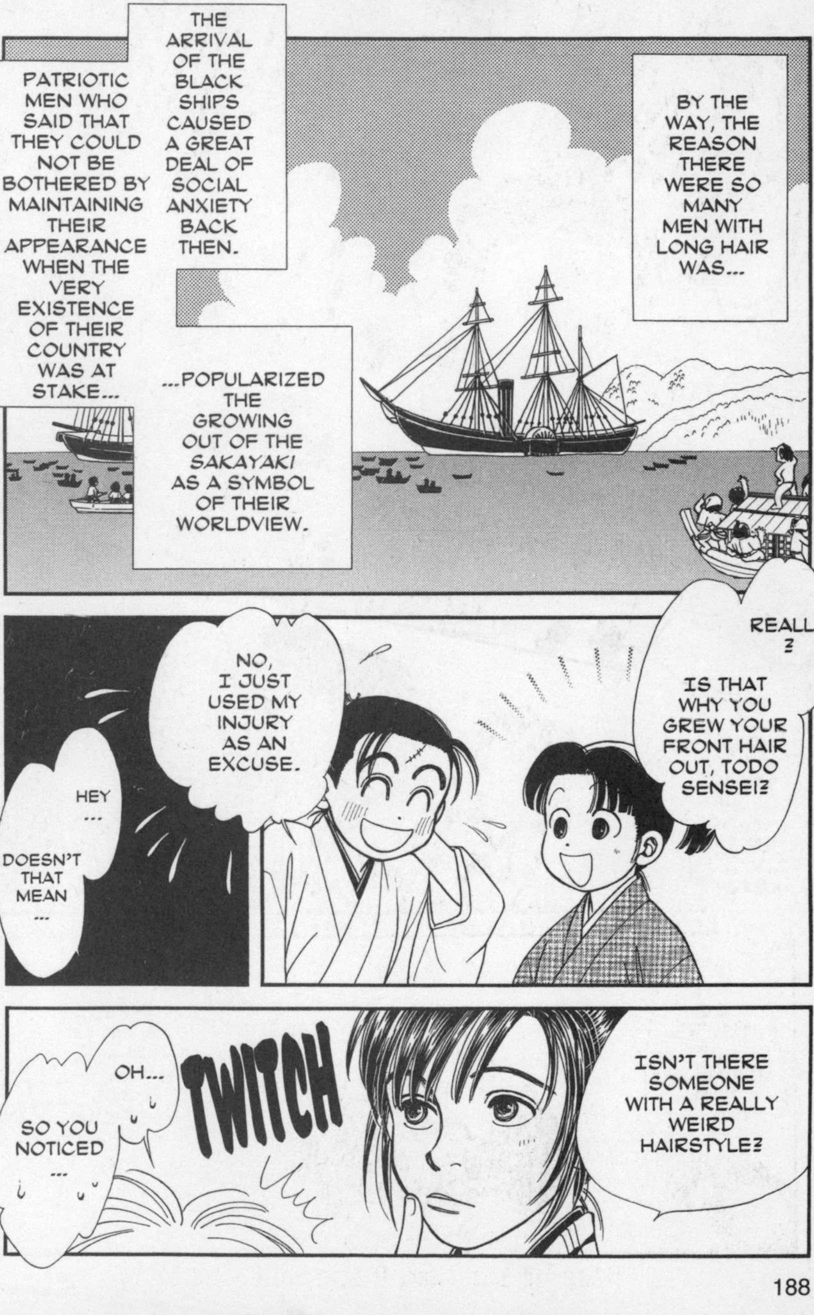
BY THE WAY, THE REASON THERE WERE SO MANY MEN WITH LONG HAIR WAS...
THE ARRIVAL OF THE BLACK SHIPS CAUSED A GREAT DEAL OF SOCIAL ANXIETY BACK THEN.
PATRIOTIC MEN WHO SAID THAT THEY COULD NOT BE BOTHERED BY MAINTAINING THEIR APPEARANCE WHEN THE VERY EXISTENCE OF THEIR COUNTRY WAS AT STAKE...
...POPULARIZED THE GROWING OUT OF THE *SAKAYAKI* AS A SYMBOL OF THEIR WORLDVIEW.
REALLY? IS THAT WHY YOU GREW YOUR FRONT HAIR OUT, TODO SENSEI?
NO, I JUST USED MY INJURY AS AN EXCUSE.
HEY... DOESN'T THAT MEAN...
ISN'T THERE SOMEONE WITH A REALLY WEIRD HAIRSTYLE?
TWITCH
OH... SO YOU NOTICED...

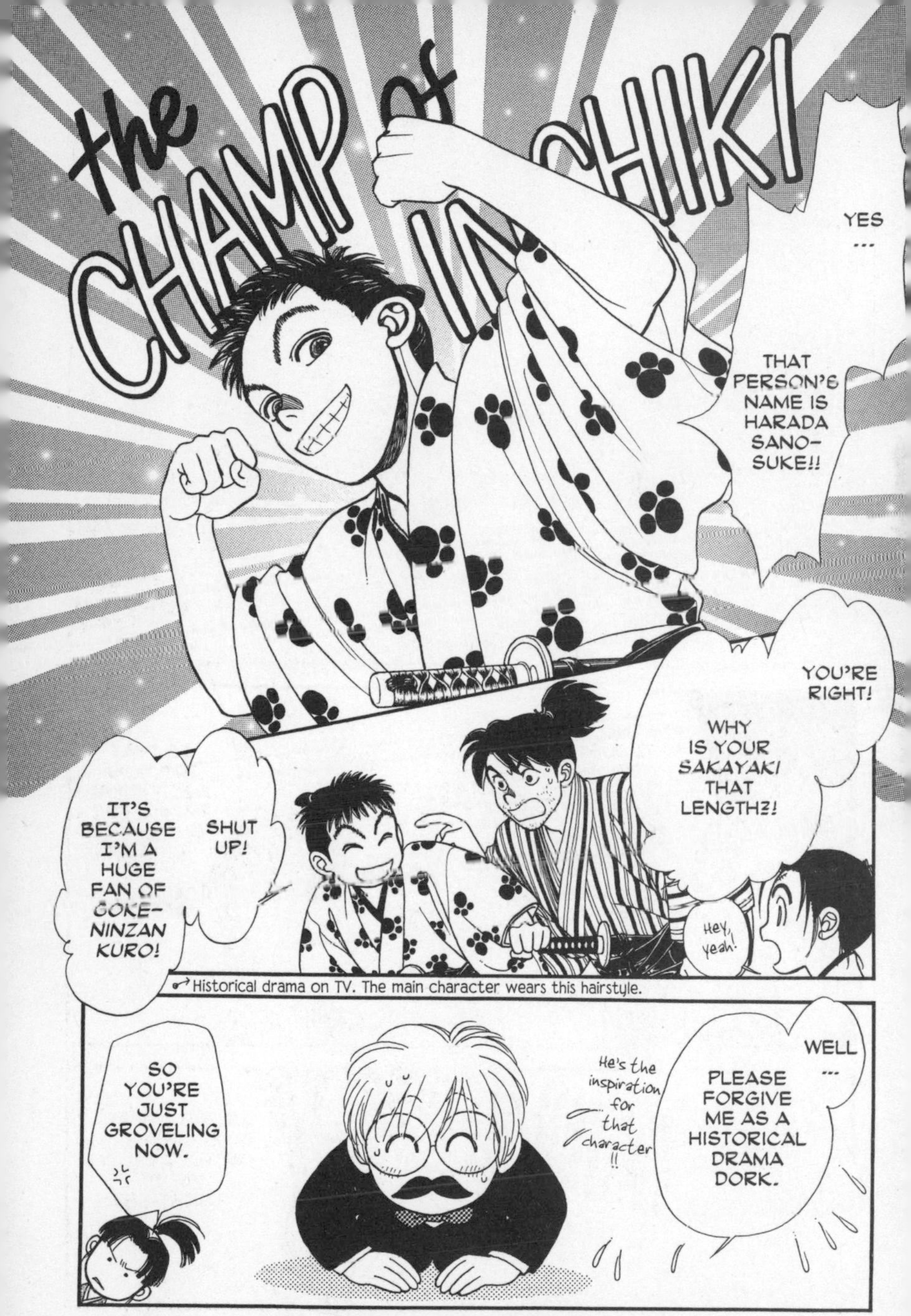
YES ...
THAT PERSON'S NAME IS HARADA SANO-SUKE!!
the CHAMP of INCHIKI!
YOU'RE RIGHT!
WHY IS YOUR SAKAYAKI THAT LENGTH?!
Hey, yeah!
SHUT UP!
IT'S BECAUSE I'M A HUGE FAN OF GOKE-NINZAN KURO!
Historical drama on TV. The main character wears this hairstyle.
WELL ...
PLEASE FORGIVE ME AS A HISTORICAL DRAMA DORK.
He's the inspiration for that character!!
SO YOU'RE JUST GROVELING NOW.

Kaze Hikaru Diary R Special!! - End

Decoding Kaze Hikaru

Kaze Hikaru is a historical drama based in 19th century Japan and thus contains some fairly mystifying terminology. In this glossary we'll break down archaic phrases, terms, and other linguistic curiosities for you, so that you can move through life with the smug assurance that you are indeed a know-it-all.

First and foremost, because *Kaze Hikaru* is a period story, we kept all character names in their traditional Japanese form—that is, family name followed by first name. For example, the character Okita Soji's family name is Okita and his personal name is Soji.

AKO-ROSHI:
The *ronin* (samurai) of Ako; featured in the immortal Kabuki play *Chushingura* (Loyalty), aka *47 Samurai*.

ANI-UE:
Literally, "brother above"; an honorific for an elder male sibling.

BAKUFU:
Literally, "tent government." Shogunate; the feudal, military government that dominated Japan for more than 200 years.

BUSHI:
A samurai or warrior (part of the compound word *bushido*, which means "way of the warrior").

CHICHI-UE:
An honorific suffix meaning "father above."

DO:
In kendo (a Japanese fencing sport that uses bamboo swords), a short way of describing the offensive single-hit strike *shikake waza ippon uchi*.

-HAN:

The same as the honorific –*san*, pronounced in the dialect of southern Japan.

-KUN:

An honorific suffix that indicates a difference in rank and title. The use of *kun* is also a way of indicating familiarity and friendliness between students or compatriots.

MEN:

In the context of *Kaze Hikaru*, *men* refers to one of the "points" in kendo. It is a strike to the forehead and is considered a basic move.

MIBU-ROSHI:

A group of warriors that supports the Bakufu.

NE'E-SAN:

Can mean "older sister," "ma'am," or "miss."

NI'I-CHAN:

Short for *oni'i-san* or *oni'i-chan*, meaning older brother.

OKU-SAMA:

This is a polite way to refer to someone's wife. *Oku* means "deep" or "further back," and comes from the fact that wives (in affluent families) stayed hidden away in the back rooms of the house.

ONI:

Literally "ogre," this is Sei's nickname for Vice-Captain Hijikata.

RANPO:

Medical science derived from the Dutch.

RONIN:
Masterless samurai.

RYO:
At the time, one *ryo* and two *bu* (four bu equaled roughly one ryo) were enough currency to support a family of five for an entire month.

-SAN:
An honorific suffix that carries the meaning of "Mr." or "Ms."

SENSEI:
A teacher, master, or instructor.

SEPPUKU:
A ritualistic suicide that was considered a privilege of the nobility and samurai elite.

SONJO-HA:
Those loyal to the emperor and dedicated to the expulsion of foreigners from the country.

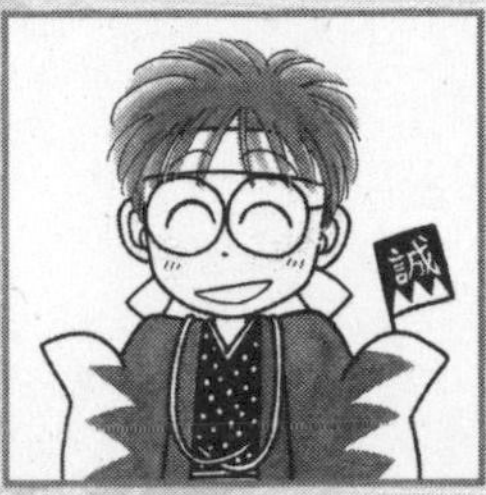
誠

One summer, I was eating at my house when I felt like someone was looking in from outside, and it freaked me out. Especially because the dining room in my house is on the second floor. I gathered myself enough to look outside and realized that it was the neighbor's large sunflower that had grown close to three meters high (heh). That is the inspiration for the cover. It seems surreal that this flower, originally from the U.S., grew in Edo era Japan, but apparently they were used for medicinal purposes rather than aesthetics.

By the way, Sei-chan is pouting in the background because she's jealous of the sunflower (heh).

Taeko Watanabe debuted as a manga artist in 1979 with her story *Waka-chan no Netsuai Jidai* (Love Struck Days of Waka). *Kaze Hikaru* is her longest-running series, but she has created a number of other popular series. Watanabe is a two-time winner of the prestigious Shogakukan Manga Award in the girls category—her manga *Hajime-chan ga Ichiban!* (Hajime-chan Is Number One!) claimed the award in 1991 and *Kaze Hikaru* took it in 2003.

Watanabe read hundreds of historical sources to create *Kaze Hikaru.* She is from Tokyo.

KAZE HIKARU VOL. 14
The Shojo Beat Manga Edition

STORY AND ART BY
TAEKO WATANABE

Translation & English Adaptation/Mai Ihara
Touch-up Art & Lettering/Rina Mapa
Design/Izumi Evers and Julie Behn
Editor/Jonathan Tarbox

Editor in Chief, Books/Alvin Lu
Editor in Chief, Magazines/Marc Weidenbaum
VP, Publishing Licensing/Rika Inouye
VP, Sales & Product Marketing/Gonzalo Ferreyra
VP, Creative/Linda Espinosa
Publisher/Hyoe Narita

KAZE HIKARU 14 by Taeko WATANABE © 2003 Taeko WATANABE
All rights reserved. Original Japanese edition published in 2003 by Shogakukan Inc., Tokyo.
The stories, characters and incidents mentioned in this publication are entirely fictional.

No portion of this book may be reproduced or transmitted in any form or by any means
without written permission from the copyright holders.

Printed in Canada

Published by VIZ Media, LLC
P.O. Box 77010
San Francisco, CA 94107

Shojo Beat Manga Edition
10 9 8 7 6 5 4 3 2 1
First printing, August 2009